Managerial Economics and Business Strategy

Managerial Economics and Business Strategy

Edited by
Rex Henson

WILLFORD PRESS
www.willfordpress.com

Published by Willford Press,
118-35 Queens Blvd., Suite 400,
Forest Hills, NY 11375, USA

ISBN: 978-1-64728-523-4

Cataloging-in-Publication Data

Managerial economics and business strategy / edited by Rex Henson.
p. cm.
Includes bibliographical references and index.
ISBN 978-1-64728-523-4
1. Managerial economics. 2. Strategic planning. 3. Economics. 4. Management. I. Henson, Rex.
HD30.22 .M36 2023
338.502 465 8--dc23

For information on all Willford Press publications
visit our website at www.willfordpress.com

Contents

Permissions

List of Contributors

Index

Preface

Managerial economics refers to a subfield of economics that deals with the use of economic methods in managerial decision-making process. It examines the internal and external factors that influence an organization. Managerial economics seeks to solve issues by using micro and macroeconomic tools. It plays an important role in assisting the businesses in identifying their strengths and weaknesses. Managerial economics assists businesses in determining where they excel and where they fall short. A business strategy is a plan that assists a business in achieving its objectives. It comprises strategies for various functions such as operations, marketing, and finance. Some of the key elements for building an effective business strategy include business objective, core values, SWOT analysis, operational strategies, and measurement. Managerial economics provides the baseline macroeconomic forecasts that drive sales and earnings projections, which are critical for making strategic business plans. This book explores all the important aspects of managerial economics and business strategy in the present day scenario. A number of latest researches have been included to keep the readers up-to-date with the global concepts in this area of study.

The information shared in this book is based on empirical researches made by veterans in this field of study. The elaborative information provided in this book will help the readers further their scope of knowledge leading to advancements in this field.

Finally, I would like to thank my fellow researchers who gave constructive feedback and my family members who supported me at every step of my research.

Editor

Modern Optimization and Simulation Methods in Managerial and Business Economics

Laura Calvet [1,2]🆔, **Rocio de la Torre** [3]🆔, **Anita Goyal** [4], **Mage Marmol** [5]🆔 **and Angel A. Juan** [1,5,*]🆔

[1] IN3—Computer Science Department, Universitat Oberta de Catalunya, 08018 Barcelona, Spain;
     lcalvetl@uoc.edu or laura.calvet@campusviu.es
[2] Business Department, International University of Valencia, 46002 Valencia, Spain
[3] INARBE Institute, Public University of Navarre, Campus de Arrosadia, 31006 Pamplona, Spain;
     rocio.delatorre@unavarra.es
[4] Indian Institute of Management, Lucknow 226013, India; anita.g@iiml.ac.in
[5] Euncet Business School, 08225 Terrassa, Spain; mage.marmol@euncet.es
[*] Correspondence: ajuanp@uoc.edu

Abstract: Managerial and Business Economics (ME/BE) aims at using quantitative and computational methods to make an efficient (ideally optimal) assignment of the scarce resources owned by firms and organizations. In the current global market, characterized by a fierce competition, an optimal use of the available resources is more important than ever for guaranteeing the economical sustainability of organizations and enterprises of any size. Heuristic optimization algorithms and simulation methods have been successfully employed to analyze and enhance complex systems and processes in a myriad of ME/BE-related fields. This paper reviews recent works on the use of these methodologies in competitive markets, as well as in imperfect markets considering externalities. The paper also discusses open challenges and how state-of-the art methods combining optimization, simulation, and machine learning can contribute to properly address them.

Keywords: managerial/business economics; heuristic optimization; simulation; microeconomics

1. Introduction

Managerial Economics (ME) is an interdisciplinary discipline that aims at efficiently assign scarce resources to achieve a managerial goal, either in an enterprise or an organization (Baye et al. 2006). ME, which is sometimes referred to as Business Economics (BE), combines concepts and methods from different knowledge areas, including: Economics (especially Microeconomics), Econometrics, Decision Sciences, Operations Management, and Management Science. ME/BE supports managers in answering complex questions such as: which price strategy allows our company to maximize revenue? how should we design our marketing campaign in order for it to be as efficient as possible? which is the right level of outsourcing in our enterprise to enhance our long-term sustainability? in which assets should the firm invest to maximize its wealthiness at the end of a time horizon? and many more (Hirschey and Bentzen 2016). ME/BE deals with different types of scenarios, ranging from competitive markets to monopolies, oligopolies, and even government decisions. Many challenges in ME/BE can be formulated as optimization problems, which are usually computationally demanding. Hence, advanced methods from Operations Research, Computer Science, Artificial Intelligence, and Behavioral Sciences are requested. The latter use to employ descriptive research—either qualitative or quantitative—and correlation research. In addition, other methods can be applied as well (Gravetter and Forzano 2018).

This paper focuses on the applications of metaheuristic algorithms and simulation methods in ME/BE. Both families of analytical methods have been successfully employed to optimize and perform what-if analyses on different ME/BE-related systems and processes. The main research questions of this work can be summarized as follows: (i) how many types of market structures have been analyzed with the use of these methodologies?; (ii) are there common characteristics in the applied methods and methodologies?; and (iii) which are the most promising research lines in the application of simulation and metaheuristics in the ME/BE-related systems and processes? To the best of our knowledge, there is not any updated review in the ME/BE literature illustrating the use and potential of the aforementioned methodologies. Hence, our paper contributes to fill this gap by: (i) classifying existing work according to the market structure (competitive and imperfect); (ii) providing a review of recent ME/BE studies that employ either one of these methods or both of them simultaneously; and (iii) discussing open challenges in research on ME/BE topics, as well as proposing the use of hybrid approaches such as simheuristics (Juan et al. 2018) and learnheuristics (Calvet et al. 2017) to deal with scenarios characterized by some degree of uncertainty or dynamism, respectively.

The rest of this paper is structured as follows. Sections 2 and 3 provide and overview of managerial economics as well as of metaheuristics and simulation methods, respectively. These sections allow the non-experts in one of these areas to have at least a good grasp of the main concepts involved. Section 4 reviews recent applications of metaheuristic algorithms and simulation methods in the context of competitive markets. Sections 5 and 6 perform a similar analysis, but this time focusing on imperfect markets and government decisions, respectively. Afterwards, Section 7 identifies and discusses common trends and open challenges, while Section 8 illustrates the potential use of simheuristics and learnheuristics in managerial economics. Finally, Section 9 highlights the main conclusions of this work.

2. Overview of Managerial Economics

After the publication of the book "Managerial Economics" (Dean 1951), this subject gained popularity in the USA and other countries. ME mainly refers to the firm's decision-making process. It could be also interpreted as "Economics of Management", since it is a bridge between both disciplines: the Management discipline focuses on the decision-making, whereas Economics relates to the optimal allocation of limited resources owned by the companies to accomplish certain objectives. Managerial Economics is sometimes referred to as "Industrial Economics" or "Business Economics". ME/BE shows how economic analysis can be used in formulating business policies. According to Agarwal and Helfat (2009) choices of resources have to be made at every stage. The author considers three economic problems: what to produce, how to produce, and for whom to produce. The knowledge of the economics is crucial to find solutions to the aforementioned problems. Since the pioneering work of Dean (1951), other studies have aroused. Spencer and Siegelman (1959) defines managerial economics as the integration of economic theory with business practice for the purpose of facilitating decision-making and forward planning by management. Douglas (1983) adds the uncertainty factor to the definition, saying that managerial economics is the application of economic principles to the decision-making process under the conditions of uncertainty. ME/BE has been popularized as a result of the increasing variability of business environments (Ahuja and Ahuja 2017). As there is a close interrelationship between economics and management, a closer look at both concepts is necessary. Regarding management, the scope of managerial economics is applied to five types of decisions (Hirschey and Bentzen 2016): (i) the selection of products to be produced or services to be offered; (ii) the choice of production methods and resources to be allocated; (iii) the determination of the best price; (iv) promotional strategies and activities; and (v) the selection of the location from which the customer is serviced.

When viewed in this way, ME/BE can be summarized as the study of allocation of resources available to a firm. Therefore, the scope of ME/BE is based on these problems in which both decision-making and resource allocation are needed: (i) resource allocation; (ii) inventory management; (iii) pricing; and (iv) investment. ME/BE can also include assessment and evaluation of funds, selection of business area, choice of products to deal with, determination of the optimum level of output, determination of the price of each product, determination of input combinations, as well as publicity and sales promotion (Agarwal and Helfat 2009). ME/BE fills the gap between the traditional economics theory and real business practices in two different ways. Firstly, it offers tools and techniques that allow managers to be more competitive in decision-making. Secondly, it is a link between all the areas in which a company operates. In addition to macroeconomics and microeconomics, capital management, profit management, and demand analysis/forecasting are also considered under the scope of ME/BE (Werden et al. 2005). Ghosh and Chowdhury (2008) considers that ME/BE applies the most useful concepts and theories from two areas, microeconomics and industrial organization, to create a systematic way of analyzing business practices and formulating strategies in the long run. Alhabeeb and Moffitt (2012) adds the concept of mathematics and statistics as supportive quantitative methods to ME/BE. They also mentioned the concept of economic scarcity, stating that it epitomized the paradox of the finite nature of resources and the infinite nature of human needs and willings.

Contrary to what many authors say, Allen et al. (2013) conclude that ME/BE differs from microeconomics because managerial economics prescribes behavior, whereas microeconomics describes the environment. This focus on managerial behavior provides powerful tools and frameworks to guide managers to better decisions and better identify the consequences of alternative courses of action. Research made by Samuelson and Marks (2015) considers the theory of the firm. The main tenet of this theory is that management strives to maximize the firm's profits although firm's revenues and costs are uncertain and accrue at different times in the future. The firm's value under this theory is defined as the present value of expected future profits. It also considers factors such as satisfactory levels of performance, maximizing total sales, and the social responsibility of business. Baye et al. (2006) considers ME/BE as the study of how to direct scarce resources in the way that most efficiently achieves a managerial goal. These authors organize the decision-making issues into categories or "forces", as defined by Porter (2011): entry, power of suppliers, power of buyers, industry rivalry, and substitute/complements. Perfect competition serves as an ideal of benchmark for other industries and that is why the study of competition is so important when defining ME/BE (Perloff and Brander 2017). Recent investigation (Hirschey and Bentzen 2016) considers ME/BE as a tool for improving management decision-making, linking economic concepts and quantitative methods. These theories can be summarized as described in Figure 1.

Hirschey and Bentzen (2016) and McGuigan (2010) add non-profit organizations, government agencies, and other organizations such as schools, hospitals, and museums to the theory of ME/BE. Hirschey and Bentzen (2016) also used the concept of multivariate optimization. This is important in ME/BE because many demand and supply relations involve more than two variables. In demand analysis, it is typical to consider the quantity sold as a function of the price of the product itself, the price of other goods, advertising, income, and other factors. In cost analysis, cost is determined by output, input prices, the nature of technology, and so on. In addition, difficult-to-predict ties between economic and political events make macroeconomic forecasting one of the toughest challenges faced in ME/BE.

Most decision-making processes can be formulated as optimization problems. Among methods to address these problems, one can mention game theory (Sadeghi and Zandieh 2011), metaheuristics (Buer and Kopfer 2014), neural networks (Göçken et al. 2016), simulation (Ivanov 2017), fuzzy sets (Graham et al. 2019), econometrics (Longo et al. 2017), and forecasting (Al Shehhi and Karathanasopoulos 2020). Linear programming (LP) (Vanderbei et al. 2015) constitutes one of the most classical and popular approaches. LP is a method of formulating and solving decision-making problems. In particular, LP returns a solution for an optimization problem consisting of a system of linear constraints and a linear objective function. Despite its popularity in ME/BE, LP presents several important limitations, mainly because most real-life problems are non-linear and too complex (*NP*-hard) (Grasas et al. 2017). This is the reason why heuristics and metaheuristics are increasingly being used in ME/BE applications. Another fundamental tool is simulation. As it will be discussed later, simulation techniques allow us to create what-if scenarios and assess the sensitive to uncertain outcomes of key economic variables. An important approach is that of innovation and new technological ventures. Karbowski (2019) suggests that a market with a high sensitivity to product quality improvements and a high competition will end up with the creation of a cartel. In addition, Monahan (2018) explores management alternatives with a behavioral economic lens and presents a new paradigm using Behavioral Sciences to account for the human factor. In this sense, the author concludes that people work for more than financial gain, and that they seek to collaborate with others. This fact challenges the dominant rational economic paradigm, which has been predominant in the existing literature.

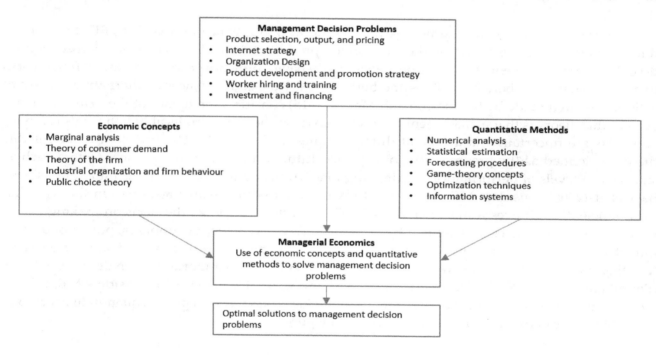

Figure 1. Concepts, problems, and methods of ME/BE. Source: based on Hirschey and Bentzen (2016).

3. Overview of Heuristic Optimization and Simulation Methods

Optimization and simulation methods are often used to analyze complex systems or processes. In the case of optimization methods, they allow obtaining optimal or near-optimal solutions for complex decision-making processes. Regarding simulation methods, these are usually employed when the system is dynamic or its behavior is stochastic (a clear example is those processes that change over time). In fact, simulation has wide applicability in different fields: from the design and analysis of networks in the supply chain to the determination of investment portfolios or the redesign of business processes. Thus, given a specific set of parameters, what-if scenarios can be analyzed. There are mainly three simulation techniques that can be used for the analysis of complex stochastic systems and processes (Law 2014):

- *Continuous simulation* refers to the modeling of a system with random variables that change continuously over time. This methodology makes use of differential equations and frequently employs numerical approaches for their resolution (Amaran et al. 2016).

- *Discrete-event simulation* points out to the modeling of a system with random variables that can vary over time (i.e., dynamic systems) but just in a discrete way (when specific events happen during a time). This approach is traditionally utilized to analyze the behavior of time-dependent network systems, such as a supply chain (Fishman 2013).

- *Monte Carlo simulation (MCS)* employs random sampling for addressing stochastic problems that do not evolve over time (i.e., static systems). This method is extensively used for dealing with not analytically tractable stochastic optimization problems (Bianchi et al. 2009).

Apart from employing simulation, optimization methods also allow to find those parameter values for which the system works best. Optimization methods are divided into exact and approximate (for example, those based on heuristics). The former guarantees the optimality of the solution to a given problem. However, as the complexity of the system grows, the time it takes to find the optimal solution also increases, sometimes exponentially, with the size of the instance problem. In order to perform the computations in a reasonable time, metaheuristic methods do not guarantee an optimal solution, but a near-optimal one instead. As a consequence, the hybridization of exact methods with metaheuristics is gaining momentum as an improved methodology for solving more complex problems (Jourdan et al. 2009). Metaheuristic algorithms can be divided into population-based—e.g., genetic algorithms (GA), particle swarm optimization (PSO), or ant colony optimization (ACO)—and single-solution—e.g., tabu search (TS), simulated annealing (SA), or iterated local search (ILS), just to name a few. According to Dunke and Nickel (2017), there are four different combinations of simulation with optimization techniques:

- *Optimization integrated with simulation*: In this approach, the optimization is used to evaluate a specific problem. Then, the result comes back to the simulation, which then re-starts its activity. For instance, the ordering of jobs could be re-scheduled according to the current state of the simulation (Dias et al. 2018).

- *Simulation as objective function*: In this case, the optimization provides a feasible solution, evaluated through the simulation. Then, these results are used by the optimization in order to generate alternative solutions. This, for instance, can be applied for determining the staff assigned to a given project (Zhang et al. 2019).

- *Simulation results as a start for optimization*: Using this combination, the simulation is conducted before the optimization, and is the one that provides the initialization parameters for the optimization process. For instance, the determination of the required staff for a certain production process and, afterward, using the optimization to allocate this staff (Rezaeiahari and Khasawneh 2020).

- *Optimization for configuring simulation*: Here, the simulation is employed to evaluate the feasibility of a solution found by the optimization (Yang et al. 2019).

A review of the literature that includes all the aforementioned can be found in Hussain et al. (2019). Moreover, some good introductory books regarding the field are Talbi (2009) and Luke (2013). As shown in Figure 2, the application of the combination of these techniques in the Business Economics and Operations Research/Management Science fields has increased over time. Furthermore, looking at Figure 3, one can conclude that the application of simulation is widely extended. Moreover, the trend in its widespread within the academia is growing for the three fields, i.e.: simulation, metaheuristics, and their combination.

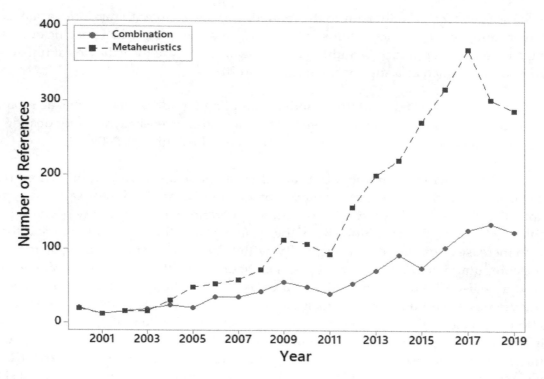

Figure 2. Time evolution of Metaheuristics and Simulation references in Business and Management in the Web of Science.

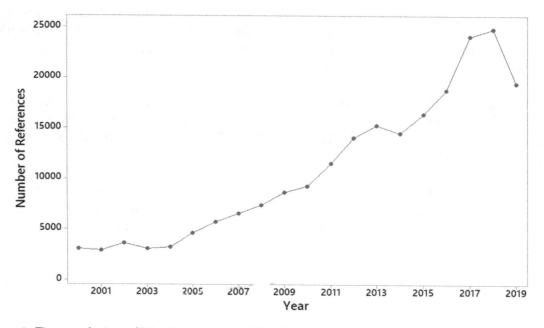

Figure 3. Time evolution of Metaheuristics and Simulation references in Business and Management in the Web of Science.

4. Applications in Competitive Markets

This section will review works in which firms benefit from the application of optimization and simulation techniques to improve their competitiveness. The existing literature provides many examples of applications. However, a series of challenges can also be identified. To limit the scope, the references will focus on recent articles in the services sector, the manufacturing sector, and the power generation markets. A common trend facing organizations is that managerial decisions are becoming increasingly complex, as they need to consider various parameters simultaneously (e.g., different types of resources) and are affected by multiple economic indicators. This is especially true for almost any decision-making exercise in collaborative networks, where metaheuristic algorithms and simulations help to suggest and provide solutions with possible better utilization of the available resources. In fact, one of the main factors that condition a firm's success is its ability to build and maintain an effective collaboration network itself. This is especially critical for companies in the Information Technology industry, for which the creation of a competitive system requires the integration of numerous resources, platforms, and skills (Brass et al. 2004). In this regard, Salamat et al. (2016) design and implement an optimization model, based on the analytic hierarchy process (AHP) and on multi-objective programming, for the decision-making process involved in the creation of a collaborative network. The idea is to use the transaction cost theory (TCT) for short-term decisions and the resource-based view for long-term decisions. The results show that the application of optimization techniques contributes to make the selection process more efficient in terms of cost, time, and development speed. Further, the designed framework provides analytical solutions and can be used as an effective tool in selecting network alternatives according to the managerial requirements. Crispim et al. (2015) advocate that the success of a virtual enterprise depends on its composition, and the selection of partners. These authors remark the inherent difficulty in this last decision, which is due to the uncertainties related to information, market dynamics, customer expectations, and technology speed-up, with a strongly stochastic decision-making context. They propose a two-stage model for cooping business environments with uncertainty: a chance-constraint multi-objective directional TS metaheuristic complemented with a 2-tuple fuzzy linguistic representation model. The results show the potential of this approach for handling partner selection problems under different scenarios.

In addition to their widespread use in companies from the service sector, metaheuristics and simulation are also frequently employed in the manufacturing industry. Being a very competitive business environment (Wang and Cao 2008), managers often seek new strategies to reduce costs, without sacrificing product quality and the reliability of the designed system or product. Ma and Lv (2019) tackle the problem of finding a solution for optimal production and scheduling with the objective of minimizing the cost per unit time in a competitive environment. They design and implemented an approach speeding up the Monte Carlo simulation to calculate the objective function, as well as to corroborate the feasibility in order to optimize the objective function by metaheuristic algorithms. To address the same problem, Lian et al. (2012) proposes a solving approach inspired by the imperialist competitive algorithm (ICA). The procedure is based on the initial population, and includes different stages: assimilation, position exchange, imperialistic competition, and elimination.

Another main goal to improve the production system is to reduce the total makespan in scheduling problems. In these cases, the use of procedures that integrate simulation and metaheuristics is widely contrasted and quite versatile, regardless of the manufacturing industry of application (from the chemical industry to the textile manufacturing one). In the case of job-shop problems, some of the most relevant manuscripts in recent years are the ones by Amelian et al. (2019) and Belkaid et al. (2016). With the main objective of enhancing competitiveness and improving effectiveness, many countries have decided to change from a monopoly-based electric power generation to one of perfect competition (Section 5). It is expected that a more competitive market helps to reduce the marginal cost (Wen and David 2001). Associated with the concept of competitiveness, the development of bidding strategies for the maximization of profits in public-service companies is inevitable. With this purpose in mind, an optimal bidding structure is needed (David and Wen 2000). In recent years, different models have been developed and implemented for bidding competitive markets based on optimization, gaming theory, and multi-agent models (Mathur et al. 2017). Thus, for example, Mousavi et al. (2015) develop and compare different metaheuristic algorithms (a GA, a SA, and a hybrid SA-GA) for optimizing bidding strategy. The authors address the problem of computing a pure Nash equilibrium for electricity markets with many players. Baringo and Amaro (2017) formulate the same problem by using a stochastic robust optimization model that takes into account uncertainties in the market prices and in the driving requirements of electric vehicles. Usually, the supplier actors of the power market are modeled as adaptive agents who can learn how to bid strategically, so they can optimize their profit through indirect interaction with other actors within the market (Azadeh et al. 2010). Following this line, Tang et al. (2017) propose a game-theoretic bidding optimization method based on bi-level programming, where the multiple power producers are formulated as a non-cooperative game with different bidding curves as strategies, while pricing is optimized simultaneously. Moreover, a distributed algorithm is implemented in order to search the solution of the generalized Nash equilibrium. Further, for verifying the feasibility and the effectiveness of the proposed optimization approach, a simulation is performed and discussed. Sadeghi and Zandieh (2011) studied a product portfolio identification problem, which was based on a customer engineering interaction model in a competitive environment. These authors approached the problem as a 2-person non-cooperative game with a Nash equilibrium point.

In the area of production scheduling, Pan et al. (2019) compared seven solving approaches, including a mixed integer linear programming model, three constructive heuristics, two variant neighborhood descent algorithms, and an iterated greedy algorithm. As they indicated, the seven algorithms were found to be effective against the sixteen algorithms presented in the existing literature. Lin et al. (2020) worked on a non-linear zero-one programming model for the courier delivery network design. The objective was to minimize the total cost including accumulation cost, transportation cost, and transfer cost, while considering facilities with a limited capacity. A simulated annealing algorithm was developed for achieving near-optimal solutions. This problem has applications in optimizing transportation routes, either to deliver courier directly or through a transfer facility. In another study for a multi-period facility location problem, Sauvey et al. (2020) coped with the problem of finding optimal locations and facilities. These need to have sufficient capacities to satisfy customers while keeping the cost as low as possible. Also, some customers required the product delivery in time, whereas other accepted a delayed delivery within a given time window. Tsao et al. (2020) worked in the context of globally competitive apparel industry to minimize the total cost considering the length of used fabric and the number of operative sections in the manufacturing process. The cut order planning problem was modeled as a mixed-integer programming model. Seven garment sizes were considered along nine cases. Several metaheuristic techniques were employed to solve the aforementioned problem, including: SA, GA, TS, a hybrid SA-GA, and a hybrid TS-GA.

5. Applications in Imperfect Markets

Imperfect competition refers to any economic market that does not meet the rigorous standards of a purely competitive market (Krugman et al. 2007). It comprises the following types of market structures: monopolies, monopsonies, monopolistic competition, oligopolies, and oligopsonies. All firms operating in different market structures face complex problems with changing consumer preferences with time, new government policies, technological advancements, scarcity of resources, and competitive landscape changing with different players entering the market with new offers. In this environment, we may find companies, for instance, that sell different products and services, set their own individual prices, fight for market share, and are protected by entry and/or exit barriers. There are such dynamic challenging situations across industries and firms operating in different market structures.

5.1. Monopolies and Monopsonies

There are different types of monopolies: (i) a pure monopoly, in which there is a single seller in the market; (ii) a soft monopoly, where the market includes several sellers but one has a very high percentage of it; and (iii) a situation in which there are several sellers but they set prices and outputs in concert (i.e., cartels). In addition, monopolies can be classified according to the factors that make possible that situation, e.g., (i) a key resource is owned by a single company; (ii) a company owns a patent to produce a good; (iii) the government grants a company the exclusive right to produce a good;

and (iv) a natural monopoly, where production costs make a single producer more efficient than many (e.g., water distribution). The decisions for a monopolist are mainly related to prices and outputs, but there are plenty of options regarding strategic entry barriers. These barriers refer to any action taken by incumbent companies in a given market with the aim of discouraging potential entrants from entering. Hostile takeovers and predatory pricing are popular examples. In a similar way in which a monopolist can influence the price for its buyers in a monopoly, in a monopsony a single entity has a strong influence over sellers. Thus, the monopsonist has also decisions to make regarding price, quantity, and behavior.

Lu et al. (2010) presents a two-stage model to investigate the location strategy and the commodity pricing strategy for a retail firm. This firm wants to enter a spatial market with multiple facilities, where a competitor firm is already operating as a monopoly. Expected market shares are calculated based on the stochastic customer behavior. The authors proof the existence and uniqueness of the pure strategy Nash equilibrium price with a specified utility function. A TS is proposed to search the optimal location-price solution. Panin et al. (2014) present a series of studies in the field of optimal facility location and pricing and propose a mathematical model for the corresponding Stackelberg game. On a different application field Zhou and Huang (2016) discussed two types of contracts for energy-saving products in a monopoly with the government's budget constraint. In this study the authors modeled a three-stage game and gave optimal design of the contracts according to the goal of minimizing the total and the average energy consumption. In a monopolistic scenario, Raza et al. (2019) presents a multi-objective model considering pricing, production, and quality decisions in a multi-objective context when the manufacturing firm experiences a demand leakage in simultaneously observed price-dependent stochastic demand. A goal programming approach combined with a simulation based optimization and a multi-objective genetic algorithm are proposed.

5.2. Monopolistic Competition

Monopolistic competition (Parenti et al. 2017) represents a popular mixture of monopoly and perfect competition. In this case, firms compete selling products that differ slightly from one another. This feature means that competing companies have some control over price. Since the demand is relatively elastic, the company may raise price without losing its entire market to competitors. There are two types of differentiation: vertical and horizontal (Besanko et al. 2009). In the first case, it can be objectively stated that the product is better or worse than the products of the competitors. Consider, for example, a producer of household appliances that uses accessories to improve the durability; all consumers appreciate the improvement, but they may not agree on its value (willingness to pay). In the case of horizontal differentiation, although the price would be the same, only a proportion of consumers would prefer a given product. Classic examples are clothing and fast food.

Feenstra (2010) states that there are three sources of gains from monopolistic competition that are not present in traditional models. The first one is the consumer gain due to the fact that she has access to new import varieties of differentiated products. Then, a second source of gains coming from self-selection of efficient firms into export markets. Last, the monopolistic competition model, allows a reduction in firm's markups due to import competition. In a scenario of monopolistic competitive markets, Kumar and Chatterjee (2015) present a mathematical programming formulation that models an entrant firm's problem, which consists in deciding on the market segments to enter and the corresponding product designs to offer. The firm's aim is to maximize its profit. The resulting non-linear programming problem is addressed by means of a heuristic. A commercial solver is used to solve a small example and compare results. Annicchiarico and Marvasi (2019) have developed a tool to understand how the underlying structure of preferences affects trade policy decisions in an environment where lobbies have their own interests that may not be the same as the ones of consumers. They show that the trade policy emerging in the political equilibrium may be either protectionist or liberal.

5.3. Oligopolies and Oligopsonies

So far, we have discussed competitive markets and monopolies. However, they constitute extreme options of market structure and there are many relevant positions between them. Oligopoly refers to the market consisting of a small number of companies. Competitive strategies are particularly important in oligopolies: in a pure monopoly there are no competitors to worry about; in competitive markets, price and output are set by supply and demand; in contrast, in oligopolies firms must correctly anticipate the actions and reactions of its rivals and respond accordingly. In fact, oligopoly market structures provide more challenging aspects to remain differentiated from each other with simultaneously following rules of the game among the competing firms –which may be governed by the leading player–, as well as the uncertainties of the environment (Robbins and Lunday 2016).

In many countries, the electricity market is no longer a monopoly, but is far from being a perfect market yet. The size of investments needed in the market represents a relevant entry barrier. Thus, producers can influence the prices by behaving strategically. In this context, Ladjici et al. (2014) presents a two settlement model consisting of a spot and a forward market. Agents aim to maximize their profit and can take part in both spot and forward transactions. The strategic interactions of the agents are modeled as a non-cooperative game. A competitive co-evolutionary algorithm is developed to calculate the Nash Equilibrium strategies ensuring the best outcome for each agent. Also in the context of the electricity market, Bhattacharya et al. (2017) develops an optimization method for bidding strategies. This method aims to maximize profits and combines GA, adaptive metropolis search, PSO and differential evolution (DE) methods. Rego et al. (2014) presents an approach designed to recommend the number, size, and composition of purchasing groups for a set of hospitals willing to cooperate. The aim is to minimize their shared supply chain costs. A hybrid variable neighbourhood search (VNS) - TS metaheuristic is put forward, while preliminary computational results are carried out for illustrative purposes and to show the potential of their approach. Robbins and Lunday (2016) studies the characterization of optimal pricing strategies for a pediatric vaccine manufacturing firm operating in an oligopolistic market. Variants of three heuristics are proposed and tested to identify the pricing scheme that maximize a manufacturer's profit: a Latin Hypercube Sampling (LHS) of the upper-level feasible region, an LHS enhanced by a Nelder–Meade search from each price point, and an LHS enhanced by a custom implementation of the Cyclic Coordinate Method from each price point. Cai et al. (2011) relate the concept of oligopoly to the study of beef packing margins. Their results show that after mandatory price regimes took effect, cooperative regimes were longer and oligopsonistic rent, as measured by average economic profit, experimented a remarkable rise. Other studies Alvarez et al. (2000) present a conceptual and empirical analysis of buyer oligopsony power in a spatial markets setting. Results show that firms may set prices above the monopsony level to minimize direct competition among them.

6. Public Sector and Public-Private Partnerships

Most economies have both private markets and a public sector. Private markets tend to offer a large number of different goods and services, but there are other things that they can not efficiently offer. Non-profit organizations will have similar offers but the need is to make decisions to have regular demand/acceptance of their services with minimum usage of resources. Government agencies providing public utilities need an optimal utilization of scarce resources to meet large scale demand (Memmah et al. 2015). National security or educational systems constitute two illustrative examples. While in private markets the optimization criteria are mainly profit and market capture maximization, the public sector has a wider range of goals, such as social cost minimization, access, efficiency, and equity. According to Samuelson and Marks (2015), the government has two main roles: (i) to regulate private markets by providing basic rules and by correcting market failures; and (ii) to provide certain desirable public goods and services that are not, or cannot, be provided via private markets. Generally, there are three causes for market failure, which we show in the following list linked to the main government responses:

- Monopoly power: (*a*) breaking up existing monopolies, (*b*) preventing monopolistic practices, (*c*) preventing mergers that reduce competition, and (*d*) preventing collusion.
- Negative externalities: (*a*) taxes, (*b*) government standards, (*c*) permits (either tradable or not), (*d*) liability rules, and (*e*) bargaining among affected parties.
- Positive externalities: (*a*) promoting literacy and education, (*b*) improving health, (*c*) promoting research, (*d*) patent system, and (*e*) copyright.
- Imperfect information: (*a*) banning some drugs, (*b*) taxing unhealthy products, (*c*) mandating compulsory education, and (*d*) requiring producers to provide information (e.g., warning labels on cigarettes).

The rest of this section describes recent works classified by field of application. We also review the models and methodologies proposed in each work, which are summarized in Figure 4.

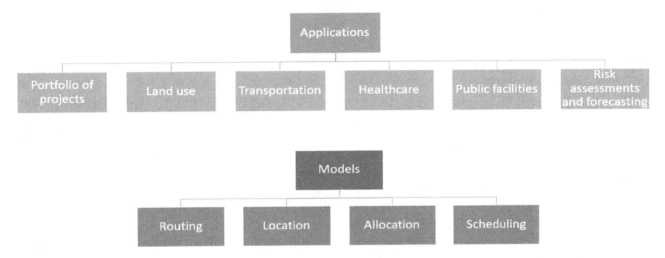

Figure 4. Applications and models of works on government decisions using metaheuristics.

6.1. Regulation

In the field of project portfolio, Manavizadeh et al. (2017) formulates and solves a multi-objective portfolio selection problem with an exact method for small instances and a non-dominated sorting GA for large sized instances. The aim is to determine the optimal portfolio for financing projects of renewable energies. The approach minimizes both the weighted cost of capital of the investors and the greenhouse gas emissions. Moreover, it maximizes net present value and job generation for urban, rural, and remote areas. Three ways to cover the required budget are considered: bonds, common stocks, and bank loans. Fernandez et al. (2013) applies a multi-criteria analysis to the problem of allocating public funds to competing programs, projects, or policies, with the subjective aim of maximizing the portfolio social return (based on either an individual or a collective decision-maker). The extended non-outranked sorting genetic algorithm (NOSGA-II) is applied for addressing this problem. The methodology is tested through two real size problems. Fonseca et al. (2015) focuses on foundations that provide grants for research projects (either public or private), which face the responsibility of selecting projects. The authors propose a TS to support the decision-making process of grant allocation, with the aim of maximizing the overall cost-benefit relation. Balderas et al. (2019) addresses the project portfolio as a multi-objective problem. The authors propose an interval-based method that considers imperfect knowledge of the contribution of projects to a portfolio, the project requirements, available resources, and preference parameters in the model. An evolutionary algorithm is used to deal with the problem. The proposal is tested both on an example from the literature and a public project portfolio with nine objective functions and large number of applicant projects.

In the field of land use optimization, Memmah et al. (2015) reviews metaheuristic algorithms for agricultural land use optimization. Land use optimization consists in allocating different species and activities to different areas in agricultural landscapes. Combining optimization techniques and simulation allow decision-makers (from private and/or public sector) to explore a large number of land use combinations. This optimization usually involve many stakeholders and decision-makers, many spatial factors, attributes and constraints, and multiple conflicting objectives (environmental, economical, and technical). Metaheuristics are quite successful in this context for several reasons: (i) the existence of a high number of integer variables; (ii) a need to take into account the points of view of many stakeholders and decision-makers; (iii) a large number of nonlinear objectives and constraints; and (iv) the need for interactive decision-support systems, which requires from fast algorithms.

6.2. Public Goods

Public transportation is a field with a large range of complex optimization problems. Because of the huge impact of public transportation, both national and local city economies, pollution reduction, and people welfare in general, many approaches have been proposed. Indeed, there are approaches for repositioning bicycles in a public bike-sharing system (Luong et al. 2014), design of feeder bus networks (Ciaffi et al. 2012), design of crew rostering problem in public bus transit (Xie et al. 2017), multi-variant optimization of traffic management (control of traffic lights) (Turek et al. 2017), disaster relief operation planning—which consists in the delivery of basic items in a post-natural-disaster scenario (Nolz et al. 2010), and design of electric transit route networks (Iliopoulou et al. 2019), among many others. Iliopoulou et al. (2019) reviews applications of metaheuristics for solving the transit route network design problem and compares them according to a benchmark network. In addition to highlight algorithmic components, solution representations and methods that tend to provide high-quality solutions, the paper identifies gaps in research and opportunities for future research. Uvaraja and Lee (2017) reviews metaheuristic approaches for urban transit scheduling, that is, for deriving useful set of routes, manageable timetabling for each transit route and transit scheduling based on available resources. They conclude that there is scarce work on parallel approaches, solving sub-problems concurrently, multi-objective approaches, and considering working preferences of the transit driver. Rodriguez et al. (2019) proposes a hyper-heuristics, which consists of a parallel combination of three metaheuristics: SA, GA, and ACO. This strategy is applied to design transport networks. Information exchanges take place between the metaheuristics and speed up the search process. The parallel implementation makes it possible for metaheuristics to run simultaneously. The hyper-heuristics achieves low computational times as well as high solution quality. Xu and Ying (2019) addresses the re-balancing problem in public bicycle systems, i.e., the problem of meeting the fluctuating demand for bicycles and for vacant lockers at each station, by actively shifting bicycles between stations with a fleet of vehicles. The authors propose a greedy randomized adaptive search procedure with a path-relinking, which is enhanced with a data mining process that makes it adaptive. This approach has been implemented in a populous city. Finally, Zhang et al. (2020) puts forward a model of transit route network design for low-mobility individuals and proposes a solving methodology. The objective function prioritizes the transit demands of low-mobility individuals followed by those of general public, and aims to minimize the weighted sum of direct traveler, transfer, and unsatisfied demand costs. A hybrid ACO-GA approach is formulated to solve the proposed model in accordance with current conditions (i.e., existing routes). Many authors have explored the use of hybrid approaches combining metaheuristics and simulation in public transportation. For instance, Fikar et al. (2016) proposes a discrete-event driven metaheuristic for dynamic home service routing with synchronized trip sharing. It is applied to home health care operations, where nurses are scheduled and routed to perform various services at clients' homes. The authors propose facilitating trip sharing and walking policies to reduce the number of required vehicles, while taking into account that, in real life, cancellations or new requests can happen at any time. Another challenging and increasingly relevant application, particularly in smart cities, is the waste collection management under uncertainty of waste levels. In this context, Gruler et al. (2017) proposes a simheuristic algorithm integrating MCS into a VNS. MCS is used to assess promising solutions and guide the search of the VNS. Hamid et al. (2019) addresses a a stochastic multi-objective and multi-period hub location problem, and applies it in public transportation. Their approach aims to minimize: (*a*) the total costs considering the possibility of investing the unused budget at each period; (*b*) the total processing time in the hub network at each period; and (*c*) the maximum distance between each pair of origin-destination nodes in the network. Three population-based metaheuristics are proposed and compared. The stochasticity in this problem resides in the fact that many types of disruptions may affect the capacity of hubs: computer-telecommunication network equipment failure, terrorist incidents, social strikes, natural disasters, etc.

In the area of public healthcare systems, Mendoza-Gómez et al. (2018) describes a problem arising in the planning of specialized diagnostic services. In particular, the problem consists in deciding which hospitals will provide the service and their capacity levels, the allocation of demand in each institution, and the reallocation of uncovered demand to other institutions or private providers. The aim is to minimize the total equivalent annual cost of investment and operating cost required to satisfy all the demand. The proposed methodology is a hybrid metaheuristic framework combining iterated greedy and variable neighborhood descent components. Marynissen and Demeulemeester (2019) reviews documents on multi-appointment scheduling problems in hospitals, in which patients need to sequentially visit multiple resource types to receive treatment or be diagnosed. Each patient is assigned a specific path over a subset of the resources and each step has to be scheduled. The aim is to let each patient visit the resources within the allotted time to receive timely care, thus avoiding a delayed diagnosis or treatment, which could result in adverse health effects. The review shows that these problems are becoming increasingly popular. For instance, Khalfalli et al. (2019) deals with the generation of a daily operating theater schedule, aiming to minimize completion time and maximum overtime while integrating real-life surgeon constraints (role, specialty, qualification, and availability). Also in the context of surgery departments, Aringhieri et al. (2015) considers the problem of determining the allocation of operating-rooms time blocks to specialties together with the subsets of patients to be scheduled within each time block. The aim is to reduce both waiting time cost and production costs measured in terms of the number of weekend stay beds required by the surgery planning. The authors propose a two level metaheuristic to address this problem.

Regarding the design and location of public facilities, Li and Li (2019) formulate the life-cycle analysis in seismic design of bridges as an interactive multi-objective optimization problem. The authors apply an evolutionary multi-objective optimization (EMO) algorithm to the seismic design of a reinforced concrete pier with four objectives: flexural strength coefficient, shear strength coefficient, reliability index of drift, and life-cycle cost coefficient. There are plenty of manuscripts on facility location in the public sector, and many of them propose heuristics/metaheuristics as solving methodologies. Haase et al. (2019) reviews recent works, highlighting the main applications: bike sharing systems, simultaneous bus scheduling and depot location planning, electric vehicle charging station planning, healthcare facility location planning, and school location planning. Hence, regarding education Xavier et al. (2020) propose location models to determine the best distribution of higher education facilities in the Amazonas State (Brazil). Castillo-López and López-Ospina (2015) present a model of location and modification of school capacity aiming to increase the efficiency of schools located in rural zones of Chile. Another interesting application is proposed by Gupta et al. (2019). It deals with the problem of setting up tele-centers (popularly known as the rural kiosks) at appropriate locations. This work proposes the combination of several metaheuristic algorithms (PSO, bat algorithm, and ACO) with traditional clustering approaches (*K*-means and fuzzy *C*-means) for the location allocation problem. The objective is that the maximum number of people can use the services with minimum travel and cost. A case study is performed with data from the Indian region. Finally, Miskovic and Stanimirovic (2016) addresses the problem of establishing the network of emergency service units, that is, locating a certain number of units at given discrete points of the region and to allocate cities to established units, aiming to balance the load of established emergency units. The authors consider a multi-period model as well as the uncertainty of the number of incidents.

Another interesting contribution is provided by Lopez-Garcia et al. (2016). The authors present a hybrid technique combining a GA with a cross entropy method to optimize fuzzy rule-based systems. This technique is applied to traffic congestion datasets in order to determine their performance in this area.

In the field of risk assessments and forecasting, Moayedi et al. (2020) address the spatial analysis of landslide susceptibility and describes a case study based on the Ardabil province of Iran. Similarly, Jaafari et al. (2019) present two predictive models that rely on an adaptive neuro-fuzzy inference system and two metaheuristic optimization algorithms for the spatially explicit prediction of wildfire probabilities. Finally, Pourghasemi et al. (2020) develop and compares four ensemble metaheuristic approaches, including the combinations of an adaptive neuro-fuzzy inference system with a GA, a SA, an ICA, and a DE. It can be concluded from these articles that metaheuristics can be useful when developing predictive models, e.g., for landslide susceptibility assessment (which can help to alleviate damages caused by this natural hazard), wildfire probabilities (which may help to effectively guide fire management plans and on-the-ground decisions on firefighting strategies), and flood assessment (that can improve flood hazard management and land use planning). As Figure 5 shows, the public sector has to deal with different applications and models to provide goods and services.

Figure 5. Wordcloud from the abstracts of works on public sector and public-private partnerships.

7. Common Trends and Open Challenges

The following research challenges and opportunities have been identified regarding the utilization of metaheuristics and simulation in the management field:

- The first challenge is the *adaptability* of the used techniques. In fact, a particular decision-making problem can be answered by different methodologies (Tsao et al. 2020) and, in other cases, a particular methodology can provide a solution for different sets of decision-making requirements. That is, within the same industry, firms are most likely to face similar problems or have similar goals. However, and independently of their goals, their necessities cannot be answered by the same methodology, since the firm environment can be diametrically opposite and can vary over time (Salamat et al. 2016). For example, collaborators (i.e., they may be based in local, national, or international region), target customers (i.e., with different demographics and living patterns) and market environment (i.e., perfect or imperfect competition), among others. Thus, it is in these cases where an intelligent design that allows adaptation and evolution of decision-making mechanisms play a fundamental role in the competitiveness of firms. In a similar line, it is also necessary to develop dynamic procedures that include uncertainty (Kumar and Chatterjee 2015; Mathur et al. 2017).

- The second challenge is the *reliability* of some of the simulation outputs. Some authors, like Zhang et al. (2019), point out about the discrepancies between the simulation outputs and the observed data in practice, due to multiple nuances that were not incorporated in the models in complex environments. This statement is particularly true in those cases where consumers' behavior may intervene (e.g., hospitals). As a consequence, the aforementioned discrepancies in output may affect the reliability of the model insights, especially when those insights are implemented in high-risk practice.

- The third challenge is the *applicability*, i.e., the horizon of repercussion to which the decision to make belongs. The previous literature review shows that firms and researchers are making an attempt to design and implement possible simulation and metaheuristic algorithms for better decision, but in most of the studies referenced in this work, the utilization of the aforementioned techniques is limited to the strategic decision level (considering the importance of these decisions for the survival of the firm). However, there is no impediment to use them as a support system in all decision making processes. Reinforcing this idea, some authors, such as Mendoza-Gómez et al. (2018), advocate its massive implementation as a support technique in the decision-making process in regular basis (i.e., tactical and operational levels).

- Finally, the fourth challenge refers to the dissemination of these techniques as a decision tool, the *uniqueness* in the solution. The procedures described in this study can provide more than one good and feasible solution, such that, according to Tang et al. (2017) this can generate controversy when making a decision. It is possible that in this scenario, in which two equally good solutions are available, the managers of the firms doubt the effectiveness of these tools and dismiss it as effective tools by not providing a single solution.

8. Potential use of Simheuristics and Learnheuristics

Decision-making processes related to ME/BE scenarios are becoming increasingly complex due to trends such as globalization, increasing scale of enterprise operations, information technologies capable of provide real-time data that needs to be analyzed, and the availability of an increasing amount of data that allows us to make more informed decisions than ever but also requires from a deeper analysis of the economical and managerial environments. Hence, there are many times in which these decision-making processes have to be done under uncertainty and/or dynamic conditions.

A concept combining simulation with metaheuristic optimization is that of simheuristics (Rabe et al. 2020). Simheuristics can be seen as an extension of metaheuristics, since a simulation module is integrated inside the metaheuristic framework to efficiently deal with *NP-hard* and large-scale stochastic optimization problems (Ferone et al. 2019). Notice that simheuristics might employ any type of simulation, e.g., discrete-event, agent-based, or MCS. These algorithms have also been used recently in multiple sectors, including: flow-shop scheduling (Gonzalez-Neira et al. 2017; Hatami et al. 2018), waste collection management (Gruler et al. 2017), arc routing (Gonzalez-Martin et al. 2018), Internet computing (Cabrera et al. 2014), finance (Panadero et al. 2020), e-commerce (Pages-Bernaus et al. 2019), and inventory routing (Gruler et al. 2018 2020). All in all, simheuristics illustrate the extraordinary potential that simulation has when combined with heuristics and metaheuristics, specially when solving stochastic versions of *NP-hard* optimization problems. While simheuristics are designed to cope with *NP-hard* optimization problems under stochastic environments, learnheuristics combine metaheuristics with machine learning methods in order to deal with *NP-hard* optimization problems under dynamic conditions, e.g., problems in which the inputs are not static but change over time or as in response to managerial decisions while the solution plan is built (Calvet et al. 2017). Thus, for instance, Calvet et al. (2016) consider how managerial decisions might dynamically influence consumers' willingness to spend (and the impact over the firm's revenues) while building a plan to assign customers to retail centers.

Similarly, Arnau et al. (2018) consider dynamic travel times while optimizing delivery plans for a transportation company.

All in all, many of the ME/BE-related challenges discussed in Section 7 might consider uncertainty and/or dynamic scenarios. Therefore, they clearly require from flexible tools, like simheuristics and learnheuristics, to efficiently deal with them. Indeed, most real-life applications related to ME/BE are characterized by a high degree of uncertainty and dynamism. Some examples are described next.

- Pricing strategies in oligopolies or monopolistic competition usually are subject to incomplete/ uncertain information, such as the pricing strategies and cost of competitors or characteristics of potential entrants. Taking into account this uncertainty is key for the economical sustainability of an organization.

- The best market segment strategy may depend on the strategies of the competitors, current and future technologies, and customer demands, among many other factors. All these factors are impossible to predict perfectly and may change over time very fast.

- Public transportation has many relevant positive externalities. To design efficient systems is required to estimate the number of users, but such predictions tend to have a high margin error. Moreover, the number of users of a given system, for instance a shuttle bus service, may depend on many factors that may change over time: prices in the car market, environmental awareness, characteristics of other public alternatives, etc.

- Public/private portfolio design is usually a multiobjective optimization problem with many restrictions. Completion times, cost and even the preferences of decision-makers and available funding may be fuzzy and change over time.

9. Conclusions

Managerial or business economics deals with the efficient assignment of scarce resources in order to enhance the performance of a firm or organization. In a context of globalization and access to huge amount of data, now more than ever only firms and organizations that are able to make an efficient use of their limited resources will be able to reach a sustainable condition (in a general sense that includes economic, environmental, and social dimensions of sustainability). In this framework, we have reviewed the applications of metaheuristic optimization algorithms and simulation methods to support informed decision-making. Hence, different recent and representative examples related to competitive markets, imperfect markets (monopolies and monopsonies, monopolitistic competition, and oligopies and oligopsonies), as well as public sector and public-private partnerships (considering works related to regulations and public goods) have been introduced and discussed. It can be concluded that the use of these methods is very extended and a high number of applications are related to routing, location, allocation, and scheduling decisions. From these examples, a series of open research challenges have been also identified, which are: (i) adaptability of the used techniques; (ii) reliability of simulation outputs; (iii) applicability (that is, implementation to support decision-making process in a more regular basis); and (iv) uniqueness of the solution (giving more than one solution may generate controversy). Finally, the paper discusses how hybrid flexible tools, combining metaheuristic optimization, simulation, and machine learning methods, can be employed to cope with increasingly complex decision-making process, under uncertainty and/or dynamic conditions. In addition, realistic examples are provided.

The use of metaheuristics and simulation methods is becoming increasingly popular due to the need of support in the complex decision-making processes of intensely competitive markets. The increasing availability of data and the unstoppable technological development is leading to a culture (both in private markets and the public sector) for evidence-based decision-making. Undoubtedly, a more efficient management represents a competitive advantage. Focusing on public sector and public-private partnerships, the existing works reviewed have shown a diverse range of applications, mainly: portfolio of projects, land use, transportation, healthcare, public facilities, and risk assessments and forecasting. This means that public policy-makers have powerful methods to support decision making processes and previous works as examples. Although most works come from the private sector, knowledge transfer could help to make better and faster decisions in the public sector. Indeed, most of the software/platforms used in the private companies could be directly applied by the public sector. However, applications in the public sector tend to have more agents involved and dissimilar and even competing objectives. Thus, multi-objective optimization approaches for the public sector represent an open, interesting and challenging line of research.

As future research lines, we plan to tackle the following ME/BE problems that have caught our eye: (i) segment discrimination and mixed bundling in e-commerce; (ii) randomized strategies in situations in which Nash equilibrium strategies cannot be easily achieved; (iii) risk analysis in lending and insurance under imperfect information; and (iv) auction methods under dynamic price conditions.

Author Contributions: Conceptualization, A.A.J. and L.C.; methodology, R.d.l.T., A.G. and M.M.; writing—original draft preparation, L.C., R.d.l.T. and M.M.; and writing—review and editing, A.A.J., A.G. and L.C. All authors have read and agreed to the published version of the manuscript.

Acknowledgments: This work has been partially supported by the Spanish Ministry of Science, Innovation, and Universities (PID2019-111100RB-C21, RED2018-102642-T) and by the SEPIE Erasmus+ program (2019-I-ES01-KA103-062602).

Abbreviations

ACO   Ant colony optimization
BE   Business economics
DE   Differential evolution
GA   Genetic algorithm
ICA   Imperialist competitive algorithm
ILS   Iterated local search
LP   Linear programming
MCS   Monte Carlo simulation
ME   Managerial economics
PSO   Particle swarm optimization
TS   Tabu search
SA   Simulated annealing
VNS   Variable neighbourhood search

References

Agarwal, Rajshree, and Constance E. Helfat. 2009. Strategic renewal of organizations. *Organization Science* 20: 281–93. [CrossRef]

Ahuja, H. L., and Amit Ahuja. 2017. *Managerial Economics: Analysis of Managerial Decision Making*. New Delhi: S Chand Limited.

Al Shehhi, Mohammed, and Andreas Karathanasopoulos. 2020. Forecasting hotel room prices in selected GCC cities using deep learning. *Journal of Hospitality and Tourism Management* 42: 40–50. [CrossRef]

Alhabeeb, Musaddak J., and L. Joe Moffitt. 2012. *Managerial Economics: A Mathematical Approach*. New York: John Wiley & Sons.

Allen, Richard, Richard Hemming, and Barry Potter. 2013. *The International Handbook of Public Financial Management*. Berlin: Springer.

Alvarez, Antonio M., Eduardo G. Fidalgo, Richard J. Sexton, and Mingxia Zhang. 2000. Oligopsony power with uniform spatial pricing: Theory and application to milk processing in Spain. *European Review of Agricultural Economics* 27: 347–64. [CrossRef]

Amaran, Satyajith, Nikolaos V. Sahinidis, Bikram Sharda, and Scott J. Bury. 2016. Simulation optimization: A review of algorithms and applications. *Annals of Operations Research* 240: 351–80.

Amelian, Sayed Shahab, Seyed Mojtaba Sajadi, Mehrzad Navabakhsh, and Majid Esmaelian. 2019. Multi-objective optimization for stochastic failure-prone job shop scheduling problem via hybrid of NSGA-II and simulation method. *Expert Systems* e12455. [CrossRef]

Annicchiarico, Barbara, and Enrico Marvasi. 2019. Protection for sale under monopolistic competition: Beyond the CES. *European Journal of Political Economy* 60: 101802. [CrossRef]

Aringhieri, Roberto, Paolo Landa, Patrick Soriano, Elena Tànfani, and Angela Testi. 2015. A two level metaheuristic for the operating room scheduling and assignment problem. *Computers & Operations Research* 54: 21–34.

Arnau, Quim, Angel A. Juan, and Isabel Serra. 2018. On the use of learnheuristics in vehicle routing optimization problems with dynamic inputs. *Algorithms* 11: 208. [CrossRef]

Azadeh, Ali, Reza Skandari, and Babak Maleki-Shoja. 2010. An integrated ant colony optimization approach to compare strategies of clearing market in electricity markets: Agent-based simulation. *Energy Policy* 38: 6307–19. [CrossRef]

Balderas, Fausto, Eduardo Fernandez, Claudia Gomez-Santillan, Nelson Rangel-Valdez, and Laura Cruz. 2019. An interval-based approach for evolutionary multi-objective optimization of project portfolios. *International Journal of Information Technology & Decision Making* 18: 1317–58.

Baringo, Luis, and Raquel Sánchez Amaro. 2017. A stochastic robust optimization approach for the bidding strategy of an electric vehicle aggregator. *Electric Power Systems Research* 146: 362–70. [CrossRef]

Baye, Michael R., Jeff Prince, and Jay Squalli. 2006. *Managerial Economics and Business Strategy*. New York: McGraw-Hill, vol. 5.

Belkaid, Fayçal, Farouk Yalaoui, and Zaki Sari. 2016. An efficient approach for the reentrant parallel machines scheduling problem under consumable resources constraints. *International Journal of Information Systems and Supply Chain Management (IJISSCM)* 9: 1–25. [CrossRef]

Besanko, David, David Dranove, Mark Shanley, and Scott Schaefer. 2009. *Economics of Strategy*. New York: John Wiley & Sons.

Bhattacharya, Anagha, Swapan Kr Goswami, and Tanima Kole Bhowmik. 2017. Developing an optimization method for bidding strategies in an open electricity market. *International Journal of Electrical Energy* 5: 71–75. [CrossRef]

Bianchi, Leonora, Marco Dorigo, Luca Maria Gambardella, and Walter J. Gutjahr. 2009. A survey on metaheuristics for stochastic combinatorial optimization. *Natural Computing* 8: 239–87.

Brass, Daniel J., Joseph Galaskiewicz, Henrich R. Greve, and Wenpin Tsai. 2004. Taking stock of networks and organizations: A multilevel perspective. *Academy of Management Journal* 47: 795–817.

Buer, Tobias, and Herbert Kopfer. 2014. A pareto-metaheuristic for a bi-objective winner determination problem in a combinatorial reverse auction. *Computers & Operations Research* 41: 208–20.

Cabrera, Guillem, Angel A. Juan, Daniel Lazaro, Joan M. Marques, and Iuliia Proskurnia. 2014. A simulation-optimization approach to deploy internet services in large-scale systems with user-provided resources. *Simulation* 90: 644–59. [CrossRef]

Cai, Xiaowei, Kyle W. Stiegert, and Stephen R. Koontz. 2011. Oligopsony fed cattle pricing: Did mandatory price reporting increase meatpacker market power? *Applied Economic Perspectives and Policy* 33: 606–22. [CrossRef]

Calvet, Laura, Jesica de Armas, David Masip, and Angel A. Juan. 2017. Learnheuristics: Hybridizing metaheuristics with machine learning for optimization with dynamic inputs. *Open Mathematics* 15: 261–80. [CrossRef]

Calvet, Laura, Albert Ferrer, M. Isabel Gomes, Angel A. Juan, and David Masip. 2016. Combining statistical learning with metaheuristics for the multi-depot vehicle routing problem with market segmentation. *Computers & Industrial Engineering* 94: 93–104.

Castillo-López, Iván, and Héctor A. López-Ospina. 2015. School location and capacity modification considering the existence of externalities in students school choice. *Computers & Industrial Engineering* 80: 284–94.

Ciaffi, Francesco, Ernesto Cipriani, and Marco Petrelli. 2012. Feeder bus network design problem: A new metaheuristic procedure and real size applications. *Procedia-Social and Behavioral Sciences* 54: 798–807. [CrossRef]

Crispim, José, Nazaré Rego, and Jorge Pinho de Sousa. 2015. Stochastic partner selection for virtual enterprises: A chance-constrained approach. *International Journal of Production Research* 53: 3661–77. [CrossRef]

David, A. Kumar, and Fushuan Wen. 2000. Strategic bidding in competitive electricity markets: A literature survey. Paper presented at 2000 IEEE Power Engineering Society Summer Meeting (Cat. No. 00CH37134), Seattle, WA, USA, March 16–20, vol. 4, pp. 2168–73.

Dean, Joel. 1951. Measurement of profits for executive decisions. *The Accounting Review* 26: 185–96.

Dias, Lisia S., Richard C. Pattison, Calvin Tsay, Michael Baldea, and Marianthi G. Ierapetritou. 2018. A simulation-based optimization framework for integrating scheduling and model predictive control, and its application to air separation units. *Computers & Chemical Engineering* 113: 139–51.

Douglas, Evan J. 1983. *Managerial Economics: Theory, Practice, and Problems*. New York: Prentice Hall.

Dunke, Fabian, and Stefan Nickel. 2017. Evaluating the quality of online optimization algorithms by discrete event simulation. *Central European Journal of Operations Research* 25: 831–58. [CrossRef]

Feenstra, Robert C. 2010. Measuring the gains from trade under monopolistic competition. *Canadian Journal of Economics/Revue canadienne d'économique* 43: 1–28. [CrossRef]

Fernandez, Eduardo, Edy Lopez, Gustavo Mazcorro, Rafael Olmedo, and Carlos A. Coello. 2013. Application of the non-outranked sorting genetic algorithm to public project portfolio selection. *Information Sciences* 228: 131–49. [CrossRef]

Ferone, Daniele, Aljoscha Gruler, Paola Festa, and Angel A. Juan. 2019. Enhancing and extending the classical GRASP framework with biased randomisation and simulation. *Journal of the Operational Research Society* 70: 1362–75. [CrossRef]

Fikar, Christian, Angel A. Juan, Enoc Martinez, and Patrick Hirsch. 2016. A discrete-event driven metaheuristic for dynamic home service routing with synchronised trip sharing. *European Journal of Industrial Engineering* 10: 323–40. [CrossRef]

Fishman, George S. 2013. *Discrete-Event Simulation: Modeling, Programming, and Analysis*. Berlin: Springer Science & Business Media.

Fonseca, Fagno, Marcelo Lisboa, David Prata, and Patrick Letouze. 2015. A decision-making technique for financial grant allocation to research projects. *International Proceedings of Economics Development and Research* 85: 119.

Ghosh, Piyali, and Purba Roy Chowdhury. 2008. *Managerial Economics*. New York: McGraw-Hill Education.

Göçken, Mustafa, Mehmet Özçalıcı, Aslı Boru, and Ayşe Tuğba Dosdoğru. 2016. Integrating metaheuristics and artificial neural networks for improved stock price prediction. *Expert Systems with Applications* 44: 320–31. [CrossRef]

Gonzalez-Martin, Sergio, Angel A. Juan, Daniel Riera, Monica G. Elizondo, and Juan J. Ramos. 2018. A simheuristic algorithm for solving the arc routing problem with stochastic demands. *Journal of Simulation* 12: 53–66. [CrossRef]

Gonzalez-Neira, Eliana Maria, Daniele Ferone, Sara Hatami, and Angel A Juan. 2017. A biased-randomized simheuristic for the distributed assembly permutation flowshop problem with stochastic processing times. *Simulation Modelling Practice and Theory* 79: 23–36. [CrossRef]

Graham, J. Edward, Carlos Lassala, and Belén Ribeiro-Navarrete. 2019. A fuzzy-set analysis of conditions influencing mutual fund performance. *International Review of Economics & Finance* 61: 324–36.

Grasas, Alex, Angel A. Juan, Javier Faulin, Jesica de Armas, and Helena Ramalhinho. 2017. Biased randomization of heuristics using skewed probability distributions: A survey and some applications. *Computers & Industrial Engineering* 110: 216–28.

Gravetter, Frederick J., and Lori-Ann B. Forzano. 2018. *Research Methods for the Behavioral Sciences*. Boston: Cengage Learning.

Gruler, Aljoscha, Christian Fikar, Angel A. Juan, Patrick Hirsch, and C. Contreras-Bolton. 2017. Supporting multi-depot and stochastic waste collection management in clustered urban areas via simulation–optimization. *Journal of Simulation* 11: 11–19. [CrossRef]

Gruler, Aljoscha, Javier Panadero, Jesica de Armas, Jose A. Moreno, and Angel A. Juan. 2018. Combining variable neighborhood search with simulation for the inventory routing problem with stochastic demands and stock-outs. *Computers & Industrial Engineering* 123: 278–88.

Gruler, Aljoscha, Javier Panadero, Jesica de Armas, Jose A. Moreno, and Angel A. Juan. 2020. A variable neighborhood search simheuristic for the multiperiod inventory routing problem with stochastic demands. *International Transactions in Operational Research* 27: 314–35. [CrossRef]

Gruler, Aljoscha, Carlos L. Quintero-Araújo, Laura Calvet, and Angel A. Juan. 2017. Waste collection under uncertainty: A simheuristic based on variable neighbourhood search. *European Journal of Industrial Engineering* 11: 228–55. [CrossRef]

Gupta, Rajan, Sunil Kumar Muttoo, and Saibal K. Pal. 2019. Meta-heuristic algorithms to improve fuzzy c-means and k-means clustering for location allocation of telecenters under e-governance in developing nations. *International Journal of Fuzzy Logic and Intelligent Systems* 19: 290–98. [CrossRef]

Haase, Knut, Lukas Knörr, Ralf Krohn, Sven Müller, and Michael Wagner. 2019. Facility location in the public sector. In *Location Science*. Berlin: Springer, pp. 745–64.

Hamid, Mahdi, Mahdi Bastan, Mojtaba Hamid, and Farrokh Sheikhahmadi. 2019. Solving a stochastic multi-objective and multi-period hub location problem considering economic aspects by meta-heuristics: Application in public transportation. *International Journal of Computer Applications in Technology* 60: 183–202. [CrossRef]

Hatami, Sara, Laura Calvet, Victor Fernandez-Viagas, Jose M. Framinan, and Angel A. Juan. 2018. A simheuristic algorithm to set up starting times in the stochastic parallel flowshop problem. *Simulation Modelling Practice and Theory* 86: 55–71. [CrossRef]

Hirschey, Mark, and Eric Bentzen. 2016. *Managerial Economics*. Boston: Cengage Learning.

Hussain, Kashif, Mohd Najib Mohd Salleh, Shi Cheng, and Yuhui Shi. 2019. Metaheuristic research: A comprehensive survey. *Artificial Intelligence Review* 52: 2191–2233. [CrossRef]

Iliopoulou, Christina, Konstantinos Kepaptsoglou, and Eleni Vlahogianni. 2019. Metaheuristics for the transit route network design problem: A review and comparative analysis. *Public Transport* 11: 487–521. [CrossRef]

Iliopoulou, Christina, Ioannis Tassopoulos, Konstantinos Kepaptsoglou, and Grigorios Beligiannis. 2019. Electric transit route network design problem: Model and application. *Transportation Research Record* 2673: 264–74. [CrossRef]

Ivanov, Dmitry. 2017. Simulation-based ripple effect modelling in the supply chain. *International Journal of Production Research* 55: 2083–2101. [CrossRef]

Jaafari, Abolfazl, Seyed Vahid Razavi Termeh, and Dieu Tien Bui. 2019. Genetic and firefly metaheuristic algorithms for an optimized neuro-fuzzy prediction modeling of wildfire probability. *Journal of Environmental Management* 243: 358–69. [CrossRef]

Jourdan, Laetitia, Matthieu Basseur, and El-Ghazali Talbi. 2009. Hybridizing exact methods and metaheuristics: A taxonomy. *European Journal of Operational Research* 199: 620–29. [CrossRef]

Juan, Angel A., W. David Kelton, Christine S. M. Currie, and Javier Faulin. 2018. Simheuristics applications: Dealing with uncertainty in logistics, transportation, and other supply chain areas. Paper presented at 2018 IEEE Winter Simulation Conference, Gothenburg, Sweden, December 9–12, pp. 3048–59.

Karbowski, Adam. 2019. Cooperative and non-cooperative R&D in product innovation and firm performance. *Journal of Business Economics and Management* 20: 1121–42.

Khalfalli, Marwa, Fouad Ben Abdelaziz, and Hichem Kamoun. 2019. Multi-objective surgery scheduling integrating surgeon constraints. *Management Decision* 57: 445–60. [CrossRef]

Krugman, Paul, Robin Wells, and Kathryn Graddy. 2007. *Economics: European Edition*. New York: Worth Publishers.

Kumar, Soumojit, and Ashis Kumar Chatterjee. 2015. A profit maximising product line optimisation model under monopolistic competition. *International Journal of Production Research* 53: 1584–95.

Ladjici, Ahmed A., Ahmed Tiguercha, and Mohamed Boudour. 2014. Nash equilibrium in a two-settlement electricity market using competitive coevolutionary algorithms. *International Journal of Electrical Power & Energy Systems* 57: 148–55.

Law, Averill M. 2014. *Simulation Modeling and Analysis*, 5th ed. McGraw-Hill Series in Industrial Engineering and Management Science. New York: McGraw-Hill.

Li, Hong-Nan, and Yu-Jing Li. 2019. Interactive multiobjective optimization for life-cycle analysis in seismic design of bridges. *Journal of Engineering Mechanics* 145: 04019050. [CrossRef]

Lian, Kunlei, Chaoyong Zhang, Xinyu Shao, and Liang Gao. 2012. Optimization of process planning with various flexibilities using an imperialist competitive algorithm. *The International Journal of Advanced Manufacturing Technology* 59: 815–28. [CrossRef]

Lin, Boliang, Yinan Zhao, and Ruixi Lin. 2020. Optimization for courier delivery service network design based on frequency delay. *Computers & Industrial Engineering* 139: 106144.

Longo, Francesco, Luigi Siciliani, Hugh Gravelle, and Rita Santos. 2017. Do hospitals respond to rivals' quality and efficiency? a spatial panel econometric analysis. *Health Economics* 26: 38–62.

Lopez-Garcia, Pedro, Eneko Osaba, Enrique Onieva, Antonio D. Masegosa, and Asier Perallos. 2016. Short-term traffic congestion forecasting using hybrid metaheuristics and rule-based methods: A comparative study. Paper presented at the Conference of the Spanish Association for Artificial Intelligence, Salamanca, Spain, September 14–16; Berlin: Springer, pp. 290–99.

Lu, Xiaoshan, Jian Li, and Fengmei Yang. 2010. Analyses of location-price game on networks with stochastic customer behavior and its heuristic algorithm. *Journal of Systems Science and Complexity* 23: 701–14. [CrossRef]

Luke, Sean. 2013. *Essentials of Metaheuristics*. Raleigh: Lulu

Luong, Binh, Pulkit Parikh, and Satish V. Ukkusuri. 2014. Metaheuristic approach for repositioning bicycles in a public bike-sharing system. Paper presented at the Transportation Research Board 93rd Annual Meeting, Washington, DC, USA, January 12–16.

Ma, Xiao-Zhi, and Wen-Yuan Lv. 2019. Joint optimization of production and maintenance using monte carlo method and metaheuristic algorithms. *Mathematical Problems in Engineering* 2019: 1–22. [CrossRef]

Manavizadeh, Neda, M. A. Yavari, and Hamed Farrokhi-Asl. 2017. Using metaheuristic algorithm to solve a multi objective portfolio selection problem: Application in renewable energy investment policy. *International Journal of Applied* 7: 21–44.

Marynissen, Joren, and Erik Demeulemeester. 2019. Literature review on multi-appointment scheduling problems in hospitals. *European Journal of Operational Research* 272: 407–419. [CrossRef]

Mathur, Somendra P. S., Anoop Arya, and Manisha Dubey. 2017. Optimal bidding strategy for price takers and customers in a competitive electricity market. *Cogent Engineering* 4: 1358545. [CrossRef]

McGuigan, Jim. 2010. Creative labour, cultural work and individualisation. *International Journal of Cultural Policy* 16: 323–35. [CrossRef]

Memmah, Mohamed-Mahmoud, Françoise Lescourret, Xin Yao, and Claire Lavigne. 2015. Metaheuristics for agricultural land use optimization: A review. *Agronomy for Sustainable Development* 35: 975–98. [CrossRef]

Mendoza-Gómez, Rodolfo, Roger Z. Ríos-Mercado, and Karla B. Valenzuela-Ocaña. 2018. An iterated greedy algorithm with variable neighborhood descent for the planning of specialized diagnostic services in a segmented healthcare system. *Journal of Industrial & Management Optimization* 13: 1.

Miskovic, Stefan, and Zorica Stanimirovic. 2016. Hybrid metaheuristic method for solving a multi-period emergency service location problem. *Information Technology and Control* 45: 321–37. [CrossRef]

Moayedi, Hossein, Mahdy Khari, Mehdi Bahiraei, Loke Kok Foong, and Dieu Tien Bui. 2020. Spatial assessment of landslide risk using two novel integrations of neuro-fuzzy system and metaheuristic approaches; ardabil province, iran. *Geomatics, Natural Hazards and Risk* 11: 230–58. [CrossRef]

Monahan, Kelly. 2018. *How Behavioral Economics Influences Management Decision-Making: A New Paradigm*. New York: Academic Press.

Mousavi, Seyed Hosein, Ali Nazemi, and Ashkan Hafezalkotob. 2015. Using and comparing metaheuristic algorithms for optimizing bidding strategy viewpoint of profit maximization of generators. *Journal of Industrial Engineering International* 11: 59–72. [CrossRef]

Nolz, Pamela C., Karl F. Doerner, Walter J. Gutjahr, and Richard F. Hartl. 2010. A bi-objective metaheuristic for disaster relief operation planning. In *Advances in Multi-Objective Nature Inspired Computing*. Berlin: Springer, pp. 167–87.

Pages-Bernaus, Adela, Helena Ramalhinho, Angel A. Juan, and Laura Calvet. 2019. Designing e-commerce supply chains: A stochastic facility–location approach. *International Transactions in Operational Research* 26: 507–528. [CrossRef]

Pan, Quan-Ke, Liang Gao, Li Xin-Yu, and Framinan M. Jose. 2019. Effective constructive heuristics and meta-heuristics for the distributed assembly permutation flowshop scheduling problem. *Applied Soft Computing* 81: 105492. [CrossRef]

Panadero, Javier, Jana Doering, Renatas Kizys, Angel A. Juan, and Angels Fito. 2020. A variable neighborhood search simheuristic for project portfolio selection under uncertainty. *Journal of Heuristics* 26: 353–75. [CrossRef]

Panin, Artem A., Mikhail G. Pashchenko, and Aleksandr V. Plyasunov. 2014. Bilevel competitive facility location and pricing problems. *Automation and Remote Control* 75: 715–27. [CrossRef]

Parenti, Mathieu, Philip Ushchev, and Jacques-François Thisse. 2017. Toward a theory of monopolistic competition. *Journal of Economic Theory* 167: 86–115. [CrossRef]

Perloff, Jeffrey M., and James A. Brander. 2017. *Managerial Economics and Strategy*. Londo: Pearson.

Porter, Michael E. 2011. *Competitive Advantage of Nations: Creating and Sustaining Superior Performance*. New York: Simon and Schuster.

Pourghasemi, Hamid Reza, Seyed Vahid Razavi-Termeh, Narges Kariminejad, Haoyuan Hong, and Wei Chen. 2020. An assessment of metaheuristic approaches for flood assessment. *Journal of Hydrology* 582: 124536. [CrossRef]

Rabe, Markus, Maik Deininger, and Angel A. Juan. 2020. Speeding up computational times in simheuristics combining genetic algorithms with discrete-event simulation. *Simulation Modelling Practice and Theory* 103: 102089. [CrossRef]

Raza, Syed Asif, Faseela Chakkalakkal Abdullakutty, Sivakumar Rathinam, and Srikrishna Madhumohan Govindaluri. 2019. Multi-objective framework for process mean selection and price differentiation with leakage effects under price-dependent stochastic demand. *Computers & Industrial Engineering* 127: 698–708.

Rego, Nazaré, João Claro, and Jorge Pinho de Sousa. 2014. A hybrid approach for integrated healthcare cooperative purchasing and supply chain configuration. *Health Care Management Science* 17: 303–20. [CrossRef] [PubMed]

Rezaeiahari, Mandana, and Mohammad T. Khasawneh. 2020. Simulation optimization approach for patient scheduling at destination medical centers. *Expert Systems with Applications* 140: 112881. [CrossRef]

Robbins, Matthew J., and Brian J. Lunday. 2016. A bilevel formulation of the pediatric vaccine pricing problem. *European Journal of Operational Research* 248: 634–45. [CrossRef]

Rodriguez, Diego A., Paola P. Oteiza, and Nélida B. Brignole. 2019. An urban transportation problem solved by parallel programming with hyper-heuristics. *Engineering Optimization* 51: 1965–79. [CrossRef]

Sadeghi, Ali, and Mostafa Zandieh. 2011. A game theory-based model for product portfolio management in a competitive market. *Expert Systems with Applications* 38: 7919–23. [CrossRef]

Salamat, Vahid Reza, Alireza Aliahmadi, Mir Saman Pishvaee, and Khalid Hafeez. 2016. Assessing partnership alternatives in an IT network employing analytical methods. *Scientific Programming* 2016: 1–18. [CrossRef]

Samuelson, William, and Stephen G. Marks. 2015. *Managerial Economics*, 8th ed. New York: John Wiley & Sons.

Sauvey, Christophe, Teresa Melo, and Isabel Correia. 2020. Heuristics for a multi-period facility location problem with delayed demand satisfaction. *Computers & Industrial Engineering* 139: 106171.

Spencer, Milton H., and Louis Siegelman. 1959. *Managerial Economics*. Merced County: Irwin.

Talbi, El-Ghazali. 2009. *Metaheuristics: From Design to Implementation*. New York: John Wiley & Sons, vol. 74.

Tang, Yi, Jing Ling, Tingting Ma, Ning Chen, Xiaofeng Liu, and Bingtuan Gao. 2017. A game theoretical approach based bidding strategy optimization for power producers in power markets with renewable electricity. *Energies* 10: 627. [CrossRef]

Tsao, Yu-Chung, Thuy-Linh Vu, and Lu-Wen Liao. 2020. Hybrid heuristics for the cut ordering planning problem in apparel industry. *Computers & Industrial Engineering* 144: 106478.

Turek, Wojciech, Leszek Siwik, Marek Kisiel-Dorohinicki, Sebastian Łakomy, Piotr Kala, and Aleksander Byrski. 2017. Real-time metaheuristic-based urban crossroad management with multi-variant planning. *Journal of Computational Science* 23: 240–48. [CrossRef]

Uvaraja, Vikneswary, and Lai Soon Lee. 2017. Metaheuristic approaches for urban transit scheduling problem: A review. *Journal of Advanced Review on Scientific Research* 34: 11–25.

Vanderbei, Robert J. 2015. *Linear Programming*. Berlin: Springer.

Wang, Jian, and De-bi Cao. 2008. Relationships between two approaches for planning manufacturing strategy: A strategic approach and a paradigmatic approach. *International Journal of Production Economics* 115: 349–61. [CrossRef]

Wen, Fushuan, and A. Kumar David. 2001. Optimal bidding strategies for competitive generators and large consumers. *International Journal of Electrical Power & Energy Systems* 23: 37–43.

Werden, Gregory J., Luke M. Froeb, and Steven Tschantz. 2005. The effects of merger efficiencies on consumers of differentiated products. *European Competition Journal* 1: 245–64. [CrossRef]

Xavier, Clahildek Matos, Marly Guimarães Fernandes Costa, and Cícero Ferreira Fernandes Costa Filho. 2020. Combining facility-location approaches for public schools expansion. *IEEE Access* 8: 24229–241. [CrossRef]

Xie, Lin, Marius Merschformann, Natalia Kliewer, and Leena Suhl. 2017. Metaheuristics approach for solving personalized crew rostering problem in public bus transit. *Journal of Heuristics* 23: 321–47. [CrossRef]

Xu, Haitao, and Jing Ying. 2019. A hybrid and adaptive metaheuristic for the rebalancing problem in public bicycle systems. *International Journal of Intelligent Transportation Systems Research* 17: 161–70. [CrossRef]

Yang, Sheng Luo, Z. G. Xu, and J. Y. Wang. 2019. Modelling and production configuration optimization for an assembly shop. *International Journal of Simulation Modelling* 18: 366–77. [CrossRef]

Zhang, Hui, Thomas J. Best, Anton Chivu, and David O. Meltzer. 2019. Simulation-based optimization to improve hospital patient assignment to physicians and clinical units. *Health Care Management Science* 23: 117–41. [CrossRef] [PubMed]

Zhang, Tao, Gang Ren, and Yang Yang. 2020. Transit route network design for low-mobility individuals using a hybrid metaheuristic approach. *Journal of Advanced Transportation* 2020: 1–12. [CrossRef]

Zhou, Wenhui, and Weixiang Huang. 2016. Contract designs for energy-saving product development in a monopoly. *European Journal of Operational Research* 250: 902–13. [CrossRef]

A Managerial Analysis of Urban Parcel Delivery: A Lean Business Approach

Luce Brotcorne [1], **Guido Perboli** [2,3,4] ⓘ, **Mariangela Rosano** [2,3,*] ⓘ and **Qu Wei** [2] ⓘ

[1]   INRIA Lille—Nord Europe, Parc scientifique de la Haute Borne 40, av. Halley-Bât A, 59650 Villeneuve d'Ascq, France; Luce.Brotcorne@inria.fr
[2]   ICT for City Logistics and Enterprises Center, Politecnico di Torino, 10129 Turin, Italy; guido.perboli@polito.it (G.P.); qu.wei@polito.it (Q.W.)
[3]   CARS@Polito, Politecnico di Torino, 10129 Turin, Italy
[4]   CIRRELT, Pavillon André-Aisenstadt, Montreal, QC H3T 1J4, Canada
*   Correspondence: mariangela.rosano@polito.it

Abstract: The improper integration of traditional transportation modes with low emissions vehicles can generate a price war that reduces the service quality, undermining the efficiency and the profitability of parcel delivery operators. This paper aims to provide managerial insights to design a win-win strategy for the co-existence of traditional and green business models. In doing so, we adopt a multi-disciplinary approach that integrates a qualitative analysis through a Lean Business methodology, named GUEST, with a quantitative analysis based on simulation-optimisation techniques. This kind of holistic vision has received little attention in the literature. The first analysis investigates the parcel delivery industry with an emphasis on the main business models involved, their costs and revenues structures, while the quantitative part aims to simulate the system and extract sustainable policies. In particular, results highlight that in deploying mixed-fleet policies, the decision-makers have to focus both on the environmental sustainability that benefits from the adoption of low-emission vehicles, and on the operational feasibility and economic sustainability of the two services. In this direction, the paper suggests some managerial insights concerning the split of the customer demand between traditional and green operators, according to the classes of parcels and geographical areas of the city.

Keywords: Last-Mile Logistics; GUEST methodology; urban delivery

1. Introduction

Urban freight transportation and parcel delivery have been subjected to significant paradigm shifts over recent decades, caused by the urbanisation and development of megacities. First, economic development in the mid-1990s led the rise of faster-growing medium-large-sized companies that specialised in the delivery of small parcels, giving birth to the Global Courier, Express, and Parcel (CEP) market [1]. Since the 2000s, the advent of e-commerce and pervasive technologies changed the logistics and freight transportation dramatically, with an increase of the deliveries to the Business-to-Consumer segments in the urban areas and the competition of e-commerce giant platform to cope with the increasing requests for fast and cheap deliveries. Moreover, the awareness of the environmental impact of transportation activities as well as the significant congestion and environmental nuisances encourage the use of non-motorized transport to move people and goods (e.g., bikes and cargo bikes), self-service kiosks (i.e., lockers), and collaborative business models [2–4]. As [5,6] point out, the integration of different delivery alternatives is unfortunately not simple due to the relationships and disputes among actors, their business models and the technologies themselves.

To cope with the different issues of such a complex system, City Logistics and new domains, such as the Physical Internet, provide initiatives to optimise the flow of traffic and jointly address the economic, operative, social, and environmental sustainability of transportation and logistics, mitigating the inefficiencies and externalities that characterize the last-mile segment of the supply chain [7]. Despite the rich literature and state-of-the-art on City Logistics, not all solutions and proposals are successfully implemented. Indeed, as [8,9] point out some City Logistics initiatives failed due to the lack of support and commitment from the different actors (with diverse expertise) in the urban areas. This gap is the result of the absence of a managerial view in the deployment of policies for sustainable freight transportation and logistics. Indeed, usually implementation and proposal are too focused on the technological aspects as platforms, or optimization tools, missing a global vision and the lack between the business and operational models. To the best of our knowledge, a holistic vision of such a complex and hyper-connected system that integrates an actors' behaviour analysis, economic and managerial considerations into simulation and optimisation tools, has little attention in the literature. In particular, works by [3,10] represent first attempts to overcome this lack. The authors in [10] developed a last-mile typology and an instrument to simulate the total last-mile costs.

Our contributions to the literature are the following:

- In terms of business models, cost and revenue schemes, and policies, we explore the implementation of green transportation modes, considering integrating them with traditional vehicles. This analysis is completely novel in the literature. Indeed, different contributions deal with the new delivery options and green vehicles, but without considering their impact on the efficiency and profitability of traditional models. In this direction, we recognize the different players in the transportation and parcel delivery system, considering several configurations of traditional vehicles (e.g., trucks and vans that use fossil fuel) and green modes (e.g., electric or hybrid vehicles, bikes, and cargo bikes). We analyze their business models and behaviors from a managerial perspective. In particular, this research adds to the literature on the issues related to incorporating the new business models (e.g., green delivery operated using cargo bikes) with traditional modes, an assessment conducted in the City of Turin (Italy).
- We derive an assessment for the computation of the cost-per-stop of a last-mile delivery operator, independently on the vehicle type in use.
- We highlight as qualitative business management tools (e.g., Business Model Canvas and SWOT analysis) provided by the Lean Business methodology named GUEST, can be useful to understand the context and, gather information and data for solving the optimisation problem and designing win-win strategies that avoid the risk of cannibalisation between models.
- We show how the mix of qualitative and quantitative models can be conjugate the results of the business models and economic analyses proposed in this paper, with quantitative approaches based on Monte Carlo-based simulation-optimisation.

The paper is organized as follows. Section 2 reviews the literature on the urban freight transportation, identifying the main research challenges. Section 3 presents the methodology adopted in this study, which is based on a Lean Business approach. Then, Section 4 describes the multi-actor system of urban parcel delivery, presenting the business models of the participating actors. The analysis of their cost structures in Section 5 brings depth of understanding to the operating costs connected to the different types of vehicles. The results are summarized in Section 6, providing relevant insights concerning the relationships between operators and defining mixed-fleet policies. Finally, some conclusions are discussed in Section 7.

2. Literature Review

In recent decades, the researchers and practitioners become more aware of the issues that affect the freight transportation and logistics in urban areas (e.g., traffic, pollution, increasing uncertainty, atomisation of parcel flow [11]). Moreover, the "zero-emissions" challenge imposed by the local authorities and European Commission fosters the researchers and practitioners to design and develop solutions to make this complex system more innovative and competitive, while reducing its inefficiencies and environmental impact. A consistent framework of the literature concerns the sustainability of urban freight transportation and parcel delivery. Different papers in this framework propose several measures grouped into four main categories [9,12,13]: material/infrastructural (e.g., infrastructure reserved for freight operations as urban consolidation centers, lay-by zones etc.), immaterial/technological (i.e., Intelligent Transportation Systems), governance/regulation (e.g., road pricing, access times, maximum parking times, heavy vehicle networks, restricted access zones, "low traffic zones" (LTZ), etc.) and collaborative systems (e.g., co-modality and multi-modality). This last category includes solutions at the planning level that regard how the freight moves within the city, fostering the collaboration among the different actors, transportation modes and integrating people and freight. Many experiences in different cities [6,14–20] address the potential of multi-modality and intermodality that integrate traditional vans with non-motorized vehicles as cargo bikes, for sustainable urban freight transport, encouraging their diffusion.

Other contributions (e.g., [21,22]) propose mathematical models to schedule and optimize the routing of heterogeneous fleet, considering costs and emissions.

As highlighted in the introduction, these contributions are focused on the technical aspects of the problem, disregarding the managerial point of view and, thus, lacking of a strategic holistic vision. Indeed, in our opinion, a gap in the literature is represented by a whole analysis of the business model of the main actors in parcel delivery systems and their business development considerations, including the discussion of costs schemes. In particular, the literature explores the implementation of green transportation modes without taking into account their impact on the overall system in terms of operations, costs and revenues, and policies when integrated with traditional modes. As above mentioned, the works by [3,10] represent first attempts to simulate the last-mile costs.

This study addresses the following two main research questions:

- Is is possible and valuable to integrate business and operational models in urban parcel delivery, through a multi-disciplinary approach?
- Which are the benefits and implications of the integration of traditional transportation modes and low-emissions vehicles in the urban context?

Our study is the first attempt to fill the above discussed gaps in the literature. The strength of the proposed analysis relies on a powerful mix of qualitative research from a business perspective of parcel delivery systems, and operations of such systems, including interactions between international couriers and third-party companies that manage the last-mile operations.

3. Methodology

As mentioned before, the literature on the parcel delivery systems is focused on operational facets, disregarding the managerial considerations and links among the main players. To overcome this gap in the literature, we adopt the GUEST methodology [23,24]. It is a Lean Business approach that arises from the works by [25] and other lean startup framework, adapted to cope with multi-actor complex systems (MACSs), such as urban freight transportation [4,26,27]. The GUEST methodology is used to analyze the actors and stakeholders requirements from the beginning of the solution design and considering them throughout the overall implementation. The result is a higher commitment from the different actors and market acceptance of the outputs, generating network effect vital for the new collaborative business models, overcoming the issues of current City Logistics measures, identified in the Section 1.

The acronym GUEST derives from the five phases of the methodology, which have been attuned to the urban parcel delivery context as follows:

- Go. In this phase, we analyse the operators in the last mile segment, investigating their company profile, their current behaviour and, internal and external forces that interact with them and affect their businesses. The aim is to collect data and information and provide a comprehensive overview of the stakeholders' profiles regarding their requirements and cost structures.

- Uniform. The information gathered in the Go phase must be expressed in a standard form to achieve a shared vision of the MACS. In this phase, the governance mechanisms and business models are investigated using the Business Model Canvas [25]. It is a graphical tool coming from the lean startup movement and it shows how the proposed solution creates value in terms of benefits, products and services, for the different stakeholders. Its strengths rely on its simplicity of use and to highlight in an intuitive and understandable manner, how the integration of traditional transportation modes and green vehicles can deal with the different operators needs and how they can obtain benefits. Moreover, opportunities and threats of this integration are identified using a SWOT analysis. It is a strategic planning method useful to identify strengths, weaknesses, opportunities, and threats related to the different business models in urban freight transportation and parcel delivery.
- Evaluate. For each transportation option, we explicitly define the cost and revenue structures. Moreover, we conduct an in-depth assessment and comparison of business models, with focus on the relevant links between business and operational model.
- Solve. Solve. The outcomes from the managerial analyses conducted in the previous phases represented the inputs by means of the simulation-optimisation tool defined in [6]. The aim is to get a global view of the complex system as a whole.
- Test. In this phase, we test and analyze the outcomes provided by the Monte Carlo simulation, to design policies adequate for heterogeneous fleet.

As the authors in [3,28] point out, we can observe a lack of available realistic benchmark dataset for testing City Logistics solutions. Indeed, the instances in the literature do not come from real or realistic settings, but they are usually based on the generalisation of classical instances or artificial data often not generated for urban applications, making difficult the assessment of new models. The reason of such unavailability of real data relies on the poor commitment of the stakeholders and their availability to share information as well as the high effort in terms of time and expertise needed to gather these realistic data and to embed them in the decision-support systems. The data streams concerning the business models, the cost structures, and the operations used in this paper are realistic and they are provided by a worldwide parcel delivery company and by stakeholders respectively involved in the two research projects URBan Electronic LOGistics (URBeLOG) and Synchro-NET [27,29,30]. In particular, we conducted interviews with the CEO, COO and marketing directors of the companies operating parcel delivery in Italy, and an in-depth analysis of their financial statements, to obtain information concerning the business models and costs structures.

4. Managerial Analysis of the Urban Parcel Delivery

The urban freight transportation and parcel delivery system involves multiple actors with sometimes conflicting goals and objectives. We identify the following five main actors:

- International courier delivery services (hereinafter, International courier). It is the company that manages the long-haul shipments at global and national levels.
- Traditional subcontractor. Once the goods coming from the long-haul shipments arrive at the urban distribution centres located in the outskirt of the city, the traditional subcontractor manages their deliveries in the last-mile segment. In the European market, it is usually a small or medium-sized company, generally organised as a legal form of cooperatives with limited financial and fleet capacity, as stated by [6].
- Green subcontractor. This is a small company that has a business model similar to those of the traditional subcontractor. However, a strong component of its value proposition relies on the low environmental impact of the transportation activities, thanks to the adoption of green vehicles as the cargo bikes.

- Customer. This category refers to the final user of transportation services. We identify different customer segment: business-to-business (B2B), business-to-consumer (B2C), consumer-to-business (C2B), consumer-to-consumer (C2C), and intra-business.
- Authority. This actor refers to the local public administration that manages the city and designs policies for freight transportation in urban areas. It seeks to reduce the environmental pollution, traffic and congestion associated with the transportation activities, as well as their social costs, while improving the quality of live in the city.

In this section, we present the analysis of the main industry-driven operators, investigating their business profiles and interactions. In doing so, we adopt a business development approach, based on the Business Model Canvas, which has not received relevant interest in the literature. In particular, Section 4.1 discusses the business models of these operators, while Section 4.2 presents the SWOT analysis.

4.1. Business Models in Urban Freight Transportation

Sections 4.1.1 and 4.1.2 discuss the business models of the international courier, traditional subcontractor and green subcontractor, respectively.

4.1.1. Business Model of International Couriers

Figure 1 depicts the Business Model Canvas of the international courier. Its main customers can be grouped in the following segments:

- B2B. It is composed by the firms that by means of couriers, move raw material, semi-finished or finished products along their logistics chain towards other companies. This segment also includes the e-commerce flows between e-retailers and between e-retailers and suppliers.
- Intra-business. It consists of the companies that uses courier services to move raw materials, semi-finished or finished products among their different plants and warehouses.
- C2B. It is represented by the flows of goods coming from the reverse logistics (e.g., waste, processing scarps, recycling end-of-life products, customer rejections).
- B2C. It comprises of companies selling products straight to end customers, bypassing distribution chains.
- C2C. This segment is composed by all the orders from private people that require the transportation of goods for personal needs.

The value proposition that the international courier offers is mainly the "time sensitive" transportation of products, due to the critical role of timing (i.e., strict time windows), flexibility and reliability of the delivery to cope with the increasing requests of the modern economy. Another component of the value proposition is a superior customer experience thanks to the benefits derived from shipment efficiency, speed, reliability, security (e.g., through "tracking and tracing") and customisation of the services received. International couriers usually manage the long-haul shipments, serving the maritime and land transport. As different authors point out [27,31,32], ports and surrounding maritime terminals act as integrated logistics centers vital for the sustainability of urban distribution of goods. However, maritime transport is affected by different challenges related to the growing fuel prices, congestion and traffic at port terminals, and environmental issues that increase the complexity of the last-mile activities. Researchers have an increasing focus on new solutions and models to reduce these issues, while improving the efficiency of operations in maritime terminals, such as the synchromodality and slow steaming [27,31,33,34], and the optimisation of berthing decisions [35]. Although maritime and land transport are strongly related, in this paper we focus on the urban freight transportation. The international courier offers to the small and medium-sized business customers, a cost optimisation service thanks to the express deliveries that allow reducing the inventory level in a Just-In-Time orientation, and the sales market extension.

These time-sensitive delivery services represent the main source of revenues for the international courier that can reach its customer segments through specific channels, as website, kiosks and retail stores.

The key resources required to make the business model work are similar to those of the other players and they are mainly tangible assets (e.g., vehicle fleets and point-of-sale systems), intangible assets (e.g., software, assignment and routing algorithms, licenses and partnerships) and the human resources represented by the drivers.

The study by [36] identifies the management of processes and operations (e.g., route planning, intermodal transportation, pickups and deliveries, monitoring) and the customer care (e.g., pre- and after-sales support, tracking and tracing of parcels, proof of delivery), as key activities for the international couriers.

The international courier establishes strong partnerships and alliances with the key partners (e.g., suppliers, subcontractors, handling agents) to improve the efficiency of its current business model, or developing new ones. Moreover, the international courier forms a close cooperation with governmental organizations and local administrations to make urban parcel delivery more sustainable and less pollutant (e.g., the URBeLOG project [29]).

The primary expenses incurred by the international courier in order to run the business model, are the costs of the key resources (e.g., fuel costs, packaging, personnel costs, acquisition and maintenance of vehicles, ICT systems), as well as the costs of marketing and advertising campaign, and the risk management consultancy.

4.1.2. Business Model of Traditional Subcontractors

Figure 2 depicts the Business Model Canvas of traditional subcontractors. As discussed in Section 4, international couriers outsource pickups, deliveries, and transportation activities in the last-mile segment of the supply chain to subcontractor couriers, obtaining operational efficiency and customer proximity. Indeed, the international courier benefits from an efficient and flexible management of urban parcel delivery operations, particularly when peaks of demand and strictly temporal constraints typical of certain events and conditions (e.g., prime customers, disaster relief [37]) exist.

Usually, traditional subcontractor reaches and activates a business with the international couriers through long-term commercial agreements and tenders. Then, a constant negotiation and information exchange along all transportation activities (e.g., tracking services and feedback) ensures the relationship between these two actors, permitting the co-creation of value for the final user. Indeed, the coordination with international courier customers represents a key activity, fundamental for the success of multimodality and the well-functioning of the on-demand logistics, with the subsequent satisfaction of final users. Other key activities for the traditional subcontractors concern the operations management, as the optimal route planning and dispatching, to achieve high performance in the service quality levels (expressed in terms of parcel delivered), while coping with the challenges such as timeline constraints, the risk of delivery failure (approximately 12% of all deliveries) [38] and the last-mile split delivery problem [39].

4.1.3. Business Model of the Green Subcontractor

New business models are raising to guarantee the sustainability and efficiency of urban transportation, particularly of the parcel deliveries in the last-mile. Looking at the business model of these companies (Figure 3), here named green subcontractors, we observe many similarities with those of traditional subcontractors. However, a great part of its value relies on the adoption of green vehicles (i.e., bikes and cargo bikes) to ensure a low environmental impact of transportation activities.

Thus, the main customer segment of the green subcontractor is the international couriers that outsource last-mile operations. Other customers are represented by the B2B and B2C segments related to the intercity and intracity postal services.

The green subcontractor offers to its customer segments a value proposition consisting of cycle-logistics service, delivering small-sized parcels, with a weight between 0 to 3 kg, or up to 6 kg. The adoption of cargo bikes and bikes allows to overcome the complexities that affect the parcel delivery in the inner city (e.g., City Logistics regulation measures, low traffic zones, unavailability of loading/unloading zones, traffic and congestion), and as a result, the customers can benefit from a more flexible, fast, punctual and reliable service. Overcoming the complexity of the last mile segment increases the economic performance of the international courier, who incurs in a cost optimization, fundamental in this industry where margins are decreasing. Moreover, in line with the increasing interest of communities to the environmental protection, the customer segments of the green subcontractor obtain a green reputation and the consequent monetary gains, to achieve the goal of sustainable supply chains.

The main channels through which customers are reached by the green subcontractors are websites and green marketing campaigns that foster the awareness and knowledge of their services (e.g., interviews published in journals specialized in sustainable urban freight transportation). Once reached, the green subcontractor maintain the relationship with its customers through regular information flows and connected services (e.g., tracking services, feedbacks, computation of the CO_2 savings).

The above mentioned value proposition provides the green subcontractor a revenue stream, which is increased by the additional incomes from the CO_2 savings and the carbon credit trading, and fees and royalties from affiliates [6].

The business model of the green subcontractor requires a set of physical assets (i.e., bikes and cargo bikes, warehouses), human resources (i.e., bikers) and intangible assets (e.g., partnerships to protect the repeatability of the model by competitors, decision support systems and ICT tools to optimize activities) [4]. In this model, the service quality and functioning are strictly dependent on the performance of bikers, as well as fatigue and external factors (e.g., weather condition).

Key Partners	Key Activities	Value Propositions	Customer Relationships	Customer Segments
• Suppliers • Subcontractors • Cargo operator and handling agent • Joint Venture • Local administration	• Process and operations management • Customer care	• Time-sensitive transportation services • Express deliveries • Superior customer experience • Costs optimization • Sales market extension	• Retail stores • Web site • Help desk • Call center • Locker • Community	• Business-to-Business (B2B) • Business-to-Consumer (B2C) • Consumer-to-Business (C2B) • Consumer-to Consumer (C2C) • Intra-Business
	Key Resources		Channels	
	• Physical assets Vehicle fleets Warehouses and retail stores • Intangible assets ICT Licenses Partnerships • Human resources		• Direct channels Web site and mobile apps Retail stores Brand identity • Indirect channels Partner web sites	

Cost Structure	Revenue Streams
• Costs of materials (e.g., fuel costs, packaging, consumables) • Personnel costs • Assets costs (e.g., vehicles, equipment, structure and warehouses, software) • Handling fees • Subcontractors fees • Marketing & advertising • Risk management • Other operative costs (auditor and governmental)	• Revenues from time-sensitive delivery services

Figure 1. Business Model Canvas of an international courier.

Key Partners
- Suppliers of strategic assets (vehicles)
- Drivers

Key Activities
- Operations and dispatchers management (ground operations)
- Anomalies management
- Coordination with international express courier

Key Resources
- Physical assets
- Vehicle fleets (van)
- Warehouses
- Human resources

Value Propositions
- Last mile parcel deliveries
- Efficiency and flexibility
- Geographical coverage
- Costs reduction
- Focus on core business activities
- Access to specialized resources and know-how

Customer Relationships
- Information exchange process (tracking and feedback)

Channels
- Commercial agreements and tenders
- Web site

Customer Segments
- International courier

Cost Structure
- Costs of materials (e.g., fuel costs, consumables)
- Personnel costs
- Assets costs (e.g., vehicles, equipment, structure and warehouses)
- Penalties

Revenue Streams
- Revenues from last mile parcel delivery services

Figure 2. Business Model Canvas of a traditional subcontractor.

Key Partners	Key Activities	Value Propositions	Customer Relationships	Customer Segments
• Technological partners • Investors • Partner • Bikers • Local administration	• Operations and dispatchers management • Anomalies management • Fund raising	• Cycle-logistics services • Costs optimization • Small sized parcel delivery (0-3 kg and 3-6 kg) • Green image and green credentials	• Information exchange process (tracking, feedback, CO_2 savings)	• International courier • B2B and B2C for intercity and intracity postal services
	Key Resources • Physical assets Vehicle fleets (bikes and cargo bikes) Warehouses • Human resources (bikers) • Intangibles assets Partnership ICT		**Channels** • Web site • Media and interviews	

Cost Structure
- Costs of materials (e.g., consumables, bags)
- Personnel costs
- Assets costs (e.g., vehicles, equipment, structure and warehouses, ICT tools)
- Marketing & advertising

Revenue Streams
- Revenues from last mile parcel delivery services
- Revenues from CO_2 savings and carbon credits trading

Figure 3. Business Model Canvas of a green subcontractor.

4.2. Swot Analysis

In this section, we present the SWOT analysis related to the traditional subcontractor (Figure 4 and the green subcontractor Figure 5). The SWOT analysis identifies and assesses the internal (i.e., inside the company) and external (i.e., in the eco-system) factors involved in the two business models. Thus, due to the strictly connection between this analysis and the Business Model Canvas, in this section we present a joint discussion of the results.

Although all business models propose a value proposition represented by time sensitive delivery, we observe the outsourcing of logistics activities to subcontractor carriers. Indeed, as [6] point out, the big international couriers companies internalize the long-haul transportation, while they entrust the last mile activities to traditional and green subcontractors carriers, achieving operational and economic efficiency, as well as the customer proximity.

The SWOT analysis (Figures 4 and 5) and the Business Model Canvas show that, for traditional subcontractors, the main sources of weaknesses and threats are their impact on the environment and the critical issues affecting European regions, like traffic and congestion, Low Traffic zones (LTZ), and the unavailability of delivery bays.These factors compromise the delivery fulfillment, inducing disadvantageous conditions (e.g., lack of parking areas) for couriers with traditional vehicles. In contrast, these same points represent strengths for green subcontractors. The latter group uses green vehicles such as bikes, in last-mile parcel deliveries, allowing them to earn additional income from the emissions reduction and carbon credit trading, as shown in the revenue streams block of the Business Model Canvas (Figure 3). However, the operational model of green subcontractors is affected by capacity constraints of bikes, which bind the size of parcels that can be loaded, thus representing the major limitation of this model. This constraint is partially overcome using next-generation cargo bikes, which have a capacity of 100–150 kg per bike, according to estimates provided by [40] based on Europe. The SWOT analysis highlights a threat related to the competition between traditional and green subcontractors. This competition is also affected by the strategy of the international courier, who can guide subcontractors using a financial lever [6]. The competition based exclusively on costs between traditional and green subcontractors operating in the same geographical area originates a price war, which reduces their profitability or their differentiation in terms of service quality perceived by the final customer.

Moreover, according to [6], a comparable case could arise when the international courier internally owns the fleet. Indeed, the partial organisational autonomy of local depot fleet managers and their strategic cost-cutting goals might have comparable impacts to a price war between traditional and green subcontractors.

Looking at the financial structure of each business model, the costs related to the vehicles and the related social costs connected to the negative externalities have a huge relevance. For this reason, we decide to investigate these costs by means of a further quantitative analysis presented in the next Section 5.

STRENGHTS	WEAKNESS
• Availability of ICTs and innovation • Tools based on Operational Research methods and models for the optimization of routes and loads • Availability of vehicles with high loading capacity to delivery large-sized parcels	• Negative externalities and associated social costs (e.g., traffic and congestion, emissions)
SWOT	
OPPORTUNITIES	THREATS
• Urbanization and demographic growth • Intermodality and integration with green vehicles • Intelligent Transportation Systems • Impact of Just-In-Time, e-Commerce, on-Demand economy	• Climate change and environmental impact of vehicles • Complexities of the last-mile segment (e.g., mobility restrictions in urban areas) • Competition with new business models based on very low environmental impact and flexibility • Pressure for fast and cheap deliveries

Figure 4. SWOT analysis referred to the traditional subcontractor.

STRENGHTS	WEAKNESS
• Availability of ICTs and innovation • Tools based on Operational Research methods and models for the optimization of routes and loads • Availability of simple vehicle	• Vehicle with limited load capacity • Biker performance subjected to physical fatigue
SWOT	
OPPORTUNITIES	THREATS
• Urbanization and demographic growth • Awareness on sustainable transportation • Complexities of the last-mile segment that affect the performance of traditional vehicles (vans) • Intelligent Transportation Systems • Impact of Just-In-Time, e-Commerce, on-Demand economy	• Complexities related to the impact of climate conditions on performance • Competitors with higher load capacity and low environmental impact (e.g., electric vans) • Pressure for fast and cheap deliveries

Figure 5. SWOT analysis referred to the green subcontractor.

5. Cost and Revenue Analysis of Vehicular and Cargo Bike Delivery

5.1. Operating Costs Analysis

The increasing awareness of the need for the environmental protection, and to increase the efficiency of delivery activities while marginal revenues are decreasing have led the operators and cities to experiment the green vehicles that use innovative propulsion systems (e.g., electric, hybrid or methane vans). In our study, we consider four main alternative vehicles: gasoline-fuelled, diesel-fuelled and totally electric vans, and cargo bikes.

This decision and the selection of the vehicles used for the benchmarking reflect the transition occurring in the industry and the common vehicles composing the fleets of the large portion of delivery couriers. For example, we consider the totally electric vehicle *e-NV200* adopted in the "GoGreen" programme [41] arose from the partnership between the automobile manufacturer Nissan Motor Co. Ltd. and the international logistics company DHL Express.

In this section, we investigate the operating and environmental costs for each class of vehicles, given their different environmental and economic impacts (e.g., investment, fleet management and maintenance requirements, emissions). In particular, we estimate the Operating Costs per Kilometre (OCK) related to each type of vehicle and then, compared them in order to identify the most cost-efficient, considering the operative performance. For the purposes of this analysis, the OCK includes both variable costs (e.g., gasoline) and the total cost of ownership, according to [42], expressed in Euro per kilometres traveled in last mile segment [€/km], which the company incurs for the use of the vehicle in a year of its technical life cycle. This cost is composed of variable costs and fixed costs. The latter are not proportional to the distance and the courier incurs regardless of the vehicles usage degree. The OCK function is:

$$OCK = (FC + VC)/TK = ((v + tx + i + p) + (f + t + mr))/TK \tag{1}$$

where:

- FC is the total annual fixed costs;
- VC is the total annual variable costs;
- TK is the total annual traveled kilometres.

The entity of each item has been estimated through primary data from market research on the commercial practices applied by the different stakeholders and has been supported by the formulation of specific assumptions on the use conditions of the vehicles benchmark. These assumptions are:

- total annual usage, in terms of traveled kilometres in the last mile segment, of about 25,000 km/year;

- a total annual usage, in terms of hours required to reach each destination and to do the delivery operations, of about 2000 h/year;

- the commercial speed of vehicles in urban areas is about 35 km/h;

- each driver must make about 80 deliveries per day, with an average time of 4.5 min per delivery, to perform all operations, from the parking of the vehicle to the collecting of the proof of delivery;

- each component of cost has charged in refers to the technical life cycle of the vehicle that has been estimated of 5 years.

The components of fixed and variable costs are briefly described as follows.

- **Purchase cost of vehicle** (v): is based on estimates realized by the fleet manager section of several car dealers, and is referred to a leasing agreement of 5 years, considering both the interest and principal payments on the loans. During this period, the company operating in the transportation and parcel delivery market on the last mile will provide a depreciation and amortisation schedule of this asset. In particular, we adopt a straight-line depreciation, which represents the simplest and most commonly used depreciation method in the market. It is based on time and thus, on the total number of years the vehicle is expected to be a useful asset for the parcel delivery company (i.e., the so-called "useful life"). In our case, we consider a life cycle of 5 years for both vehicles and batteries.

- **Vehicle taxes** (tx): are referred to the expenditures and taxes related to the vehicles, according to the current regulations, such as the ownership tax.

- **Insurance** (i): is the cost of the truck liability insurance based on the capacity of the vehicle and the third party cargo insurance, while it excludes the theft and fire insurances, included in the leasing agreement. Due to the liberalisation process that have interested in the 2014 the insurance industry in different country including the Italy, and that have imposed the right to determine independently the contract conditions and the tariffs, the amount of the policy considered refers to an average value of the prices offered by several insurance companies, as emerged by a secondary research conducted in this work.

- **Personnel costs** (p): is defined as the total remuneration payable by a driver, and also include taxes and employees' social security contributions, according to the National Collective Labour Agreement prescribed for the category to which they belong.

- **Vehicle fuelling** (f): are referred to the costs related to the fuel supply, both fossil and diesel, and to the powertrain. Their values are estimated considering the consumption derived from the technical specifications provided by the manufacturer. For the petrol and diesel fuel, prices are measured by the average monthly domestic prices from the statistical data elaborated by the Italian Ministry of Economic Development for 2018. Otherwise, the electricity price is evaluated as an average cost from the prices charged by major suppliers operating in the energy industry, to a business customer.

- **Tyres costs** (t): are based on the list prices charged, by the leading manufacturers, discounted by a corrective factor of 15% for the purchase of high quantities for the whole fleet. It is also considered the average duration of a set of about 50,000 km/year referring to the capacity and the wear out of the vehicle.

- **Maintenance and repair costs** (mr): estimated from the data provided by the Automobile Club Italia (ACI) [43], they are related to the expenditures for the activities required to maintain the effectiveness of the vehicle performance, along his life cycle, known the travelled distance. These activities are classified in time or condition-based maintenance, which have the aim to prevent negative events and to maintain the normal conditions of use. Otherwise, breakdown maintenance or repair, which is conducted after a failure occurrence.

Tables 1–3 show the different cost items for the fossil-fuelled, diesel-fuelled and electric vehicles.

Table 1. Operating Costs per Kilometre related to the fossil fuelled vehicle.

Cost Item	Benchmark Value [€]	Technical Life Cycle [years]	Annual Cost [€]	Commercial Speed [km/h]	Total km [km]	OCK [€/km]
Purchasing cost of vehicle						
Advance payment	5000.00	5	1000.00	35	25,000	0.0400
Lease fees and other insurance	11,820.00	5	2364.00	35	25,000	0.0946
Stamp duty	16.00	5	3.20	35	25,000	0.0001
VAT 22%	3703.92	5	740.78	35	25,000	0.0296
Total purchasing cost of vehicle	20,539.92		4107.98			**0.1643**
Vehicle taxes						
IPT	319.00	5	63.80	35	25,000	0.0026
DMV costs and PRA	100.00	5	20.00	35	25,000	0.0008
Stamp duty	208.98		208.98	35	25,000	0.0084
Total vehicle taxes	627.98		292.78			**0.0117**
Insurance						
Average truck liability insurance costs			2680.33	35	25,000	0.1072
Total insurance cost						**0.1072**
Maintenance and repair costs						
Maintenance and repair costs						0.0573
Total maintenance and repair costs						**0.0573**
Tyres costs						
Average tyres costs			311.15	35	25,000	0.0124
Average tyres costs						**0.0124**
Personnel costs						
Personnel costs			56,000.00	35	25,000	2.2400
Total personnel costs						**2.2400**
Vehicle Fuelling						

		Price per Litre [€/l]	Consumption [€/100km]	Commercial Speed [km/h]	Total km [km]	Cost per Kilometre [€/km]
Average manufacturing price	0.5375	0.072	35	25,000		0.0387
Average production tax		1.0069	0.072	35	25,000	0.0725
Total vehicle fuelling costs						**0.0112**
				TOTAL OCK	€/km	**2.7042**

Table 2. Operating Costs per Kilometre related to the diesel fuelled vehicle.

Cost Item	Benchmark Value [€]	Technical Life Cycle [years]	Annual Cost [€]	Commercial Speed [km/h]	Total km [km]	OCK [€/km]
Purchasing cost of vehicle						
Advance payment	5000.00	5	1000.00	35	25,000	0.0400
Lease fees and other insurance	13,740.00	5	2748.00	35	25,000	0.1099
Stamp duty	16.00	5	3.20	35	25,000	0.0001
VAT 22%	4126.32	5	825.26	35	25,000	0.0330
Total purchasing cost of vehicle	22,882.32		4575.46			**0.1831**
Vehicle taxes						
IPT	319.00	5	63.80	35	25,000	0.0026
DMV costs and PRA	100.00	5	20.00	35	25,000	0.0008
Stamp duty	170.28		170.28	35	25,000	0.0017
Total vehicle taxes	627.98		292.78			**0.0102**
Insurance						
Average truck liability insurance costs			2680.33	35	25,000	0.1072
Total insurance cost						**0.1072**
Maintenance and repair costs						
Maintenance and repair costs						0.0625
Total maintenance and repair costs						**0.0625**
Tyres costs						
Average tyres costs			311.15	35	25,000	0.0124
Average tyres costs						**0.0124**
Personnel costs						
Personnel costs			56,000.00	35	25,000	2.2400
Total personnel costs						**2.2400**
Vehicle Fuelling						

		Price per Litre [€/l]	Consumption [€/100 km]	Commercial Speed [km/h]	Total km [km]	Cost per Kilometre [€/km]
Average manufacturing price	0.5593	0.048	35	25,000		0.0268
Average production tax		0.8763	0.048	35	25,000	0.0421
Total vehicle fuelling costs						**0.0689**
				TOTAL OCK	€/km	**2.6843**

Table 3. Operating Costs per Kilometre related to the electric vehicle.

Cost Item	Benchmark Value [€]	Technical Life Cycle [years]	Annual Cost [€]	Commercial Speed [km/h]	Total km [km]	OCK [€/km]
Purchasing cost of vehicle						
Advance payment	5000.00	5	1000.00	35	25,000	0.0400
Lease fees and other insurance	21,756.00	5	4351.20	35	25,000	0.1740
Battery rental fee	4320.00	5	864.00	35	25,000	0.0346
Stamp duty	16.00	5	3.20	35	25,000	0.0001
VAT 22%	6840.24	5	1368.05	35	25,000	0.0547
Total purchasing cost of vehicle	37,932.24		7586.45			**0.3035**
Vehicle taxes						
IPT	319.00	5	63.80	35	25,000	0.0026
DMV costs and PRA	100.00	5	20.00	35	25,000	0.0008
Stamp duty	-		-			-
Total vehicle taxes	419.00		83.80			**0.0034**
Insurance						
Average truck liability insurance costs			932.50	35	25,000	0.0373
Total insurance cost						**0.0373**
Maintenance and repair costs						
Maintenance and repair costs						0.0540
Total maintenance and repair costs						**0.0540**
Tyres costs						
Average tyres costs			230.92	35	25,000	0.0092
Average tyres costs						**0.0092**
Personnel costs						
Personnel costs			56,000.00	35	25,000	2.2400
Total personnel costs						**2.2400**

Vehicle Fuelling		Average Price of Electricity [€/kWh]	Consumption [kWh/km]	Commercial Speed [km/h]	Total km [km]	Cost per Kilometre [€/km]
Average price of electricity	0.0672	0.1650	35	25,000	0.0111	
Total vehicle fuelling costs						**0.0111**
			TOTAL OCK		**€/km**	**2.6584**

5.2. Environmental Costs Analysis

In compliance with the technical specification ISO/TS 14067:2013 "Greenhouse gases—Carbon footprint of product—Requirements and guidelines for quantification and communication", we compute the carbon footprint of the last-mile deliveries, as the total direct (i.e., generated by fuel combustion process) and indirect (i.e., originated by the fossil fuel production and the energy consumed during the charging of batteries) greenhouses gas emitted by logistics activities. Concerning the source of electricity considered in our study, we refer to the current practice in Italy and Europe where the adoption of coal and crude oil is decreasing over the last 10 years, according to [44]. In particular, we consider that less than the 7% of the energy comes from the coal, 38% from natural gas, 20% from renewable sources and the remaining part is oil. As we concentrate on the last-mile operations, we omit emissions from long-haul transportation, vehicles manufacturing and their disposal. We also take into account all the pollutants generated by the transportation activities (e.g., nitrogen oxides, particulate) which are converted into CO_2, considering a conversion rate equals to 4.7 kg of CO_2 per liter of fuel consumed [45].

Finally, in Table 4, we computed the social costs paid by the courier due to its environmental impact. In particular, by applying a Pigouvian tax, named carbon tax, which refers to the price paid for CO_2 emissions in the atmosphere, we express the carbon footprint in monetary terms. This tax mechanism aims to push the transportation operators in switching to innovative technologies and tools that could make them more efficient and less pollutant, discouraging non-green behaviours.

As the carbon tax is not the same in all the countries, we consider two main levels of tariffs: 17 €/t and 150 €/t, according to the French [46] and Swedish [47] taxation systems, respectively [46].

Table 4. Cost analysis results.

Costs	Tariffs Carbon Tax [€/tons]	Fossil Fuel Vehicle	Diesel Fuel Vehicle	Electric Vehicle	Bike
TCK [€/km]					
Annual kilometre cost		2.70	2.68	2.66	1.50
Environmental costs [€]					
Direct CO_2 Emissions [tons]		4.15	3.38		
Indirect CO_2 Emissions [tons]		4.15	3.38		
Equivalent CO_2 Emissions [tons]		8.46	5.52		
Total Emissions [tons]		16.76	12.28		
Carbon Tax [€]	17.00	284.92	208.63		
	30.00	502.80	368.18		
	90.00	1508.40	1104.53		
	150.00	2514.00	1840.88		
Electric Battery Emissions [tons]				3.08	
Carbon Tax [€]	17.00			52.31	
	30.00			92.31	
	90.00			276.94	
	150.00			461.56	
Direct CO_2 Emissions [tons]					0.00

Tables 2 and 3 show that the traditional subcontractors using fossil fuel vehicles incurs in a higher cost than the green subcontractors. Electric vehicles enable reduced insurance tariffs and exemption from ownership tax, obtaining cost savings than traditional vans. However, few electric vehicles are still used in the market due to their high setup costs related to the purchasing cost of the van and battery rental fees. The reduced costs of bikes and personnel costs, given that the riders do not need any driving license and the working hours are limited, increase the economic efficiency of the bike couriers. Indeed, they incur in a operative costs equal to 1.50 €/km.

Moreover, the green subcontract benefits from the additional income by the selling of carbon credits. In fact, as shown by Table 5, when the carbon credit prices are 30% lower than the carbon tax tariffs, the engagement of green subcontractors generate an additional revenue equals to 0.02 € per stop, which becomes notably, considering high volumes of parcels that have as a destination the city.

Table 5. Revenue streams from carbon credit trading.

Buyer Emissions [tons]	Seller Emissions [tons]	Δ Emissions [tons]	Carbon Credit Prices [€/tons]	Revenue [€]
Fossil Fuel Vehicle vs. Electric Vehicle				
16.76	0.02	16.74	11.90	199.21
			21.00	351.54
			63.00	1054.62
			105.00	1757.70
Diesel Vehicle vs. Electric Vehicle				
12.27	0.02	12.25	11.90	145.80
			21.00	257.30
			63.00	771.91
			105.00	1286.51
Fossil Fuel Vehicle vs. Bike				
0.000421	0.00	0.000421	11.90	0.005
			21.00	0.009
			63.00	0.027
			105.00	0.044
Diesel Vehicle vs. Bike				
0.000308	0.00	0.000308	11.90	0.004
			21.00	0.006
			63.00	0.019
			105.00	0.032

6. Results

The findings emerged in the costs analysis have been used as input in a decision-support system developed for designing appropriate policies for heterogeneous fleet. The overall system is based on the simulation-optimisation approach integrating a Monte Carlo simulation, a last-mile optimisation meta-heuristic, and data aggregation and analytic module. The interested reader is referred to [6], for the complete description of the decision-support system and technical details of the simulator.

To conduct the computational experiments, we considered three instance settings I1, I2, and I3, with a number of parcels in the range [1000; 4000]. These instances are created from realistic analytics gathered during three weeks at the end of 2014 and the beginning of 2015 by a medium-sized courier.

As shown by Table 6, this data set is heterogeneous in terms of parcels composition as it considers three types of parcels, according to the classification proposed by the European Commission and [6]. Thus, we classify parcels as follows: "mailer," (0–3 kg), "small parcels" (3–6 kg), and "large deliveries" (more than 6 kg). Mailers cover the largest portion of the parcels that have as destination the city, given the increasing impact of e-commerce. Moreover, these parcels are easy to handle for the green subcontractors and to moved by bikes. Thus, mailers are more profitable for both subcontractors, counting a great part of their critical mass to make their business models sustainable.

Table 6. Classes of parcels and delivery locations.

Parcel Delivery Features	n. Delivery	%
In center	3395	22.51
Out of center	11,688	77.49
0–3 kg	8577	56.87
3–6 kg	1915	12.70
>6 kg	4590	30.43
Total deliveries	15,083	100.00

Combining the information related to the classes of parcels and the geographical area served by the green subcontractors, we define five operational scenarios:

- Scenario S_0. The traditional subcontractor manages all deliveries in the considered area:
- Scenario S_3_C. The green subcontractor delivers mailer parcels in the inner city, while the traditional subcontractor manages all remaining categories in both the central and semi-central areas.
- Scenario S_3_S. Compared to the previous scenario, the green subcontractor delivers mailers also in the semi-central areas, while the traditional subcontractor manages the small parcels and large deliveries.
- Scenario S_5_C. In this scenario, the mailers and small parcels in the central area are outsourced to the green subcontractor. The traditional subcontractor manages the large deliveries in the whole city and the small parcels in semi-central areas.
- Scenario S_5_S. In this scenario, the green subcontractor deliver mailer and small parcels in both the central and semi-central area, while the traditional one delivers only large parcels.

To evaluate the integration of traditional vehicles and those with a low environmental impact, particularly the cargo bikes, we measured different key performance indicators (KPIs), that reflect the following perspectives:

- Economic Sustainability. As discussed above, the subcontracts incur in operating costs related to fleet management and maintenance, and personnel costs associated with drivers. To monitor this aspect, we compute the number of equivalent vehicles used by the subcontractors (Veh Eq) and we consider the OCK costs derived in Section 5. As in the study by [6], we express the VehEq measure related to bikes in terms of vans, according to the duration of a working day of a traditional subcontractor in the European countries, composed by six-and-a-half hours. This conversion makes possible the comparison between the performance of the traditional and of the green subcontractors.

- Environmental Sustainability. As highlighted by the managerial analysis, the value proposition of new business models based on cargo bikes is to reduce the environmental impact of transportation and parcel delivery activities. Thus, we compute the kilograms of CO_2 (in compliance with the regulation ISO/TS 14067:2013) not emitted in the scenarios with cargo bikes, and we express this measure as the CO_2 savings (CO_2 Sav). Due to the negative impact of these emissions on society, we need to consider also the social costs paid by the traditional subcontractors for their externalities. Thus, we express these CO_2 saving in monetary terms as social costs savings, applying the carbon tax used in Table 4.
- Operational Sustainability. Finally, to evaluate in what extents the introduction of green delivery vehicles impacts on the operative performance and the efficiency of the traditional courier, we compute the number of parcels delivered per hour (nD/h).

Table 7 presents the results obtained by the experiments. On the one hand, the delivery of mailers and small parcels using cargo bikes allows reducing the total emissions of about 14 tons per year, corresponding to an amount of CO2 savings equals to more than 40%. Notice that the value of the CO_2 savings in each scenario is computed as the emissions in that scenario minus the emission in the scenario (S_0), then expressed in terms of social costs savings. Another valuable outcome is that the area served by using bike has a huge role in that result. Indeed, the scenarios in which the green subcontractors access to both the central and semi-central areas (i.e., S_3_S and S_5_S) have higher CO2 savings than scenarios S_3_C and S_5_C. The reason is that the traditional subcontractors no longer serve these areas, and thus the routes traveled by vans are reduced by 25%, with consequent benefits in terms of emissions and costs.

On the other hand, outsourcing mailers and small parcels to one or more green subcontracts that own their green fleets leads to a reduction of the traditional subcontractor performance, in terms of the operational efficiency and profitability. For example, in scenarios S_5_C and S_5_S the traditional subcontractor manages only large parcels, which usually require much time to be handled and delivered, with consequent reduction of the needed vehicles (e.g., in Set I1 the value of VehEq fall from 7.49 to less more than 2 or 3), increase of the total service time and reduction of the number of deliveries fulfilled in a day. This number is also undermined by the rapid saturation of vans capacity (due to the large sized of handled parcels) that imposes to the traditional subcontractors, frequent returns to the depots. Indeed, Table 7 highlights a reduction of up to five deliveries per hours moving from scenario to S_0 to the other scenarios using bikes. This reduction corresponds to a loss of efficiency of about 15% ad more than 30% when respectively mailers and, mailers and small parcels are handled by the green subcontractors.

To guarantee a well-functioning of the system, the inefficiency of the traditional subcontractor should be mitigated by an increase of the 130 deliveries per day managed by the green subcontractors, which represents an unfeasible target to achieve. Moreover, considering that the actual contractual schemes imply revenues based on the operational performance and penalties on the failed deliveries, the above-mentioned result may be compromising for the profitability of both operators.

These findings suggest some insights to the managers operating in the urban freight transportation and parcel delivery to derive sustainable policies and the balanced mix of traditional and green delivery modes. In particular, when the traditional subcontractor owns its fleet, it should outsource only the mailers in central and semi-central areas and small parcels in downtown, to avoid a large decrease of efficiency, while increasing the service quality perceived by customers. In this case, the green subcontractor will be able to deliver all the demand of assigned mailers and small parcels in the areas most affected by traffic and congestion, where its value proposition becomes strong, thus reaching the critical mass to sustain its model. In the case of the external fleet, the traditional subcontract should internalise the green fleet or outsource mailers in central and semi-central areas, while the outsourcing of small parcels requires the changing of the contractual scheme, to avoid the erosion of the margins. Moreover, the green subcontractor should balance the reduced revenues (due to fewer deliveries to manage, compared with the previous case), by the reselling of so-called "green credits".

Table 7. KPIs values generated by the Monte Carlo simulation. Note that in the scenario S_0, the KPIs referred to the green subcontractor have no values, as it is not involved in the parcel delivery.

KPI	Instances	Traditional Subcontractor					Green Subcontractor				
		S_0	S_3_C	S_3_S	S_5_C	S_5_S	S_0	S_3_C	S_3_S	S_5_C	S_5_S
nD/h	I1	15.65	12.82	12.98	10.44	10.38	NA	11.94	11.24	12.47	11.94
	I2	16.18	13.79	13.77	10.92	10.73	NA	12.03	11.36	12.51	12.06
	I3	15.47	13.29	13.01	10.50	10.21	NA	11.82	11.16	12.56	12.04
VehEq	I1	7.49	2.16	3.53	2.28	3.62	NA	3.70	6.55	3.88	6.88
	I2	9.89	3.03	4.86	3.07	4.98	NA	4.96	8.39	5.45	9.02
	I3	8.40	2.54	4.18	2.70	4.41	NA	3.85	6.89	4.12	7.14
CO2Sav	I1	NA	22%	34%	27%	45%					
	I2	NA	16%	34%	26%	44%					
	I3	NA	16%	41%	20%	48%					

7. Conclusions

In this paper, we analysed from a managerial standpoint the co-existence of traditional (i.e., based on the adoption of vans) and new green (i.e., using low emissions vehicles as cargo bikes) business models to perform the freight transportation and parcel delivery within the city areas. The failure of several City Logistics initiatives was highlighted, as such integration is no small matter. Indeed, a proper balance between these models must be guaranteed by the decision-makers to avoid the cannibalisation of the two services and a damaging price war that erodes the margins and the profitability of the companies involved. In doing so, it is important to have a system view of this industry, considering the business profiles of the different stakeholders involved, as well as their costs and revenues structure. Unfortunately, this type of holistic vision does not receive too much attention in the literature.

We contributed to overcoming this gap first proposing a complete analysis of the business models of the major stakeholders playing a key role in the integration of traditional and green delivery systems. Moreover, we understood the features and competitiveness of the eco-system, identifying opportunities, threats and strategies' potential profitability. Then, we investigate the costs and revenues structures of the companies (we referred to the traditional and green subcontractor couriers, respectively) that manage the urban parcel delivery. These analyses have been conducted by means of lean business tools and techniques. Finally, we presented some relevant results and managerial insights derived by applying simulation-optimisation tools to the outcomes of the previous analyses.

We can use these results to make some recommendations. First, the decision-makers have to design mixed-fleet policies, which do not aim only at the environmental sustainability that, however, would benefit from the adoption of low emission vehicles, but also look at the feasibility and, operational and economic sustainability of both traditional and green business models. Second, to deploy a winning strategy for all the actors involved in the system, a holistic vision is needed. This must integrate qualitative and quantitative approaches linked in a proper way to assess the co-existence of different transportation modes, which are not considered individually, but parts of a unique whole system. Third, the green business models based on the adoption of cargo bikes have beneficial effects on the environmental protection, but also on the operations. In fact, they emerge as the most flexible transportation modes to cope with the increasing uncertainty (e.g., related to demand and travel times) originated by the growing requests connected to the on-demand economy.

Despite the interesting results, this paper presents some limitations, which will be the subject of future research. First, the decision-support system developed do not cover all the operational issues (e.g., the crowdsourcing) and modes (e.g., automatic vehicles, drones and fully electric vehicles). Second, the related study in [6] proposes a sensitivity analysis on the composition of the demand, which is one of the most relevant parameters affected by uncertainty in the urban context. However, the current study lacks of further sensitivity analyses. In particular, to our vision, an interesting one considers the tariff schemes paid to the contractor. This analysis requires the development of a bi-level programming optimisation model, which is still not available in the literature, for the time being. Thus, it could be an interesting direction for future research.

Author Contributions: Authors contributed equally to design the research and writing the paper. All authors proofread and approved the final manuscript.

Acknowledgments: While working on this paper, the second author was the Director of the ICT for City Logistics and Enterprises Lab and the the head of the Urban Mobility and Logistics Systems (UMLS) initiative of the interdepartmental Center for Automotive Research and Sustainable mobility (CARS) at Politecnico di Torino, Italy.

References

Dablanc, L. City distribution, a key element of the urban economy: Guidelines for practitioners. In *City Distribution and Urban Freight Transport: Multiple Perspectives*; Edward Elgar Publishing: Cheltenham, UK, 2011; Volume 1, pp. 13–36.

Taefi, T.T.; Kreutzfeldt, J.; Held, T.; Fink, A. Supporting the adoption of electric vehicles in urban road freight transport—A multi-criteria analysis of policy measures in Germany. *Transp. Res. Part A* **2016**, *91*, 61–79. [CrossRef]

Perboli, G.; Rosano, M.; Saint-Guillain, M.; Rizzo, P. Simulation-optimization framework for City Logistics. An application on multimodal last-mile delivery. *IET Intell. Transp. Syst.* **2018**, *12*, 262–269. [CrossRef]

Perboli, G.; Rosano, M. A Decision Support System for Optimizing the Last-Mile by Mixing Traditional and Green Logistics. In *Information Systems, Logistics, and Supply Chain. ILS 2016. Lecture Notes in Business Information Processing*; Temponi, C., Vandaele, N., Eds.; Springer: Cham, Switzerland, 2018; Volume 262, pp. 28–46.

Tadei, R.; Fadda, E.; Gobbato, L.; Perboli, G.; Rosano, M. An ICT-Based Reference Model for E-grocery in Smart Cities. *Lect. Notes Comput. Sci.* **2016**, *9704*, 22–31.

Perboli, G.; Rosano, M. Parcel delivery in urban areas: Opportunities and threats for the mix of traditional and green business models. *Transp. Res. Part C* **2019**, *99*, 19–36. [CrossRef]

Perboli, G.; De Marco, A.; Perfetti, F.; Marone, M. A New Taxonomy of Smart City Projects. *Transp. Res. Procedia* **2014**, *3*, 470–478. [CrossRef]

Marcucci, E.; Gatta, V.; Marciani, M.; Cossu, P. Measuring the effects of an urban freight policy package defined via a collaborative governance model. *Res. Transp. Econ.* **2017**, *65*, 3–9. [CrossRef]

Russo, R.; Comi, A. A classification of city logistics measures and connected impacts. *Procedia Soc. Behav. Sci.* **2010**, *2*, 6355–6365. [CrossRef]

Gevaersa, R.; Van de Voorde, E.; Vanelslera, T. Cost Modelling and Simulation of Last-mile Characteristics in an Innovative B2C Supply Chain Environment with Implications on Urban Areas and Cities. *Procedia Soc. Behav. Sci.* **2014**, *125*, 398–411. [CrossRef]

Morganti, E.; Seidel, S.; Blanquart, C.; Dablanc, L.; Lenz, B. The Impact of E-commerce on Final Deliveries: Alternative Parcel Delivery Services in France and Germany. *Transp. Res. Procedia* **2014**, *4*, 178–190. [CrossRef]

Taniguchi, E. Concepts of city logistics for sustainable and liveable cities. *Procedia Soc. Behav. Sci.* **2014**, *151*, 310–317. [CrossRef]

De Marco, A.; Mangano, G.; Zenezini, G. Classification and benchmark of City Logistics measures: An empirical analysis. *Int. J. Logist. Res. Appl.* **2018**, *21*, 1–19. [CrossRef]

Leonardi, J.; Browne, M.; Allen, J. Before-After Assessment of a Logistics Trial with Clean Urban Freight Vehicles: A Case Study in London. *Procedia Soc. Behav. Sci.* **2012**, *39*, 146–157. [CrossRef]

Dablanc, L. City distribution, a key element of the urban economy: Guidelines for practitioners. *City Distrib. Urban Freight Transp.* **2011**, *1*, 13–36.

Conway, A.; Fatisson, P.; Eickemeyer, P.; Cheng, J.; Peters, D. Urban micro-consolidation and last mile goods delivery by freight-tricycle in Manhattan: Opportunities and challenges. In Proceedings of the Conference proceedings. Transportation Research Board 91st Annual Meeting, Washington, DC, USA, 22–26 January 2012.

Janjevic, M.; Ndiaye, A.B. Development and application of a transferability framework for micro-consolidation schemes in urban freight transport. *Procedia Soc. Behav. Sci.* **2014**, *125*, 284–296. [CrossRef]

Schliwa, G.; Armitage, R.; Aziz, S.; Evans, J.; Rhoades, J. Sustainable city logistics. Making cargo cycles viable for urban freight transport. *Res. Transp. Bus. Manag.* **2015**, *15*, 50–57. [CrossRef]

Lenz, B.; Riehle, E. Bikes for urban freight. *Transp. Res. Rec. J. Transp. Res. Board* **2013**, *2379*, 39–45. [CrossRef]

Navarro, C.; Roca-Riu, M.; Furió, S.; Estrada, M. Designing new models for energy efficiency in urban freight transport for smart cities and its application to the Spanish case. *Transp. Res. Procedia* **2016**, *12*, 314–324. [CrossRef]

Baldacci, R.; Battarra, M.; Vigo, D. Routing a Heterogeneous Fleet of Vehicles. In *The Vehicle Routing Problem: Latest Advances and New Challenges*; Springer: Boston, MA, USA, 2008; Volume 43, pp. 3–27.

Molina, J.C.; Eguia, I.; Racero, J.; Guerrero, F. Multi-objective vehicle routing problem with cost and emission functions. *Procedia Soc. Behav. Sci.* **2014**, *160*, 254–263. [CrossRef]

The GUEST Initiative. 2017. Available online: http://www.theguestmethod.com (accessed on 19 April 2019).

Perboli, G. The GUEST Methodology. 2017. Available online: http://staff.polito.it/guido.perboli/GUEST- site/docs/GUEST_Metodology_ENG.pdf (accessed on 19 April 2019).

Osterwalder, A.; Pigneur, Y. *Business Model Generation. A Handbook for Visionaries, Game Changers, and Challengers*; John Wiley and Sons, Inc.: Hoboken, NJ, USA, 2010.

Perboli, G.; Ferrero, F.; Musso, S.; Vesco, A. Business models and tariff simulation in car-sharing services *Transp. Res. Part A Policy Pract.* **2018**, *115*, 32–48.

Perboli, G.; Musso, S.; Rosano, M.; Tadei, R.; Godel, M. Synchro-modality and slow steaming: New business perspectives in freight transportation. *Sustainability* **2017**, *9*, 1843. [CrossRef]

Kim, G.; Ong, Y.S.; Heng, C.K.; Tan, P.S.; Zhang, N.A. City Vehicle Routing Problem (City VRP): A Review. *IEEE Trans. Intell. Transp. Syst.* **2015**, *16*, 1654–1666. [CrossRef]

URBeLOG Project Web Site. Available online: http://www.urbelog.it/ (accessed on 11 April 2019)

De Marco, A.; Mangano, G.; Zenezini, G.; Cagliano, A.C.; Perboli, G.; Rosano, M.; Musso, S. Business Modeling of a City Logistics ICT Platform. In Proceedings of the 2017 IEEE 41st Annual Computer Software and Applications Conference (COMPSAC), Turin, Italy, 4–8 July 2017.

Giusti, R.; Iorfida, C.; Li, Y.; Manerba, D.; Musso, S.; Perboli, G.; Tadei, R.; Yuan, S. Sustainable and De-Stressed International Supply-Chains Through the SYNCHRO-NET Approach. *Sustainability* **2019**, *11*, 1083. [CrossRef]

Montwiłł, A. The role of seaports as logistics centers in the modelling of the sustainable system for distribution of goods in urban area *Procedia Soc. Behav. Sci.* **2014**, *151*, 257–265. [CrossRef]

Bonney, J. Carriers Move Full Speed into Slow Steaming. *JOC* **2010**. Available online: http://www.joc.com/ maritime/carriers-move-full-speed-slow-steaming (accessed on 31 May 2019).

Lee, C.Y.; Lee, H.; Zhang, J. The impact of slow ocean steaming on delivery reliability and fuel consumption. *Transp. Res. Part E* **2015**, *76*, 176–190. [CrossRef]

Venturini, G.; Iris, Ç.; Kontovas, C.A.; Larsen, A. The multi-port berth allocation problem with speed optimization and emission consideration. *Transp. Res. Part D* **2017**, *54*, 142–159. [CrossRef]

Caroli, M.G.; Monarca, U.; Simonelli, F.; Valentino, A. The Nusiness Model of International Express Couriers. From Value Chain to Policy Indications, LUISS Business School and AICAI. 2010. Available online: http://www.aicaionline.it/kdocs/48400/AICAI_SUMMARY_UK.pdf (accessed on 19 April 2019).

Cook, R.A.; Lodree, E.J. Dispatching policies for last-mile distribution with stochastic supply and demand. *Transp. Res. Part E* **2017**, *106*, 353–371. [CrossRef]

Visser, J.; Nemoto, T.; Browne, M. Home delivery and the impacts on urban freight transport: A review. *Procedia Soc. Behav. Sci.* **2014**, *125*, 15–27. [CrossRef]

Zhang, Y.; Sun, L.; Hu, X.; Zhao, C. Order consolidation for the last-mile split delivery in online retailing. *Transp. Res. Part E* **2019**, *122*, 309–327. [CrossRef]

Riehle, E.B. *Cargo Bikes as Transportation Vehicles for Urban Freight Traffic. Study on European Business Examples to Estimate the Parameters and Potential for German Cities*; Faculty of Spatial Planning, TU Dortmund University: Dortmund, Germany, 2012.

NISSAN. Nissan and DHL Test e-NV200. Available online: http://www.nissan-global.com/EN/NEWS/ 2013/_STORY/130712-01-e.html (accessed on 5 December 2018).

Canadian Automobile Association. *Driving Cost Beyond the Price Tag: Understanding Your Vehicle's Expenses*; Canadian Automobile Association: Ontario, ON, Canada. Available online: https://www.caa.ca/wp- content/uploads/2016/09/CAA_Driving_Cost_English_2013_web.pdf (accessed on 11 June 2019).

Automobile Club Italia. Available online: http://www.aci.it (accessed on 19 April 2019).

International Energy Agency. *World Energy Balances 2018 Edition*; Data & Publications: Paris, France, 2018. Available online: https://webstore.iea.org/world-energy-balances-2018 (accessed on 11 June 2019).

Knörr, W. *EcoPassenger: Environmental Methodology and Data*; Final Report; IFEU—Institut für Energie-und Umweltforschung Heidelberg GmbH: Heidelberg, Germany, 2008.

Elbeze, J. The reform of energy taxation: An extension of carbon pricing in France. *Policy Brief* **2014**, *6*.

Johansson, B. Economic Instruments in Practice 1: Carbon Tax in Sweden. Swedish Environmental Protection Agency. Available online: https://www.oecd.org/sti/inno/2108273.pdf (accessed on 3 January 2019).

3

Financial Development and Income Inequality in Emerging Markets: A New Approach

Thang Cong Nguyen [1,*] , Tan Ngoc Vu [1], Duc Hong Vo [1] and Dao Thi-Thieu Ha [2]

[1]   Business and Economics Research Group, Ho Chi Minh City Open University,
       Ho Chi Minh City 70000, Vietnam; Tan.vn@ou.edu.vn (T.N.V.); duc.vhong@ou.edu.vn (D.H.V.)
[2]   International Economics Faculty, Banking University Ho Chi Minh City, Ho Chi Minh City 70000, Vietnam;
       daohtt@buh.edu.vn
*   Correspondence: thang.ngc@ou.edu.vn

Abstract: Financial development has been considered an efficient and effective mechanism for the sustainable economic growth and development of emerging markets in past decades. However, various concerns have emerged in relation to the influences of financial sector development on income inequality. It is the claim of this paper that findings from the current literature are incomplete. This is because various proxies have been utilized inconsistently for both financial development and income inequality in previous empirical studies. This study extends the current literature on this important finance–inequality nexus by examining a sample of 21 emerging countries for the period of 1961–2017. Various estimation techniques were employed with the aim of ensuring robust findings. Findings from this paper confirm the existence of an inverted U-curve relationship between financial development and income inequality, implying that income inequality may rise at the early stage of financial development and fall after a certain level is achieved. Policy implications have emerged from the findings of this study.

Keywords: financial development; income inequality; FMOLS; DOLS; emerging markets

JEL Classification: O11; O12; O15; F62; F63

1. Introduction

It is generally accepted that financial development fosters economic growth by enabling the efficient allocation of capital together with reducing financial constraints (Rousseau and Yilmazkuday 2009; Yilmazkuday 2011; Vo et al. 2019a, 2019b). However, the current literature appears to largely overlook the effect of financial development on income inequality. Debates have emerged in relation to the influences of the financial sector on income inequality, especially after the global financial crisis in 2008. Understanding the relationship between financial development and income inequality is important because policymakers can assess the indirect impact of the financial sector on growth via income inequality.

The literature on the finance–inequality linkage is inconclusive. Greenwood and Jovanovic (1990) argued that income inequality increased at the early stage of financial development and then the degree of inequality decreased after a certain level of financial development. Galor and Zeira (1993) and Banerjee and Newman (1993) stated that income inequality would be lower when financial markets were fully developed. Similarly, a well-functioning financial market was said to be essential for reducing income inequality (Younsi and Bechtini 2018). In contrast, Rajan and Zingales (2003) posited that the development of the financial sector may widen existing income inequality.

In addition, a theoretical guide to the measurement of financial development has not been properly developed, although market-based and/or bank-based indicators are commonly used in empirical studies.

Various proxies for financial development have been utilized, including the domestic credit to private sector–GDP ratio (Sehrawat and Giri 2015; Batuo et al. 2010; Law et al. 2014; Park and Shin 2017); the share of market capitalization-to-GDP ratio (Sehrawat and Giri 2015; Park and Shin 2017); and deposit money banks as a share of GDP (Kim and Lin 2011; Kappel 2010), among others. As such, the use of various proxies can influence the findings of empirical studies of the finance–inequality nexus.

In addition, previous empirical studies have been devoted to the examination of the short-run relationship between financial development and income inequality; this relationship in the long run has been largely ignored. We consider that a single-country investigation is necessary to provide useful policy implications. However, an examination of a group of various countries that share many similarities in relation to the level of financial development and economic growth is also desirable. As such, on the grounds of the theoretical ambiguity of the finance–inequality nexus and the lack of a theoretical guide to the measurement of financial development, we are motivated to consider the following fundamental questions: (i) How does financial development affect income inequality in the long-run? (ii) Does the foregoing relationship vary with the choice of a proxy for financial development? In response to these objectives, the aim of this study was to validate the relationship between financial development and income inequality in the long run and to verify the validity of the nexus by employing various variables as proxies for financial development.

On the grounds of the above considerations, emerging countries have attracted our attention. Two superpower economies—China and India—are generally recognized as emerging markets. These two countries continue to be increasingly influential players globally. Emerging markets play the key role in global economic growth and stability, according to the World Bank. However, despite the tremendous growth of emerging markets over the past decade, empirical analyses on the impact of financial development on income inequality have largely been ignored. As such, this study extends the current literature on the finance–inequality nexus through an investigation using available data for 21 emerging countries over the period of 1961–2017. Various robustness checks were conducted to ensure that the estimated results are unbiased.

The remainder of this paper is structured as follows. Section 2 provides an overview of the current literature on the issue. Data and methodology are presented in Section 3. Empirical results are discussed in Section 4, followed by a robustness check in Section 5. Section 6 provides concluding remarks.

2. An Overview of the Literature

The relationship between financial development and income inequality has received great attention from academics, practitioners, and in particular, policymakers in recent decades (Agnello et al. 2012; Ang 2010; Claessens and Perotti 2007; Clarke et al. 2006; De Haan and Sturm 2017), in addition to the determinants of income inequality (Afonso et al. 2010; Atkinson 2003; Dowrick and Akmal 2005; Roine et al. 2009; Malinen 2012; De Gregorio and Lee 2002; Huber and Stephens 2014; Li et al. 1998; Milanović 2000; Pan-Long 1995; Nguyen et al. 2019; Malinen 2012). For example, Atkinson (2003) considered explanatory factors of income inequality for nine OECD countries over the period of 1945–2001. The author found that various determinants could significantly affect income inequality variation, such as technological change, globalization, public policy, and sources of income. De Gregorio and Lee (2002) examined the relationship between human capital and income inequality for a broad range of countries from 1960 to 1990. Their empirical results showed an inverted U curve in the relationship, although a significant proportion of income inequality variation remains unexplained. In addition, Roine et al. (2009) investigated long-run determinants of income inequality for a group of 16 countries over the period of 1900 to 2000. They stated that income inequality was significantly affected by economic growth and financial development. In contrast, trade openness had no clear impact on income inequality.

Various studies were conducted to figure out how financial development affects income inequality. Empirical findings can be classified into three different groups. First, the finance–inequality widening hypothesis proposed by Rajan and Zingales (2003) posited that the development of financial sectors increases income inequality. Second, finance–inequality narrowing hypothesis suggested by Galor and Zeira (1993) and Banerjee and Newman (1993) argued that a better-functioning financial system reduced income inequality. Finally, the inverted U-shaped hypothesis suggested by Greenwood and Jovanovic (1990) fundamentally combined the two foregoing outcomes, where the finance–inequality linkage is non-linear. Specifically, this hypothesis suggests that income inequality increases at the early stage of financial development and then decreases after a certain level of financial sector development.

Some studies found a positive relationship between financial development and income inequality (Jauch and Watzka 2016; Seven and Coskun 2016; Jaumotte et al. 2013). For instance, Jauch and Watzka (2016) examined the relationship between financial development and income inequality in 138 developing and developed countries over the period of 1960–2008. Using the fixed effect and generalized method of moments (GMM) techniques, their results indicated that financial development provided a significantly positive effect on income inequality, indicating a rejection of a negative impact of financial development on income inequality or the finance–inequality narrowing hypothesis. Similarly, as countries were classified based on four different levels (e.g., high-income, upper-middle-income, lower-middle-income, and low-income), empirical findings on a sample including various countries also confirmed that there appeared to be a positive relationship between financial development and income inequality. Seven and Coskun (2016) found a statistically significant contribution of bank development on the growth effect of income inequality. The results emerged from the use of GMM techniques from a database of 45 emerging countries over the period 1987–2011. Prior to these studies, Jaumotte et al. (2013) stated that an increase of income inequality was associated with an increase of financial globalization, which was the case for 20 advanced countries as well as 31 developing and emerging countries for the research period from 1981 to 2003.

On the other hand, various scholars have demonstrated that the reduction of income inequality was triggered by the enhancement of financial sectors (Batuo et al. 2010; Hamori and Hashiguchi 2012; Kappel 2010; Mookerjee and Kalipioni 2010; Law et al. 2014). In other words, the development of the financial sector was negatively related to income inequality. For example, Hamori and Hashiguchi (2012) utilized a multi-step study, starting with fixed-effects estimation and then moving on with a dynamic panel model. In relation to the fixed-effects estimations, the authors found that the estimates of M_2–GDP ratio and domestic credit to private sector as a percentage of GDP, which represented the development of finance, were negative and statistically significant at the level of 1%. In addition, for the dynamic panel model where difference GMM was utilized, the contribution of financial development to income inequality was considered. Findings from this study presented evidence confirming the finance–inequality narrowing hypothesis, regardless of the proxies for financial development.

In addition, various empirical studies found a non-linearity in the relationship between financial development and income inequality (Kim and Lin 2011; Park and Shin 2017; Younsi and Bechtini 2018; Zhang and Chen 2015). Park and Shin (2017) confirmed that the impact of financial development on income inequality varied depending on the level of financial development. At the early stage of financial development, the development of the financial sector alleviated income inequality. In contrast, income inequality increased as financial development was further increased. Additionally, a non-linear effect of financial development on income inequality was found in a group of 65 countries from 1960 to 2005 (Kim and Lin 2011). Using a threshold regression technique, which allows one to simultaneously deal with endogeneity and to account for threshold nonlinearity, the authors found that after a certain level of financial development, income inequality would be reduced through the growth of finance and that income inequality would be counteracted by financial development.

In relation to various finance–inequality linkages, scholars have also been motivated by different types of proxies for financial development. Various proxies for financial development have been proposed, including the domestic credit to private sector–GDP ratio (Sehrawat and Giri 2015; Batuo et al. 2010; Law et al. 2014; Park and Shin 2017); the share of market capitalization-to-GDP ratio (Sehrawat and Giri 2015; Park and Shin 2017); deposit money in banks as a share of GDP (Kim and Lin 2011;

Kappel 2010), among others. As such, it is noticeable that the use of proxies for financial development influences the interpretation of its influence on the finance–inequality nexus.

3. Data and Model

3.1. Data

This paper employed unbalanced panel data of 21 emerging countries as classified by the International Monetary Fund (IMF) where required data were available. Only Venezuela and Russia, two emerging markets, were excluded due to a lack of required data. Data were collected from the World Development Indicators (WDI) from the World Bank. Annual data of economic growth per capita, financial development, inflation, and government expenditure–GDP ratio are available and accessible. Unfortunately, the WDI does not provide sufficient data on income inequality. In response to the problem, the Standardized World Income Inequality Database (SWIID), proposed by Solt (2016), was utilized. Our choice was largely based on data availability. Together with emerging countries, the SWIID also covers income inequality data for other countries, constituting a database of 192 countries, with the first observation dated back to 1960. Noted that only the Gini coefficient is provided in the SWIID database.

Although various methods have been developed to measure income inequality, the use of the Gini coefficient proposed by Deininger and Squire (1996) appears to be appropriate for the purpose of this paper, and the measurement is also widely adopted. As such, the Gini coefficient was utilized in this work to measure income inequality. Our choice was based on the following two considerations. First, the use of the Gini coefficient allows our results to be compared with previous studies. Second, the Gini coefficient achieves a high-quality standard (Li and Zou 1998; De Dominicis et al. 2008). In addition to the WDI, our dataset also incorporates the index of financial development (Svirydzenka 2016) developed by the IMF Strategy, Policy, and Review Department, in order to ensure that empirical findings achieved from the paper are robust. Details of variables are reported in Table 1. The descriptive statistics are presented in Table 2.

Our dataset consists of 21 emerging countries, including Argentina, Bangladesh, Brazil, Bulgaria, Chile, China, Colombia, Hungary, India, Indonesia, Malaysia, Mexico, Pakistan, Peru, the Philippines, Poland, Romania, South Africa, Thailand, Turkey, and Ukraine. Note that available data for Argentina, Brazil, and the Philippines are from 1961 to 2017, whereas the period is shorter for other countries.

Table 1. Summary of variables. IMF: International Monetary Fund; SWIID: Standardized World Income Inequality Database; WDI: World Development Indicators.

Variable	Definition	Proxy	Source
Gini	Income inequality measurement	Post-tax, post-transfer income	SWIID
		Pre-tax, pre-transfer income	SWIID
g	Economic growth	Annual percentage growth rate of GDP per capita	WDI
Inflation	A measurement of the overall level of prices in the economy	Percentage change in the cost to the average consumer of acquiring a basket of goods and services	WDI
GovExp/GDP	General government final consumption expenditure as a share of GDP	Ratio of government final consumption expenditure–GDP ratio	WDI

Table 1. *Cont.*

Variable	Definition	Proxy	Source
FD	A measurement of financial development	Domestic credit to private sector–GDP ratio	WDI
		Domestic credit to private sector by banks–GDP ratio	WDI
		Domestic credit to private sector by financial sector–GDP ratio	WDI
		Stock market capitalization as percentage of GDP	WDI
		New broad-based index of financial development	IMF

Table 2. Descriptive statistics.

Variable	Gini	g	FD	Inflation	GovExp/GDP
Min	26	−22.55	1.38	−7.63	2.97
Max	59.1	13.63	166.50	7481.66	27.39
Mean	42.45	2.75	43.52	63.60	12.46
S.D.	7.94	4.24	34.63	401.53	4.10
Observations	830	830	830	783	823

Note: The above table employs post-tax, post-transfer income as proxy for the Gini coefficient and the domestic credit to private sector–GDP ratio as proxy for financial development.

3.2. Model

This paper employs the following equation to consider the effects of financial development on income inequality. Following Kuznets (1955), we incorporate both linear and non-linear, proxied as a squared term of economic growth, denoted by g and g^2 respectively. We also add a set of control variables, denoted by X_{it}, including inflation and government consumption–GDP ratio.[1] This is because wealthy people can hedge better against inflation through access to financial markets while the poor, who are generally geared with debt, tend to experience unexpected consequences from high inflation since the contracts are written in nominal terms (Yilmazkuday 2012). Moreover, a large proportion of government consumption-to-GDP ratio can be a consequence of either redistributing income or rent-seeking activities (Jauch and Watzka 2016):

$$Gini_{it} = \alpha + \beta_1 FD_{it} + \beta_2 FD^2{}_{it} + \beta_3 g_{it} + \beta_4 g^2{}_{it} + \beta_j X_{it} + \varepsilon_{it}.$$

The sign and significance of β_1 and β_2 reveal how financial development affects income inequality. Following the finance–inequality narrowing hypothesis, β_1 should be significant and negative and β_2 should be insignificant. According to the finance–inequality widening hypothesis, β_1 should be significant and positive and β_2 should be insignificant. As the inverted U-shaped hypothesis suggests, β_1 should be significant and positive and β_2 should be significant and negative.

There is extensive literature on the finance–inequality nexus using the fixed effect (FE) method and generalized method of moments (GMM). However, some issues have emerged in these techniques,

[1] We would like to thank an anonymous referee for suggesting other control variables, such as human capital and trade openness. It is arguable that human capital and trade openness may play an important role in determining a variation of income inequality. However, for the purpose of this paper, these two variables were not utilized for the following reasons. In relation to human capital, Milanović (2000) stated that human capital and economic growth should not be used concurrently due to a severe collinearity between them. In relation to trade openness, various empirical studies considered that its effects on income inequality were still a matter of controversy (Bensidoun et al. 2011; Mahesh 2016; Urata and Narjoko 2017).

leading to biased estimates. It is argued that the FE comes at a cost, and the GMM technique suffers from the problem of instrument proliferation as the time dimension increases (De Dominicis et al. 2008); (Grijalva 2011). In addition, these techniques are dedicated to the estimation of short-run relationships, which is not the focus of this study. As such, this paper utilizes the dynamic OLS (DOLS) and fully modified OLS (FMOLS).

It is widely noted that the relationship between income inequality and economic growth is endogenous. Therefore, estimations without considering a potential endogeneity will produce misleading results. Fortunately, the above issue can be reduced by employing FMOLS and DOLS regression techniques. Al Mamun et al. (2018) considered that endogeneity can be alleviated using the FMOLS regression technique. Risso et al. (2013) stated that the FMOLS and DOLS estimators deal with the problem of endogeneity.

4. Empirical Findings

In this section, we use appropriate econometric techniques to reveal the underlying relationship between income inequality and financial development for a sample of 21 emerging markets.

4.1. Slope Homogeneity Test

Table 3 reports the mean of each investigated variable. Variations in the averages could suggest heterogeneity across panels. For example, while the average GDP per capita growth was quite high in China (8.67%), Bulgaria (4.52%), and Thailand (4.48%), it was low in South Africa (0.46%) and Ukraine (−0.45%). Similarly, the magnitudes of financial development and inflation varied significantly across the analyzed countries. Breitung (2005) stated that if the panel was heterogeneous, the estimated coefficients would be biased.

Table 3. The mean of each variable.

Country	Gini	g	FD	Inflation	GovExp/GDP	Observed Period
Argentina	40.13	1.31	17.71	185.73	11.16	1961–2015
Bangladesh	32.50	2.76	21.00	6.32	4.83	1974–2016
Brazil	50.61	2.27	45.86	335.17	14.72	1961–2015
Bulgaria	33.09	4.52	50.24	4.10	17.73	2001–2016
Chile	46.87	2.63	56.18	45.42	11.79	1968–2015
China	36.28	8.67	95.37	5.44	13.91	1978–2015
Colombia	50.86	2.24	33.02	15.79	13.43	1970–2015
Hungary	27.86	2.30	45.94	4.24	21.11	2001–2016
India	43.03	3.81	29.91	7.54	10.97	1980–2017
Indonesia	35.81	3.49	32.24	9.83	8.94	1980–2017
Malaysia	44.72	3.93	90.24	3.53	13.97	1970–2016
Mexico	47.90	1.77	22.18	21.07	9.50	1963–2016
Pakistan	34.59	2.37	24.32	8.75	11.13	1964–2013
Peru	52.25	1.41	19.41	293.18	11.09	1972–2011
Philippines	43.05	1.70	27.89	9.10	9.90	1961–2015
Poland	31.45	3.64	39.23	2.23	18.37	2001–2016
Romania	31.38	3.60	23.09	22.87	15.31	1996–2016
South Africa	57.17	0.46	104.65	9.67	17.78	1975–2015
Thailand	42.79	4.48	71.22	4.62	11.88	1962–2013
Turkey	42.69	3.03	29.05	41.31	12.48	1987–2016
Ukraine	28.03	−0.45	36.31	264.86	19.64	1992–2016

Source: The above table employs post-tax, post-transfer income as a proxy for the Gini coefficient and a domestic credit to private sector–GDP ratio as a proxy for financial development.

4.2. Cross-Section Dependence Test

Correlation of the residual across entities seems to be common in macro data where a group of highly connected countries are examined. Spill-over effects across countries are often considered as sources of the linkages. Estimations which ignore cross-section dependence will result in inconsistent estimates or lead to inaccurate conclusions. Thus, in order to verify the existence of cross-section dependence, we conducted the CD test proposed by Pesaran (2015). The empirical results are reported in Table 4.

Table 4. Results from Pesaran's CD test for cross-section dependence.

Variable	Gini	g	g^2	FD	FD^2	Inflation	GovExp/GDP
CD test	1.30	17.65 ***	4.88 ***	23.78 ***	22.27 ***	17.69 ***	1.12
p-value	0.19	0.00	0.00	0.00	0.00	0.00	0.26

Note: *** significant at 1% level. Null hypothesis is of cross-section independence.

For our dataset, the null hypothesis of cross-section independence was rejected at the 1% level of significance to some variables of economic growth, financial development, and inflation, suggesting that cross-section dependence should be accounted for in the regression techniques.

4.3. Panel Unit Root Test

On the grounds of the issue of heterogeneous panels and cross-section dependence, we employed the t-test for unit roots, as proposed by Pesaran (2003). As presented in Table 5, referring to the p-value in the first and second columns, it is suggested that all variables contained unit roots. However, the statistical estimates in the third and fourth columns indicate that the first difference of those was stationary. In summary, the considered variables were integrated of order one, or I(1).

Table 5. Results from panel unit root test.

Variable	Level		First Difference		Order of Integration
	Constant (1)	Constant and Trend (2)	Constant (3)	Constant and Trend (4)	
Gini	0.77 (0.77)	1.74 (0.96)	−11.50 *** (0.00)	−9.55 *** (0.00)	I (1)
g	0.01 (0.50)	0.53 (0.70)	−13.41 *** (0.00)	−11.04 *** (0.00)	I (1)
g^2	0.52 (0.70)	1.07 (0.85)	−1.70 ** (0.04)	−4.62 *** (0.00)	I (1)
FD	2.56 (0.99)	4.48 (1.00)	−4.38 *** (0.00)	−3.28 *** (0.00)	I (1)
FD^2	2.04 (0.97)	3.37 (1.00)	−4.40 *** (0.00)	−2.93 *** (0.00)	I (1)
Inflation	0.55 (0.71)	1.27 (0.89)	−11.45 *** (0.00)	−9.64 *** (0.00)	I (1)
GovExp/GDP	−1.03 (0.15)	0.25 (0.60)	−6.03 *** (0.00)	−3.78 *** (0.00)	I (1)

Note: The p-values are reported in parentheses. The Z[t-bar] is reported. ** significant at 5% level, *** significant at 1% level. Null hypothesis assumes that all series are non-stationary.

4.4. Panel Cointegration Test

We continued to conduct another test—the panel cointegration test—before determining how financial development affects income inequality. To examine the existence of a long-run equilibrium relationship between the variables of interest, we employed the tests of Kao (1999); Pedroni (1999, 2004); and Westerlund (2005). Findings are presented in Table 6. The results of the Pedroni and Kao tests were statistically significant at the level of 1%, and significant estimates emerged from the Westerlund test. These results indicate that the variables were cointegrated in all panels or there was a long-run equilibrium relationship between them.

Table 6. Panel cointegration test results.

Cointegration Test	Statistics
Pedroni	
Phillips–Perron t	3.58 *** (0.00)
Panel ADF statistic	3.85 *** (0.00)
Kao	
Modified Dickey–Fuller t	2.61 *** (0.00)
Dickey–Fuller t	2.83 *** (0.00)
Augmented Dickey–Fuller t	3.09 *** (0.00)
Unadjusted modified Dickey–Fuller t	2.40 *** (0.00)
Unadjusted Dickey–Fuller t	2.55 *** (0.00)
Westerlund	
Variance Ratio	1.42 * (0.07)

Note: The p-values are reported in parentheses. * significant at 10% level, *** significant at 1% level. Null hypothesis assumes no cointegration.

4.5. Estimation Results

Table 7 presents the long-run estimates of a pool of 21 selected emerging countries. We proceeded in several steps, starting with the panel FMOLS and then dealing with the DOLS estimators. Note that the domestic credit to private sector–GDP ratio and the post-tax income were employed to measure financial development and income inequality, respectively.

Table 7. Regression results (post-tax, post-transfer income).

Regressors	FMOLS	DOLS
g	0.037 * (0.096)	1.435 *** (0.000)
g^2	−0.002 (0.536)	−0.083 *** (0.001)
FD	0.197 *** (0.000)	0.295 * (0.052)
FD^2	−0.003 *** (0.000)	−0.006 * (0.064)
Inflation	−0.010 (0.122)	−0.175 *** (0.000)
GovExp/GDP	0.017 (0.542)	0.679 *** (0.000)
Number of observations	754	705
R^2	0.499	0.93

Note: * significant at 10% level, *** significant at 1% level. p-values are in parentheses. DOLS: dynamic OLS; FMOLS: fully modified OLS.

Regardless of the estimation techniques employed in this paper, the results were similar to the estimates of economic growth. The coefficient of g was positive and significant and the coefficient of g^2 was negative, although it was only significant under the FMOLS estimation. The results imply that the income inequality–economic growth nexus follows the prediction of Kuznets (1955). Furthermore, they indicate a turning point for annual percentage growth rate of GDP per capita of 9.25 and 8.6 for FMOLS and DOLS, respectively.

Both FMOLS and DOLS estimators support an inverted U curve between financial development and income inequality. At the level of 10%, the coefficient of FD was positive while that of FD^2 was negative, indicating that the hypothesis of Greenwood and Jovanovic (1990) is confirmed in our study. The estimated turning point for FD was 32.8 and 24.5 for the above two estimations.

This finding is also supported by the study of Younsi and Bechtini (2018), in which the BRICS members were investigated, or the study of Zhang and Chen (2015), which is dedicated to China. From another point of view, the results also indicate a rejection of the linearity of the financial development–inequality nexus.

Regardless of the control variables, we suggest that their effects on income inequality were quite consistent across estimations. Particularly, inflation was negatively related to income inequality, indicating that as inflation increases, income inequality decreases. Jauch and Watzka (2016) argued that debtors would benefit from high inflation due to a reduction in their debt obligation, as most contracts are written in nominal terms. That relationship was also found in the study of Park and Shin (2017). On the other hand, the government expenditure–GDP ratio was positively associated with income inequality. Jauch and Watzka (2016) stated that a large share of government expenditure in the economy operated by the elite through rent-seeking activities could widen inequality.

Overall, the use of the domestic credit to private sector–GDP ratio as a measure of financial development rejects the linearity of the financial development–inequality nexus and supports its non-linearity, as presented in Table 7. However, the conclusion seems to be somewhat arbitrary due to the choice of proxy for income inequality and financial development. Thus, in the following section, we perform robustness checks in relation to the use of various proxies for financial development.

5. Robustness Checks

Thus far, this paper has used inequality in disposable (post-tax, post-transfer) income. As such, we use the inequality in market (pre-tax, pre-transfer) income as a robustness check.

The results from Table 8 suggest that there is an inverted U curve in the relationship between income inequality and economic growth as well as between income inequality and financial development. The results not only further strengthen the findings presented in Table 7 but also confirm the inverted U curve hypothesis of Greenwood and Jovanovic (1990).

Table 8. Regression results (pre-tax, pre-transfer income).

Regressor	FMOLS	DOLS
g	0.044 * (0.07)	0.499 (0.379)
g^2	−0.003 (0.239)	−0.031 (0.381)
FD	0.254 *** (0.000)	0.423 *** (0.009)
FD^2	−0.004 *** (0.000)	−0.008 ** (0.022)
Inflation	−0.011 (0.140)	−0.103 ** (0.047)
GovExp/GDP	−0.045 (0.148)	−0.319 (0.208)
Number of observations	754	705
R^2	0.529	0.913

Note: * significant at 10% level, ** significant at 5% level, *** significant at 1% level. *p*-values are in parentheses.

Development finance refers to economic analysis of the role of financial resources and financial institutions in the development of an economy (Rao 2003). Ouyang and Li (2018) argued that financial development was a multifaceted phenomenon. From that argument, they stated that using only one proxy variable to measure financial development would provide misleading conclusions. Indeed, it is observable that financial structure, financial market size, and the efficiency of financial intermediaries for each country are quite different from their counterparts in other countries (Ang 2008). Thus, in addition to the domestic credit to private sector–GDP ratio variable, we also employed other variables as proxies for financial development, including (i) stock market capitalization as percentage of GDP, (ii) domestic credit to private sector by banks-to-GDP ratio, (iii) domestic credit provided by financial sector-to-GDP ratio, and (iv) the IMF-proposed financial development index. The first three variables were obtained from the WDI while the last is available in the IMF database.

The IMF-proposed financial development index is an overall index which accounts for the depth, access, and efficiency of the financial sector. It was developed on a sample of 183 countries and is available on an annual basis over the period of 1980–2013. As such, we expected that the variable would provide a comprehensive picture of how financial development affects income inequality. Empirical estimates are presented in Table 9.

Table 9. Regression results using various proxies for financial development including stock market capitalization as percentage of GDP, domestic credit to private sector by banks-to-GDP ratio, domestic credit provided by financial sector-to-GDP ratio, and the IMF-proposed financial development index.

Regressors	Gini (Disposable Income)		Gini (Market Income)	
	FMOLS	DOLS	FMOLS	DOLS
Panel A: Stock market capitalization as percentage of GDP				
g	0.219 ***	0.105 *	−0.053	0.147
	(0.000)	(0.096)	(0.494)	(0.405)
g^2	−0.016 **	0.009	0.003	0.040 *
	(0.016)	(0.397)	(0.762)	(0.084)
FD	0.014	−0.045 ***	0.012	0.083 *
	(0.348)	(0.001)	(0.477)	(0.081)
FD^2	−0.000 ***	0.000 ***	−0.001 ***	−0.002 ***
	(0.000)	(0.001)	(0.001)	(0.000)
Inflation	−0.025	−0.035 **	−0.017	−0.02
	(0.184)	(0.020)	(0.392)	(0.715)
GovExp/GDP	−0.083	0.179 **	−0.108	0.285
	(0.324)	(0.036)	(0.199)	(0.223)
Number of observations	436	214	436	214
R^2	0.502	0.982	0.58	0.914
Panel B: Domestic credit to private sector by banks-to-GDP ratio				
g	0.027	−0.034 *	0.056 **	−0.058 **
	(0.210)	(0.078)	(0.047)	(0.019)
g^2	−0.001	−0.002	−0.005	0.004
	(0.572)	(0.280)	(0.124)	(0.125)
FD	0.147 ***	0.054 ***	0.227 ***	0.084 ***
	(0.000)	(0.000)	(0.000)	(0.000)
FD^2	−0.002 ***	−0.000 ***	−0.004 ***	−0.000 ***
	(0.000)	(0.000)	(0.000)	(0.000)
Inflation	−0.012 *	0.000	−0.017	0.000 *
	(0.064)	(0.105)	(0.102)	(0.086)
GovExp/GDP	0.028	−0.405 ***	−0.042	−0.360 ***
	(0.300)	(0.000)	(0.292)	(0.000)
Number of observations	754	712	754	712
R^2	0.506	0.951	0.611	0.925

Table 9. *Cont.*

Regressors	Gini (Disposable Income)		Gini (Market Income)	
	FMOLS	**DOLS**	**FMOLS**	**DOLS**
Panel C: Domestic credit provided by financial sector-to-GDP ratio				
g	0.118 ***	−0.146 ***	0.089 ***	−0.029
	(0.000)	(0.000)	(0.000)	(0.328)
g^2	−0.009 ***	−0.003	−0.009 ***	0.008 **
	(0.002)	(0.313)	(0.000)	(0.020)
FD	0.201 ***	0.031 ***	0.118 ***	0.030 ***
	(0.000)	(0.000)	(0.000)	(0.002)
FD^2	−0.001 ***	−0.000 ***	−0.000 **	−0.000 *
	(0.000)	(0.000)	(0.035)	(0.063)
Inflation	−0.014	0.000 ***	−0.006	0.008 **
	(0.141)	(0.000)	(0.491)	(0.010)
GovExp/GDP	0.062	−0.023	−0.070 *	0.004
	(0.168)	(0.203)	(0.067)	(0.881)
Number of observations	709	709	709	711
R^2	0.5252	0.936	0.536	0.934
Panel D: IMF-proposed financial development index				
g	0.083 *	0.015	0.115 **	0.029
	(0.063)	(0.755)	(0.010)	(0.646)
g^2	−0.041	0.001	−0.043	0.003
	(0.381)	(0.896)	(0.365)	(0.743)
FD	10.479 ***	7.375	7.933 ***	10.982 *
	(0.000)	(0.116)	(0.000)	(0.0600)
FD^2	−18.003 ***	−18.614 ***	−12.283 ***	−25.116 ***
	(0.000)	(0.000)	(0.000)	(0.000)
Inflation	−0.024	0.002	−0.027	0.002
	(0.278)	(0.190)	(0.226)	(0.181)
GovExp/GDP	0.058 ***	−0.003	0.083 ***	0.118
	(0.001)	(0.966)	(0.000)	(0.130)
Number of observations	652	473	652	474
R^2	0.558	0.970	0.632	0.974

Note: * significant at 10% level, ** significant at 5% level, *** significant at 1% level. *p*-values are in parentheses. The IMF-proposed financial development index starts in 1980 and ends in 2013.

It is observed that the impact of financial development on income inequality holds firmly. That is, there is an inverted U curve in the relationship between them. These findings imply that the growth of the financial sector exacerbates income inequality at its early stages of development before it narrows income inequality after a certain threshold.

6. Concluding Remarks

The relationship between financial development and inequality has attached great attention from academics, practitioners, and policymakers in the past few decades. Various debates have emerged in relation to the influences of the financial sector on income inequality, especially after the global financial crisis of 2008. In addition, a theoretical consensus on the finance–inequality nexus has not been reached among scholars. As such, this study was conducted to provide additional empirical evidence on the influence of financial development, which is heavily pursued by many emerging markets, on income inequality. We extended the finance–inequality nexus framework through an investigation on a sample of 21 emerging countries over the period of 1961–2017. Various proxies of financial development were utilized in this paper. In addition, this paper employed various estimation techniques, focusing on the long-run relationship between financial development and income inequality, accounting for endogeneity in order to ensure that the estimated findings are robust.

Our results indicate that there is an inverted U curve relationship between financial development and income inequality in emerging markets. That is, it seems that at the early stage of financial development, the expansion of a financial sector is likely to be associated with an increase in income inequality. Once a certain level of a financial development is achieved, income inequality is expected to fall. These findings hold for various proxies of financial development as well as income inequality.

The empirical findings of this paper offer additional evidence for the governments of emerging countries to formulate and implement their respective economic policies. As there is a tradeoff between income inequality and the development of a national financial sector, it is necessary for any policy to ensure that the achievements of the economic development are redistributed to the people—especially those at the bottom of the national income distribution level. In addition, it appears to be crucial to target financial development towards the poor in society, and to the small and medium firms. Our results also indicate that income inequality is expected to be reduced after a certain level of financial development. In other words, financial development is essential for reducing income inequality. Moreover, there is no doubt that financial development plays a key role in sustainable economic growth and development. Overall, these considerations suggest that the development of a financial sector should receive proper attention from policy makers. Financial development continues to be considered as an important and effective mechanism to achieve sustainable economic growth and development of the emerging markets. However, financial reform should be carefully implemented. Policy makers should be aware of valuable lessons learned from the global financial crisis of 2008.

Author Contributions: Conceptualization, D.T.-T.H.; Methodology, D.H.V.; Software, T.C.N. and T.N.V.; Validation, T.C.N. and D.H.V.; Formal Analysis, T.C.N.; Investigation, T.C.N. and D.H.V.; Resources, T.C.N.; Data Curation, T.N.V.; Writing-Original Draft Preparation, T.C.N. and D.T.-T.H.; Writing-Review & Editing, D.H.V.; Visualization, T.N.V. and D.T.-T.H.; Supervision, D.H.V.; Project Administration, D.H.V.; Funding Acquisition, T.C.N. and D.H.V.

Acknowledgments: For financial support, the first author is most grateful to Ho Chi Minh City Open University (E2018.13.2). We are grateful to the three anonymous referees for their constructive comments. We also thank the participants at the 3rd Vietnam's Business and Economics Research Conference VBER2019 (Ho Chi Minh City Open University, Vietnam, 18–20 July 2019) for their helpful suggestions. The authors wish to acknowledge financial supports from Ho Chi Minh City Open University. The authors are solely responsible for any remaining errors or shortcomings.

References

Afonso, António, Ludger Schuknecht, and Vito Tanzi. 2010. Income distribution determinants and public spending efficiency. *The Journal of Economic Inequality* 8: 367–89. [CrossRef]

Agnello, Luca, Sushanta K. Mallick, and Ricardo M. Sousa. 2012. Financial reforms and income inequality. *Economics Letters* 116: 583–87. [CrossRef]

Al Mamun, Md, Kazi Sohag, Muhammad Shahbaz, and Shawkat Hammoudeh. 2018. Financial markets, innovations and cleaner energy production in OECD countries. *Energy Economics* 72: 236–54. [CrossRef]

Ang, James B. 2008. A survey of recent developments in the literature of finance and growth. *Journal of Economic Surveys* 22: 536–76. [CrossRef]

Ang, James B. 2010. Finance and inequality: the case of India. *Southern Economic Journal* 76: 738–61. [CrossRef]

Atkinson, Anthony Barnes. 2003. Income inequality in OECD countries: Data and explanations. *CESifo Economic Studies* 49: 479–513. [CrossRef]

Banerjee, Abhijit V., and Andrew F. Newman. 1993. Occupational Choice and the Process of Development. *Journal of Political Economy* 101: 274–98. [CrossRef]

Batuo, Michael Enowbi, Francesco Guidi, and Kupukile Mlambo. 2010. Financial Development and Income Inequality: Evidence from African Countries. Available online: https://mpra.ub.uni-muenchen.de/25658/ (accessed on 5 March 2019).

Bensidoun, Isabelle, Sébastien Jean, and Aude Sztulman. 2011. International trade and income distribution: reconsidering the evidence. *Review of World Economics* 147: 593–619. [CrossRef]

Breitung, Jörg. 2005. A parametric approach to the estimation of cointegration vectors in panel data. *Econometric Reviews* 24: 151–73. [CrossRef]

Claessens, Stijin, and Enrico Perotti. 2007. Finance and inequality: Channels and evidence. *Journal of comparative Economics* 35: 748–73. [CrossRef]

Clarke, Geogre R. G., Lixin Colin Xu, and Heng-Fu Zou. 2006. Finance and income inequality: what do the data tell us? *Southern Economic Journal* 72: 578–96. [CrossRef]

De Dominicis, Laura, Raymond J. G. M. Florax, and Henri L. F. de Groot. 2008. A Meta-Analysis on the Relationship between Income Inequality and Economic Growth. *Scottish Journal of Political Economy* 55: 654–82. [CrossRef]

De Haan, Jakob, and Jan-Egbert Sturm. 2017. Finance and income inequality: A review and new evidence. *European Journal of Political Economy* 50: 171–95. [CrossRef]

Deininger, Klaus, and Lyn Squire. 1996. A New Data Set Measuring Income Inequality. *World Bank Economic Review* 10: 565–91. [CrossRef]

Dowrick, Steve, and Muhammad Akmal. 2005. Contradictory trends in global income inequality: A tale of two biases. *Review of Income and Wealth* 51: 201–29. [CrossRef]

Galor, Oded, and Joseph Zeira. 1993. Income Distribution Macroeconomics. *The Review of Economic Studies* 60: 35–52. [CrossRef]

Greenwood, Jeremy, and Boyan Jovanovic. 1990. Financial Development, Growth, and the Distribution of Income. *Journal of Political Economy* 98: 1076–107. [CrossRef]

De Gregorio, José, and Jong-Wha Lee. 2002. Education and income inequality: New evidence from cros-country data. *Review of Income and Wealth* 48: 395–416. [CrossRef]

Grijalva, Diego F. 2011. Inequality and Economic Growth: Bridging the Short-run and the Long-run. EScholarship, Univ of California. Available online: http://escholarship.org/uc/item/4kf1t5pb (accessed on 5 March 2019).

Hamori, Shigeyuki, and Yoshihiro Hashiguchi. 2012. The effect of financial deepening on inequality: Some international evidence. *Journal of Asian Economics* 23: 353–59. [CrossRef]

Huber, Evelune, and John D. Stephens. 2014. Income inequality and redistribution in post-industrial democracies: demographic, economic and political determinants. *Socio-Economic Review* 12: 245–67. [CrossRef]

Jauch, Sebastian, and Sebastian Watzka. 2016. Financial development and income inequality: A panel data approach. *Empirical Economics* 51: 291–314. [CrossRef]

Jaumotte, Florence, Subir Lall, and Chris Papageorgiou. 2013. Rising income inequality: technology, or trade and financial globalization? *IMF Economic Review* 61: 271–309. [CrossRef]

Kao, Chihwa. 1999. Spurious regression and residual-based tests for cointegration in panel data. *Journal of Econometrics* 90: 1–44. [CrossRef]

Kappel, Vivien. 2010. The Effects of Financial Development on Income Inequality and Poverty. Available online: https://ssrn.com/abstract=1585148 (accessed on 8 January 2019).

Kim, Dong-Hyeon, and Shu-Chin Lin. 2011. Nonlinearity in the financial development-income inequality nexus. *Journal of Comparative Economics* 39: 310–25. [CrossRef]

Kuznets, Simon. 1955. Economic Growth and Income Inequality. *American Economic Review* 45: 1–28. [CrossRef]

Law, Siong Hook, Hui Boon Tan, and W. N. W. Azman-Saini. 2014. Financial Development and Income Inequality at Different Levels of Institutional Quality. *Emerging Markets Finance and Trade* 50: 21–33. [CrossRef]

Li, Hongyi, and Heng-Fu Zou. 1998. Income inequality is not harmful for growth: theory and evidence. *Review of Development Economics* 2: 318–34. [CrossRef]

Li, Hongyi, Lyn Squire, and Heng-fu Zou. 1998. Explaining international and intertemporal variations in income inequality. *The Economic Journal* 108: 26–43. [CrossRef]

Mahesh, Malvika. 2016. The effects of trade openness on income inequality: Evidence from BRIC countries. *Economics Bulletin* 36: 1751–61.

Malinen, Tuomas. 2012. Inequality and growth: Another look with a new measure and method. *Journal of International Development* 25: 122–38. [CrossRef]

Milanović, Branko. 2000. *Equality, Participation, Transition*. London: Palgrave Macmillan, pp. 48–79.

Mookerjee, Rajen, and Paul Kalipioni. 2010. Availability of financial services and income inequality: The evidence from many countries. *Emerging Markets Review* 11: 404–8. [CrossRef]

Nguyen, Cong Thang, Vo The Anh, Pham Ngoc Thach, Do Thanh Trung, and Vo Hong Duc. 2019. Gender-Based Attitudes toward Income Inequality in the Asia-Pacific Region. *Emerging Markets Finance and Trade*, 1–15. [CrossRef]

Ouyang, Yaofu, and Peng Li. 2018. On the nexus of financial development, economic growth, and energy consumption in China: New perspective from a GMM panel VAR approach. *Energy Economics* 71: 238–52. [CrossRef]

Pan-Long, Tsai. 1995. Foreign direct investment and income inequality: Further evidence. *World Development* 23: 469–83. [CrossRef]

Park, Donghyun, and Kwanho Shin. 2017. Economic Growth, Financial Development, and Income Inequality. *Emerging Markets Finance and Trade* 53: 2794–25. [CrossRef]

Pedroni, Peter. 1999. Critical Values for Cointegration Tests in Heterogeneous Panels with Multiple Regressors. *Oxford Bulletin of Economics and Statistics* 61: 653–70. [CrossRef]

Pedroni, Peter. 2004. Panel cointegration: Asymptotic and finite sample properties of pooled time series tests with an application to the PPP hypothesis. *Econometric Theory* 20: 597–625. [CrossRef]

Pesaran, M. Hashem. 2003. A Simple Panel Unit Root Test in the Presence of Cross-Section Dependence. Available online: http://www.econ.cam.ac.uk/research-files/repec/cam/pdf/cwpe0346.pdf (accessed on 5 March 2019).

Pesaran, M. Hashem. 2015. Testing Weak Cross-Sectional Dependence in Large Panels. *Econometric Reviews* 34: 1089–117. [CrossRef]

Rajan, Raghuram G., and Luigi Zingales. 2003. *Saving Capitalism from the Capitalists*. New York: Crown Business.

Rao, Pinninti K. 2003. *Development Finance*. New York: Springer. [CrossRef]

Risso, W. Andrián, Lionello F. Punzo, and Edgar J. Sánchez Carrera. 2013. Economic growth and income distribution in Mexico: A cointegration exercise. *Economic Modelling* 35: 708–14. [CrossRef]

Roine, Jesper, Jonas Vlachos, and Daniel Waldenström. 2009. The long-run determinants of inequality: What can we learn from top income data? *Journal of Public Economics* 93: 974–88. [CrossRef]

Rousseau, Peter L., and Hakan Yilmazkuday. 2009. Inflation, financial development, and growth: A trilateral analysis. *Economic Systems* 33: 310–24. [CrossRef]

Sehrawat, Madhu, and A. K. Giri. 2015. Financial development and income inequality in India: An application of ARDL approach. *International Journal of Social Economics* 42: 64–81. [CrossRef]

Seven, Unal, and Yener Coskun. 2016. Does financial development reduce income inequality and poverty? Evidence from emerging countries. *Emerging Markets Review* 26: 34–63. [CrossRef]

Solt, Frederick. 2016. The Standardized World Income Inequality Database. *Social Science Quarterly* 97: 1267–81. [CrossRef]

Svirydzenka, Katsiaryna. 2016. Introducing a New Broad-Based Index of Financial Development. International Monetary Fund. Available online: https://www.imf.org/external/pubs/ft/wp/2016/wp1605.pdf (accessed on 3 March 2019).

Urata, Shujiro, and Dionisius A. Narjoko. 2017. International Trade and Inequality. Available online: https://www.adb.org/publications/international-trade-and-inequality (accessed on 5 September 2019).

Vo, Hong Duc, Huynh Van Son, Vo The Anh, and Ha Thi Thieu Dao. 2019a. The importance of the financial derivatives markets to economic development in the world's four major economies. *Journal of Risk and Financial Management* 12: 35. [CrossRef]

Vo, Hong Duc, Nguyen Van Phuc, Nguyen Minh Ha, Vo The Anh, and Nguyen Cong Thang. 2019b. Derivatives Market and Economic Growth Nexus: Policy Implications for Emerging Markets. *The North American Journal of Economics and Finance*. [CrossRef]

Westerlund, Joakim. 2005. New simple tests for panel cointegration. *Econometric Reviews* 24: 297–316. [CrossRef]

Yilmazkuday, Hakan. 2011. Thresholds in the finance-growth nexus: A cross-country analysis. *The World Bank Economic Review* 25: 278–95. [CrossRef]

Yilmazkuday, Hakan. 2012. Inflation thresholds and growth. *International Economic Journal* 27: 1–10. [CrossRef]

Younsi, Moheddine, and Marwa Bechtini. 2018. Economic Growth, Financial Development and Income Inequality in BRICS Countries: Evidence from Panel Granger Causality Tests. Available online: https://mpra.ub.uni-muenchen.de/85182/1/MPRA_paper_85181.pdf (accessed on 6 August 2019).

Zhang, Quanda, and Rongda Chen. 2015. Financial development and income inequality in China: An application of SVAR approach. *Procedia Computer Science* 55: 774–81. [CrossRef]

4

The Impact of Urbanization on Income Inequality

Nguyen Minh Ha [1,*], Nguyen Dang Le [2] and Pham Trung-Kien [3]

[1] Business and Economics Research Group, Ho Chi Minh City Open University, 97 Vo Van Tan Street, District 3, Ho Chi Minh City 700000, Vietnam

[2] Department of Financial Informatics and Statistics, Ministry of Finance, Ho Chi Minh City 700000, Vietnam

[3] Faculty of Economics, Binh Duong University, 504 Binh Duong Avenue, Binh Duong Province 590000, Vietnam

* Correspondence: ha.nm@ou.edu.vn

Abstract: This paper explores the impact of urbanization on income inequality in Vietnam, using the regression estimation method with panel data including Driscoll and Kraay, and Pooled Mean Group. The research data cover 63 provinces in Vietnam from 2006 to 2016. The results show that in the long term, urbanization has an impact on reducing income inequality. In the short term, urbanization has a negligible impact on income inequality. The hypothesis of an inverted-U-shaped relationship between urbanization and income inequality is confirmed. The high school enrollment rate and the proportion of agriculture have an effect on reducing income inequality.

Keywords: urbanization; income inequality; Driscoll and Kraay; PMG

1. Introduction

Many economists argue that increasing inequality is the root cause of economic crises (Stiglitz 2009). Meanwhile, the world faces serious income inequality. The gap between the rich and other groups has increased significantly. In 2015, the richest 1% of the population owned more assets than the other 99%. In Asia, the income of the poorest 70% has decreased, while that of the richest 10% has increased significantly (Hardoon et al. 2016).

The relationship between income inequality and development has long been a topic of particular interest to researchers in developed as well as developing countries. Many studies have tried to determine whether countries must make a trade-off between income inequality and growth. If so, what is the specific model of the relationship and why?

Kuznets (1955) was the first to introduce the idea of a link between inequality and development, pointing out that development involves a shift in population from traditional activities to modern activities. "An invariable accompaniment of growth in developed countries is the shift away from agriculture, a process usually referred to as industrialization and urbanization", he wrote (Kuznets 1955, p. 7). Therefore, in a simple model, income distribution among the entire population can be viewed as a combination of income distribution among those in rural and urban areas. We observe that income per capita is often lower in rural areas than in urban areas, and inequality in income distribution is lower than in rural areas in urban areas. What conclusions can we draw from these observations? First, under the same conditions, increasing the share of the urban population does not necessarily reduce economic growth: in fact, some evidence indicates that growth may be higher because urban per capita productivity increased faster in agriculture. If this is true, inequality in income distribution increases. This ideal was highlighted and clarified by Bourguignon and Morrisson (1998), Piketty (2006).

Industrialization and urbanization are closely related to economic development. The process of industrialization and urbanization affects income distribution, causing income inequality. In the short term, urbanization can increase income inequality because wages are higher for urban jobs than rural work. However, in the long term, when urbanization is highly developed, the difference in income distribution in the two regions may decrease, and income inequality will decrease.

In Vietnam today, urbanization and industrialization have progressed considerably. Vietnam's urbanization level is still low compared to the global average but, in recent years, higher than the average in other developing countries as well as countries in Southeast Asia. In terms of Gini data, income inequality in Vietnam increased until 2008 and then decreased, and in 2014 began to increase again. So, does urbanization increase income inequality? This is the question that we address in this study.

2. Literature Review

Income inequality refers to an unequal distribution of income among individuals or households. To calculate the degree of income inequality, scholars often rely on the percentage of income held by different shares of the population. Income inequality is often associated with unfairness, such as when rich people hold a significantly larger share of national income relative to their proportion of the population (Todaro 1989).

Income inequality can be measured by various methods, such as using quintiles to measure income gaps between the poorest and the richest; using World Bank Standard 40, measured with the Lorenz curve (Lorenz 1905), the Gini coefficient (Gini 1913, 1921), and the Theil index (Akita et al. 1999). In this research, we use the Gini coefficient to represent income inequality.

Urbanization concerns the physical, human, and economic development of cities. This term also includes the concentration of people and social activities on the settlement model characterized by the development of land with high population density. The result of urbanization is partly due to the increase in population, natural and by migration, as well as economic, social, and technological changes that motivate people to migrate to urban areas, which have many jobs and opportunities. Market rules and government policies promote urbanization and create related changes in people's livelihoods, land use, health, and natural resource management. Job placement decisions, rural-urban transformation and production systems, and government development and distribution policies often create urban immigration and focus on economic activities in cities (Gotham 2012).

According to Bloom et al. (2010), a basic concept commonly used to determine the level of urbanization is the proportion of the population living in urban areas, represented by Urbant and defined using the following equation:

$$Urban_t = \frac{PU_t}{PU_t + PR_t}$$

in which PU_t and PR_t represent urban and rural population respectively.

2.1. How Does Urbanization Affect Income Inequality?

An economic model including urban and rural areas has four main elements of income inequality: (1) the level of urbanization; (2) the urban-rural income gap; (3) urban income inequality; and (4) rural income inequality. By keeping urban and rural disparities and rural and urban inequalities constant, Kuznets (1955) outlines an inverted-U-shaped relationship between inequality and urbanization. In this study, urbanization is viewed as an important factor affecting income inequality, and we examine Kuznets's inverted-U-shape hypothesis based on Vietnam's provinces.

A great deal of evidence supports the idea that urbanization promotes economic growth, at least in the early stages of development, implying that a balance exists between economic growth and equal income distribution, at least geographically. Brülhart and Sbergami (2009) argue that poor countries face an awkward choice between inequality reduction and higher economic growth. In fact, the relationship between development and income inequality described by Kuznets is highly relevant to urbanization.

The classic dual economic model examining structural change shows that inequality is an inevitable result of urbanization that is characteristic of economic development (Harris and Todaro 1970; Lewis 1954; Rauch 1993). Similarly, the New Economic Geography helps explain how economic development is associated with increased urbanization and inequality in its early stages (Krugman 1991). Both models show an increasing profit from industrial activities. In fact, many good workers are concentrated in urban areas with higher industrial wages. Economic growth is facilitated by structural changes in the economy, allowing it to enjoy the benefits of increasing profits and the economics of urbanization.

The process of urbanization brings about changes in economic structure, with people and resources being reallocated from agricultural activities to industrial activities. This process is associated with increased inequality, with higher incomes in urban areas than in rural areas. In this sense, both higher inequality and greater urbanization can enhance the concentration of production factors necessary for growth, at least in the early stages of development. And this focus further strengthens the reallocation of labor from rural to urban areas (Ross 2000). Therefore, both inequality and geographic concentration indicate, to some extent, capital accumulation (both physical and human). However, in the later stages of development, especially urban growth and the growth of a large concentration—urban accumulation—is linked to increasing inequality (Behrens and Robert-Nicoud 2014).

2.2. Previous Related Studies

Kanbur and Zhuang (2013) studied the impact of the change of two sectional economic structure and urbanization that affect inequality in Asia. Based on the Kuznets model and the inequality measurement method using the Theil index, this study analyzes four specific countries: China, India, Indonesia, and the Philippines. Their results show the following.

First, the effect of urbanization and the economic structure change on income inequality depends on the specific country. Urbanization contributes about 300% to the increase in inequality in the Philippines, more than 50% in Indonesia, and nearly 15% in India. However, it reduces inequality in China. Meanwhile, the change in the urban-rural income gap reduces inequality in Indonesia and the Philippines, but it increases inequality in India and China. Moreover, in China, the increase in income inequality is mainly due to the raise of 43% rural inequality. This is contrary to the popular point of view that increasing income inequality is the result of the expansion in the urban–rural income gap and the rising urban inequality.

Second, how urbanization will affect inequality in the future depends on the status urbanization of the country. If a country passes its "turning point", urbanization will reduce inequality in, for example, China. In contrast, urbanization will increase inequality in countries such as India, Indonesia, and the Philippines.

Third, there are four factors driving inequality in the Asian country including the degree of urbanization, urban–rural income gap, and urban and rural inequality. Among them, the urban-rural income gap is expected to have the largest marginal impact on inequality.

Sagala et al. (2014) studied the relationship between inequality in expenditure and urbanization in Indonesia. A panel data regression analysis was carried out to test the Kuznets inverted-U-shaped hypothesis based on a dataset of 33 provinces in 2000–2009. The results of the study supported the inverted-U-shaped hypothesis, regardless whether the Gini coefficient or Theil index is used as a measure of inequality. Inequality in expenditure is expected to peak at an urbanization rate of about 46–50%. Because the urbanization rate in Indonesia in 2010 was 50%, this indicates that inequality in spending has reached its highest value. Therefore, further urbanization will reduce inequality in expenditure, with other factors constant.

Oyvat (2016) studied the impact of agricultural structure and urbanization on income inequality. The author investigated the empirical relationship between inequality in land holding, urbanization, and income inequality using cross-data sets. The estimated results indicated that the inequality of land holding has a significant impact on urbanization and urban income and inequality. Moreover, the analysis found that excessive urbanization increases income inequality. The results of the study showed that policy makers need to have a broader view of the importance of agricultural policies. An issue of progressive land reform and subsidies to protect small farmers rogressive land reform and subsidies to protect small farmers could also reduce urban income inequality and poverty in the long term.

Wu and Rao (2017) studied inequality in China, focusing on identifying the main causes of inequality. The main objective of the study was to examine the relationship between urbanization and income inequality using provincial data. Panel data in 20 provinces was collected from the China Statistical Yearbook for five years include 1998, 2000, 2002, 2005, and 2010. The empirical analysis was based on ordinary least squares estimator and fixed and random effects models, showing a strong inverted-U-shaped relationship between inequality and urbanization. An urbanization rate of 0.53 has been determined, with the implication that provinces with higher levels of urbanization can reduce income inequality.

However, Angeles (2010) used urban population density to represent the urbanization rate, and its square as an explanatory variable in the regression analysis of panel data on income inequality. With panel data on 226 countries and regions in 1960–2005, a U-shaped relationship was found, not an inverted-U-shaped relationship. Although it is not statistically significant, this result does not support Kuznets's hypothesis.

3. Methodology and Data

3.1. Empirical Framework

Based on the theory related to urbanization and income inequality, the impact of urbanization on income equality, and the research model of Sagala et al. (2014), Wu and Rao (2017), and related studies, we present a quantitative model assessing the impact of urbanization on income inequality as follows:

$$INEQ_{it} = \alpha + \beta_1 URB_{it} + \beta_2 URB\_sq_{it} + \beta_3 GRDPpc_{it} + \beta_4 GRDPpc\_sq_{it} + \beta_5 initialINEQGRDPpc_{it} + \beta_6 rEXP_{it} + \beta_7 rGOV_{it} + \beta_8 rEDU_{it} + \beta_9 rAGR_{it} + \varepsilon_{it} \tag{1}$$

Definition of variables in research model are summarized in Table 1.

Table 1. Definition of variables in research model.

Variable Label	Definition	Expected Sign
	Dependent variable	
INEQ	Gini index	
	Independent variable	
URB	Urban population as a share of the average population in the province	+
URB_sq	Square of URB	−
GRDPpc	Gross regional domestic product per capita	+
GRDPpc_sq	Square of GRDPpc	−
initialINEQGRDPpc	Variable interaction between initial inequality and GRDPpc	
rEXP	Export value as a share of the province's GRDP	−
rGOV	Public expenditure as a share of the province's GRDP	−
rEDU	Students entering high school as a share of the average population in the province	−
rAGR	Agricultural value as a share of the province's GRDP	−

3.2. Data

Due to limited access to Vietnam's statistical data and availability of the dataset Vietnam Household Living Standard Survey (VHLSS), this study uses panel data on 63 provinces in Vietnam for every two years from 2006 to 2016. The total number of observations is 378 (6 years × 63 provinces).

The data used in our quantitative analysis include the Gini coefficient, representing income inequality, which was calculated by the author from VHLSS, and secondary data was collected from reports and surveys conducted by the General Statistics Office of Vietnam every two years.

The research uses urban population as a share of total population to proxy for urbanization. This variable is commonly used in previous studies (Nguyen and Nguyen 2018).

Data for independent and control variables used in quantitative models include urbanization, gross regional domestic product (GRDP) per capita, export volume as a share of the province's GRDP, public expenditure as a share of the province's GRDP, students entering high school as a share of the average population of the province, and agricultural value as a share of the province's GRDP, which were collected from the annual statistical yearbook of the General Statistics Office and the Provincial Statistics Office in Vietnam.

The study uses regression methods to estimate static panel data with OLS, FE, RE, and regression correction techniques proposed by Driscoll and Kraay (1998) and pooled mean group (PMG) estimation (Pesaran et al. 1999; Pesaran and Smith 1995).

4. Empirical Results

4.1. Descriptive Statistics of Variables in the Research Model

Table 2 summarizes the descriptive statistics of all the variables used in the model. The mean value of *INEQ* is 0.3794, its standard deviation is 0.0537, its minimum is 0.2498, and its maximum is 0.5883. Thus, our sample does not have much difference in the income inequality index. For *URB*, the mean is 0.2597, the standard deviation is 0.1640, the minimum is 0.0736, and the maximum is 0.8746—this shows a significant disparity in the level of urbanization among provinces during the study period. Like *URB*, *GRDPpc*, *rEXP*, *rGOV*, and *rAGR* also have large differences among provinces. For *rEDU*, the average is 0.0313, and the standard deviation is 0.0082, indicating a relatively small difference.

Table 2. Descriptive Statistics.

Variable	Obs.	Mean	S.D.	Min.	Max.
INEQ	378	0.3794	0.0537	0.2498	0.5883
URB	378	0.2597	0.1640	0.0736	0.8746
GRDPpc	378	0.3002	0.3693	0.0356	3.9169
rEXP	378	0.4413	0.6613	0.7863	6.2757
rGOV	378	0.3450	0.2512	0.1322	1.8091
rEDU	378	0.0313	0.0082	0.0123	0.0575
rAGR	378	0.2870	0.1444	0.0083	0.6241

4.2. Correlation Matrix and Multicollinearity

The correlation between variables in the regression model indicates the presence of multicollinearity that can affect the accuracy of the regression results. The results of the correlation analysis between variables in Table 3 show that the pairs of independent variables are not significantly correlated. However, to ensure accurate estimation results, we conduct a test on the multicollinearity phenomenon between variables in Table 4.

Table 3. Correlation matrix.

Variable	URB	GRDPpc	rEXP	rGOV	rEDU	rAGR
URB	1.000					
GRDPpc	0.4223 *	1.000				
rEXP	0.2164 *	0.2254 *	1.000			
rGOV	−0.2579 *	−0.2675 *	−0.3093 *	1.000		
rEDU	−0.100	−0.1489 *	−0.1449 *	−0.050	1.000	
rAGR	−0.5279 *	−0.4605 *	−0.3387 *	0.1350 *	−0.101	1.000

*** $p < 0.01$, ** $p < 0.05$, * $p < 0.1$.

In Table 4, the results show that the coefficient VIF of the variables is quite small (<2), so the model has no multicollinearity.

Table 4. Checking multicollinearity.

Variable	VIF	SQRT VIF	Tolerance	R-Squared
URB	1.56	1.25	0.6417	0.3583
GRDPpc	1.46	1.21	0.6855	0.3145
rEXP	1.29	1.14	0.7753	0.2247
rGOV	1.24	1.11	0.8074	0.1926
rEDU	1.15	1.07	0.8678	0.1322
rAGR	1.80	1.34	0.555	0.445
Mean VIF	1.42			

4.3. Assessing the Impact of Urbanization on Income Inequality

First, the implementation of static panel data regression estimation methods follows that in model (1). To assess the impact of urbanization (URB) on income inequality (INEQ), without considering the relevant factors, we revised this model by excluding URB_sq, GRDPpc_sq, and initialINEQGRDPpc in model (2):

$$INEQ_{it} = \alpha + \beta_1 URB_{it} + \beta_3 GRDPpc_{it} + \beta_6 rEXP_{it} + \beta_7 rGOV_{it} + \beta_8 rEDU_{it} + \beta_9 rAGR_{it} + \varepsilon_{it} \quad (2)$$

To test the inverted-U-shaped hypothesis between income inequality and urbanization, we added URB_sq to model (2), revised as model (3):

$$INEQ_{it} = \alpha + \beta_1 URB_{it} + \beta_2 URB\_sq_{it} + \beta_3 GRDPpc_{it} + \beta_6 rEXP_{it} + \beta_7 rGOV_{it} + \beta_8 rEDU_{it} + \beta_9 rAGR_{it} + \varepsilon_{it} \quad (3)$$

To test the inverted-U-shaped hypothesis between income inequality and economic growth, we added GRDPpc_sq to model (2), revised as model (4):

$$INEQ_{it} = \alpha + \beta_1 URB_{it} + \beta_3 GRDPpc_{it} + \beta_4 GRDPpc\_sq_{it} + \beta_6 rEXP_{it} + \beta_7 rGOV_{it} + \beta_8 rEDU_{it} + \beta_9 rAGR_{it} + \varepsilon_{it} \quad (4)$$

To analyze the effects of initial inequality on the impact of economic growth on income inequality, we added initialINEQGRDPpc to model (2), revised as model (5):

$$INEQ_{it} = \alpha + \beta_1 URB_{it} + \beta_3 GRDPpc_{it} + \beta_5 initialINEQGRDPpc_{it} + \beta_6 rEXP_{it} + \beta_7 rGOV_{it} + \beta_8 rEDU_{it} + \beta_9 rAGR_{it} + \varepsilon_{it} \quad (5)$$

Finally, to analyze the impact of URB on INEQ under the simultaneous influence of all factors, we constructed model (6):

$$INEQ_{it} = \alpha + \beta_1 URB_{it} + \beta_2 URB\_sq_{it} + \beta_3 GRDPpc_{it} + \beta_4 GRDPpc\_sq_{it} + \beta_5 initialINEQGRDPpc_{it} + \beta_6 rEXP_{it} + \beta_7 rGOV_{it} + \beta_8 rEDU_{it} + \beta_9 rAGR_{it} + \varepsilon_{it} \quad (6)$$

To select an estimation method that is consistent with the dataset, we chose between pooled OLS and FE methods through F-testing with the hypothesis "H_0: Pooled OLS method is appropriate ($u_i = 0$)". The regression result of the FE method in Table 5 shows that "F-test $u_i = 0$" has a p-value = $0.000 < 0.01$ in all models, which indicates that the FE method is more appropriate than pooled OLS. The results in Table 5 also show that the F-test has a p-value < 0.01 in all models, indicating that at the 1% significance level, the models are statistically significant. Then, to choose between FE and RE, the study uses the Hausman test with the hypothesis "H_0: RE model is appropriate". The test results show (Prob > Chi2) = $0.0000 < 0.01$ in all models, which demonstrates sufficient statistical evidence to reject H_0, indicating that the more efficient FE model should be selected.

However, the results of post-regression tests with the FE model have the following violations: aWald test with the hypothesis "H_0: constant variance" gives the result Prob > Chi2 = $0.0000 < 0.01$ in all empirical models, rejecting H_0 at a significance level of 1%, which means that the existing models of variance change. The Wooldridge autocorrelation test with the hypothesis "H_0: no autocorrelation" gives the statistical result Prob > F = $0.0000 < 0.05$ in all models, rejecting H_0 at a significance level of 5%, which means that the model has autocorrelation. The result from testing Pesaran cross-sectional dependence with the hypothesis "H_0: Cross-sectional independence" is (Prob > z) <0.01 in all models, rejecting the H_0 hypothesis at a significance level of 1%, which means that cross-sectional dependence exists in models. The study also uses the Durbin-Wu-Hausman test for endogeneity of explanatory variables with the hypothesis "H_0: explanatory variables are exogenous," i.e., not correlated with residuals. The results show that $rEXP$ and $rGOV$ are endogenous in the model.[1]

Table 5. Results of fixed effects regression.

Variables	(2) INEQ	(3) INEQ	(4) INEQ	(5) INEQ	(6) INEQ
URB	−0.307 *** (0.0680)	−0.00200 (0.237)	−0.247 *** (0.0727)	−0.323 *** (0.0728)	0.0657 (0.238)
URB_sq		−0.319 (0.237)			−0.353 (0.234)
GRDPpc	−0.0233 (0.0151)	−0.0229 (0.0150)	−0.0891 *** (0.0327)	0.0631 (0.144)	0.289 * (0.158)
GRDPpc_sq			0.0150 ** (0.00662)		0.0281 *** (0.00824)
initialINEQGRDPpc				−0.215 (0.356)	−1.083 ** (0.439)
rEXP	−0.00584 (0.00504)	−0.00753 (0.00518)	−0.00527 (0.00501)	−0.00619 (0.00507)	−0.00843 (0.00513)
rGOV	0.00847 (0.0202)	0.00820 (0.0202)	0.00416 (0.0202)	0.00934 (0.0203)	0.00440 (0.0200)
rEDU	−1.302 ** (0.658)	−1.006 (0.692)	−2.133 *** (0.750)	−1.182 * (0.687)	−1.932 ** (0.766)
rAGR	−0.0839 * (0.0468)	−0.0746 (0.0472)	−0.124 ** (0.0497)	−0.0821 * (0.0469)	−0.140 *** (0.0505)
Constant	0.531 *** (0.0339)	0.470 *** (0.0563)	0.570 *** (0.0380)	0.528 *** (0.0342)	0.527 *** (0.0578)
Observations	378	378	378	378	378
F-test (p-value)	0.0000	0.0000	0.0000	0.0001	0.0000
R-squared	0.093	0.098	0.108	0.094	0.132
F-test $u_i = 0$ (p-value)	0.0000	0.0000	0.0000	0.0000	0.0000
Number of id	63	63	63	63	63

Standard errors in parentheses: *** $p < 0.01$, ** $p < 0.05$, * $p < 0.1$.

---

[1] The results of estimating OLS and RE regression, Hausman test, and post-regression tests are detailed in the Appendix A.

The models have an endogenous element caused by $rEXP$ and $rGOV$, but this is not the main research focus, so we ignore this problem.

A regression model can be used for analysis of the estimation results, and statistical inference techniques should be used for appropriate revisions. Technical studies revise regressions following Driscoll and Kraay (1998), whose method resolves violations in the FE model, such as changes in the variance, autocorrelation, and cross-dependence. The results are in Table 6.

Finally, the impact of urbanization on income inequality in the short and long term is assessed. The technical econometric dynamic panel regression estimatation method used in this study is PMG (Pesaran et al. 1999; Pesaran and Smith 1995). Because the number of years of observation is not long enough, the study assesses only the impact of urbanization on income inequality unaffected by other factors. The results in Table 7 show that urbanization affects income inequality in the long term but not in the short term.

Table 6. Results of Driscoll and Kraay regression.

Variables	(2)	(3)	(4)	(5)	(6)
	INEQ	INEQ	INEQ	INEQ	INEQ
URB	−0.307 *** (0.0729)	−0.00200 (0.0489)	−0.247 ** (0.0907)	−0.323 *** (0.0708)	0.0657 (0.0419)
URB_sq		−0.319 ** (0.0920)			−0.353 ** (0.103)
GRDPpc	−0.0233 ** (0.00884)	−0.0229 ** (0.00882)	−0.0891 * (0.0370)	0.0631 (0.194)	0.289 (0.194)
GRDPpc_sq			0.0150 (0.00771)		0.0281 *** (0.00675)
initialINEQGRDPpc				−0.215 (0.484)	−1.083 * (0.484)
rEXP	−0.00584 (0.00579)	−0.00753 (0.00615)	−0.00527 (0.00619)	−0.00619 (0.00638)	−0.00843 (0.00693)
rGOV	0.00847 (0.0121)	0.00820 (0.0127)	0.00416 (0.00794)	0.00934 (0.0107)	0.00440 (0.00804)
rEDU	−1.302 (0.722)	−1.006 (0.696)	−2.133 *** (0.302)	−1.182 * (0.469)	−1.932 *** (0.338)
rAGR	−0.0839 *** (0.0197)	−0.0746 *** (0.0166)	−0.124 ** (0.0459)	−0.0821 ** (0.0218)	−0.140 ** (0.0437)
Constant	0.531 *** (0.0297)	0.470 *** (0.0219)	0.570 *** (0.0111)	0.528 *** (0.0266)	0.527 *** (0.0160)
Observations	378	378	378	378	378
Number of groups	63	63	63	63	63

Standard errors in parentheses: *** $p < 0.01$, ** $p < 0.05$, * $p < 0.1$.

Table 7. Results of PMG regression.

Variables	Long Run	Short Run
__ec		−0.889 ***
		(0.0959)
D.URB		−1.199
		(1.940)
URB	−0.500 ***	
	(0.0129)	
Constant		0.457 ***
		(0.0466)
Observations	315	315

Standard errors in parentheses: *** $p < 0.01$, ** $p < 0.05$, * $p < 0.1$.

5. Discussion of Results

The results of the econometric models lead to the following findings.

URB has a negative regression coefficient with a statistical significance of 1% in model (2), indicating the negative impact of urbanization on income inequality in Vietnamese provinces. This means that higher urbanization contributes to reducing income inequality, which is consistent with the impact of urbanization on income inequality in models (3), (4), and (5). This result is consistent with Johansson and Wang (2014) and contrary to Beladi et al. (2017). In fact, in Vietnam, urbanization is associated with the formation of industrial zones and clusters. People who have little or no land in rural areas migrate to cities to work in factories with higher wages than previous jobs in rural areas, which raises their income. Therefore, urbanization contributes to reducing income inequality in Vietnam. This impact is consistent with the PMG method in the long term.

URB_sq, the impact of urbanization on income inequality, may be nonlinear, in other words, this effect may be in accordance with the inverted-U-shaped hypothesis. *URB_sq* is included in models (3) and (6) to test this hypothesis, and the estimation results show that its impact on *INEQ* is negatively significant at the 5% level. Model (6), which includes with regression coefficients for *URB* and *URB_sq*, shows the nonlinear relationship between urbanization and income inequality. Urbanization increases income inequality in the early stages until it reaches a certain threshold, after which it reduces income inequality. This result is consistent with Sagala et al. (2014) in Indonesia and Wu and Rao (2017) in China.

GRDPpc, which has a negative regression coefficient with a statistical significance of 5% in model (2), shows the negative impact of per capita income on income inequality in Vietnam provinces, which means that higher per capita income contributes to reducing income inequality. This result is consistent with the impact of per capita income on income inequality in models (3) and (4), consistent with Jin (2009) who studies China in 1990–2006. In addition, the interaction variable between initial economic growth and inequality (*initialINEQGRDPpc*) has no significant regression coefficients. The results of model (5) show that the effect of economic growth on income inequality in Vietnam in 2006–2016 is not affected by the level of initial inequality. The results are contrary to those of Johansson and Wang (2014).

The regression coefficients of *GRDPpc_sq*, which are not statistically significant in model (4), shows that the inverted-U-shape hypothesis between economic growth and income inequality in Vietnam is not confirmed from 2006 to 2016. The results are contrary to those of Sagala et al. (2014), who found evidence supporting the inverted-U-shape hypothesis in Indonesia between 2000 and 2009.

rEXP, which is not statistically significant, shows that trade, which represents the share of exports in GDP, has a negligible effect on income inequality in Vietnam. This result is similar to that of Johansson and Wang (2014).

rGOV, which is not statistically significant, shows that the government spending in the provinces has a negligible effect on income inequality in Vietnam. This result is similar to that of Johansson and Wang (2014) and Beladi et al. (2017).

rEDU, which represents human capital, has a negative regression coefficient, showing the negative impact of education on income inequality. Although the level of statistical significance is not consistent in all empirical models, the results show that education plays a role in decrease income inequality in Vietnam. This result contrasts with Jin (2009), showing the education increased income inequality in China between 1990 and 2006, with Johansson and Wang (2014), which found no impact of education on income inequality in 90 countries in 1981–2005.

rAGR, which has a negative regression coefficient and is statistically significant at the 1% significance level in models (2) and (3) and 5% in models (4) and (5) shows the negative effect of the proportion of agricultural value to income inequality. This result is consistent with that of Wu and Rao (2017).

6. Conclusions and Policy Implications

This study analyzed and evaluated the impact of urbanization on income inequality in Vietnam in the period 2006–2016. We used the following econometric techniques and methods: the estimation methods with static panel data regression used are OLS, FE, RE, and Driscoll and Kraay. The method used for estimating dynamic panel data regression is PMG, enabling us to consider the impact of urbanization on income inequality in the short and long term.

Our research results lead us to draw the following conclusions. Urbanization helps reduce income inequality in Vietnam, including in the long term. We confirm the inverted-U-shaped relationship between urbanization and income inequality in Vietnam, where economic growth reduces income inequality. The impact of economic growth on income inequality is not affected by the initial level of inequality. The hypothesis on an inverted-U-shaped relationship between economic growth and income inequality is not confirmed during the study period. The share of exports has a negligible effect on income inequality in Vietnam. Public spending does not significantly affect income inequality in Vietnam. The high school enrollment rate and the proportion of agriculture influence reductions in income inequality.

Because urbanization has the effect of reducing income inequality, even in the long term, Vietnam needs to continue to promote urbanization. Economic growth has the effect of reducing income inequality, therefore policies to increase economic growth and social welfare should be maintained to reduce the gap between rich and poor. As improving intellectual standards will help reduce inequality, more supportive policies are needed to improve education. Because high value agricultural development will contribute to reducing inequality, appropriate policies are needed to support and develop agriculture, farmers, and rural areas.

Author Contributions: All authors contributed equally and reviewed the final manuscript.

Acknowledgments: We are grateful to the three anonymous referees for their constructive comments. We also thank the participants at the 3rd Vietnam's Business and Economics Research Conference VBER2019 (Ho Chi Minh City Open University, Vietnam, 18–20 July 2019) for their helpful suggestions. The authors wish to acknowledge financial supports from Ho Chi Minh City Open University. The authors are solely responsible for any remaining errors or shortcomings.

Appendix A

Table A1. Results of pooled OLS regression.

Variables	(2)	(3)	(4)	(5)	(6)
	INEQ	INEQ	INEQ	INEQ	INEQ
URB	−0.00142	0.0299	0.00526	0.00115	−0.00203
	(0.0191)	(0.0585)	(0.0194)	(0.0184)	(0.0573)
URB_sq		−0.0371			0.00174
		(0.0654)			(0.0637)
GRDPpc	0.0146*	0.0140 *	−0.0219	−0.415 ***	−0.421 ***
	(0.00822)	(0.00830)	(0.0222)	(0.0787)	(0.0804)
GRDPpc_sq			0.0106 *		−0.00286
			(0.00598)		(0.00636)
initialINEQGRDPpc				1.036 ***	1.074 ***
				(0.189)	(0.209)
rEXP	−0.00500	−0.00521	−0.00406	0.00191	0.00193
	(0.00431)	(0.00433)	(0.00434)	(0.00434)	(0.00438)
rGOV	0.0799 ***	0.0803 ***	0.0763 ***	0.0699 ***	0.0705 ***
	(0.0111)	(0.0112)	(0.0113)	(0.0109)	(0.0110)
rEDU	−0.642 *	−0.647 **	−0.854 **	−1.021 ***	−0.977 ***
	(0.328)	(0.328)	(0.348)	(0.323)	(0.338)
rAGR	0.0507 **	0.0493 **	0.0351	0.0246	0.0279
	(0.0234)	(0.0235)	(0.0249)	(0.0230)	(0.0243)
Constant	0.356 ***	0.352 ***	0.374 ***	0.388 ***	0.384 ***
	(0.0191)	(0.0204)	(0.0218)	(0.0193)	(0.0222)
Observations	378	378	378	378	378
R-squared	0.189	0.189	0.195	0.250	0.250

Standard errors in parentheses: *** $p < 0.01$, ** $p < 0.05$, * $p < 0.1$.

Table A2. Results of RE regression.

Variables	(2)	(3)	(4)	(5)	(6)
	INEQ	INEQ	INEQ	INEQ	INEQ
URB	−0.0314	0.0527	−0.0217	−0.0193	0.0273
	(0.0258)	(0.0812)	(0.0262)	(0.0239)	(0.0745)
URB_sq		−0.0990			−0.0514
		(0.0896)			(0.0822)
GRDPpc	−0.00198	−0.00349	−0.0510 **	−0.388 ***	−0.376 ***
	(0.0100)	(0.0101)	(0.0230)	(0.0903)	(0.0931)
GRDPpc_sq			0.0135 **		0.00272
			(0.00574)		(0.00637)
initialINEQGRDPpc				0.949 ***	0.895 ***
				(0.219)	(0.245)
rEXP	−0.00627	−0.00682	−0.00557	−0.00156	−0.00185
	(0.00456)	(0.00459)	(0.00454)	(0.00455)	(0.00459)
rGOV	0.0564 ***	0.0568 ***	0.0520 ***	0.0535 ***	0.0544 ***
	(0.0136)	(0.0136)	(0.0136)	(0.0129)	(0.0129)
rEDU	−0.682 *	−0.668 *	−1.110 **	−1.125 ***	−1.166 ***
	(0.395)	(0.397)	(0.434)	(0.388)	(0.408)
rAGR	0.0153	0.0130	−0.0126	−0.00103	−0.00458
	(0.0286)	(0.0288)	(0.0308)	(0.0276)	(0.0290)
Constant	0.388 ***	0.377 ***	0.420 ***	0.413 ***	0.409 ***
	(0.0226)	(0.0253)	(0.0261)	(0.0226)	(0.0266)
Observations	378	378	378	378	378
Number of id	63	63	63	63	63

Standard errors in parentheses: *** $p < 0.01$, ** $p < 0.05$, * $p < 0.1$.

Table A3. Hausman test results.

Statistical Parameters	(2)	(3)	(4)	(5)	(6)
Chi2	58.27	58.63	55.59	49.78	68.39
Prob > chi2	0.0000	0.0000	0.0000	0.0000	0.0000

Table A4. Wald test of constant variance.

Statistical Parameters	(2)	(3)	(4)	(5)	(6)
Chi2	8920.95	12,922.50	6332.03	9820.80	16,898.79
Prob > chi2	0.0000	0.0000	0.0000	0.0000	0.0000

Table A5. Wooldridge test inspection of autocorrelation.

Statistical Parameters	(2)	(3)	(4)	(5)	(6)
$F_{(1,62)}$	6.297	5.556	6.457	5.997	5.207
Prob>F	0.0147	0.0216	0.0136	0.0172	0.0259

Table A6. Pesaran test inspection dependence between units.

Statistical Parameters	(2)	(3)	(4)	(5)	(6)
Pesaran's test	3.915	3.520	3.945	3.979	3.675
Prob > z	0.0001	0.0004	0.0001	0.0001	0.0002
abs	0.401	0.403	0.395	0.403	0.397

Table A7. Durbin-Wu-Hausman test on the endogenousness of explanatory variables.

Variables	(2)	(3)	(4)	(5)	(6)
URB					
Chi-sq	0.36863	0.41196	0.37807	0.21610	0.19385
p-value	0.54375	0.52098	0.53864	0.64203	0.65973
URB_sq					
Chi-sq		0.61870			0.30912
p-value		0.43153			0.57822
GRDPpc					
Chi-sq	0.37675	0.38193	0.02666	0.88462	0.67078
p-value	0.53935	0.53657	0.87030	0.34694	0.41278
GRDPpc_sq					
Chi-sq			0.75805		0.05507
p-value			0.38394		0.81446
initial INEQGRDPpc					
Chi-sq				0.64876	0.46360
p-value				0.42056	0.49595
rEXP					
Chi-sq	3.67900	3.65990	4.37889	7.78901	7.89755
p-value	*0.05510*	*0.05574*	*0.03639*	*0.00526*	*0.00495*
rGOV					
Chi-sq	3.91847	3.93987	3.64679	3.52257	3.44806
p-value	*0.04776*	*0.04715*	*0.05618*	*0.06054*	*0.06333*
rEDU					
Chi-sq	0.02895	0.02656	0.12883	0.09891	0.13693
p-value	0.86490	0.87053	0.71965	0.75314	0.71135
rAGR					
Chi-sq	0.07408	0.07707	0.00048	0.03788	0.06896
p-value	0.78548	0.78131	0.98260	0.84569	0.79286

References

Akita, Takahiro, Rizal Affandi Lukman, and Yukino Yamada. 1999. Inequality in the Distribution of Household Expenditures in Indonesia: A Theil Decomposition Analysis. *The Developing Economies* 37: 197–221. [CrossRef]

Angeles, Luis. 2010. An alternative test of Kuznets' hypothesis. *The Journal of Economic Inequality* 8: 463–73. [CrossRef]

Behrens, Kristian, and Frédéric Robert-Nicoud. 2014. Survival of the fittest in cities: agglomeration, polarization, and inequality. *The Economic Journal* 124: 1371–400. [CrossRef]

Beladi, Hamid, Chi-Chur Chao, Mong Shan Ee, and Daniel Hollas. 2017. *Urban Development, Excessive Entry of Firms and Wage Inequality in Developing Countries*. ADBI Working Paper Series, ADBI Working Paper 653; Tokyo: Asian Development Bank Institute.

Bloom, David E., David Canning, Günther Fink, Tarun Khanna, and Patrick Salyer. 2010. *Urban Settlement: Data, Measures, and Trends*. UNU-WIDER Working Paper. Helsinki: World Institute for Development Economic Research (UNU-WIDER).

Bourguignon, François, and Christian Morrisson. 1998. Inequality and Development: The Role of Dualism. *Journal of Development Economics* 57: 233–57. [CrossRef]

Brülhart, Marius, and Federica Sbergami. 2009. Agglomeration and growth: cross-country evidence. *Journal of Urban Economics* 65: 48–63. [CrossRef]

Driscoll, John C., and Aart C. Kraay. 1998. Consistent Covariance Matrix Estimation with Spatially Dependent Panel Data. *Review of Economics and Statistics* 80: 549–60. [CrossRef]

Gini, Corrado. 1913. Variabilita e Mutabilita. *Journal of the Royal Statistical Society* 76: 326–27.

Gini, Corrado. 1921. Measurement of inequality of incomes. *The Economic Journal* 31: 124–26. [CrossRef]

Gotham, Kevin Fox. 2012. Urbanization. In *The Wiley-Blackwell Companion to Sociology*. Edited by G. Ritzer Malden. Hoboken: Wiley-Blackwell, pp. 488–503.

Hardoon, Deborah, Sophia Ayele, and Ricardo Fuentes-Nieva. 2016. *An Economy for the 1%*. Nairobi: Oxfam.

Harris, John R., and Michael P. Todaro. 1970. Migration, Unemployment, and Development: A Two Sector Analysis. *American Economic Review* 60: 126–42.

Jin, Furong. 2009. Foreign Direct Investment and Income Inequality in China. *Seoul Journal of Economics* 22: 311–39.

Johansson, Anders C., and Xun Wang. 2014. Financial sector policies and income inequality. *China Economic Review* 31: 367–78. [CrossRef]

Kanbur, Ravi, and Juzhong Zhuang. 2013. Urbanization and inequality in Asia. *Asian Development Review* 30: 131–47. [CrossRef]

Krugman, Paul R. 1991. *Geography and Trade*. Cambridge: MIT Press.

Kuznets, Simon. 1955. Economic Growth and Income Inequality. *American Economic Review* 45: 1–28.

Lewis, W. Arthur. 1954. Economic Development with Unlimited Supplies of Labor. *Manchester School* 22: 139–91. [CrossRef]

Lorenz, Max O. 1905. Methods of Measuring the Concentration of Wealth. *Publications of the American Statistical Association* 9: 209–19. [CrossRef]

Nguyen, Ha Minh, and Le Dang Nguyen. 2018. The relationship between urbanization and economic growth: An empirical study on ASEAN countries. *International Journal of Social Economics* 45: 316–39. [CrossRef]

Oyvat, C. 2016. Agrarian Structures, Urbanization, and Inequality. *World Development* 83: 207–30. [CrossRef]

Pesaran, M. Hashem, and Ron Smith. 1995. Estimating Long-run Relationships from Dynamic Heterogeneous Panels. *Journal of Econometrics* 68: 79–113. [CrossRef]

Pesaran, M. Hashem, Yongcheol Shin, and Ron P. Smith. 1999. Pooled Mean Group Estimation of Dynamic Heterogeneous Panels. *Journal of the American Statistical Association* 94: 621–34. [CrossRef]

Piketty, Thomas. 2006. The Kuznets Curve, Yesterday and Tomorrow. In *Understanding Poverty*. Edited by Abhijit Banerjee, Roland Benabou and Dilip Mookherjee. New York: Oxford University Press, pp. 63–72.

Rauch, James E. 1993. Economic development, urban underemployment, and income inequality. *Canadian Journal of Economics* 26: 901–18. [CrossRef]

Ross, Jaime. 2000. *Development Theory and the Economics of Growth*. Ann Arbor: The University of Michigan Press.

Sagala, Perdamen, Takahiro Akita, and Arief Anshori Yusuf. 2014. Urbanization and expenditure inequality in Indonesia: Testing the Kuznets hypothesis with provincial panel data. *Letters in Spatial and Resource Sciences* 7: 133–47. [CrossRef]

Stiglitz, Joseph. 2009. The global crisis, social protection and jobs. *International Labour Review* 148: 1–2. [CrossRef]

Todaro, Michael P. 1989. *Economic development in the Third World*, 4th ed. London and New York: Longman.

Wu, Dongjie, and Prasada Rao. 2017. Urbanization and Income Inequality in China: An Empirical Investigation at Provincial Level. *Social Indicators Research* 131: 189–214. [CrossRef]

5

Cultural Distance and Entry Modes in Emerging Markets: Empirical Evidence in Vietnam

Nguyen Minh Ha [1,*] , **Quan Minh Quoc Binh** [2] **and Pham Phi Dang** [3]

[1] The Business and Economics Research Group, Ho Chi Minh City Open University, 97 Vo Van Tan Street, District 3, Ho Chi Minh City 700000, Vietnam

[2] Faculty of Economics and Public Management, Ho Chi Minh City Open University, 97 Vo Van Tan Street, District 3, Ho Chi Minh City 700000, Vietnam; binh.qmq@ou.edu.vn

[3] Department of Planning and Investment Binh Thuan Province, 290 Tran Hung Dao Street, Phan Thiet City 800000, Vietnam; dangpp@skhdt.binhthuan.gov.vn

* Correspondence: ha.nm@ou.edu.vn

Abstract: Cultural distance is acknowledged as a crucial factor that significantly affects the entry mode selection of multinational enterprises. The purpose of this article is to analyze the relationship between cultural distance and entry mode choice by exploring a novel dataset of 5236 firms in Vietnam with foreign investment during the period 2005–2016. Although many studies were conducted about the cultural distance and entry mode nexus, most of the research mainly focuses on developed and developing countries, where a market economy is already established. It is important to expand the research to a transition economy such as Vietnam, where the government is committed to attracting foreign investment. The results indicate that, when the cultural difference between Vietnam and their home country is high, foreign-invested firms prefer wholly-owned subsidiaries (WOS) over equity joint ventures (EJV). The study contributes to the general understanding about cultural distance and entry mode decision of foreign-invested firms in emerging markets.

Keywords: cultural distance; entry mode; equity joint venture; wholly owned subsidiary

1. Introduction

Multinational companies invest in foreign markets for a variety of reasons: Some may find new markets for their goods and services, while others are attracted by the cheap and abundant resources of the host country (Dunning 2002). During the pre-investment stage, the choice of market entry mode is the essential strategy that will affect the survival and development of firms in the future (Anderson and Gatignon 1986). Many scholars believe that the cultural distance between the investing and host countries is one of the most important factors that influences the entry mode choice by investors (Kogut and Singh 1988; Agarwal and Ramaswami 1992; Erramilli 1996). However, the way in which cultural distance affects the entry mode is still controversial among scholars. According to transaction cost theory, there are two opposing arguments about the impacts of cultural distance on entry mode selection. The first argument states that cultural distance influences the perception of costs and uncertainty of the investing firm (Kogut and Singh 1988). A larger cultural distance between home and host countries encourages multinational corporations to select equity joint ventures (EJV) over wholly owned subsidiaries (WOS) to limit their exposure to uncertainty and risk. The second argument states that it is difficult for foreign firms to acquire accurate information about the local partners, as well as understand the behavior of these partners in an environment with a large cultural distance (Chang et al. 2012). Therefore, foreign firms would select WOS to gain full control of their business and avoid opportunistic behaviors by the partners (Sutcliffe and Zaheer 1998). However, most studies on the entry mode and cultural distance focus on developed economies. Many researchers (Meyer and

Nguyen 2005; Dikova 2012) state that the entry mode strategy is totally different in transition countries and developed countries due to different institutional frameworks.

The question of whether the WOS or EJV can be selected in a transition country when the cultural distance between an investing country and a host country is large, remains unanswered. Our research in the context of a transition country contributes to the body of knowledge about entry mode selection.

To address the research gap, we aim to explore the impact of cultural difference on entry mode selection using a novel dataset of 5236 foreign-invested firms in Vietnam in the period 2005–2016. This research objective is achieved by adopting the transaction cost theory. The transaction cost approach contributes new insights into how the cultural distance influences the entry mode choice of foreign-invested firms into a transition economy. Theoretical argument about the role of cultural distance and entry mode selection is developed in a transition country context. As suggested by Michailova (2011) about the importance of context-specific theory development in international business research, we believe that our theoretical argument can contribute a new knowledge in international business literature.

Vietnam is a suitable country for this study for many reasons. First, Vietnam is an emerging country with a high economic growth rate in recent years, and continues in transition with commitments from the government for important reforms, such as attracting foreign direct investment (FDI), so it is a good case for research on the entry mode. Vietnam's Investment Law 2015 introduces positive change, but the cultural distance between the home and host countries is still the main obstacle, in addition to restrictions on investors who are considering investment in Vietnam (Van Dut et al. 2018). Therefore, comprehensive research on the relationship between cultural distance and entry mode choice to promote foreign investment in Vietnam is needed. Second, little research about entry mode selection in emerging countries covers Vietnam. Most research on this topic mainly discusses developed or developing countries, where a market economy is already formed (Kogut and Singh 1988; Agarwal and Ramaswami 1992). It is important to expand the research to a transition economy such as Vietnam, and it makes a contribution to the theory development in a specific context, as suggested by Michailova (2011).

The structure of the paper is as follows: In the next section we present a brief review of the literature. We then present the methodology in Section 3, followed by a discussion of the results in Section 4. Section 5 concludes our paper.

2. Literature Review

When conquering new markets, multinational enterprises need to select an entry mode as their important internationalization strategy (Agarwal and Ramaswami 1992). Entry mode is defined by Sharma and Erramilli (2004, p. 2) as "a structural agreement that allows a firm to implement its product market strategy in a host country either by carrying out only marketing operations (i.e., via export modes) or both production and marketing operations there by itself or in a partnership with others (contractual modes, joint venture, wholly owned operations)." The choice of entry mode has a significant impact on the survival and development of firms in the future (Porter 1987). In the past two decades, researchers identified different types of entry modes, mainly divided into two groups: Equity mode and non-equity mode. The equity mode group includes joint venture and wholly owned subsidiaries (Root 1994). The non-equity mode group includes exporting, licensing/contractual agreement, R and D contracts, franchising, and strategic alliance (Root 1994). Different types of entry modes have different levels of control, resource commitment, and risk (Hill et al. 1990). In this research, we consider two important modes of entry in Vietnam: Equity joint ventures (EJV) and wholly-owned subsidiaries (WOS) (Tsang 2005). Another reason for only considering EJV and WOS in this study is the nature of the data that we collected. Our sample consists of 4070 WOS projects (77.27%), 1116 EJV projects (22.14%), six build-operate-transfer (BOT), build–transfer (BT) and build–transfer–operate (BTO) projects (0.11%), and 25 business cooperation contract (BCCs) projects (0.47%). We omit the data on BOT, BT, BTO and BCCs from the sample because they are small in number, and have special characteristics.

Based on previous empirical research, scholars divide the determining factors of entry mode into three groups: Country-specific factors, firm-specific factors and industry factors (see Luo 2001; Tsang 2005; Shieh and Wu 2012). Country-specific factors represent the characteristics of investing and recipient countries such as the country risk, market potential and cultural distance. Industry-specific factors refer to characteristics of the industry. Lastly, firm-specific factors are concerned with the characteristics of foreign-invested firms, and this study examines investment amount, project orientation, investment duration and year of investment. When we move from macro to micro determinant factors, the role of transaction cost theory is increasingly more important.

Prior research often emphasizes that cultural distance (a country-specific factor) has significant impacts on entry mode choice (Yiu and Makino 2002). Cultural distance is defined as "the degree to which shared norms and values differ from one country to another" (Hofstede 2001). In order to explore the cultural distance and entry mode relationship, international business scholars tend to rely on transaction cost theory (Anderson and Gatignon 1986; Kogut and Singh 1988). Transaction cost theory was first articulated in the seminal work of Ronald Coase (1937), who was awarded the Nobel Memorial Prize in economics for his research on the nature of the firm. In addition, Williamson (1975) also received the Nobel Prize in economics for his research on transaction costs economics theory (TCT), and the concept of transaction cost was first applied to entry mode by Anderson and Gatignon (1986). TCT is the most widely-adopted and applied in international business on market entry mode choice (Canabal and White 2008). The theory states that the selection of market entry mode by foreign firms is affected by the desire to minimize transaction costs (Anderson and Gatignon 1986). Transaction costs occur when firms do business with their partners. These costs include the cost of compiling a contract and negotiating with business partners, as well as cost of monitoring contract performance. The theory suggests two opposing arguments about the impacts of cultural distance on entry mode selection. The first argument states that cultural distance influences the perception of costs and the uncertainty of the investing firm (Kogut and Singh 1988). A larger cultural distance between home and host countries encourages multinational corporations to select equity joint ventures (EJV) over wholly-owned subsidiaries (WOS) to limit their exposure to uncertainty and risk. Empirical evidence from Kogut and Singh (1988), Erramilli and Rao (1993), and Pak and Park (2004) support this argument. The second argument states that it is difficult for foreign firms to acquire accurate information about the local partners, as well as understand the behavior of these partners in an environment with a large cultural distance (Chang et al. 2012). In this case, the cost of negotiating, monitoring, and enforcing contracts with local firms is even higher. Therefore, foreign firms would select WOS to gain full control of their business and avoid opportunistic behaviors by the partners (Sutcliffe and Zaheer 1998). Empirical studies by Shane (1994), as well as Chen and Hu (2002), provide evidence that supports the hypothesis of choosing WOS when the cultural difference is large. However, most studies on the entry mode and cultural distance focus on developed economies. Given the debate, we argue that the role of cultural distance on entry mode selection cannot be ignored in the context of the transition economy. In transition countries, the main difficulty faced by foreign-invested firms is the selection between WOS or EJV. The reason is that foreign-invested firms first need to select between employing local resources or conquering the transition country on their own (Van Dut et al. 2018). When the cultural distance between host country with a transition economy and the home country is large, firms need the local knowledge and local resources to overcome the risk and uncertainty (Van Dut et al. 2018). Adopting the transaction cost approach, we expect a large cultural difference and inefficient cooperation with local counterparts to encourage foreign investors to select WOS. The discussion leads to the hypothesis:

Hypothesis 1 (H1): *WOS are preferred to EJV when the cultural distance between Vietnam and investing countries is large.*

3. Methodology

3.1. Data

The study explores the linkage between entry mode choice and the cultural distance of foreign firms in Vietnam, a developing country in the transition process with reform commitments by the government to attract FDI. The data, from 2005 to 2016, were compiled by the Ministry of Planning and Investment of Vietnam, totaling 4070 wholly-owned subsidiaries (WOS) (77.27%), 1116 equity joint ventures (EJV) (22.14%), six build-operate-transfer (BOT), build–transfer (BT), and build–transfer–operate (BTO) (0.11%), and 25 business cooperation contract (BCCs) (0.47%). The data on BOT, BT, BTO, and BCCs were omitted from this study because of their small number and special characteristics. These foreign-invested projects came from 78 countries in the world. The sample consisted of 1064 foreign-invested projects from Korea, 876 from Europe, 792 from Singapore, 654 from Chinese regions (mainland China, Hong Kong, Macau, and Taiwan), and 274 from the US.

3.2. Variables

3.2.1. Dependent Variable

The dependent variable is the entry mode choice of foreign investors when entering Vietnam. This is a dummy variable that takes a value of 1 if foreign investors establish EJV, and 0 for WOS (Slangen and Hennart 2008).

3.2.2. Independent Variable

Cultural distance is the most important variable in this study. We measure cultural distance between Vietnam and investing countries along the six cultural dimensions developed by Hofstede (1980): Power distance, individualism, masculinity, uncertainty avoidance, long-term orientation and indulgence. Hofstede's cultural metrics are used because they enable us to conduct international comparisons between cultures. These data are widely employed in international business and cross-cultural psychology studies (Shenkar 2001). These data are adjusted and computed from 0 to 100 (percentage), and are available at Hofstede's website, https://geerthofstede.com. Based on the equation of Kogut and Singh (1988), we calculate a cultural distance index between Vietnam and other countries. Because culture is a multidimensional concept, using cultural distance data at an aggregate level can fully measure all aspects of culture. In addition, if we use data from each dimension, some of them may be incompatible with Vietnam.

$$CD_j = \sum_{i=1}^{6} \left\{ \frac{\left(I_{ij} - I_{iv}\right)^2}{V_i} \right\} / (6)$$

where CD_j is the cultural distance between investing countries and Vietnam, I_{ij} is the cultural aspect i of home countries j, I_{iv} is the ith cultural aspect of Vietnam, v is Vietnam, and V_i is the variance of the ith cultural aspect. The larger the value of this indicator is, the larger the cultural distance between Vietnam and the investing countries.

3.2.3. Control Variables

To account for country-specific factors that might affect entry mode choice, we included variables for country risk and market potential. Anderson and Gatignon (1986) define country risk as unpredictable changes in the business environment in a particular country (cited in Shieh and Wu 2012), and these risks decrease the profitability of firms conducting business in this country. In high-risk host countries, foreign investors often avoid committing to investment in large projects to minimize losses in case they want to withdraw from the market (Kim and Hwang 1992). Previous empirical studies predict that in an unpredictable business environment FDI firms prefer a joint venture, rather than a WOS (Agarwal and Ramaswami 1992).

This is because when investment risks increase, multinational corporations (MNCs) seek information and knowledge through joint ventures with local companies. Joint ventures allow firms to enjoy lower long-term costs due to having better information (Beamish and Banks 1987). We follow Manh Chien and Tu (2012) in using the political risks of Vietnam as a proxy for country risk. The data can be obtained from the website of Political Risk Services at http: //www.prsgroup.com/ICRG_Methodology.aspx.

Market potential is a crucial factor in entry mode selection. A country with a rapid and stable economic growth rate encourages foreign-invested firms to commit all their financial resources to development, and thus establish a company with 100% foreign capital (Agarwal and Ramaswami 1992). We employ Vietnam's GDP growth rate in the year that an investment project is initiated as a proxy for market potential. This is the one-year GDP growth rate, and the data come from the General Statistics Office of Vietnam, at https://gso.gov.vn.

We also add a dummy variable to distinguish between manufacturing (coded as 1) and services (coded as 0) (Brouthers and Brouthers 2003). According to Erramilli and Rao (1993) (cited in Brouthers and Brouthers 2003), manufacturing firms often require higher capital investment than service firms. Investing in manufacturing requires a large amount of capital to build factories and buy equipment when entering a foreign country (Gatignon and Anderson 1988). Manufacturing firms that make large capital-intensive investment are assumed to prefer WOS to EJV because doing so helps them protect their business secrets better and avoid opportunistic behavior by joint venture partners.

Firm-specific factors include investment amounts, duration, project orientation and investment year as crucial factors in entry mode choice. Investment amount represents the financial commitment of a parent company to its subsidiaries (Wei et al. 2005). According to transaction cost theory, the level of financial commitment has a significant impact upon the market entry mode of foreign firms. When a small amount of capital is invested, WOS is a preferred option because it allows the parent company to control the subsidiary and retain the profits (Luo 2001). However, when the company participates in a large project and requires a large amount of investment capital, EJV can provide solid financial support, as well as share the risks with the local partners (Luo 2001). Therefore, a higher investment amount increases the likelihood that EJV is chosen for entry in Vietnam. Investment capital is calculated by total investment in a project (USD). The data come from the Ministry of Planning and Investment. We take the natural log of this variable to reduce the variable scale.

Investment duration is the period during which a foreign company commits to investment in the host country, and it is a source of bargaining power (Pan 1996). When the duration is short, foreign companies do not earn the necessary profits or exploit the full potential of the business. Therefore, foreign-invested firms with shorter investment duration are reluctant to choose WOS because they cannot obtain higher returns (Shan 1991). In this paper, investment duration is measured by the number of years that the project lasts. The data come from the Ministry of Planning and Investment.

Project orientation (exporting or serving the domestic market) affects the distribution strategy, marketing capability and performance of MNCs, and this affects the company's governance structures, as well as the entry mode selection (Luo 2001). If a project is set up to serve the domestic market, it interacts with the domestic environment more deeply than an export project. Partnering with local companies can reduce the risk of change in the domestic business environment. Most business transactions in emerging economies are based on relationships with individuals or organizations, and consumers tend to be loyal to businesses that have long experience (Xin and Pearce 1996) (cited in Luo 2001). Collaboration with local companies is necessary for MNCs seeking local market expansion. However, when a project is export-oriented, contributions by local companies become less important. Instead, MNCs can choose 100% foreign capital to facilitate business processes (Luo 2001). This variable is a dummy variable. It takes a value of 1 if the investment project is for exporting purposes, and 0 if the investment project only serves the domestic market.

Investment year has a significant impact on the entry mode choice of the firms. In 2008, after it became a member of the World Trade Organization (WTO), Vietnam increased its socio-economic achievements and created a favorable business environment for domestic and foreign investors. For example, Vietnam's GDP growth rate in 2018 was 7.08%, the highest since 2008, making Vietnam one of the fastest-growing countries in the region and the world (GSO 2018). In addition, the introduction of an Investment Law in 2014 has contributed to an improvement in the investment climate in Vietnam. Therefore, investors are more confident about choosing WOS as an entry mode. This variable is also a dummy variable. It takes a value of 1 for the period after 2008, when Vietnam joined the WTO; otherwise, 0.

3.3. Analytical Methodology: Logit Regression Model

Based on the measurement of dependent variable described in Section 3.2, we employ the Logit (logistic unit) regression model to examine the impacts of cultural distance between Vietnam and investing countries on the entry mode selection of FDI firms. The Logit regression model allows us to explain the actual coefficients in the model. The estimation model can be described with the equation:

$$Y = \beta_0 + \beta_1 X_1 + \beta_2 X_2 + \beta_3 X_3 + \beta_4 X_4 + \beta_5 X_5 + \beta_6 X_6 + \beta_7 X_7 + \beta_8 X_8 + \varepsilon$$

where

Y is the entry mode choice of foreign-invested firms (Y = 1 for EJV, and Y = 0 for WOS)
β_0 is the intercept
β_1 is the regression coefficient of cultural distance
X_1 is the value of the cultural distance variable
$\beta_{2 \to 8}$ is the regression coefficients of other control variables (country risk, market potential, investment capital, duration, project orientation, industry, WTO)
$X_{2 \to 8}$ is the value of control variables
ε is the error term

4. Results and Discussion

4.1. Descriptive Statistics

Table 1 describes the means, standard deviation (SD) and correlations for the entry mode choice of foreign-invested firms in Vietnam. The average capital investment of a project is USD 5.1 million, and the average project duration is 22 years. About 2% of foreign-invested projects in Vietnam are for exporting. About 83% of projects in Vietnam with foreign investment post-date Vietnam's WTO membership.

Table 1. Mean, Standard Deviation, and Correlation (n = 5236).

	VIF	Mean	Std. Dev	1	2	3	4	5	6	7	8	9
1. Entry mode		0.22	0.41	1								
2. Culture distance	1.02	0.89	0.58	−0.03	1							
3. Country risk	1.72	0.80	0.03	−0.004	−0.02	1						
4. Market potential	2.45	6.18	0.64	−0.03	−0.01	0.4	1					
5. Investment Capital	1.10	5.1	6.55	0.07	−0.09	0.1	0.04	1				
6. Duration	1.23	22.11	16.67	0.02	−0.05	−0.02	0.33	0.17	1			
7. Project orientation	1.13	0.02	0.15	−0.07	0.03	0.18	0.26	0.001	−0.0006	1		
8. Industry	1.12	0.239	0.42	−0.08	−0.06	0.23	0.15	0.18	0.02	0.15	1	
9. WTO	3.08	0.83	0.375	0.01	−0.004	−0.62	−0.72	−0.10	−0.13	−0.31	−0.23	1

In terms of market potential, Vietnam's economic growth rate in the period 2005–2016 was 6.18%. Vietnam is considered a country with low political risk, and the average level of political risk in that period was 0.8.

Regarding the cultural distance between Vietnam and the investment country, Vietnam has the lowest cultural difference (minimum value is 0.07) with countries in Southeast Asia, such as Brunei, Cambodia, Myanmar and Indonesia. The cultural gap increases in the sample with European countries and the US. Vietnam has the largest cultural gap (2.34) with Nigeria.

4.2. Results of Regression Models

The findings in our research contribute to a general understanding of the entry mode selection in emerging countries.

In cross-sectional data regression, heteroskedasticity may be a serious problem that we need to address. To deal with heteroskedasticity, we use a White heteroskedasticity consistent covariance matrix for each coefficient standard error. In addition, the variance inflation factor (VIF) test provides no evidence of multicollinearity in our model (Hair et al. 2016). We include four regression models to examine the impacts of country-specific factors, firm-specific factors, and industry factors on entry mode choice. The estimates remain robust in term of significant level and sign. The Pseudo-R^2 has improved from 0.0022 in model 1 to 0.0230 in model 4. Therefore, we choose model 4 as our final model to interpret the results.

In H1, we assume that the greater the cultural distance between Vietnam and the investing countries is, the more likely it is that foreign investors will choose WOS over EJV as an entry mode. Regression results in Table 2 support this hypothesis: When cultural difference increases by one percentage point, the probability of selecting WOS increases 1.8%. The finding is consistent with transaction cost theory, which emphasizes that the structure chosen by a firm with foreign investment is affected by a desire to minimize the transaction costs (Anderson and Gatignon 1986; cited in Luo 2001). These transaction costs include the cost of drafting contracts, negotiating with business partners, and monitoring the partner (Luo 2001). When the transaction costs are high, firms are more likely to select WOS as an entry mode because it enables them to operate independently and to avoid opportunistic behavior by their local partners. For example, in Vietnam, in the era of doi moi, foreign investors preferred joint ventures to WOS because this investment form helped them to overcome inefficient government bureaucracy and gain more market information from their local partners and it also had a lower sunk cost for new entrants (Simonet 2012).

However, joint ventures have many disadvantages, such as lacking flexibility, and many joint venture companies ended up in litigation. For example, Sapharco bought the share of its French partner to change Roussel Vietnam into a 100% locally-owned enterprise in 2002 (Simonet 2012). In this kind of situation, great cultural difference and inefficient cooperation with local counterparts encourages foreign investors to select WOS to ensure a lower failure rate. According to Simonet (2012), the overall failure rate of foreign-invested firms from 1988 to 1997 was 16% (694 out of 4514 projects were dissolved), and the failure rate of joint venture projects is twice as high as the overall rate. New foreign investors in Vietnam hear stories about unsuccessful EJV from previous investors. Therefore, they prefer WOS for entry. In 2015, the share of WOS in investment in Vietnam was high, comprising 70.5% of investment projects compared to 3.8% that were EJV (Ministry of Planning and Investment 2015).[1] The same was seen in China, where in 2004, WOS made up 65% of investment projects, whereas EJV accounted for 30% (Simonet 2012). Our findings suggest that the cultural distance between home and host transition country is an important factor to consider when foreign-invested firms want to invest in a transition country with a high level of uncertainty. The study contributes to the discussion of entry mode selection in transition countries.

---

[1]   This information comes from http://www.mpi.gov.vn/en/Pages/tinbai.aspx?idTin=38605&idcm=109/

Table 2. The Effect of Cultural Distance on the Entry Mode Choice of Foreign-Invested Firms in Vietnam (Marginal Effect of the Logit Model).

	Model 1	**Model 2**	**Model 3**	**Model 4**
Country-Specific Factors				
Cultural distance	−0.022 ***			−0.018 ***
	(0.01)			(0.009)
Country risk	0.107			0.146
	(0.15)			(0.18)
Market potential	−0.025 **			−0.032 **
	(0.009)			(0.013)
Industry-Specific Factors				
Industry sector		−0.08 *		−0.09 *
		(0.01)		(0.01)
Firm-Specific Factors				
Investment amount			0.015 *	0.017 *
			(0.003)	(0.003)
Duration			0.0003	0.0005
			(0.0003)	(0.0003)
Project orientation			−0.192 *	−0.182 *
			(0.017)	(0.02)
Year of investment			0.006	−0.048 ***
			(0.01)	(0.02)
No. of obs.	5194	5236	5236	5194
Wald chi-square	12.10	40.48	43.91	93.95
(Prob. > chi-square)	(0.0070)	(0.0000)	(0.0000)	(0.0000)
Pseudo chi-square	0.0022	0.0079	0.0118	0.0230

Notes: * significant at 1%, ** significant at 5%, *** significant at 10%. White heteroskedasticity consistent standard errors are reported in parentheses. Industry sector: Manufacturing (coded as 1) and services (coded as 0).

As hypothesized, we find that manufacturing firms prefer WOS to EJV, and service firms are more likely to select EJV over WOS. This is because manufacturing firms often require greater capital investment than service firms (Erramilli and Rao 1993). Selecting WOS allows foreign-invested firms to enjoy lower transaction costs and avoid opportunistic behavior by joint venture partners (Brouthers and Brouthers 2003).

These findings support Shieh and Wu (2012), who find that investors in Vietnam in the Greater Chinese Economic Region were more likely to select WOS when investing in manufacturing, and EJV in services.

The regression results show that markets with greater potential have a higher likelihood that investors will select WOS over EJV. A country with a fast and stable economic growth rate encourages foreign investors to commit resources toward its development. In this context, market potential stimulates investors to establish WOS in order to maximize profits (Agarwal and Ramaswami 1992). The finding is consistent with those in previous empirical studies (Hill et al. 1990).

As expected, foreign-invested enterprises with high investment capital are more likely to choose EJV over WOS to share the risks with domestic partners. When capital investment increases by 1%, the likelihood that a foreign-invested firm will choose EJV as its entry mode increases by 1.7%. Investment capital represents the financial commitment of the parent company to the subsidiary (Wei et al. 2005). According to transaction cost theory, financial commitment has a significant impact on the market entry mode of foreign-invested enterprises. When a relatively small amount of capital is being invested, WOS is the preferred option, as this form of investment allows the parent company to fully control the subsidiary and retain all of the profit (Luo 2001). However, when the company participates in a large project and requires a large amount of capital investment, EJV can provide solid financial support and help to share risks with local partners (Luo 2001). This result is similar to those in previous studies (Kogut and Singh 1988; Tsang 2005; Shieh and Wu 2012).

The coefficient of the project orientation variable is negative and statistically significant at 1% with the entry mode choice. This means that if the project is established for the purpose of exporting, foreign-invested firms choose WOS. If a project is set up to serve the domestic market, it will certainly interact more intensively and extensively with the domestic environment than an export project (Luo 2001). Partnering with local companies can help reduce the risks of change in the domestic business environment and explore business potential. However, when a project is export oriented, the contributions of local companies will become less important. Instead, MNCs choose WOS to facilitate business processes.

We conjecture that foreign investors would be more likely to choose WOS over EJV after Vietnam joined the WTO. Regression results in Table 1 support this hypothesis. After becoming an official WTO member, Vietnam had great socio-economic achievements and created a favorable business environment for domestic and foreign investors. Thanks to significant changes in the investment environment, foreign investors feel more secure when investing in Vietnam and selecting WOS.

However, we do not find a statistically significant relationship between country risk and entry mode choice in Vietnam. This is because Vietnam has low investment risk (especially political risk). The political risk index fluctuates over a range of only 0.76–0.86. Therefore, the investors do not consider political risk an important factor when choosing their entry mode in Vietnam.

We expect that if the investment duration is long, the likelihood that investors will choose WOS is higher than that of EJV. Our regression results do not support this hypothesis. The duration variable is not statistically significant in the model.

5. Conclusions

This study broadens our knowledge of the entry mode choice of foreign-invested firms in a transition economy, in this case, Vietnam. The study is based on transaction cost theory to explore the link between cultural difference between Vietnam and investing countries and their entry mode selection. We employ a novel dataset of 5236 foreign-invested firms in Vietnam from 2005 to 2016, and our empirical results indicate that foreign-invested firms prefer WOS over EJV when the cultural difference between Vietnam and their home country is large. The study contributes to a general understanding of the investment strategy of foreign-invested firms and academic discussion of the entry mode in many ways. First, although cultural distance is widely accepted as having a significant influence on the entry mode choice, the question of whether a high level of cultural difference is connected with the choice of WOS or EJV in Vietnam remains unanswered. Our paper fills the research gap.

Our findings are consistent with transaction cost theory, which emphasizes that the structure chosen by a foreign-invested firm is affected by a desire to minimize the transaction cost. When the cultural distance and transaction costs are high, firms are more likely to select WOS as their entry mode because it enables them to operate independently, and to avoid opportunistic behavior by their local partners. Second, our findings have practical implications for the Vietnamese government. Given that a larger cultural distance leads to more WOS selection by foreign investors, this investment form hinders the positive spillover effects of transferring advanced technology, as well as good management practices. This is because the establishment of WOS makes it easy for MNCs to engage in production and minimize the risk of technology exposure to domestic firms. In fact, for many years, Vietnam has encountered many difficulties in promoting technology transfer, as well as learning advanced technology from foreign firms (Ministry of Planning and Investment 2015). The Vietnamese government should improve the investment climate and the quality of governance if it wishes to attract foreign firms to establish EJV with domestic firms.

Author Contributions: Conceptualization, N.M.H.; Q.M.Q.B.; Methodology, N.M.H.; Q.M.Q.B.; Software, Q.M.Q.B.; Validation N.M.H; Q.M.Q.B.; Formal Analysis, N.M.H.; Q.M.Q.B.; P.P.D.; Investigation, Q.M.Q.B.; Resources, N.M.H.; Data Curation, P.P.D.; Q.M.Q.B.; Writing—Original Draft Preparation, N.M.H.; Q.M.Q.B.; Writing—Review and Editing, Q.M.Q.B.; Visualization, P.P.D.; Supervision, N.M.H.; Q.M.Q.B.; Project

Administration, N.M.H.; Q.M.Q.B.; Funding Acquisition P.P.D. All authors have read and agreed to the published version of the manuscript.

Acknowledgments: We are grateful to the three anonymous referees for their constructive comments. We also thank the participants at the 3rd Vietnam's Business and Economics Research Conference (Ho Chi Minh City Open University, Ho Chi Minh City, Vietnam, 18–20 July 2019) for their helpful suggestions. The authors are solely responsible for any remaining errors or shortcomings.

References

Agarwal, Sanjeev, and Sridhar N. Ramaswami. 1992. Choice of foreign market entry mode: Impact of ownership, location and internalization factors. *Journal of International Business Studies* 23: 1–27. [CrossRef]

Anderson, Erin, and Hubert Gatignon. 1986. Modes of foreign entry: A transaction cost analysis and propositions. *Journal of International Business Studies* 17: 1–26. [CrossRef]

Beamish, Paul W., and John C. Banks. 1987. Equity joint ventures and the theory of the multinational enterprise. *Journal of International Business Studies* 18: 1–16. [CrossRef]

Brouthers, Keith D., and Lance Eliot Brouthers. 2003. Why service and manufacturing entry mode choices differ: The influence of transaction cost factors, risk and trust. *Journal of Management Studies* 40: 1179–204. [CrossRef]

Canabal, Anne, and George O. White III. 2008. Entry mode research: Past and future. *International Business Review* 17: 267–84. [CrossRef]

Chang, Yi-Chieh, Ming-Sung Kao, Anthony Kuo, and Chih-Fang Chiu. 2012. How cultural distance influences entry mode choice: The contingent role of host country's governance quality. *Journal of Business Research* 65: 1160–70. [CrossRef]

Chen, Haiyang, and Michael Y. Hu. 2002. An analysis of determinants of entry mode and its impact on performance. *International Business Review* 11: 193–210. [CrossRef]

Coase, Ronald Harry. 1937. The nature of the firm. *Economica* 4: 386–405. [CrossRef]

Dikova, Desislava. 2012. Entry mode choices in transition economies: The moderating effect of institutional distance on managers' personal experiences. *Journal of East-West Business* 18: 1–27. [CrossRef]

Dunning, John H. 2002. *Global Capitalism, FDI and Competitiveness*. Cheltenham: Edward Elgar, vol. 2.

Erramilli, M. Krishna. 1996. Nationality and subsidiary ownership patterns in multinational corporations. *Journal of International Business Studies* 27: 225–48. [CrossRef]

Erramilli, M. Krishna, and Chatrathi P. Rao. 1993. Service firms' international entry-mode choice: A modified transaction-cost analysis approach. *Journal of Marketing* 57: 19–38.

Gatignon, Hubert, and Erin Anderson. 1988. The multinational corporation's degree of control over foreign subsidiaries: An empirical test of a transaction cost explanation. *JL Econ. & Org.* 4: 305.

GSO. 2018. *Statistical Yearbook of Vietnam 2018*. Hanoi: General Statistics Office of Vietnam.

Hair, Joseph F., Jr., G. Tomas M. Hult, Christian Ringle, and Marko Sarstedt. 2016. *A Primer on Partial Least Squares Structural Equation Modeling (PLS-SEM)*. Beverly Hills: Sage.

Hill, Charles W. L., Peter Hwang, and W. Chan Kim. 1990. An eclectic theory of the choice of international entry mode. *Strategic Management Journal* 11: 117–28. [CrossRef]

Hofstede, Geert. 1980. *Culture's Consequences: International Differences in Work-Related Values*. Beverly Hills: Sage.

Hofstede, Geert. 2001. *Culture's Consequences: Comparing Values, Behaviors, Institutions and Organizations across Nations*. Beverly Hills: Sage.

Kim, W. Chan, and Peter Hwang. 1992. Global strategy and multinationals' entry mode choice. *Journal of International Business Studies* 23: 29–53. [CrossRef]

Kogut, Bruce, and Harbir Singh. 1988. The effect of national culture on the choice of entry mode. *Journal of International Business Studies* 19: 411–32. [CrossRef]

Luo, Yadong. 2001. Determinants of entry in an emerging economy: A multilevel approach. *Journal of Management Studies* 38: 443–72. [CrossRef]

Manh Chien, Vu, and Phan Thanh Tu. 2012. Entry mode of MNEs in Vietnam: An eclectic model of the choice between international joint ventures and wholly owned subsidiaries. *Journal of Economics and Development* 14: 91–100. [CrossRef]

Meyer, Klaus E., and Hung Vo Nguyen. 2005. Foreign investment strategies and sub-national institutions in emerging markets: Evidence from Vietnam. *Journal of Management Studies* 42: 63–93. [CrossRef]

Michailova, Snejina. 2011. Contextualizing in international business research: Why do we need more of it and how can we be better at it? *Scandinavian Journal of Management* 27: 129–39. [CrossRef]

Ministry of Planning and Investment. 2015. Understanding the Implementation of Millennium Development Goals in Vietnam; Results Achieved and Lessons Learned. Available online: http://www.mpi.gov.vn/en/Pages/default.aspx (accessed on 15 April 2018).

Pak, Yong Suhk, and Young-Ryeol Park. 2004. Global ownership strategy of Japanese multinational enterprises: A test of internalization theory. *Management International Review* 44: 3–22.

Pan, Yigang. 1996. Influences on foreign equity ownership level in joint ventures in China. *Journal of International Business Studies* 27: 1–26. [CrossRef]

Porter, Michael E. 1987. *Competitive Strategy*. New York: Basic Books.

Root, Franklin R. 1994. *Entry Strategies for International Markets*. New York: Lexington Books.

Shan, Weijian. 1991. Environmental risks and joint venture sharing arrangements. *Journal of International Business Studies* 22: 555–78. [CrossRef]

Shane, Scott. 1994. The effect of national culture on the choice between licensing and direct foreign investment. *Strategic Management Journal* 15: 627–42. [CrossRef]

Sharma, Varinder M., and M. Krishna Erramilli. 2004. Resource-based explanation of entry mode choice. *Journal of Marketing theory and Practice* 12: 1–18. [CrossRef]

Shenkar, Oded. 2001. Cultural distance revisited: Towards a more rigorous conceptualization and measurement of cultural differences. *Journal of International Business Studies* 32: 519–35. [CrossRef]

Shieh, Bih-Lian, and Tzong-Chen Wu. 2012. Equity-based entry modes of the Greater Chinese Economic Area's foreign direct investments in Vietnam. *International Business Review* 21: 508–17. [CrossRef]

Simonet, Daniel. 2012. Entry modes of European firms in Vietnam. *EMAJ: Emerging Markets Journal* 2: 9–16. [CrossRef]

Slangen, Arjen H. L., and Jean-François Hennart. 2008. Do multinationals really prefer to enter culturally distant countries through greenfields rather than through acquisitions? The role of parent experience and subsidiary autonomy. *Journal of International Business Studies* 39: 472–90. [CrossRef]

Sutcliffe, Kathleen M., and Akbar Zaheer. 1998. Uncertainty in the transaction environment: An empirical test. *Strategic Management Journal* 19: 1–23. [CrossRef]

Tsang, Eric W. K. 2005. Influences on foreign ownership level and entry mode choice in Vietnam. *International Business Review* 14: 441–63. [CrossRef]

Van Dut, Vo, Yusaf H. Akbar, Nguyen Huu Dang, and Nguyen Kim Hanh. 2018. The impact of institutional distance on the choice of multinational enterprise's entry mode: Theory and empirical evidence from Vietnam. *Asian Journal of Business and Accounting* 11: 71–95.

Wei, Yingqi, Bo Liu, and Xiaming Liu. 2005. Entry modes of foreign direct investment in China: A multinomial logit approach. *Journal of Business Research* 58: 1495–505. [CrossRef]

Williamson, Oliver E. 1975. *Markets and Hierarchies*. New York: Free Press.

Xin, Katherine K., and Jone L. Pearce. 1996. Guanxi: Connections as substitutes for formal institutional support. *Academy of Management Journal* 39: 1641–58.

Yiu, Daphne, and Shige Makino. 2002. The choice between joint venture and wholly owned subsidiary: An institutional perspective. *Organization Science* 13: 667–83. [CrossRef]

6

Fiscal Decentralisation and Economic Growth across Provinces: New Evidence from Vietnam using a Novel Measurement and Approach

Phuong Duy Nguyen [1], **Duc Hong Vo** [2], **Chi Minh Ho** [2] **and Anh The Vo** [2,*]

[1]   Ho Chi Minh City Market Surveillance Department, Vietnam Directorate of Market Surveillance, Ho Chi Minh City 72400, Vietnam

[2]   Business and Economics Research Group, Ho Chi Minh City Open University, Ho Chi Minh City 70000, Vietnam

*   Correspondence: anh.vt@ou.edu.vn

Abstract: Fiscal decentralisation has attracted great attention from governments, practitioners, and international institutions with the aims of enhancing economic growth in the last 5 decades. However, satisfactorily measuring the degree of fiscal decentralisation across countries has appeared to be problematic. In addition, the link between fiscal decentralisation and economic growth across provinces has largely been ignored, in particular for emerging markets such as Vietnam. As such, this study is conducted to determine the extent of fiscal decentralisation and to assess its impact on economic growth based on data from all 63 provinces of Vietnam in the period after the 2008 financial crisis. Instead of using traditional measures of fiscal decentralisation, the study uses the Fiscal Decentralisation Index (FDI) together with the two most important and inseparable components of the index, those being (i) the Fiscal Importance (FI) and (ii) the Fiscal Autonomy (FA). The Difference Generalised Method of Moments (DGMM) is utilised to correct for the potential problem of endogeneity between fiscal decentralisation and economic growth. Results show that the two indicators (FI and FDI) have a negative impact while FA has a positive impact on economic growth across provinces. On the ground of these empirical findings, implications for specific policies have emerged for Vietnam and other emerging markets on the extent of fiscal decentralisation, and its major determinants, which positively support economic growth in the future.

Keywords: fiscal autonomy; fiscal decentralisation; fiscal importance; DGMM; Vietnam

JEL Classification: C33; O47; H72

1. Introduction

A decision regarding fiscal division has never been a purely economic decision. The relationship between economic growth and fiscal decentralisation is always a pertinent matter to different actors in the economy. Many theoretical and quantitative studies seeking to understand, evaluate and quantify growth effect of the fiscal decentralisation have been conducted (Lin and Liu 2000; Oates 1972; Thiessen 2005; Thornton 2007; Woller and Phillips 1998; Zhang and Zou 1998).

Distinguished from other studies, Vo (2010, 2019) and Vo et al. (2019) argue that the theories on fiscal decentralisation can be presented and summarised on two main aspects: (i) Fiscal Autonomy (FA) and (ii) Fiscal Importance (FI). On that basis, the author has developed the Fiscal Decentralisation Index (FDI) and applied it to different countries. In this study, for the first time, the FDI is adopted and fully applied on a provincial level in the context of Vietnam. As such, fiscal decentralisation by provincial governments will be more thoroughly evaluated through the FDI that reflects Fiscal Autonomy and Fiscal Importance.

In this study, we focus on whether increasing fiscal decentralisation will help or hinder provincial economic growth in Vietnam. Few studies on fiscal decentralisation are conducted in Vietnam due to difficulties in gathering data for quantitative research (Nguyen and Anwar 2011). Moreover, when assessing the extent of fiscal decentralisation in provincial governments, most of the previous studies focus on calculating the ratio of provincial revenue and provincial expenditure over total fiscal revenue and total fiscal expenditure, respectively. This assessment, though simple, is unable to shed light on the most fundamental features of the fiscal decentralisation process. As such, we employ the framework of Vo (2010) in order to clarify the growth effect of fiscal decentralisation in the context of Vietnam.

According to reports from Vietnam's Ministry of Finance (MOF), in 2015, Vietnam's public debt level was at 61.30% Gross Domestic Product (GDP). The fiscal deficit was around 5.00% GDP. In the composition of Vietnam's public debt, the government's debt has always accounted for a large percentage compared to provincial debts. The evidence shows that most of the resources for investment and development are held by the Ministries, and then partially allocated to the provinces.

Currently, only 13 out of 63 provinces in Vietnam achieve fiscal balance. Ho Chi Minh City (HCMC), despite being an economic powerhouse, still has difficulty in balancing its budget. On the other hand, many provinces and cities still rely on provisions from the central government. As a result, fiscal decentralisation reforms have become an urgent problem to the government in the process of public re-investment. However, fiscal decentralisation, the transfer of budget responsibilities from the central government to the provincial government, should follow a roadmap with specific programs and plans and be carefully assessed.

Our study significantly contributes to policy influences as well as to the current literature of fiscal decentralisation. First, although the link between fiscal decentralisation and economic growth is critical, few studies have been conducted in Vietnam. For example, Vo (2009b) compared the level of fiscal decentralisation in Vietnam to other Asian countries. The study focused on a macroeconomics level of fiscal decentralisation and its potential impact to economic growth for the case of Vietnam. Su et al. (2014) examined the effect of fiscal policies on the sustainability of economic growth at a provincial level in Vietnam, but their focus was on the long-run relationship between the two key variables with a very crude measurement of fiscal decentralisation. Our study is distinct and different from previous studies. First, a more appropriate measure of fiscal decentralisation is utilised in this study. This measure of fiscal decentralisation takes into account both major aspects of fiscal decentralisation including (i) fiscal autonomy and (ii) fiscal importance of subnational governments. Second, we attempt to empirically investigate the relationship between fiscal decentralisation and economic growth in Vietnam based on an appropriate econometrics approach. Based on important findings from this study, we can offer proper policies and recommendations for the appropriate extent of the fiscal decentralisation not only for Vietnam's Governments but also for other developing countries. Third, and the first of its kind in Vietnam, we utilize a panel of Vietnam provinces for the analysis which is in contrast to another study which was conducted by Nguyen (2009), who used the cross-sectional data of all provinces in Vietnam. An obvious advantage of panel data is not only taking such heterogeneity explicitly into account by controlling for individual variances, but also utilizing more information and less collinearity among the selected variables, more degrees of freedom, and more estimation efficiency (Gujarati and Porter 2009). As such, our study provides additional and important empirical evidence on the link between fiscal policy and economic growth.

Following this introduction, the paper is constructed as follows: The literature review is examined in Section 2. Section 3 introduce the fiscal decentralisation and its measurement in previous studies while Section 4 discusses the research methodology. Section 5 presents empirical results and discussions, followed by conclusions and policy recommendations in Section 6.

2. Literature Review

2.1. *Theoretical Background*

Besides empirical research, many scholars assess the effect that fiscal decentralisation has on economic growth. Fiscal decentralisation can affect economic growth in two different directions. Firstly, fiscal decentralisation can lead to economic growth due to the public spending aspect. Secondly, fiscal decentralisation can cause a destabilisation of the macroeconomics, meaning a negative impact on economic growth. Thirdly, the impact of fiscal decentralisation on economic growth differs between developed and developing countries, specifically a positive impact in developed countries but a negative one in developing countries. The reason is that in developing countries, the provincial government lacks management capability when decentralised, leading to budget leaks or wasteful and inefficient public investments.

Oates (1993) argues that public spending on infrastructure and social elements has a positive effect on provincial economic development as the local government better understands the features of local population as well as their needs, thus distributing public resources more efficiently than the central government. Similarly, Zhang and Zou (1998) argue that the local government has more advantages in providing public services locally than the central government. As a result, the decentralisation of revenue sources and spending responsibilities to the provincial government is a way to improve the efficiency of public sector investment, reducing fiscal deficits and helping to develop the economy.

Vo (2010) presents an assessment of the main channels through which fiscal decentralisation will have a positive impact on the local economy. Firstly, fiscal decentralisation brings efficiency in distributing resources. This tends to ensure that local preferences will be met with minimum expenses, as the relatively more accessible local government, compared to the central government, helps to reduce the costs of providing public goods and services. Secondly, competition among provincial governments will increase when there is decentralisation—the pressure of re-selecting provincial leadership will motivate higher productivity and reduce careless spending, thus growing the local economy. Since the size of each provincial government is smaller than that of the state, it can lead to an optimal scale of education, medical services and infrastructure provision, trimming administrative expenses and raising efficiency. Thirdly, fiscal decentralisation induces economic growth by reducing corruption. The extent of corruption is often related to bad management, impeding economic growth by draining government revenue and increasing wasteful spending.

On the other hand, there are opposing theoretical views on the impact of fiscal decentralisation on economic growth. According to Prud'Homme (1995) and Tanzi and Schuknech (1996), given the assumptions that fiscal decentralisation matches spending responsibilities and that the provincial government lacks capability and accountability, fiscal decentralisation can have a negative effect on economic growth. Prud'Homme (1995) and Tanzi and Schuknech (1996) argue that the provincial government cannot be efficient in delivering public goods and services on a national level due to the economies of scale. Fiscal decentralisation incurs the risks of corruption and self-interests at the provincial level as the power of authority lies with the provincial leadership.

2.2. *Empirical Studies in Foreign Countries*

There are several empirical studies on the relationship between fiscal decentralisation and economic growth in different countries. Most utilise panel data of different provinces of one country or of across countries. China is a representative case study on this relationship from a provincial angle. Zhang and Zou (1998) used panel data of 28 provinces of China in the 1986—1992 period, concluding that the extent of fiscal decentralisation affects economic growth negatively. On the other hand, Lin and Liu (2000) discovered the positive effect of fiscal decentralisation on growth by using panel data of Chinese provincial governments from 1970–1993. As such, these studies covering different periods of time appeared to report significantly different results. Moreover, these two studies were interested in the economic reform in China in 1978. While Zhang and Zou (1998) excluded the period with major economic reform in China in the data utilised in their analysis, Lin and Liu (2000) utilised the longest possible period of data. However, Lin and Liu (2000) did not take into account any technique in order to exclude the potential impact of the economic reform on the growth effect of fiscal decentralisation. As such, systematic shocks in a long time period may possibly bias the empirical results when the major events are not satisfactorily controlled for.

In Romania, Adrian and Petronela (2015) conducted research on the relationship between fiscal autonomy and provincial development at a district level in the 2008–2011 period. An increase in provincial fiscal autonomy tends to increase the extent of development in that province. From these results, it can be implied that that the higher the extent of provincial fiscal autonomy, the higher the capability of provincial public authorities in meeting the needs of local communities, hence raising local economic growth.

National panel data are also extensively used in other research. Martinez-Vazquez and McNab (2006) use panel data from 66 developed and developing countries between 1997 and 2002. The Ordinary Least Squares (OLS) technique is employed to analyse the relationship between fiscal decentralisation, macroeconomic stability and economic growth. The authors concluded that fiscal decentralisation in developed countries has a negative impact on economic growth while in developing countries, the impact is unclear.

Ezcurra and Rodríguez-Pose (2013) used panel data from 21 Organisation for Economic Cooperation and Development (OECD) countries in Central and Eastern Europe between 1990 and 2005. Based on OLS regression results, the study concluded that fiscal decentralisation negatively affects economic growth. Similar results were found in a study by Baskaran and Feld (2013) in 23 OECD countries between 1975 and 2008 based on a fixed effect model.

2.3. Studies in Vietnam

Some studies on fiscal decentralisation have been recently conducted in Vietnam. Nguyen (2009), based on the endogenous economic growth theory, the fiscal theory, and the relationship model between economic growth and fiscal decentralisation, determined a relationship between fiscal decentralisation and economic growth in 64 provinces of Vietnam in two different time periods, 1997–2001 and 2002–2007.

Another study by Su et al. (2014), based on the endogenous growth model, used panel data from 62 provinces between 2000 and 2011 and utilised the Pooled Mean Group (PMG) and Difference Generalized Method of Moments (DGMM) technique by Arellano and Bond (1991) to empirically analyse the relationship between fiscal policies and economic growth in Vietnam. The study puts forward the following conclusions: (i) Fiscal decentralisation and economic growth are positively correlated in the long term, however, when the economy detracts from the long-term equilibrium, government efforts in adjusting fiscal policies have little effectiveness, (ii) Revenue decentralisation is positively correlated with economic growth in the long term, while expenditure decentralisation is negatively correlated with economic growth, and (iii) Regular expenditure on education and training, scientific research, environment and medical services, positively affects economic growth, while investment spending has a negative impact. Su et al. (2014) discussed various aspects of fiscal policies, however, they estimated fiscal decentralisation as a simple ratio of provincial fiscal expenditure or revenue over total fiscal expenditure or revenue. Nevertheless, it is argued that they focused on the growth effect of fiscal policy instead of a growth effect of fiscal decentralisation.

Vo (2009b) looked into the status of fiscal decentralisation in Vietnam based on lessons from other Asian countries. The study points out that the degree of fiscal autonomy of provincial governments in Vietnam is the lowest among comparable Association of Southeast Asian Nations (ASEAN) countries (Indonesia, Philippines and Thailand) and China. If the government of Vietnam wants to reform fiscal decentralisation to improve provincial fiscal autonomy, factors that can help to boost fiscal decentralisation include allowing provincial governments to set appropriate fees in the local context and lowering the tax remittance rate to the central government. Although Vo (2009a) did a great comparison of fiscal decentralisation between Vietnam and other Asian countries using a strong foundation of theories and historical fiscal data, he did not make further steps to identify the influence of fiscal decentralisation to economic growth in his paper using a quantitative approach.

3. Fiscal Decentralisation and Measurement

3.1. Fiscal Decentralisation

Fiscal decentralisation, also known as financial decentralisation, is the transfer of partial power from the upper government to lower tiers of the government. This is part of public sector reforms, creating a competitive environment for different levels of government in providing optimal public goods and services to the society and stimulating economic growth (Bird et al. 1993; Liu et al. 2017; Martinez-Vazquez et al. 2016).

Fiscal decentralisation is understood as the process of shifting rights and responsibilities from the central government to the provincial government or to the private sector. Fiscal decentralisation is concerned with the distribution of public resources between the central and provincial government, focusing on the two main issues that are the division of revenue sources and spending responsibilities (Woller and Phillips 1998). Fiscal decentralisation can also be defined as the delegation of rights, responsibilities and interests between different levels of government in budgetary management and execution.

3.2. Measurements of Fiscal Decentralisation

There are various measurements of fiscal decentralisation in empirical research, based on two main indicators, (i) expenditure ratio and (ii) revenue ratio. Each author has his own assessment on the extent of decentralisation and the features of each country or region in order to construct a measurement of fiscal decentralisation (Rodriguez-Pose and Krøijer 2009; Rodríguez-Pose et al. 2009).

A number of previous studies have measured the extent of fiscal decentralisation from a spending angle (Law et al. 2014; Rodríguez-Pose et al. 2009; Zhang and Zou 1998). Additional spending financed by the central government for assigned programmes and missions is deducted from total expenditure by the provincial government. As a result, total fiscal spending is equal to total spending by provincial governments after deducting additional spending made by the central government to the provincial government. The Expenditure Ratio (ER) is calculated as follows:

$$ER = \frac{Total\ spending\ by\ provincial\ government}{Total\ fiscal\ spending}$$

Other scholars measure fiscal decentralisation from a revenue angle (Lin and Liu 2000; Thornton 2007). The revenue ratio is calculated as the total revenue by the provincial government over the total fiscal revenue, in which total provincial revenue includes the revenue that the province receives in full and the portion of revenue between the provincial and central government after deducting additional provisions from central budget. The Revenue Ratio (RR) is calculated as follows:

$$RR = \frac{Total\ revenue\ by\ provincial\ government}{Total\ fiscal\ revenue}$$

The closer ER and RR get to 1, the higher the extent of revenue decentralisation.

In a different approach, Vo (2008, 2009a) developed the Fiscal Decentralisation Index (FDI), which comprises Fiscal Autonomy (FA) and Fiscal Importance (FI). First, fiscal autonomy is the transfer of taxing powers and assignment of responsibilities for the delivery of public goods and services. It is affected by regulations regarding fiscal transfers between the central and provincial government as well as provincial borrowings (Vo 2008, 2009a). Fiscal autonomy is calculated as follows:

$$FA = \frac{\sum_{i=1}^{p} OSR_i}{\sum_{i=1}^{p} E_i}$$

In which: OSR_i is the own-sourced revenue and E_i is the own-sourced expenditure of the province i, and p is the number of provinces.

The formula implies that the value of FA is within the (0,1) range, with a minimum value of 0 and a maximum value of 1. If FA is equal to 1, the province has sufficient budgetary revenue to match its budgetary spending, reflecting a high level of autonomy and independence from the central budget, allowing the province to be proactive and innovative in growing its economy. Conversely, if FA is low or close to 0, the province is almost entirely dependent on the central budget as its own revenue cannot cover its spending.

Secondly, fiscal importance is the relative significance of fiscal activities undertaken by the province compared to those by the state. Provincial fiscal autonomy implies that by decentralisation regulations, the provincial government can balance its revenue sources by managing its tax bases in order to finance the expenses incurred in delivering public goods and services. In Vo (2008, 2009a), public expenditure representing fiscal activities is calculated as follows:

$$FI = \frac{\sum_{i=1}^{p} E_i}{TE}$$

In this formula, FI is the fiscal importance of province i, TE is the total public sector expenditure by all levels of government in the country, while E_i is the public expenditure incurred by the province i. The value of FI is within the (0,1) range. The closer FI gets to 1, the higher the percentage of the total fiscal spending by the country accounted for by the public spending of the province, reflecting the significant standing of the province. Conversely, if FI gets close to 0, the public spending by the province is very low relative to the country, implying a minor role in national economic development.

Combining the two aforementioned indicators, Vo (2008, 2009a) proposed the Fiscal Decentralisation Index (FDI), calculated as follows:

$$FDI = \sqrt{FA \times FI} = \sqrt{\frac{\sum_1^p OSR_i}{\sum_1^p E_i} \times \frac{\sum_1^p E_i}{TE}}$$

The FDI of the provincial government is capped at unity (1.0). Accordingly, there are 4 degrees of FDI measurement:

- *Perfect fiscal decentralisation*: FDI = 1
- *Relative fiscal decentralisation*: 0.5 < FDI < 1
- *Relative fiscal centralisation*: 0 < FDI < 0.5
- *Perfect fiscal centralisation*: FDI = 0

4. Research Methodology and Data

4.1. Research Model and Data

The research applies the endogenous growth model to empirically study the impact of fiscal decentralisation on provincial economic growth. The regression equation is as follows:

$$LnY_{it} = \beta_0 + \beta_1 LnY_{it-1} + \beta_2 PC_{it} + + \beta_3 CON_{it} + e_{it}$$

In which: i and t denote data from province i ($i = 1, 2, \dots , 63$) in year t ($t = 2008, \dots , 2013$).

Economic growth is measured as the log of provincial GDP per capita: LnY_{it} is a function of the lagged variable LnY_{it-1}, PC_{it} is the degree of fiscal decentralisation and CON_{it} are the control variables. Details of the variables utilised in this study are carefully presented in Table A1 in the Appendix A. According to Vo (2008, 2009a), the degree of fiscal decentralisation is measured by the following three indicators: (i) Fiscal Autonomy (FA), (ii) Fiscal Importance (FI), and (iii) Fiscal Decentralisation Index (FDI). The selected control variables are (i) investment capital in the province, (ii) labour force growth rate, (iii) inflation rate of the province, and (iv) trade openness. Table 1 summarises the definition of variables used in previous studies.

Table 1. Summary of variables used in the study.

No.	Variable	Definition	Study	Expectation
Dependent variable				
1	Y	GDP per capita		
Fiscal Decentralisation (PC) includes				
2	FA	Fiscal autonomy	Vo (2008, 2009a)	+
3	FI	Fiscal importance	Vo (2008, 2009a)	+
4	FDI	Fiscal decentralisation index	Vo (2008, 2009a)	+
Control Variables (CON) includes				
5	POP	Labour force growth rate	Zhang and Zou (1998)	+
6	INF	Inflation rate	Hanif et al. (2014), Zhang and Zou (1998)	−
7	CAP	Investment capital in the province	Zhang and Zou (1998)	+
8	OP	Trade openness	Zhang and Zou (1998)	+

Based on mixed findings from Zhang and Zou (1998) and Lin and Liu (2000), we consider that including two extremes of the world economy (the global financial crisis in 2007 and the world recession in 2014) can possibly affect the macroeconomic fundamentals in Vietnam. As such, in order to consider the effects arising from these potential influences, we reasonably consider that it is appropriate to conduct the analysis covering the period from 2008 to 2013. In addition, we note that historical data on public finances at the provincial level are very limited in Vietnam in terms of availability. As such, the data set used for the research are the balanced panel data of 63 provinces of Vietnam within the six years from 2008 to 2013 with 378 observations. The data are sourced from Ministry of Finance (MOF), General Statistics Office (GSO), and Annual Abstract of Statistics on provinces of Vietnam.

On the basis of relevant theories and empirical results on fiscal decentralisation and economic growth from other previous studies, we provide the following expectations, as indicated in Table 1.

4.2. Regression Methodology

Although different econometric methods have been employed to study the relationship between fiscal decentralisation and provincial economic growth, in this research, the authors used the Difference Generalized Method of Moments (DGMM) by Arellano and Bond (1991). The DGMM method helps to solve several problems. Firstly, as the variables in the model can be considered endogenous, panel data regression on the relationship between fiscal decentralisation and economic growth can occur in two directions, from the independent variables to the dependent variables or vice versa. The regression of these variables can lead to a correlation with the error term, which means there exists bias coefficients. Secondly, fixed effect potentially involves characteristics of unobserved factors and errors of presented variables. Thirdly, the introduction of the lagged variable in the equation will lead to autocorrelation. Fourthly, panel data used in the study has a short time period (short T) and a large number of panel members (large N).

5. Results and Discussions

The sample is formed from data collection of 63 provinces of Vietnam from 2008 to 2013, with 378 observations. Table 2 depicts the descriptive statistics. Figure 1 shows the degree of fiscal autonomy, Ha Noi and Ho Chi Minh City (HCMC), the two largest cities, have high FA ratios in 2013 (78.28%

and 82.64%, respectively) as these two cities have large revenue sources, supporting their own fiscal autonomy. Ha Giang had the lowest FA ratio in 2013 at 11.94%. Ha Giang, being a poverty-stricken province in the northwest mountainous region, has no advantageous factors to appeal to businesses. As such, it has little revenue source that cannot cover its expenditure needs and has to rely almost entirely on provisions from the central government. Ha Noi, HCMC and Da Nang have higher FA ratios than other provinces in the country.

Table 2. Descriptive statistics of variables in the model.

Variable	Observations	Unit	Mean	Standard Variation	Min	Max
Fiscal autonomy	378	%	42.63%	16.90%	11.94%	99.71%
Fiscal importance	378	%	1.59%	1.71%	0.37%	12.37%
Fiscal Decentralisation Index	378	%	7.74%	4.17%	3.65%	30.16%
Inflation	378	%	−0.35%	7.93%	−22.48%	23.70%
Labour force growth rate	378	%	2.11%	3.14%	−16.12%	17.80%
Trade openness	378	%	78.20%	107.45%	0.19%	898.55%
Ln (investment capital)	378		30.06	0.86	27.71	33.26
Ln (GDP per capita)	378		16.91	0.60	15.45	19.79
Ln (lag of GDP per capita)	378		16.73	0.69	15.25	22.71

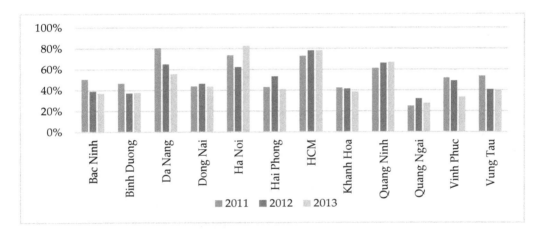

Figure 1. Fiscal autonomy ratio of selected provinces in Vietnam over the 2011–2013 period.

Looking at Fiscal importance (FI) in Figure 2, Ha Noi had the highest FI ratio in the country (11.2% in 2010). Budget spending of provinces in the Red River Delta region was consistently among the highest in the country. Tra Vinh had the lowest FI ratio, at 0.365% in 2011.

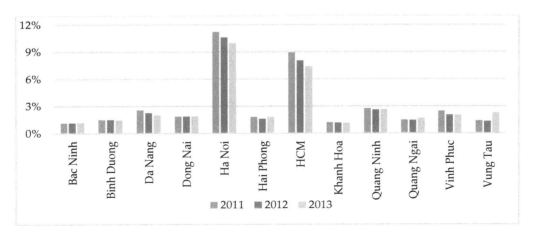

Figure 2. Fiscal importance ratio of selected provinces in Vietnam over the 2011–2013 period.

In Table 3, Ha Noi had the highest FDI of the country (30.16% in 2009), followed by HCMC, as tax revenue sources are concentrated in these two cities and they also have significantly higher economic development than other provinces. When the FDI calculation proposed by Vo (2008, 2009a) was applied, the portion of tax revenue split between the central and provincial government was deducted from the own-sourced revenue of the province. Since this tax revenue source accounts for a higher percentage in HCMC's budget revenue composition than Hanoi's, HCMC's FDI was lower than that of Hanoi, even though HCMC had the highest budget revenue sum in the country. Ca Mau had the lowest FDI value (3.65% in 2009).

Table 3. The value of fiscal decentralisation index for 13 provinces in 2008–2013 (%).

Province	2008	2009	2010	2011	2012	2013
Bac Ninh	7.15	6.82	7.94	7.50	6.59	6.53
Binh Duong	10.83	12.80	8.56	8.27	7.37	7.32
Da Nang	15.41	14.38	14.95	14.30	12.06	10.54
Dong Nai	11.18	10.10	10.40	8.96	9.24	9.02
Ha Noi	29.84	30.16	29.43	28.69	25.62	28.67
Hai Phong	8.25	8.08	9.16	8.76	9.18	8.51
HCM	27.92	26.66	25.42	25.47	24.98	24.01
Khanh Hoa	8.96	8.69	8.14	7.13	6.87	6.56
Quang Ninh	11.98	10.21	11.60	12.95	13.02	13.21
Quang Ngai	7.37	6.98	6.57	6.00	6.72	6.72
Vinh Phuc	7.86	10.70	10.76	11.26	9.93	8.16
Vung Tau	10.53	9.47	8.70	8.54	7.24	9.36

We initially consider the correlation among the variables in the proposed model by looking at a correllation matrix, which is shown in Table A2 in the Appendix A. It can be observed that there is a strong correlation among FDI, FI and FA. Thus, we separately use those three explanatory variables in different estimations. Estimation results in Table 4 show that fiscal decentralisation has an impact on economic growth in Vietnam in terms of DGMM estimations.[1] In particular, positive FA (statistically significant at the 5% significance level) implies a positive effect on provincial economic growth. This is consistent with a study by Adrian and Petronela (2015), which states that the degree of fiscal autonomy helps to boost the economic growth of the province. This fiscal autonomy allows the provincial government to proactively and flexibly manage its responsibilities, independent of the central government.

On the other hand, FI has a negative impact on provincial economic growth, as seen from its negative coefficient at the 1% significance level. FDI has a negative impact, although at a lower extent compared to FI. This can be explained by the fact that in most provinces in Vietnam, fixed expenses account for a major portion of total fiscal spending. As a result, if regular spending can be lowered while investment spending is increased, provincial economic growth can be stimulated. In addition, the extent of fiscal decentralisation in provincial governments in Vietnam is very low, with large gaps in FDI among provinces. The FDI values of provinces in Vietnam belong to the Relative Fiscal Centralisation category. This is in line with the theory which argues that the impact of fiscal decentralisation on economic growth in developing countries is negative, as well as with previous

---

[1]   We have utilised the fixed and random effects model and our analyses indicate that the fixed effect mode appears to be more appropriate than the later on the ground of the Hausman test. Detailed analyses of these approaches are available upon request. However, we consider that with the apperance of the lagged value of the dependent variable in the regression, the estimated coefficients using both fixed and random effect models may be biased. As such, in this study, we used the Difference Generalised Method of Moments (DGMM) to correct the potential problem of endogeneity between fiscal decentralisation and economic growth. Thus, necessary statistical tests, including AR(1), AR(2), and Sargan tests were conducted and presented to ensure the appropriateness of the DGMM.

studies (Zhang and Zou 1998; Martinez-Vazquez and McNab 2006; Ezcurra and Rodríguez-Pose 2013; Baskaran and Feld 2013).

The lag of economic growth has a positive effect on its current value, as seen from the positive estimation coefficient at the 1% significance level in all of the three regression equations. The estimation coefficients of labour force growth rate and trade openness, the control variables, are mostly positive but are statistically insignificant. The results concur with studies by Nguyen (2009) Nguyen (2009). Trade openness has a positive coefficient that is statistically significant when the fiscal decentralisation variable is FDI. This is consistent with results from the study by Zhang and Zou (1998). The investment capital variable has a positive coefficient at the 1% significance level, except for the FA model. As such, it can be concluded that investment has a positive effect on provincial economic growth.

Table 4. Results (using the Difference Generalized Method of Moments (DGMM)).

Dependent Variable: Economic Growth (LnGDPPC)			
Fiscal Decentralisation Variable	**FA**	**FI**	**FDI**
Fiscal autonomy	0.30 **		
Fiscal importance		−6.08 ***	
Fiscal decentralisation index			−1.84 **
Labour force growth rate	−0.03	0.07	0.06
Trade openness	0.00	0.01	0.02 **
Investment capital	0.02	0.20 ***	0.18 ***
Inflation rate	0.48 ***	0.43 ***	0.43 ***
Lag of Economic growth	0.89 ***	0.74 ***	0.73 ***
Constants	1.17 ***	−1.39	−0.64
AR (1)	0.00	0.00	0.00
AR (2)	0.27	0.51	0.46
Sargan test	0.07	0.11	0.13
Legend:		*** $p < 0.01$; ** $p < 0.05$	
Number of observations		378	

Notes: ***, and ** indicate significance levels of 1%, and 5%, respectively. LnGDPPC—the logarithm of Gross Domestic Product per capita.

Results from the model also show that inflation rate has a positive coefficient at the 1% significance level. In other words, inflation rate in the 2008–2013 period has a positive impact on provincial economic growth. This contradicts the author's expectation but falls in line with Nguyen (2009).

6. Conclusions and Recommendations

This study was conducted to determine and quantify the degree of fiscal decentralisation in 63 provinces of Vietnam between 2008 and 2013. The fiscal decentralisation index used in this study is based on the Fiscal Decentralisation Index developed by Vo (2008, 2009a). In this index, two important and inseparable constituent elements, Fiscal autonomy and Fiscal importance, are considered and utilised. The DGMM technique was employed to correct for the endogeneity in the model. The study has identified the degree of fiscal decentralisation in different provinces in Vietnam as well as the Fiscal autonomy and Fiscal importance capability of the 63 provinces. At the same time, the main focus of this study was to discover and quantify the relationship between fiscal decentralisation and provincial economic growth in Vietnam in the 2008—2013 period.

Based on the results of the study, certain macroeconomic policy implications can be summarised as follows. Initially, the government should improve provincial autonomy in finding revenue sources as provincial governments face constraints due to central government regulations. As of now, provincial governments are only authorised to set certain fees and rates within the current legal framework. Revenue from these fees and rates is in fact very small, accounting for only 10% of the provincial budget revenue. Provincial governments have limited means to create revenue sources, little control over the revenue collected and no incentives for prospective revenue sources. Taxing power lies with the central government, including both tax rates and tax bases, thus leaving limited space for provincial autonomy. As a result, provincial governments are compelled to raise revenue from land sources, a source fully delegated to local governments but volatile due to its dependence on the real estate sector. Therefore, it is advisable to let provinces have the authority to set certain taxes appropriate for the local context, to adjust certain tax rates and to increase the retained portion of tax revenue meant to be split with central government. These measures will help provincial governments to balance their budget, reducing their reliance on the central government.

Government offices need to tighten control over spending, ensuring budget revenue matches expenditure needs, thereby avoiding budget deficits. Government spending should be publicised to prevent redundancy or budget leaks, while expenditure should be linked to accountability of provincial leadership, increasing transparency and reducing deficits. Government fixed expenses should be lowered through public finance reforms and workforce simplification in order to increase spending on investment to stimulate economic growth.

Additionally, Vietnam is a developing country, with vastly different levels of development among provinces. Rapidly increasing fiscal decentralisation will incur risks in resource management at the provincial level as key personnel at provincial governments are not sufficiently competent in macroeconomic management. Moreover, corruption and self-interests are also cause for concern. As a result, fiscal decentralisation should be implemented with a roadmap of specific plans and programmes to ensure effectiveness. The government needs to fight corruption and self-interests while training provincial governments to be more competent in order to enhance economic growth. At the same time, the following results were achieved through this study.

The government should increase investment capital, including state capital, on key regions as well as regions with economic and social disadvantages to narrow the gap in economic development among provinces. At the same time, incentives should be in place to raise non-public capital and foreign direct investments to help with provincial economic development. Also, inflation rate should be maintained at an appropriate level for macroeconomic stability, keeping consumer prices at a suitable level. The State Bank of Vietnam should have an enhanced role in setting interest rates that are accessible to businesses.

Global integration should be intensified to create new jobs and to seek new export markets for Vietnamese goods. Other than traditional ones, Vietnam should identify new export markets to increase its inbound foreign currencies. The investment environment should be continuously improved to assist businesses. The government also needs specific solutions to help companies prepare and improve their competitive advantage in an increasingly open market that embraces international standards.

This paper has its own limitations which should be considered in future studies. First, although the number of observations were sufficient for this paper and relevant for the purpose of this study focusing on a particular period of time (around the times with major economic events such as the global financial crisis and recessions) to consider the effects of fiscal decentralisation on economic growth across provinces, a full period of data may need to be considered in empirical studies in the future. Second, as Vo (2010) has advocated the subnational governments, including both provincial and district levels, studies in the future may also need to consider the second level of subnational governments (the district level).

Author Contributions: Conceptualization, D.H.V.; Methodology, P.D.N. and C.M.H.; Software, P.D.N. and C.M.H.; Validation, D.H.V. and A.T.V.; Formal Analysis, P.D.N. and A.T.V.; Investigation, D.H.V. and P.D.N.; Resources, A.T.V. and C.M.H.; Data Curation, A.T.V. and C.M.H.; Writing—Original Draft Preparation, D.H.V. and P.D.N.; Writing—Review and Editing, D.H.V. and A.T.V.; Visualization, A.T.V. and C.M.H.; Supervision, D.H.V.; Project Administration, P.D.N. and C.M.H.; Funding Acquisition, D.H.V. and P.D.N.

Acknowledgments: We are grateful to the three anonymous referees for their constructive comments. We also thank the participants at the 3rd Vietnam's Business and Economics Research Conference VBER2019 (Ho Chi Minh City Open University, Vietnam, 18–20 July 2019) for their helpful suggestions. The authors wish to acknowledge financial support from Ho Chi Minh City Open University. The authors are solely responsible for any remaining errors or shortcomings.

Appendix A

Table A1. Data source of variables.

No.	Variable	Definition	Measurement	Source
1	GDP	Economic growth	Ln (Provincial GDP / provincial population)	GSO
2	FA	Fiscal autonomy	Provincial own-sourced revenue/ Provincial own-sourced spending	MOF
3	FI	Fiscal importance	Provincial own-sourced spending/ Total fiscal spending of country	MOF
4	FDI	Fiscal decentralisation index	$\sqrt{FA \times FI}$	MOF
5	POP	Labour force growth rate	(Labour force year $t + 1$—Labour force year t)/Labour force year t	GSO
6	INF	Inflation rate	(CPI year $t + 1$—CPI year t)/CPI year t (%)	GSO
7	CAP	Investment capital in the province	State capital + non-state capital + foreign capital	GSO
8	OP	Trade openness	Export + import volume (%GDP)	GSO

Notes: MOF—Ministry of Finance; GSO—General Statistics Office.

Table A2. The correlation matrix among variables.

Variable	FA	FI	FDI	INF	POP	OP	CAP	GDP
FA	1.00							
FI	0.33	1.00						
FDI	0.63	0.93	1.00					
INF	0.06	−0.02	0.00	1.00				
POP	0.05	0.04	0.05	−0.09	1.00			
OP	0.26	0.25	0.31	−0.02	0.17	1.00		
CAP	0.37	0.70	0.74	−0.08	0.02	0.47	1.00	
GDP	0.25	0.30	0.37	−0.09	−0.02	0.43	0.70	1.00

References

Adrian, Liviu Scutariu, and Scutariu Petronela. 2015. The link between financial autonomy and local development: The case of Romania. *Procedia Economics and Finance* 32: 542–49.

Arellano, Manuel, and Stephen Bond. 1991. Some tests of specification for panel data: Monte Carlo evidence and an application to employment equations. *Review of Economic Studies* 58: 277–97. [CrossRef]

Baskaran, Thushyanthan, and Lars P. Feld. 2013. Fiscal decentralization and economic growth in the OECD countries: Is there a relationship? *Public Finance Review* 41: 421–45. [CrossRef]

Bird, Richard M., Robert D. Ebel, and I. Christine. 1993. *Decentralization of Socialist State a Regional and Sectoral Study*. Washington, DC: World Bank.

Ezcurra, Roberto, and Andrés Rodríguez-Pose. 2013. Political decentralization, economic growth and regional disparities in the OECD. *Regional Studies* 47: 388–401. [CrossRef]

Gujarati, Damodar N., and Dawn C. Porter. 2009. *Basic Econometrics*, 5th ed. Singapore: Mc Graw Hill.

Hanif, Imran, Imran Sharif Chaudhry, and Sally Wallace. 2014. Fiscal autonomy and economic growth nexus: Empirical evidence from Pakistan. *Pakistan Journal of Social Sciences* 34: 767–80.

Law, Marc T., Yunsen Li, and Cheryl X. Long. 2014. Local government autonomy and city growth: Evidence from China. In *Wang Yanan Institute for Studies in Economics (WISE)*. Fujian: Xiamen University, Available online: https://economics.ucr.edu/seminars_colloquia/2014-15/applied_economics/ (accessed on 16 July 2019).

Lin, Justin Yifu, and Zhiqiang Liu. 2000. Fiscal decentralization and economic growth in China. *Economic Development and Cultural Change* 49: 1–21. [CrossRef]

Liu, Yongzheng, Jorge Martinez-Vazquez, and Alfred M. Wu. 2017. Fiscal decentralization, equalization, and intra-provincial inequality in China. *International Tax Public Finance* 24: 248–81. [CrossRef]

Martinez-Vazquez, Jorge, and Robert M. McNab. 2006. Fiscal Decentralization, Macrostability, and Growth. *Hacienda Pública Española/Revista de Economía Pública* 179: 25–49.

Martinez-Vazquez, Jorge, Santiago Lago-Peñas, and Agnese Sacchi. 2016. The impact of fiscal decentralisation: A survey. *Journal of Economic Surveys* 31: 1095–129. [CrossRef]

Nguyen, Lan Phi. 2009. *Fiscal Decentralisation and Economic Growth at Provincial Levels in Vietnam.* Hanoi: Department of Economics, Monetary Statistics, State Bank of Vietnam.

Nguyen, Lan Phi, and Sajid Anwar. 2011. Fiscal decentralisation and economic growth in Vietnam. *Journal of the Asia Pacific Economy* 16: 3–14. [CrossRef]

Oates, Wallace E. 1972. *Fiscal Federalism.* New York: Harcourt Brace Jovanovich, ISBN 978-085-793-994-4.

Oates, Wallace E. 1993. Fiscal decentralization and economic development. *National Tax Journal* 46: 237–43.

Prud'Homme, Remy. 1995. The dangers of decentralization. *The World Bank Research Observer* 10: 201–20. [CrossRef]

Rodriguez-Pose, Andres, and Anne Krøijer. 2009. Fiscal decentralization and economic growth in Central and Eastern Europe. *Growth and Change* 40: 387–417. [CrossRef]

Rodríguez-Pose, Andrés, Sylvia A. R. Tijmstra, and Adala Bwire. 2009. Fiscal decentralisation, efficiency, and growth. *Environment and Planning A* 41: 2041–62. [CrossRef]

Su, Dinh Thanh, Hoai Bui Thi Bui, and Lam Dinh Mai. 2014. The nexus between fiscal policy and sustained economic growth over the 2011–2020. *Journal of Economic Development* 280: 2–21. (In Vietnamese).

Tanzi, Vito, and Ludger Schuknech. 1996. Reforming government in industrial countries. *The Journal of Finance and Development- English Edition* 33: 2–5.

Thiessen, Ulrich. 2005. Fiscal decentralisation and economic growth in high-income OECD Countries. *Fiscal Studies* 24: 237–74. [CrossRef]

Thornton, John. 2007. Fiscal decentralization and economic growth reconsidered. *Journal of Urban Economics* 61: 64–70. [CrossRef]

Vo, Duc Hong. 2008. Fiscal decentralisation indices: A comparison of two approaches. *International Journal of Economics and Law* 2: 1–29.

Vo, Duc Hong. 2009a. Fiscal Federalism. *International Encyclopedia of Public Policy* 2: 230–40.

Vo, Duc Hong. 2009b. Fiscal decentralisation in Vietnam: Lessons from selected Asian nations. *Journal of Asia Pacific Economy* 14: 399–419. [CrossRef]

Vo, Duc Hong. 2010. The economics of fiscal decentralisation. *Journal of Economic Survey* 24: 657–79. [CrossRef]

Vo, Duc Hong. 2019. Information Theory and an Entropic Approach to an Analysis of Fiscal Inequality. *Entropy* 21: 643. [CrossRef]

Vo, Duc Hong, Thuan Nguyen, Dao Thi-Thieu Ha, and Ngoc Phu Tran. 2019. The Disparity of Revenue and Expenditure among Subnational Governments in Vietnam. *Emerging Markets Finance and Trade*, 1–12. [CrossRef]

Woller, Gary M., and Kerk Phillips. 1998. Fiscal decentralisation and IDC economic growth: An empirical investigation. *Journal of Development Studies* 34: 139–48. [CrossRef]

Zhang, Tao, and Heng-fu Zou. 1998. Fiscal decentralization, public spending, and economic growth in China. *Journal of Public Economics* 67: 221–40. [CrossRef]

7

An Empirical Test of Capital Structure Theories for the Vietnamese Listed Firms

Hoang Huy Nguyen [1], Chi Minh Ho [2] and Duc Hong Vo [2,*]

[1]   Vietnam—The Netherlands Economics Program, Ho Chi Minh City 7000, Vietnam
[2]   Business and Economics Research Group, Ho Chi Minh City Open University,
     Ho Chi Minh City 7000, Vietnam
*   Correspondence: duc.vhong@ou.edu.vn

Abstract: Raising capital efficiently for the operations is considered a fundamental decision for any firms. Since the 1960s, various theories on capital structure have been developed. Various empirical studies had also been conducted to examine the appropriateness of these theories in different markets. Unfortunately, evidence is mixed. In the context of Vietnam, a rising powerful economy in the Asia Pacific region, this important issue has been largely ignored. This paper is conducted to provide additional evidence on this important issue. In addition, different factors affecting the capital structure decisions from the Vietnamese listed firms are examined. The Generalized Method of Moment approach is employed on the sample of 227 listed firms in Ho Chi Minh City stock exchange over the period from 2008 to 2017. Findings from this study suggest that the Vietnamese listed firms follow the trade-off theory to determine their capital structure (i.e., to determine the optimal debt level). In contrast, no evidence has been found to confirm that the pecking order theory can explain the financing decisions of the Vietnamese listed firms, as previously expected. In addition, findings from this study also indicate that 'Fund flow deficit' and 'Change in sales' are the most two important factors that affect the amount of debt issued for the Vietnamese listed firms. Implications for academics, practitioners, and the Vietnamese government have also been emerged from the findings of this paper.

Keywords: pecking order theory; trade off theory; capital structure; GMM; Vietnam

1. Introduction

Capital always plays a crucial role in all firm activities. As such, raising capital efficiently for the operational activities is considered a fundamental decision for any firms. Since the 1960s, various theories and empirical researches have been conducted to examine the impacts of the capital structure decisions on firm's value. Among the number of capital structure theories, three notable theories are highly recognized including: (i) the pecking order theory; (ii) the trade-off theory; and (iii) the market timing theory. An intensive literature review indicates that both trade-off and pecking order theories have always been playing a dominate role in firms' financing decisions. However, debates have also emerged whether which theory that best explains for capital structure decisions of firms. The trade-off theory indicates that profitable firms have a tendency to increase debt to utilize the benefits from tax shields. In contrast, the pecking order theory argues that profitable firms prioritize internal funds first in order to reduce their debt or firms will use external funds when retained earnings are inadequate. Market-timing theory also receives supports, albeit limited, from empirical studies that managers tend to issue new stocks in the good timing of the market. Agha et al. (2013) considered that all three theories exhibit their own weaknesses. In the case of the trade-off theory, even though the theory extensively explains the decision for a capital structure, it ignores an important fact that debt is negatively correlated with profitability. The pecking order theory on the other hand provides a straightforward explanation for this relationship. However, mixed evidence has also emerged.

Shyam-Sunder and Myers (1999) and Yu and Aquino (2009) suggested that the pecking order theory can explain better for capital structure decisions from firms. Shyam-Sunder and Myers (1999) considered that the pecking order model is more robust than the target adjustment model although the model, once independently tested, appears to perform well. Yu and Aquino (2009) found that the pecking order theory better explains financing behavior of the Philippine listed firms than the trade-off theory.

In contrast to the arguments from Shyam-Sunder and Myers (1999) and Yu and Aquino (2009), Frank and Goyal (2003), and Razak and Rosli (2014) considered that the trade-off theory can better explain the capital structure decisions of firms than the pecking order theory. Frank and Goyal (2003) found that internal financing is insufficient to cover investment expenditures on average. A much stronger relationship between net equity issued and financing deficit is observed than net debt issuance and financing deficit. Razak and Rosli (2014) emphasized that the trade-off theory showed a stronger explanation on financing decisions of selected firms than the pecking order theory.

In practice, private enterprises frequently confront with the problems of capital structure and issued debt. In Vietnam, during the period of 2010–2015, after the global financial crisis in 2008 and the world depression in 2012, deposit interest rate was around 6–8%, while lending interest rate, which firms can issue from banks, was more than 10%, on average. Due to these global economic issues, the tightening monetary policy from the State Bank of Vietnam (SVB) gave pressure on domestic production. It was hard for firms to issue formal debt in order to foster their production, although private enterprises, especially small and medium enterprises account for a large proportion of Vietnamese GDP (approximately 43% in 2010 and 43.2% in 2015).

Since 2014 after the two recent global crisis, SVB changed its direction to loosening policy, in which SBV lowered and stabilized the lending interest rate around 7–8%. Later on, in 2018, Decree number 168 from the Vietnamese Government on the problem of private bond loosed its previous regulation in order to encourage firms to raise their financial funds and diversify their capital structure. In previous Decree (Decree number 90 activated in 2011), firm can only issue private bond if it had positive profit in the previous year. That requirement was removed from the current activated Decree (Decree number 168). Even that, in 2018, total private bond issued from Vietnamese private corporations was approximately 7% of GDP. That was a relatively low rate compared to the average level of the region (21%). These efforts from the Vietnamese Government and SVB seemed to weakly affect to the capital structure of private firms.

Due to the mixed evidence from previous studies, in particular for the case of an emerging market such as Vietnam, this paper is conducted to examine the importance of the capital structure theories in the context of Vietnam and to consider an appropriate model for Vietnamese listed firms to consider when conducting financing decisions. In addition, the paper also considers different factors which have also greatly contributed to the financing decisions of Vietnamese listed firms.

In order to obtain the above objectives, the paper utilizes various models on the ground of previous studies from Shyam-Sunder and Myers (1999), and Frank and Goyal (2003), Yu and Aquino (2009), and Razak and Rosli (2014). The pecking order theory is tested using two distinct models including the (original) pecking order model and the partially aggregated pecking order model. In addition, the trade-off theory is tested using the target adjustment model. In addition, the study uses the effect of factors on leverage model to measure the impact of different factors on capital structure decisions from the Vietnamese listed firms. The paper employs a Generalized Method of Moment (GMM) approach on the ground of a panel dataset of 227 firms from all sectors listed in Ho Chi Minh City stock exchange (HOSE) over the period from 2008 to 2017. The data set excludes listed firms from finance, insurance, and investment sectors.

The paper is structured as follows. Following this introduction, Section 2 reviews relevant literature. Then, Section 3 describes the research methodology utilized in this paper. Data and empirical results are presented in Section 4, followed concluding remarks in Section 5.

2. Literature Review

Corporate capital structure has been widely considered in empirical studies with the focus on the determinants of financing decisions. Various aspects have been studied including the effect of corporate governance (Giroud and Mueller 2010, 2011; Morellec et al. 2012; Wen et al. 2002) or the influence of managerial characteristics (Berger et al. 1997; Coles and Li 2018; Friend and Lang 1988). Findings from these studies indicated that corporate capital structure is mostly affected by firm's characteristics. However, it is noted that none of these studies investigated the appropriateness of the theories on firms' financing decision to explain the corporate capital structure.

To test for the appropriateness and the validity of the theoretical models on financing decision, a number of papers have been conducted. The pecking order theory was validated to explain firm's financing decisions in studies by Shyam-Sunder and Myers (1999), Vijayakumar (2011), Atiyet (2012), Sheikh et al. (2012), Pacheco (2016), Balios et al. (2016), Maças Nunes and Serrasqueiro (2017), Trinh et al. (2017). Razak and Rosli (2014) supported the extended pecking order model whereas Yu and Aquino (2009) argued that the trade-off theory was more appropriate than the pecking order theory in explaining firms' financing decisions. However, Chirinko and Singha (2000) criticized the validity of the tests adopted in Shyam-Sunder and Myers (1999). This paper presents and discusses selected papers on this important research issue in order to identify and highlight the research gap in the context of an emerging market such as Vietnam.

To test traditional capital structure models against the pecking order model, Shyam-Sunder and Myers (1999) used a dataset of 157 US firms over the period from 1971 to 1989. The study started with the year-end values of the book debt ratio of each firm in 1971. Then, the book debt ratios of the later years were generated by ascertaining the funds flow deficit which is calculated by real investment, dividends, operating cash flow and others. The firm is supposed to retire debt in the case of negative deficit, and issue debt in the case of positive deficit. The key empirical results are briefly described as follows: (i) the pecking order model best describes firm's financing behavior; (ii) the adjustment target model, once independently tested, appeared to perform well; (iii) when the two models were jointly tested, the significance of the estimated coefficients from the pecking order model did not vary whereas the performance of the target adjustment model reduced even though the estimated coefficients from the model were still statistically significant; and (iv) firms not only intended to use debt to finance the need of cash in the short term but also in the case when the deficits were unexpected. These findings demonstrate the robustness of the pecking order model in explaining firms' behavior to capital structure decisions.

Yu and Aquino (2009) tested the validity of the pecking order model and the trade-off model to explain a financing behavior of the Philippine listed firms over the period 1990 to 2001. Findings from this study supported for the pecking order model due to the negative relationship between profitability and leverage, while the annual change in total liabilities is mostly explained by financing deficit. Yu and Aquino (2009) used the model of Shyam-Sunder and Myers (1999) and added dummy variable for years 1992–2001 to control time fixed effects when the pecking order model was tested. The results showed that firms followed the trade-off model in selecting capital structure model.

Chirinko and Singha (2000) indicated that the empirical evidence of Shyam-Sunder and Myers (1999) did not evaluate both the pecking order and static trade-off models. Chirinko and Singha considered the plausibility of three alternative external financing patterns and raised a question in relation to the validity of Shyam-Sunder and Myers (1999) conclusions. Chirinko and Singha (2000) argued that using the model of Shyam-Sunder and Myers (1999) provided difficulties in evaluating the validity of the pecking order model. As a result, they suggested that it is essential to have alternative tests to identify capital structure determinants and to distinguish one from other hypotheses.

Frank and Goyal (2003) employed a dataset of the American public trading firms from the 1971 to 1998 period to test the validity of the pecking order theory. Two different approaches were applied in the paper. The first approach is that the fund flow deficit was utilized in order to account for the net debt issued. The second approach is that leverage was used. Frank and Goyal (2003) concluded that internal financing is insufficient to cover investment expenditures on average. This conclusion is in contrast to what is usually suggested. External financing is considerably used.

Razak and Rosli (2014) examined various theories of the capital structure and tested the static trade-off theory and the pecking order theory. The study used data from 200 listed firms in Malaysia over the period 2007 to 2012. Three models were tested including the pecking order model, the extended pecking order model, and the static trade-off model, to explain financing decision of firms in relation to new debt issuance. Findings from this study presented that the issuance of new shares was not affected by internal fund deficits. As such, the pecking order hypothesis expecting firms to issue debt to finance internal fund deficit was statistically rejected. However, findings from the extended pecking order model presented another story. The hypothesis supporting a positive relationship between financial activities and issuance of new debt is statistically accepted. Razak and Rosli (2014) continuously conducted further regression analysis to test the hypothesis of the extended pecking order model. The results indicated that new debt issuance was positively influenced by a long-term debt repayment and capital expenditure.

Kopecky et al. (2018) provided an alternative equilibrating process which markedly differs from the Modigliani (Modigliani and Miller 1958) and Miller (Miller 1977) theorem in terms of the prediction of debt uses, to achieve the same optimal level for firm values. This alternative process reinstitutes the prospect of capital structure irrelevancy. The study indicates that the takeover market can alter the stock market valuations such that firms may find it optimal not to recapitalize, even though predictions of the standard discounted cash flow model with recapitalization costs suggested that they have to recapitalize.

3. Methodology

This paper utilizes four different models on the ground of various studies of Shyam-Sunder and Myers (1999), Frank and Goyal (2003), Yu and Aquino (2009), and Razak and Rosli (2014) in the context of Vietnam. The pecking order theory is tested by two models including the original pecking order model and the partially aggregated pecking order model. In addition, the trade-off theory is tested using the target adjustment model. Together with these analyses, the paper also uses the effect of factors on leverage model to examine the impact of different factors on capital structure decisions from the Vietnamese listed firms. This study uses the panel Generalized Method of Moment (GMM) estimation to test the robustness of the pecking order theory as well as the trade-off theory and to measure the impact of different factors on capital structure decisions of the Vietnamese listed firms. Flannery and Rangan (2006) and Nunkoo and Boateng (2010) observed that recent studies in developed countries have a tendency to use the GMM estimation technique to conduct empirical analyses on the capital structure issues. In addition, Kannadhasan et al. (2018) emphasized that the GMM consistently estimates the dynamic model and deals with the endogenous problems by employing efficient instrumental variable (IV) techniques.

The pecking order model is tested on the ground of the model of Shyam-Sunder and Myers (1999) which has been widely used in previous studies including Frank and Goyal (2003), Yu and Aquino (2009), and Razak and Rosli (2014). The model can be expressed as below:

$$\Delta D_{it} = \alpha + b_{PO}DEF_{it} + e_{it} \qquad (1)$$

where ΔD_{it} represents the amount of debt issued or retired by firm i in year i. b_{PO} is the pecking order coefficient and e_{it} is the error term. DEF_{it} is the fund flow deficit of firm i in year i and is calculated using the following equation:

$$DEF_{it} = DIV_{it} + CFI_{it} + \Delta NWC_{it} - CFO_{it}$$

where DIV_{it}, CFI_{it}, ΔNWC_{it}, and CFO_{it} are dividend payments, net investment, change in net working capital, operating cash flows for firm i in year i respectively.

The partially aggregated pecking order model was based on Frank and Goyal (2003) which proposed to use the fund flow deficit (DEF) equation to estimate the amount of debt issued or retired (ΔD).

$$\Delta D_{it} = a + b_{DIV}DIV_{it} + b_{CFI}CFI_{it} + b_{NWC}\Delta NWC_{it} - b_{CFO}CFO_{it} + e_{it} \qquad (2)$$

where ΔD_{it} represents the amount of debt issued or retired by firm i in year t. CFO_{it} is the operating cash flows of firm i in year t. DIV_{it} represents dividend payments of firm i in year t. CFI is the investing cash flow of firm i in year t. ΔNWC_{it} represents the change in net working capital of firm i in year t. e_{it} is the error term.

The target adjustment model on the ground of Shyam-Sunder and Myers (1999) study was used to test the validity of the trade-off theory.

$$\Delta D_{it} = \alpha + b_{TA}\Delta D_{it}^* + e_{it} \qquad (3)$$

where ΔD_{it} is the amount of debt issued or retired by firm i in year t. D_{it}^* represents the target debt level for firm i in year t calculated by multiplied the historical mean of the debt ratio for each firm with total capital. b_{TA} is the target-adjustment coefficient and e_{it} is the error term.

Frank and Goyal (2003) used other factors to account for firm's leverage. The leverage regression was developed utilizing five factors: profitability (P), log sales (LS), market-to-book ratio (MTB), tangibility of assets (T), and fund flow deficit (DEF).

As such, the effect of factors on leverage model specification is as follows:

$$\Delta D_{it} = a + b_T\Delta T_{it} + b_{MTB}\Delta MTB_{it} + b_{LS}\Delta LS_{it} + b_P\Delta P_{it} + b_{DEF}DEF_{it} + e_{it} \qquad (4)$$

where ΔD_{it} represents the amount of debt issued or retired by firm i in year t. ΔT_i is Change in assets of firm i in year t. ΔP_{it} represents the change in profitability of firm i in year t. ΔLS_{it} is the change in log sales of firm i in year t. ΔMTB_{it} is the change in market-to-book ratio of firm i in year t. DEF_{it} represents fund flow deficit of firm i in year t.

4. Data and Results

Data were collected from financial reports, and annual reports of listed firms operating in all sectors in Ho Chi Minh Stock Exchange (HOSE) over the period 2008 to 2017 except for firms operating in finance, insurance, and investment sectors. Firms with missing or incomplete data were excluded from the analysis. The remaining data forms a balanced panel dataset. Table 1 presents the outcome of descriptive statistics for all variables used in this study. All variables have 2268 observations, except change in log sales (ΔLS) which has 2267 observations.

Table 1. Descriptive Statistics.

Variable	Obs.	Mean	Std. Dev.	Min	Max
ΔD	2268	0.1424	1.5380	(59.1252)	10.6219
DEF	2268	(0.2350)	1.6005	(13.7638)	61.6392
DIV	2268	(0.0588)	0.0736	(1.2161)	0.0730
CFI	2268	(0.0892)	1.4522	(3.3698)	66.0117
ΔNWC	2268	0.0192	0.8129	(17.6784)	16.3728
CFO	2268	0.1063	0.5968	(7.4473)	12.7931
ΔD *	2268	0.1102	1.4033	(41.2042)	9.3302
ΔT	2268	(0.0095)	3.0170	(101.0872)	101.8906
ΔMTB	2268	0.0627	1.1848	(20.7629)	20.8969
ΔLS	2267	0.1038	0.5555	(4.2825)	12.6414
ΔP	2268	(0.0359)	2.1643	(63.4109)	53.3619

Notes: ΔD_{it}: the amount of debt issued; DEF_{it}: Fund flow deficit; DIV_{it}: Dividend payments; CFI: Investing cash flow; ΔNWC_{it}: Change in net working capital; CFO_{it}: Operating cash flows; ΔD_{it}^* is the target debt ratio; ΔT_i: Change in assets; ΔMTB_{it}: Change in market-to-book ratio; ΔLS_{it}: Change in log sales; ΔP_{it}: Change in profitability.

This study employed the panel Generalized Method of Moment (GMM) estimation to test the validity of the models and to measure the impact of different factors on capital structure decisions from Vietnamese listed firms. Table 2 shows the results for different estimations for the pecking order model.

Table 2. Estimation results of the pecking order model.

Explanatory Variable	Dependent Variable Amount of Debt Issued (ΔD)
Fund Flow Deficit (DEF)	−0.572 ***
	(0.029)
Constant	82.09 ***
	(14.750)
Number of observations	2268
Number of firms	227

Notes: Standard deviations in parenthesis. *** Significant at 0.01 level.

The hypothesis of the pecking order model is that the amount of debt issued has a positive relationship with the fund flow deficit ($b_{PO} > 0$) indicating that firms prefer to issue debt to finance the fund flow deficit. However, the regression coefficient of the model is negative ($b_{PO} = -0.572$) and statistically significant at the level of one percent ($p < 0.01$). This indicates that the results do not support the pecking order theory in the context of the Vietnamese market. In a nut shell, Vietnamese listed firms do not prefer to issue debt to finance the fund flow deficit.

Table 3 describes Arellano–Bond test for first-order autocorrelation AR(1) and second-order autocorrelation AR(2) in the first-differenced errors which are conducted to verify the consistent degree and robustness of the empirical results. The estimated values confirm that second order autocorrelation is not in existence.

Table 3. Arellano–Bond Test for the pecking order model.

Arellano-Bond	System GMM	
	Z-Value	Pr > z
First-order autocorrelation AR(1)	−3.61	0.000
Second-order autocorrelation AR(2)	−1.44	0.149

Table 4 presents the results obtained for different estimations of the Partially Aggregated Pecking Order Model.

Table 4. Estimation results of the partially aggregated pecking order model.

Explanatory Variables	Dependent Variable Amount of Debt Issued (ΔD)
Dividend Payments (DIV)	−0.821 * (0.423)
Investing Cash Flow (CFI)	−1.117 *** (0.052)
Change in Net Working Capital (ΔNWC)	0.030 (0.125)
Operating Cash Flow (CFO)	−1.272 *** (0.166)
Constant	16.720 (16.240)
Number of observations	2268
Number of firms	227

Notes: Standard deviations in parenthesis. * Significant at 0.1 level, *** Significant at 0.01 level.

The regression coefficient of dividend payments (DIV) is negative (−0.82) and statistically significant at the level of 10 percent. The result is consistent with the findings of Vo and Nguyen (2014) and Tran and Vo (2015) who reported a negative relationship between dividend and firm leverage. The regression coefficient of operating cash flows (CFO) and investing cash flow (CFI) are also negative and significant at the level of one percent. Operating cash flow and investing cash flow have negative relationships with the amount of debt issued (ΔD) while there is no impact of the net working capital (ΔNWC) on the amount of debt issued (ΔD).

The hypothesis of the partially aggregated pecking order model is that the amount of debt issued or retired is positively related to dividend payments (DIV), investing cash flow (CFI) and change in net working capital (ΔNWC) but is negatively related to operating cash flows of firm (CFO). However, the empirical results do not support the hypothesis of the partially aggregated pecking order model.

Table 5 describes Arellano–Bond test for first-order autocorrelation AR(1) and second-order autocorrelation AR(2) in the first-differenced errors are conducted to verify the consistent degree and robustness of the model results. The testing values confirm that second order autocorrelation is absent.

Table 5. Arellano-Bond test for the partially aggregated pecking order model.

Arellano–Bond	System GMM	
	Z-Value	Pr > z
First-order autocorrelation AR(1)	−4.45	0.000
Second-order autocorrelation AR(2)	−0.60	0.549

Tables 6 and 7 present estimation's results and validation test of the target adjustment model (Shyam-Sunder and Myers 1999). Table 8 reports the results attained for different estimations of the effect of factors on leverage model using the system GMM.

Table 6. Estimation Results of the Target Adjustment Model.

Explanatory Variable	Fixed Effects	Random Effects
	Dependent Variable Amount of Debt Issued (ΔD)	
Target Debt Ratio (ΔD^*)	0.714 ***	0.739 ***
	(0.018)	(0.017)
Constant	0.137 *	0.131 *
	(0.075)	(0.075)
Number of observations	2268	2268
Number of firms	227	227

Notes: Standard deviations in parenthesis. * is significant at 0.1 level, *** is significant at 0.01 level.

Table 7. Statistics Test of the Target Adjustment Model.

Statistics Tests	System GMM	
	Chi-Square	Pr > Chi-Square
Hausman	9.78	0.1342
Breusch-Pagan Lagrange multiplier (LM)	152.76	0.0000

Table 8. Estimation results of the effect of factors on leverage model.

Explanatory Variables	Dependent Variable Amount of Debt Issued (ΔD)
Fund Flow Deficit (DEF)	−0.530 ***
	(0.057)
Change in Log Sales (ΔLS)	0.512 ***
	(0.177)
Change in Market to Book Ratio (ΔMTB)	(0.040)
	(0.097)
Change in Profitability (ΔP)	(0.023)
	(0.036)
Change in Tangibility (ΔT)	0.080
	(0.071)
Constant	51.74 **
	(22.200)
Number of observations	2267
Number of firms	227

Notes: Standard deviations in parenthesis. ** is significant at 0.05 level, *** is significant at 0.01 level.

The regression coefficient of fund flow deficit *(DEF)* is negative ($b_{DEF} = -0.530$) and statistically significant at the level of one percent ($p < 0.01$). Change in log of sales (ΔLS) has a positive relationship with amount of debt issued (0.178) and is statistically significant at the level of one percent.

We consider that the above findings are consistent with our observations of the economic environment in Vietnam. Lending interest rate in Vietnam has been maintained at the average level of around 7.8 percent per year for the last five years. This stability of interest rate in Vietnam encourages Vietnamese firms to absorb more debt in order to take the advantage of the financial leverage. Findings from this paper reconfirm this position and observation. Figure 1 below illustrates the lending interest rate in Vietnam from 2008 to 2017.

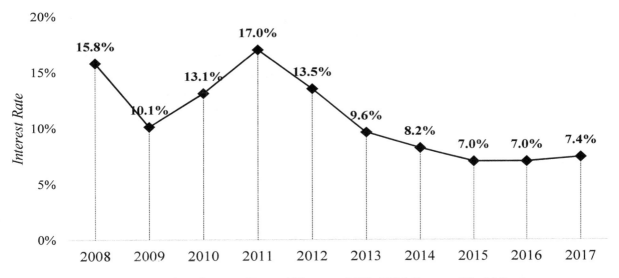

Figure 1. Lending Interest Rate of Vietnam 2008–2017. Source: World Bank.

5. Concluding Remarks

Financing decision is always important for any firm. As such, an appropriate model for firms to follow in making their financing decisions is desired. Unfortunately, mixed evidence has been emerged in previous empirical studies. In addition, limited number of studies addressed this important question in the context of Vietnam. As such, this study is conducted to examine an appropriate model in which the Vietnamese firms employ to determine their capital structures. In addition, the study also measures the impact of different factors on capital structure decisions of the Vietnamese listed firms.

The study develops four models based on studies of Shyam-Sunder and Myers (1999), Frank and Goyal (2003), Yu and Aquino (2009), and Razak and Rosli (2014). The pecking order theory is tested by two models including the original pecking order model and the partially aggregated pecking order model. In addition, the trade-off theory is tested using the target adjustment model. The study also utilizes the effect of factors on leverage model to measure the impact of different factors on capital structure decisions of Vietnamese listed firms. Unlike many other studies, a panel dataset of 227 HOSE listed firms over the period 2008 to 2017 and Generalized Method of Moment (GMM) approach are used. The use of GMM and panel data analysis help to effectively control unobservable firm-specific fixed effects but are very critical in capital structure decisions of firms.

The study finds no evidence that the pecking order theory can explain financing decisions of Vietnamese listed firms over the period 2008 to 2017. On the contrary, the empirical results strongly support that Vietnamese listed firms have followed the trade-off theory to determine their capital structures. The empirical results from the effect of factors on leverage model also suggest fund flow deficit has a negative impact on the amount of debt issued which is consistent with the result from the pecking order model, and change in sales has a positive influence on the amount of debt issued.

On the grounds of the findings from this paper, implications are drawn for academics, investors and firms, and also the Vietnamese government.

First, for academics, the study provides additional empirical evidence to answer one of the most arguable topics in the corporate finance in relation to how firms determine their capital structure. This paper provides empirical evidence that listed firms in Vietnam do not follow the pecking order theory. They have followed the trade-off theory to determine their optimal capital structure. The study also contributes to the capital structure study in Vietnam where the finance literature has not been thoroughly investigated. However, for robustness, studies in the future should consider the potential limitation of this paper as discussed further below.

Second, Vietnamese firms may consider the findings from this paper as a reference and a starting point to choose an appropriate capital structure in order to maximize firm's value. Vietnamese firms appear to have a tendency to substitute between debt and equity to move towards the target debt ratio.

Third, for the Vietnamese government, Vietnamese firms depend heavily on debt to finance their capital structure and Vietnam's financial markets have not yet developed with a variety of choices. According to the NFSC (the National Finance Supervisory Commission) report, the banking system is the main capital supply source for the economy accounting over 60 percent of total supply. Depending heavily on banking loans brings risks to firms in relation to meet their obligations to pay interest expenses and debt repayment, in particular when lending interest rate increases. As a result, the Vietnamese government should put more effort to improve the financial market in terms of products and choices.

This study exhibits some limitations. For example, an extended period is desirable to consider a potential difference between various periods, in particular crisis and normal periods. Advanced techniques on risk measurements can also be considered and utilized such as credit risk measurements (Powell et al. 2017, 2018). In addition, this study only focuses on the Ho Chi Minh City stock market which may not be the complete proxy for the Vietnamese listed firms. The sample should be extended to include firms listed in Ha Noi stock market as well. It is because the ruling of listings between these two markets is significantly different. Last but not least, in addition to testing the appropriateness and validity of the three typical models, the characteristics of firms included in the study should be carefully considered as the difference in firms' characteristics is expected to influence firms' financing decisions.

Author Contributions: H.H.N.: Methodology, Data curation, Formal analysis, Software, Writing—original draft. C.M.H.: Writing—review & editing, Analysis, Resources, Validation. D.H.V.: Conceptualization, Writing—original draft, Writing—review & editing, Validation, Supervision.

Acknowledgments: We are grateful to the three anonymous referees for their constructive comments. We also thank the participants at the 3rd Vietnam's Business and Economics Research Conference VBER2019 (Ho Chi Minh City Open University, Vietnam, 18–20 July 2019) for their helpful suggestions. The authors wish to acknowledge financial supports from Ho Chi Minh City Open University. The authors are solely responsible for any remaining errors or shortcomings.

References

Agha, Jahanzeb, Saif-Ur-Rehman Khan, Norkhairul Hafiz Bajuri, Meisam Karami, and Aiyoub Ahmadimousaabad. 2013. Trade-off theory, pecking order theory and market timing theory: A comprehensive review of capital structure theories. *International Journal of Management and Commerce Innovations* 1: 11–18.

Atiyet, Ben Amor. 2012. The Pecking Order Theory and the Static Trade off Theory: Comparison of the Alternative Explanatory Power in French Firms. *Journal of Business Studies Quarterly* 4: 1–14.

Balios, Dimitris, Nikolaos Daskalakis, Nikolaos Eriotis, and Dimitrios Vasiliou. 2016. SMEs capital structure determinants during severe economic crisis: The case of Greece. *Cogent Economics & Finance* 4: 1–12.

Berger, Philip, Eli Ofek, and David Yermack. 1997. Managerial entrenchment and capital structure decisions. *The Journal of Finance* 52: 1411–38. [CrossRef]

Chirinko, Robert, and Anuja Singha. 2000. Testing static tradeoff against pecking order models of capital structure: A critical comment. *Journal of Financial Economics* 58: 417–25. [CrossRef]

Coles, Jeffrey L., and Zhichuan Frank Li. 2018. Managerial attributes, incentives, and performance. *SSRN*. [CrossRef]

Flannery, Mark, and Kasturi Rangan. 2006. Partial adjustment toward target capital structures. *Journal of Financial Economics* 79: 469–506. [CrossRef]

Frank, Murray, and Vidhan Goyal. 2003. Testing the pecking order theory of capital structure. *Journal of Financial Economics* 67: 217–48. [CrossRef]

Friend, Irwin, and Larry Lang. 1988. An empirical test of the impact of managerial self-interest on corporate capital structure. *The Journal of Finance* 43: 271–81. [CrossRef]

Giroud, Xavier, and Holger Mueller. 2010. Does corporate governance matter in competitive industries? *Journal of Financial Economics* 95: 312–31. [CrossRef]

Giroud, Xavier, and Holger Mueller. 2011. Corporate governance, product market competition, and equity prices. *The Journal of Finance* 66: 563–600. [CrossRef]

Kannadhasan, M., Bhanu Thakur, C. Gupta, and Parikshit Charan. 2018. Testing capital structure theories using error correction models: Evidence from China, India, and South Africa. *Cogent Economics & Finance* 6: 1443369.

Kopecky, Kenneth, Zhichuan Li, Timothy Sugrue, and Alan Tucker. 2018. Revisiting M&M with Taxes: An Alternative Equilibrating Process. *International Journal of Financial Studies* 6: 10.

Maças Nunes, Paulo, and Zélia Serrasqueiro. 2017. Short-term debt and long-term debt determinants in small and medium-sized hospitality firms. *Tourism Economics* 23: 543–60. [CrossRef]

Miller, Edward. 1977. Risk, Uncertainty, and Divergence of Opinion. *The Journal of Finance* 32: 1151–68. [CrossRef]

Modigliani, Franco, and Merton Miller. 1958. The cost of capital, corporation finance and the theory of investment. *American Economic Review* 48: 261–97.

Morellec, Erwan, Boris Nikolov, and Norman Schürhoff. 2012. Corporate governance and capital structure dynamics. *The Journal of Finance* 67: 803–48. [CrossRef]

Nunkoo, Pravish, and Agyenim Boateng. 2010. The empirical determinants of target capital structure and adjustment to long-run target: Evidence from Canadian firms. *Applied Economics Letters* 17: 983–90. [CrossRef]

Pacheco, Luís. 2016. Capital structure and internationalization: The case of Portuguese industrial SMEs. *Research in International Business and Finance* 38: 531–45. [CrossRef]

Powell, Robert, Duc H. Vo, and Thach N. Pham. 2017. The long and short commodity tails and their relationship to Asian equity markets. *Journal of Asian Economics* 52: 32–44. [CrossRef]

Powell, Robert, Duc H. Vo, and Thach N. Pham. 2018. Economic cycles and downside commodities risk. *Applied Economics Letter* 25: 258–63. [CrossRef]

Razak, Nazrul, and Mohd Rosli. 2014. A test between Pecking Order Hypothesis and Static Trade-Off Theory: An Analysis from Malaysian Listed Firms for Periods of Year 2007 To 2012. *International Journal of Business and Commerce* 3: 99–117.

Sheikh, Jibran, Wajid Ahmed, and Muhammad Masood. 2012. Pecking at pecking order theory: Evidence from Pakistan's non-financial sector. *Journal of Competitiveness* 4: 86–95. [CrossRef]

Shyam-Sunder, Lakshmi, and Stewart Myers. 1999. Testing static tradeoff against pecking order models of capital structure. *Journal of Financial Economics* 51: 219–44. [CrossRef]

Tran, Minh, and Duc Vo. 2015. The appropriateness of the pecking order theory in corporate capital structure in Vietnam. *Banking Technology Review* 106–107: 25–42.

Trinh, Huong, Makoto Kakinaka, Donghun Kim, and Tae Yong Jung. 2017. Capital structure and investment financing of small and medium-sized enterprises in Vietnam. *Global Economic Review* 46: 325–49. [CrossRef]

Vijayakumar, Ashvin. 2011. An empirical investigation of the trade-off and pecking order hypotheses on Indian automobile firms. *International Journal of Research in Commerce, Economics & Management* 1: 94–100.

Vo, Duc, and Van Nguyen. 2014. Managerial ownership, leverage and dividend policies: Empirical evidence from Vietnam's listed firms. *International Journal of Economics and Finance* 6: 274–99. [CrossRef]

Wen, Yu, Kami Rwegasira, and Jan Bilderbeek. 2002. Corporate governance and capital structure decisions of the Chinese listed firms. *Corporate Governance: An International Review* 10: 75–83. [CrossRef]

Yu, Darwin, and Rodolfo Aquino. 2009. Testing capital structure models on Philippines listed firms. *Applied Economics* 41: 1973–90. [CrossRef]

8

Modeling the Impact of Agricultural Shocks on Oil Price in the US: A New Approach

Tan Ngoc Vu [1],*, Duc Hong Vo [1] ⓘ, Chi Minh Ho [1] and Loan Thi-Hong Van [2]

[1]   Business and Economics Research Group, Ho Chi Minh City Open University,
      Ho Chi Minh City 7000, Vietnam; duc.vhong@ou.edu.vn (D.H.V.); chiminhho.1003@gmail.com (C.M.H.)
[2]   School of Advanced Study, Ho Chi Minh City Open University, Ho Chi Minh City 7000, Vietnam;
      loan.vth@ou.edu.vn
*   Correspondence: tan.vn@ou.edu.vn

Abstract: The current literature has generally considered prices of the agricultural commodity as an endogenous factor to crude oil price. As such, the role of the agricultural market in the energy sector has been largely ignored. We argue that the expansion of agricultural production may trigger a significant increase in oil price. In addition, the world has recently witnessed a growth in biofuel production, leading to an increase in the size of the agricultural sector. This study is conducted to examine the impact of different agricultural shocks on the oil and agricultural markets in the US for the period from 1986 to 2018. The study utilizes the Structural Vector Autoregressive (SVAR) model to estimate the relationship between the agricultural market and the crude oil market. Moreover, the variance decomposition is also used to quantify the contribution of agricultural demand shocks on oil price variations. Findings from this paper indicate that different agricultural shocks can have different effects on oil price and that corn use in ethanol plays an important role in the impact of corn demand shocks on oil price. We find evidence that the agricultural market can have an impact on oil prices through two main channels: indirect cost push effect and direct biofuel effect. Of these, the biofuel channel unexpectedly suggests that the expansion of bioethanol may in fact foster the dependency of the economy on fossil fuel use and prices.

Keywords: agricultural commodity prices; volatility; crude oil prices; structural vector autoregressive model; impulse response functions

---

1. Introduction

The correlation of crude oil price and agricultural commodity prices during the food price crisis of 2007–2008 has led to a rich array of studies on the impact of crude oil price and biofuel expansion on agricultural prices. According to these studies, the increase in crude oil price has increased the prices of many agricultural crops and damaged global food security, as crude oil is one of the main factors of agricultural production (Bayramoğlu et al. 2016; Persson 2015; Adam et al. 2018; Wang et al. 2014). Furthermore, the increase in crude oil price also raised the demand for biofuel as an alternative energy source. The coincidence of biofuel expansion and the occurrence of the food price crisis during 2007–2008 has raised serious concerns about the causality from the former to the latter (Lucotte 2016; Ma et al. 2016; Ahmadi et al. 2016). In particular, the increase in biofuel production has led to an increase in corn demand, as corn is the main feedstock of bio-ethanol in the US. The increase in corn demand led to an increase in corn price and the prices of other agricultural commodities, as these crops compete for planted acreage and other agricultural resources (Wang et al. 2014). Furthermore, the demand for biofuel was strengthened as many developed countries imposed several renewable energy mandates, which greatly increased biofuel consumption. Since then, biofuel has played a key role in connecting the agricultural market and the energy market (De Gorter et al. 2013).

However, the correlation between crude oil price and agricultural commodity prices does not always mean causation from the former to the latter. Previous studies often focused on the causality from crude oil price to agricultural commodity prices, so the possibility of reverse causality is often ignored in the literature. Baumeister and Kilian (2014) argued that the mechanization of agricultural production may increase the energy consumption in the agricultural sector. Therefore, an increase in agricultural production is likely to increase fuel demand and crude oil price. Moreover, an increase in the size of the agricultural and biofuel sectors makes the reverse causality more likely to happen.

Despite its scarcity, the empirical literature has recognized the causality from food prices to energy prices (Su et al. 2019; Vacha et al. 2013; Avalos 2014; Natanelov et al. 2011; Zhang et al. 2010). However, these studies often employed only the price data without including further information about the agricultural supply and demand. Baumeister and Kilian (2014) and Serra and Zilberman (2013) criticized these time-series models for their inability to identify the transmission mechanisms of the price spillovers between the two markets. Theoretically, the agricultural sector can influence crude oil price through both indirect input cost and direct biofuel channels (Ciaian 2011). The author showed that the two channels can have different impacts on the crude oil price. In particular, the increase in agricultural supply may lead to a decrease in crude oil demand and crude oil price. However, the increase in agricultural demand caused by ethanol expansion may either increase energy demand or increase energy supply. Therefore, we find that the existing empirical studies are inconclusive about the transmission mechanisms in which the agricultural market can influence the crude oil price.

The contribution of this paper is twofold. Firstly, we confirm the results derived from the theoretical model in Ciaian (2011) that different shocks from the agricultural market can have different effects on oil price. We use the agricultural supply and demand shocks of different crops to test the existence of the indirect input cost and the direct biofuel channels. Our results confirm the existence of the indirect input cost channel in the barley market and the direct biofuel channel in the corn and sorghum market. For the corn market, we identify that agricultural demand shocks play a larger role in the fluctuation of crude oil price, compared to the effect of the agricultural supply shock.

Secondly, our results have important policy implications for the biofuel sector. We find that an increase in corn use in ethanol can have a positive influence on the crude oil price. This is in contrast to the original expectation that the expansion of biofuel can increase the total fuel supply and reduce the dependency of the domestic economy on fossil fuel. Our results show that an increase in corn use in ethanol may lead to an increase in fuel demand and crude oil price, which is an unexpected consequence of biofuel. Such conclusions could not be reached if the analysis only included agricultural prices.

Moreover, the use of corn in ethanol has an additional advantage over using corn price in the sense that corn price and crude oil price are likely to react to changes in monetary and trade policies, global business cycle, and aggregate demand. However, the expansion of corn use in ethanol is most likely to be the result of the renewable energy mandate, which is exogenous to changes of the macroeconomic variables. Therefore, the impact of corn use in ethanol on crude oil price is not likely to be correlated with global economic events.

In general, the novelty of our study is that we include variables which are different in nature, such as oil prices, agricultural prices, agricultural supplies, and corn use in ethanol. This approach differs from existing studies, that often focus on the price spillover effects between the two markets. Our approach is interesting because we can observe a number of interconnected relationships, which might be missed if the analysis only included price variables. In particular, we confirm that the agricultural market can have feedback effects on oil prices. Previous studies did not disentangle the impact of agricultural supply and demand shocks, which can potentially have different effects on oil prices, according to Ciaian (2011). By observing variables other than prices, we find evidence that the agricultural market is more likely to affect oil prices through the direct biofuel channel. We also find that biofuel expansion can lead to an increase in agricultural production, which will eventually increase oil demand.

The following section of this paper is a review of the studies related to the current research. Section 3 presents the methodology and the models used in the empirical section. Section 4 shows the data and preliminary tests. Section 5 presents the results of the empirical analysis and the discussion of the outcomes. Section 6 concludes our research.

2. Literature Review

The literature on the nexus of food versus energy often investigates the relationship between biofuel, agricultural commodity, and crude oil prices. Regarding the studies on biofuel and agricultural markets, many efforts have been devoted to research on price and volatility transmission. Many studies have shown that shocks from the corn market can have an impact on ethanol price, due to corn being a feedstock of bioethanol. Kristoufek et al. (2016) employed the wavelet coherence methodology to study the relationship between ethanol and agricultural commodities in the US and Brazil. The results show that the impact of corn price on ethanol price is unidirectional. The relationships are robust, both in short- and long-term periods. Similarly, Dutta et al. (2018) argued that the volatility in the corn market can have an impact on ethanol price. The paper employed conditional Generalized Autoregressive Conditional Heteroskedasticity (GARCH)-jump models with daily US ethanol and corn prices, both series are based on future contracts. The study found that the relationship is asymmetric because only positive shocks on corn price volatility can induce an increase in ethanol price. Bentivoglio et al. (2016) employed a vector error correction model with the Granger causality test, impulse response function, and forecast error variance decompositions to illustrate that ethanol price is impacted by fluctuations in oil and corn prices, but not the reverse. Dutta (2018) also showed similar results using the Autoregressive Distributed Lag (ARDL) model and the Kyrtsou–Labys nonlinear causality test.

On the other hand, Hao et al. (2017) showed that the ethanol market can also impact agricultural commodity prices. The authors focused on the consequences of biofuel production expansion in the US on the welfare of the poor in developing countries. Hao et al. (2017) investigated the influences of the US ethanol market on the maize prices of developing countries using the panel structural vector autoregression model (panel SVAR). The study divided the developing countries into groups with different political and geographical characteristics, which have potential impacts on the vulnerability of these countries to changes in the US ethanol and maize market. The authors found that the dependency of a country on US Food Aid may have a positive impact on the response of domestic maize prices to US ethanol supply shock. Similarly, coastal countries were found to be more likely to be affected by US ethanol demand shock.

Some studies pointed out that the causal relationship between the agricultural and ethanol markets can run in both ways. Apergis et al. (2017) employed a threshold error correction model (TECM) to show that biofuel and agricultural commodity prices have a bi-directional causal relationship. The study used the daily prices of seasonal biodiesel and agricultural commodities, including corn, sugar, sugarcane, soybean oil, sunflower oil, palm oil, and camelina oil. The results show that the relationships between biofuel price and agricultural commodity prices are non-linear. The non-linear relationships suggest that the analysis of the relationship should be divided into two periods, where the two markets have a stronger bond during the second periods. Chiu et al. (2016) confirmed a bidirectional relationship between corn and ethanol price using the Granger causality test and impulse response function in the Vector Autoregressive (VAR) model and Vector Error Correction Model (VECM).

Most of the studies on this relationship focused on price transmissions. However, there are studies confirming the volatility spillover effect. Chang et al. (2018) showed that there is a strong volatility transmission between the bioethanol market and the agricultural markets. The study employed the diagonal BEKK (named after the authors of the model: Baba, Engle, Kraft, and Kroner) to investigate the spot prices and future prices of corn, sugarcane, and bioethanol. The results show that future prices of bioethanol and agricultural commodities have stronger co-volatility spillovers than their spot prices. These outcomes suggest that the future prices can be used for risk management purpose.

Saghaian et al. (2018) also confirmed the volatility spillover between the corn and ethanol markets. The authors showed that the relationship is bidirectional. However, the spillover effect from the ethanol to the corn market can only be observed using the daily data.

Enciso et al. (2016) employed the Aglink-Cosimo model to investigate the impact of removing biofuel-related policies on the biofuel and agricultural commodity prices and volatilities. According to their results, the biofuel policies can increase biofuel production, consumption, and prices, and reduce their volatilities. Similarly, Zhou and Babcock (2017) showed that corn prices could decrease 5% or 6% if the US biofuel mandates were to be reduced, using the competitive storage model.

The food versus fuel nexus also attracts many studies on the relationship between agricultural commodity and crude oil prices. In this literature, VAR models have been widely used to capture the impact of crude oil price changes on agricultural commodity prices (Lucotte 2016; Ma et al. 2016; Ahmadi et al. 2016). Some studies included the exchange rate and the global business cycle in the analysis of the relationship, as these variables can have an effect on both crude oil and agricultural commodity price (Adam et al. 2018; Wang et al. 2014; Vo et al. 2019). Adam et al. (2018) employed a vector autoregressive model (VAR) to analyze the crude oil price, the rice price, and the exchange rate. Their results show that crude oil price has a unidirectional relationship with rice price, however, the relationship only exists in the short term. The reason is that oil price changes can cause fluctuations in rice price, because crude oil is an important input factor in rice production.

The relationship between crude oil and agricultural commodity prices was impacted by the food price crisis during 2007–2008. Wang et al. (2014) used the SVAR approach to analyze the impact of different oil-related shocks on various agricultural commodity prices. SVAR approach has been widely used as well (Vo et al. 2018; Nguyen and Vo 2019). The study found that the impact of oil-specific demand shocks on the many agricultural commodity prices was only significant after the food price crisis. Han et al. (2015) also argued that the changes in crude oil price and agricultural commodity price relationship are most likely to be affected by the last financial crisis, of 2007–2008. Their analysis employed the multivariate normal mixture models to analyze the interactions of energy price and agricultural commodity prices. Their results show that industrial commodity prices are more likely to affect one another when the price and volatility transmission have a higher possibility to happen after the financial crisis. Using a VECM model, Chen and Saghaian (2015) showed that the relationship between oil, ethanol, and sugar has become stronger after 2008 in Brazil, where oil price tends to impact the other two variables, while sugar price tends to impact ethanol price. Most of the studies capturing the correlation between oil and agricultural markets interpret such correlations as the transmissions and spillovers from the former to the latter (Koirala et al. 2015; Zafeiriou et al. 2018; Allen et al. 2018).

The reason for the stronger bond between the two markets might be caused by renewable energy mandates. Several studies argued that the expansion of biofuel production has attracted land use, water, and other agricultural resources. Because these resources are limited, the expansion may lead to the reduction of food crop supplies (Büyüktahtakın and Cobuloglu 2015; De Martino Jannuzzi 1991; Fradj and Jayet 2016; Herrmann et al. 2017). To and Grafton (2015) provided evidence that a global increase in oil price and biofuel demand has contributed a significant role in agricultural commodity price fluctuations.

On the other hand, some studies also recognized the potential impact of agricultural shocks on the crude oil price. Ciaian's theoretical model (Ciaian 2011) suggests that agricultural shocks can affect crude oil price through different channels. According to this study, when food demand is inelastic, surges in agricultural supply resulting from positive productivity shocks accompanied may reduce the farmers' profit margin and therefore trigger a reduction in production activities and fuel demand. On the contrary, with an elastic food demand, an increase in agricultural productivity may result in an increase in fuel demand, due to the increase in food consumption. Besides the indirect input cost channel, the theoretical framework shows that an increase in biofuel production can lead to opposite effects on crude oil price. On the one hand, biofuel expansion will increase the energy supply and have a negative effect on crude oil price. On the other hand, agricultural production expansion due to an increase in demand for ethanol feedstock will increase fuel demand and crude oil price. In general, the direct biofuel channel has an ambiguous effect on crude oil price.

Su et al. (2019) showed that the bidirectional relationships between crude oil price and agricultural commodity prices are more likely to be found in the sub-sample periods using the sub-sample rolling estimation. Furthermore, the study also pointed out that agricultural commodities that are not feedstocks of biofuel production can also have bidirectional relationships with oil price.

The existing studies suggest the increasing roles of agricultural shocks in energy markets, specifically the ethanol and crude oil markets. It has been shown that agricultural shocks can be divided into supply and demand shocks, with each type of shock having potentially different impacts. However, the existing studies only employed agricultural commodity prices to investigate the relationship between agricultural and energy markets. Within the extent of our knowledge, our study is the first one to attempt to investigate the impact of agricultural shocks on oil price using agricultural demand and supply shocks. The study reveals that supply and demand shocks can have different impacts on oil price and thus, should be studied individually.

3. Methodology

In this paper, we used the SVAR model to estimate the relationship between agricultural markets and the crude oil market. It has been pointed out that agricultural commodity prices are endogenous to oil price, and vice versa (Zhang et al. 2010; Natanelov et al. 2011; Vacha et al. 2013; Avalos 2014; Su et al. 2019). Therefore, standard regression models cannot capture the bidirectional relationship between the two commodities. Even though VAR models can be used to treat the endogeneity problem, such models are said to have little power to establish a causal relationship between oil and agricultural commodity prices (Baumeister and Kilian 2014). Cooley and LeRoy (1985) pointed out that the estimations of VAR models are often based on ad-hoc assumptions, which may be arbitrary. Thus, we employed the following SVAR model, with exclusion restrictions based on the economic theories and empirical evidence:

$$Az_t = \alpha + \sum_i^p \omega_i z_{t-1} + \varepsilon_t. \tag{1}$$

In the first model, we have $z_t = (\Delta oilpro_t, \Delta aggre_t, \Delta oilpr_t, \Delta agripr_t)$, where $oilpro_t$ denotes the logs of world crude oil production, $aggre_t$ denotes the aggregate demand captured by the Kilian's index (Kilian 2018), $oilpr_t$ denotes the US real imported crude oil price, and $agripr_t$ represents the real agricultural commodity prices. ε_t represents the vector of mutually uncorrelated structural shocks in each equation of the system. Δ is the first order difference operator. We ran this model on the full sample period from January 1986 to May 2018.

We imposed matrix A so that its inverse had the following recursive structure:

$$A^{-1} = \begin{pmatrix} a_{11} & 0 & 0 & 0 \\ a_{21} & a_{22} & 0 & 0 \\ a_{31} & a_{32} & a_{33} & 0 \\ a_{41} & a_{42} & a_{43} & a_{44} \end{pmatrix}.$$

The reduced-form of Equation (1) becomes:

$$z_t = \beta + \sum_i^p \Omega_i z_{t-1} + \epsilon_t,$$

where $\epsilon_t = \begin{pmatrix} \epsilon_t^{\Delta oilpro} \\ \epsilon_t^{\Delta aggre} \\ \epsilon_t^{\Delta oilpr} \\ \epsilon_t^{\Delta agripr} \end{pmatrix} = \begin{pmatrix} a_{11} & 0 & 0 & 0 \\ a_{21} & a_{22} & 0 & 0 \\ a_{31} & a_{32} & a_{33} & 0 \\ a_{41} & a_{42} & a_{43} & a_{44} \end{pmatrix} \begin{pmatrix} \varepsilon_t^{\Delta oilpro} \\ \varepsilon_t^{\Delta aggre} \\ \varepsilon_t^{\Delta oilpr} \\ \varepsilon_t^{\Delta agripr} \end{pmatrix}.$$

We ran the SVAR model for the vector $z = \left(\Delta oilpro_t, \Delta aggre_t, \Delta oilpr_t, \Delta agripr_t, \Delta agripro_t \right)$ for the second model, where $agripro_t$ denotes the agricultural supplies of corn, sorghum, and barley. We ran the third model for the vector $z = (\Delta oilpr_t, \Delta cornethanol_t, \Delta cornpr_t, \Delta cornpro_t)$, where $cornethanol$ denotes the logs of corn use in ethanol, $cornpr$ denotes the corn price, and $cornpro$ represents the corn supply.

The orders of the variables in the vectors reflect the exclusion restrictions, which are widely agreed in the economic theories and empirical literature. Firstly, studies on the link between the oil market and the agricultural markets often agreed on the exogeneity of the former to the latter (Kilian 2009; Wang et al. 2014; Qiu et al. 2012; McPhail et al. 2012; Mcphail 2011; To et al. 2019). Therefore, oil-related variables have higher orders in the vector of endogenous variables. Within the oil market, oil supply is assumed to only respond to its own shock within the same period. This assumption is based on the fact that major oil producers often have a long-term plan for their production. Therefore, these oil producing countries do not respond to temporary fluctuations in demand shock. The global economic activities often respond to the disruptions of oil supply caused by political events from the Organization of Petroleum Exporting Countries (OPEC), while the global oil supply does not respond contemporarily to the aggregate demand shock. On the other hand, oil prices do not have a contemporaneous impact on the global industrial demand, while the aggregate demand can have an impact on oil demand, as reflected by Kilian (2009).

Within the agricultural market, agricultural demand shocks often have a stronger impact on agricultural commodity prices than agricultural supply shocks (Qiu et al. 2012). The reason is that the agricultural stocks and trade liberalization tend to lessen the impact of agricultural supply shocks on crop prices (Jha and Srinivasan 2001). Therefore, the agricultural prices and corn use in ethanol have a higher order of exogeneity than the agricultural supply variables. For the third model, the response of ethanol demand to shocks to the corn market is considered lagging because ethanol demand is more likely to be affected by the renewable energy mandates (Qiu et al. 2012; McPhail et al. 2012), which explains the exogeneity of corn use in ethanol to other corn demand shocks.

The fluctuations of the global aggregate demand, crude oil demand, and supply shocks, which are often the results of an increase in trade openness, changes in monetary and trade policies, contribute simultaneously and significantly to the fluctuation in demand for agricultural products and crude oil price. The SVAR helps us to disentangle the impact of the agricultural supply and demand shocks from the common factors by decomposing the error terms into mutually uncorrelated shocks.

4. Data and Tests

The main purpose of this paper is to investigate the impact of different agricultural shocks on the US crude oil price over the period from January 1986 to May 2018. In this paper, we used the imported crude oil price to capture the domestic oil price. The real monthly average imported crude oil price and world crude oil production were obtained from the Energy Information Administration (EIA) (https://www.eia.gov/). The nominal agricultural commodity prices, agricultural supplies, and corn use in ethanol were collected from the Feed Grains Database of Economic Research Service, USDA (https://www.ers.usda.gov/). The nominal agricultural commodity prices were deflated by the Consumer Price Index of the total all items for the United States, retrieved from the Federal Reserve Economic Data (FRED) (https://fred.stlouisfed.org). By using the real prices of agricultural commodities and crude oil, we effectively controlled for the simultaneous inflationary effects of monetary policies on both commodity prices. Therefore, we can disentangle the effects of the agricultural supply and demand shocks from the common factor of monetary policies. The changes in global demand for industrial commodities can be captured by the changes in demand for transport services, which are reflected in the variation in ocean freight rate (Kilian 2009). Therefore, we used an index developed by Kilian (Kilian 2018) as a proxy for the aggregate demand[1].

---

[1]   The data can be obtained from the following website: https://sites.google.com/site/lkilian2019/research/data-sets.

Regarding the decision of structural breaks and subsample periods, we recognize that there are other important economic and political events that might have a significant impact on crude oil and agricultural prices. For example, Baumeister and Kilian (2016) stated in their work that several supply and demand shocks during 2014 played a large role in the fluctuations of the oil price and other commodities. During this year, the production expansion of both OPEC and non-OPEC countries increased the global oil supply. Additionally, the price reduction of other commodities and the decline in oil stocking behaviors put downward pressure on the oil demand.

On the other hand, Chiu et al. (2016) recognized that the relationship between crude oil prices and agricultural prices has changed over time due to multiple structural shifts. In particular, the authors observed that the causal relationship from agricultural prices to oil prices was strengthened during 1998–1999 (after the Asian financial crisis) and 2008–2009 (during the Global financial crisis and Global food crisis). As a result, we recognize that these events are worthy of exploration for future research. However, we decided to focus on the impact of the Energy Policy Act of 2005 on the relationship between oil prices and the agricultural market in this paper.

For the first model, we divided the full sample into two subsamples, including the first period, from January 1986 to December 2005, and the second period, from January 2006 to May 2018. Barley, corn, and sorghum supply series were only available in quarterly data. For the second model, the marketing year of barley supply began on 1 June, and its four quarters included June–August, September–November, December–February, and March–May.

Therefore, the first period of barley supply series was Q3 1985 to Q3 2005 and the second period was from Q4 2005 to the Q4 2017 in the barley marketing year. Similarly, the marketing year of corn and sorghum supply began on 1 September, and its four quarters included September–November, December–February, March–May, and June–August. Thus, the first period of corn and sorghum supply was from Q2 1985 to the Q2 2005 and their second period was from Q3 2005 to Q3 2017 in the corn and sorghum marketing year. For the third model, the first period of corn use in ethanol was from Q1 1986 to Q2 2005 and its second period was from Q3 2005 to Q3 2017 in the corn marketing year.

The partition of the dataset was motivated by the implementation of the Energy Policy Act of 2005. Previous studies pointed out that agricultural and energy markets are more likely to interact with each other after the event (Su et al. 2019; Avalos 2014; Wang et al. 2014; Baumeister and Kilian 2014). Moreover, the shocks of the food crisis and the global financial crisis, which can trigger changes in the joint dynamics between the two markets, also happened during this period. Baumeister and Kilian (2014) argued that the increase in the mechanization of the agricultural production in major agricultural countries can also increase the strength of the relationship between the agricultural and fuel markets. Therefore, the causal relationship from the former to the latter, if any, is more likely to be found during this period, compared to the previous periods.

Table 1 shows the descriptive statistics of the commodity prices, the agricultural supplies, and corn use in ethanol. The commodity prices had higher means and standard deviations during the second period. For each period, corn supply was larger in mean and more volatile than the supplies of other agricultural commodities. Moreover, the mean and volatility of the corn supply increased, while those of the barley and sorghum supplies decreased during the second period. Similarly, there was also an expansion of alcohol supply for fuel use during the second period.

Table 1. Data Description.

January 1986–December 2005

Variable	Mean	SD	Max	Min	Skewness	Kurtosis
Oil supply	11.06	0.08	11.22	10.90	0.14	2.14
Kilian index	−0.98	41.72	125.00	−81.10	1.08	4.34
Oil price	34.85	10.32	75.68	14.45	1.30	5.70
Barley price	3.58	0.70	5.97	2.43	1.28	4.60
Corn price	3.59	0.91	6.69	2.09	0.67	3.26
Sorghum price	3.33	0.85	6.49	1.89	0.72	3.63
Barley supply	366.48	169.31	937.11	125.11	1.10	4.07
Corn supply	6924.41	2908.72	13,228.27	1720.75	0.22	2.06
Sorghum supply	484.69	350.66	1489.88	70.39	1.01	3.34
Biofuel demand	4.85	0.48	5.96	4.12	0.67	2.62

January 2006–May 2018

Variable	Mean	SD	Max	Min	Skewness	Kurtosis
Oil supply	11.25	0.04	11.32	11.19	0.40	1.72
Kilian index	3.23	79.92	188.00	−164.00	0.58	2.57
Oil price	81.73	27.55	147.58	28.39	0.05	2.02
Barley price	5.03	0.93	6.78	2.94	−0.19	2.36
Corn price	4.45	1.38	7.87	2.38	0.78	2.46
Sorghum price	4.28	1.32	7.12	2.10	0.63	2.25
Barley supply	199.79	61.10	321.26	98.99	0.46	2.11
Corn supply	8999.50	4061.65	16,908.16	2805.80	0.27	1.93
Sorghum supply	226.60	144.28	618.76	34.33	0.94	3.09
Biofuel demand	6.97	0.34	7.26	6.01	−1.54	4.19

In our structural VAR model, we decomposed the agricultural commodity price variance into agricultural supply shock and agricultural demand shocks in the second model. The third model further divided the corn demand shocks into corn use in ethanol shock and other corn demand shocks. For the oil market, we decomposed oil-related shocks into oil supply shock, aggregate demand shock, and other oil-specific demand shocks.

In this paper, we used the unit root tests based on the augmented Dickey and Fuller (ADF) (Dickey and Fuller 1979), Phillips and Perron (PP) (Phillips and Perron 1988), and Kwiatkowski–Phillips–Schmidt–Shin (KPSS) methods (Kwiatkowski et al. 1992). The null hypothesis of the ADF and PP tests is that the time series has a unit root, while the null hypothesis of the KPSS test is that the time series is stationary. For the ADF test in Table 2A, we cannot reject that 7 out of 10 series were non-stationary at 5% significance level. According to the PP test, there were 5 series that had a unit root. The KPSS statistics reject the hypothesis that nine series followed stationary processes. For the first order difference series, the three tests indicate stationarity at 1% significance level for all series, except for the KPSS statistics of the corn use in ethanol.

118 — Managerial Economics and Business Strategy

Table 2. (A) Unit root tests without structural break. (B) Unit root test with a structural break.

(A)

Variables	ADF		PP		KPSS	
	Original Series	First Order Difference	Original Series	First Order Difference	Original Series	First Order Difference
Oil production	−0.42	−6.75 ***	−1.07	−21.32 ***	0.14 *	0.03
Kilian index	−2.69 *	−7.03 ***	−3.02 **	−14.21 ***	0.26 ***	0.03
Oil price	−1.78	−9.7 ***	−2.18	−11.11 ***	0.21 **	0.07
Barley price	−2.24	−10.95 ***	−2.27	−20.08 ***	0.3 ***	0.05
Corn price	−2.94 **	−5.34 ***	−2.72 *	−12.57 ***	0.2 **	0.05
Sorghum price	−2.56	−8.12 ***	−2.94 **	−14.63 ***	0.18 **	0.04
Barley supply	−4.12 ***	−4.58 ***	−5.96 ***	−25.4 ***	0.35 ***	0.02
Corn supply	−1.97	−5.71 ***	−11.15 ***	−25.19 ***	0.22 ***	0.02
Sorghum supply	−3.19 ***	−4.94 ***	−5.94 ***	−24.57 ***	0.42 ***	0.02
Bio demand	−0.36	−4.43 ***	−0.19	−10.27 ***	0.37 ***	0.16 **

(B)

Variables	Model A1: Breaks in Intercept		Model A2: Breaks in Trend		Model A3: Breaks in Intercept and Trend	
	Original Series	First Order Difference	Original Series	First Order Difference	Original Series	First Order Difference
Oil production	−5.96 ***	−11.16 ***	−5.49 ***	−11.08 ***	−5.95 ***	−11.15 ***
Kilian index	−4.29	−11.51 ***	−3.6	−11.34 ***	−4.71	−11.69 ***
Oil price	−4.86 **	−10.05 ***	−4.1	−9.66 ***	−5.15 **	−10.03 ***
Barley price	−4.23	−11.11 ***	−3.03	−11.02 ***	−4.01	−11.13 ***
Corn price	−4.28	−12.92 ***	−3.29	−12.67 ***	−4.64	−13.06 ***
Sorghum price	−4.64 *	−9.04 ***	−3.83	−8.83 ***	−5.59 **	−9.22 ***
Barley supply	−3.77	−5.05 **	−3.18	−5.67 ***	−3.4	−5.62 ***
Corn supply	−2.36	−5.27 **	−2.68	−5.19 ***	−2.56	−5.34 **
Sorghum supply	−1.94	−5.93 ***	−6.78 ***	−5.54 ***	−4.22	−6.01 ***
Bio demand	−3.08	−6.01 ***	−2.06	−5.69 ***	−2.43	−6.12 ***

Notes: *, **, *** denote significance at the 10%, 5%, 1% level respectively.

The conventional unit root tests may fail to reject the unit root hypothesis when the alternative stationarity is true and the series contains structural breaks. Taking account of this possibility, many studies have come up with unit root tests with structural breaks. These tests are more likely to reject the null hypothesis of unit root compared to the traditional Dickey–Fuller unit root test (Zivot and Andrews 2002; Perron 1989). However, the limitation of the model using one structural break is that it may still fail to reject the null hypothesis if the series contains two structural breaks (Perron and Vogelsang 1992; Clemente et al. 1998; Lumsdaine and Papell 1997). Moreover, according to Lee and Strazicich (2003), the null hypothesis of these models assumes a unit root without breaks. Therefore, rejection of the null hypothesis does not necessarily mean that the series is trend-stationary with breaks. In contrast, the rejection of the null suggests that the series may contain a unit root with breaks.

In Table 2B, we employed the unit root test with the assumption that the series contained a structural break developed by Zivot and Andrews (2002). The test has three models with different assumptions. The first model assumes that the time series has a structural break in the intercept, the second model assumes a structural break in trend, while the third model tests the stationarity of the series under the assumption of both intercept and trend. The three models show that most of the time series is integrated with the order of one.

5. Empirical Results

5.1. Agricultural Commodity Price and Oil Price Shocks

In the literature of crude oil price and its relationship with agricultural commodity prices, several studies found it helpful to add oil supply and global economic activity as control variables (Kilian 2009; Wang et al. 2014). The reason for this is that oil price might be endogenous to oil supply and the global business cycle, while the global business cycle can affect both oil and agricultural commodity prices. Following previous studies, we first investigated the price relationship using the monthly data and the following model, during the period from 1986m1 to 2018m5:

$$z = \left(\Delta oilpro_t, \Delta aggre_t, \Delta oilpr_t, \Delta agripr_t\right).$$

We considered the Akaike information criterion (AIC) to choose the optimal number of lags. The information criterion suggests two lags for the period 1986m1 to 2005m12 and one lag for the period 2006m1 to 2018m5. Figure 1A,B plots the accumulative response of agricultural commodity prices to the oil-specific demand shocks and the responses of oil price to agricultural commodity price shocks. During the first period, we can see that the agricultural commodity prices did not respond significantly to oil-specific demand shock. The only exception is the marginally significant response of corn price in the second month. However, the effect disappears shortly after that.

The situation changed sharply during the second period. The responses of corn price and sorghum price were positive and statistically significant, while the response of barley price was still insignificant. The response of corn price was significant in a very short period of time, while the effect on sorghum price lasted for 8 months.

Regarding the impact of agricultural shocks on oil price, there was no significant response during the first period. During the second period, the impact of barley-related shocks was still insignificant. On the other hand, corn-related shocks inflicted a significant and lasting impact on oil price (up to 8 months), while the effect of sorghum-related shocks was only marginally significant in the first month.

In general, the relationship between crude oil and agricultural commodity prices depends on the time period and the commodities under investigation. The links between the two markets appear to have been stronger during the second period. There are many studies attributing the difference between the two periods to the expansion of biofuel production. According to our results, corn and sorghum appear to have a stronger connection with crude oil price, compared to barley. In the US, corn and sorghum are used as feedstocks for biofuel production. Thus, these commodity prices are more likely to react to oil price fluctuations, as well as to trigger changes in the oil market.

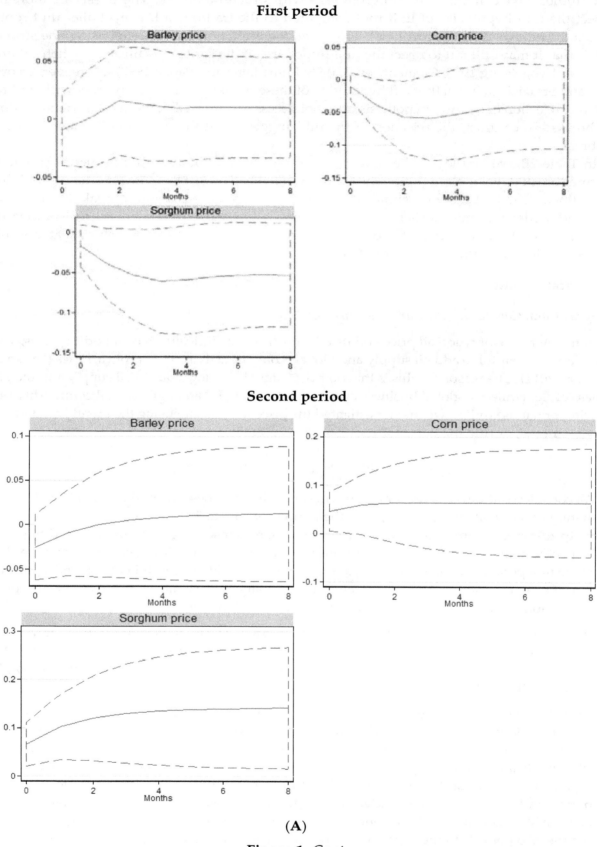

(A)

Figure 1. *Cont.*

First period

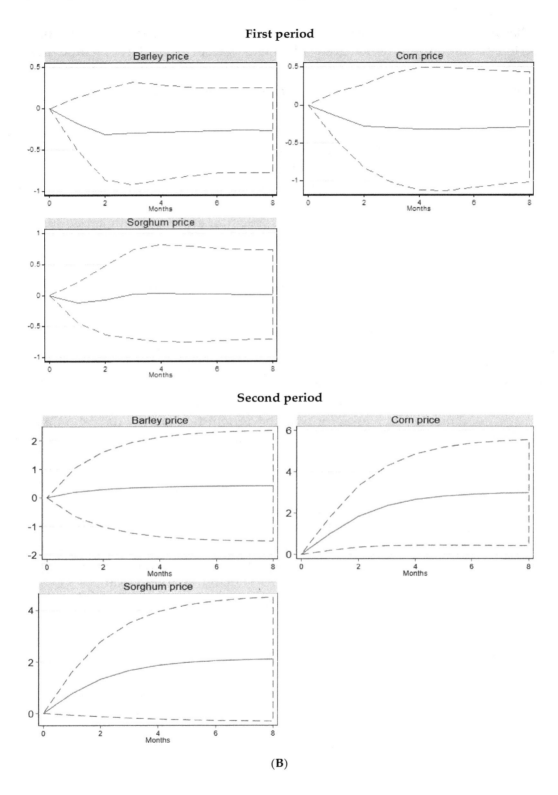

(B)

Figure 1. (A) Response of agricultural commodity prices to oil-specific demand shocks; **(B)** response of oil price to agricultural related-shocks. Notes: Red lines represent cumulative orthogonalized impulse–response functions while blue lines represent 95% confidence intervals.

The results suggest that the corn market can have an influence on crude oil price. According to the descriptive statistics, corn has far a larger supply than other agricultural commodities, which suggests that corn production may consume more energy than other agricultural sectors. In the US, corn is the main source of feedstock for ethanol production. Since 2006, the Energy Act 2005 by the US

Government has increased ethanol consumption exponentially. The expansion of corn production due to an increase in ethanol consumption might explain why corn price can have an influence on oil price.

5.2. *The Responses of Agricultural Commodity Prices to Supply and Demand Shocks*

In the second model, our main objective was to differentiate the effects of agricultural shocks on oil price changes. According to the previous section, it has been shown that shocks in the agricultural markets can have a significant impact on crude oil price. However, agricultural shocks can be divided into supply and demand-related shocks. Therefore, using only agricultural commodity prices does not allow us to identify which agricultural shocks are responsible for crude oil responses. Thus, it is helpful to include agricultural supplies in the model specification, along with agricultural commodity prices. Similar practices can be found in Qiu et al. (Qiu et al. 2012). We used the following model:

$$z = \left(\Delta oilpro_t, \ \Delta aggre_t, \ \Delta oilpr_t, \ \Delta agripr_t, \ \Delta agripro_t\right).$$

In this model, we used the dummy variables as the exogenous variables of the SVAR system to control for the seasonality in agricultural supplies. The inclusion of the exogenous variables helped to increase the stability of the models, which tend to be unstable due to the inclusion of the agricultural supply data[2]. In Qui et al. (Qiu et al. 2012), the authors used the cubic spline interpolation to convert the quarterly agricultural supplies into monthly supplies. The disadvantage of this technique is that there should be a good theoretical reason for why the agricultural supply data should behave like a cubic function. In this paper, we decided to use the quarterly data of the agricultural supplies and the quarterly average of the other monthly variables. The consideration of the Akaike information criterion suggests four lags in both periods.

In prior to analyze the effects of agricultural shocks on oil price, we first plotted the response of agricultural commodity prices to the supply and demand shocks in Figure 2A–C. We can see that the responses of corn and sorghum price to real economic activity shocks are positive but not significant, while the impact of aggregate demand on barley price is marginally significant.

The shocks to barley, corn, and sorghum supplies did not have a significant impact on their own prices. In contrast, agricultural-specific demand shocks were the main factors contributing to the agricultural commodity price fluctuations. It can be seen that the responses of barley, sorghum, and corn price to their own specific demand shocks were positive and significant for eight quarters. The results confirm the hypothesis that the supply shock has a lesser impact on agricultural commodity prices than the demand shocks. The reason for this might be buffer stocking behaviors and trade liberalization. In times of crisis, the lack of supply from one region can be neutralized by the abundant supplies from other regions, thanks to free trade.

---

[2]   The results of the stability tests are available upon request.

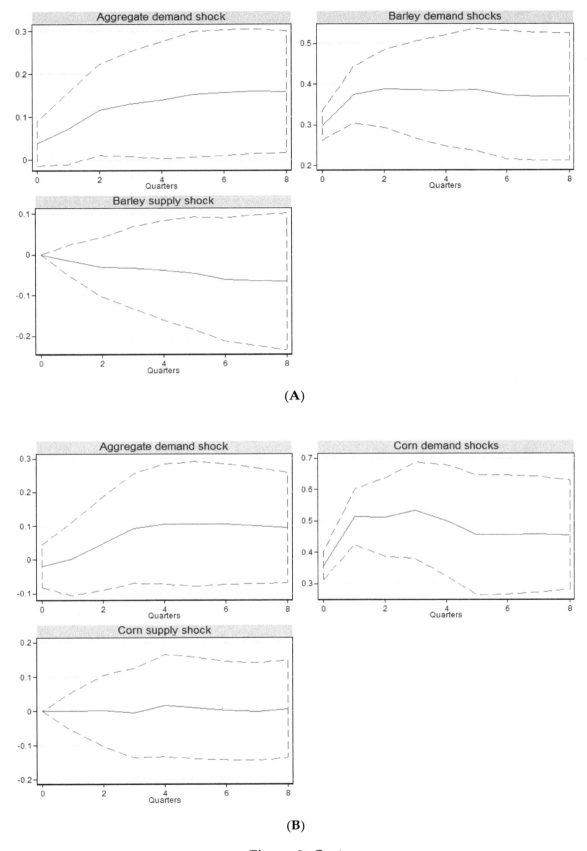

Figure 2. *Cont.*

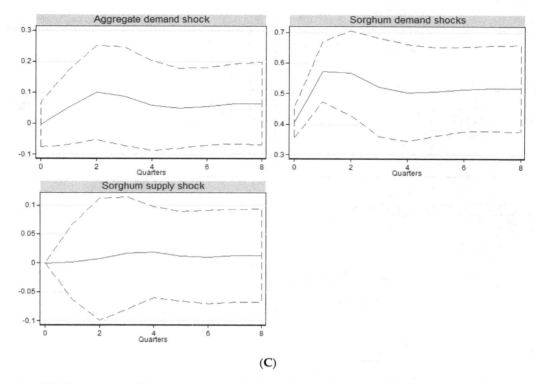

(C)

Figure 2. (**A**) Response of barley price to barley-related shocks. (**B**) Response of corn price to corn-related shocks. (**C**) Response of sorghum price to sorghum-related shocks. Notes: Red lines represent cumulative orthogonalized impulse–response functions while blue lines represent 95% confidence intervals.

5.3. The Responses of Oil Price to Agricultural Supply and Demand Shocks

In the previous section, we analyzed the impacts of agricultural shocks on agricultural commodity prices. In this section, we will investigate the impact of these shocks on crude oil price. Figure 3A–C shows the responses of crude oil price to different agricultural shocks. During the first period, we can see that the oil price did not respond significantly to agricultural shocks. The results are consistent with the unresponsiveness of oil price to agricultural commodity price shocks during the first period in Figure 1B.

During the second period, Figure 3A shows that the response of oil price to barley demand shocks was still insignificant. However, the response of oil price to barley supply shock was significantly negative. The reason for this might be that a positive productivity shock in the barley market reduced the demand for crude oil (Ciaian and Kancs 2011).

For the corn and sorghum case, Figure 3B,C shows that corn and sorghum supply shocks did not have a significant impact on crude oil price during the second period, even though we can see significant responses of oil price to corn and sorghum price shocks in Figure 1B. This can be explained by the insignificant impact of agricultural supply shocks on agricultural commodity prices observed in Figure 2A–C.

Figure 3B,C shows that the responses of crude oil price to corn and sorghum demand shocks were significantly positive during the second period. The effects of corn and sorghum demand shocks lasted for the first three quarters. After that, the impact of the sorghum demand disappeared, while the response of oil price to corn demand shocks became marginally significant from quarter five to eight.

In general, we observed that the significant response of oil price to corn and sorghum price shocks observed in Figure 1B was due to the impact of agricultural demand shocks on oil price, while the agricultural supply shocks played an insignificant role. The reason for this is the insignificant impact of agricultural supplies on their own prices observed in Figure 2B,C. Additionally, we observed that the responses of oil price to barley, corn, and sorghum supply and demand shocks were different.

For the barley case, the agricultural commodity is indirectly used in biofuel production. Therefore, the crop can only impact oil price through the indirect input cost channel, which is triggered by the productivity shocks. For the corn and sorghum cases, these two commodities are directly used in biofuel production. Thus, they are more likely to impact oil price through the direct biofuel channel, which is triggered by the increase in demand for biofuel feedstocks.

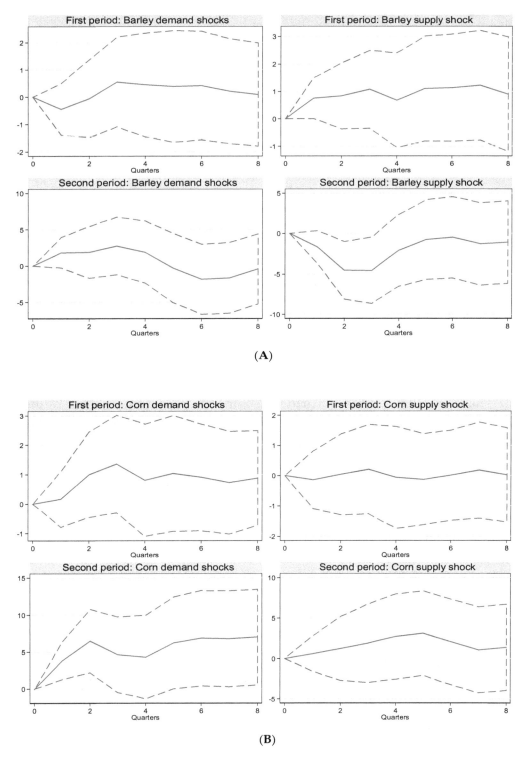

Figure 3. *Cont.*

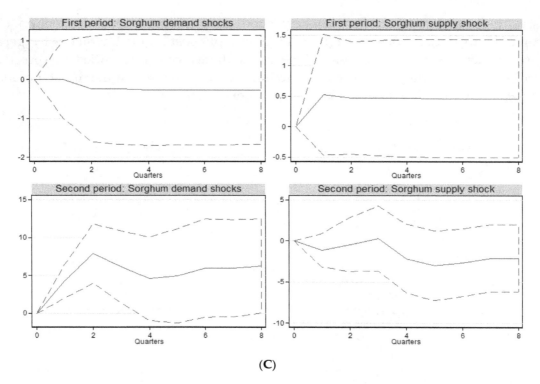

(C)

Figure 3. (**A**) Response of oil price to barley supply and demand shocks. (**B**) Response of oil price to corn supply and demand shocks. (**C**) Response of oil price to sorghum supply and demand shocks. Notes: Red lines represent cumulative orthogonalized impulse–response functions while blue lines represent 95% confidence intervals.

After the Energy Act 2005 by the US Government, the expansion in ethanol production has led to an increase in corn demand, besides the demand from the animal feed industry and human consumption. Therefore, we decided to further decompose corn demand shocks into corn use in ethanol and other corn demand shocks, using the following model, in the period 1986Q1 to 2005Q3 and period 2005Q4 to 2017Q3 (corn marketing year):

$$z = (\Delta oilpr_t, \ \Delta cornethanol_t, \ \Delta cornpr_t, \ \Delta cornpro_t).$$

The consideration of the Akaike information criterion suggests four lags for this model. Figure 4A,B shows the response of corn use in ethanol to oil price changes and the response of crude oil price to corn-related shocks after decomposing corn demand shocks into corn use in ethanol and other corn demand shocks. According to Figure 4A, oil price did not have a significant impact on corn use in ethanol during the first period. However, the response of corn use in ethanol to oil price variance became significant during the second period. The results suggest that the increase in oil price has created an incentive for more ethanol consumption, which ultimately transfers into the increase in the quantity of corn use in ethanol. On the other hand, such phenomena can only be observed during the second period, when the biofuel mandate became effectively implemented. The timing suggests that the biofuel mandate was successful in inducing consumers to increase biofuel consumption when oil prices increased.

Table 3 shows that the null hypothesis that crude oil price does not Granger-causes corn use in ethanol cannot be rejected during the first period. However, the null is rejected at 5% during the second period. The results suggest that during this period, surges in oil price tended to make biofuel a more viable alternative to fossil fuel, which increased corn demand for ethanol production.

Table 3. Granger causality.

Direction of Causality	1986m1–2005m12	2006m1–2018m5
Oil price → Barley price	1.32	0.90
Barley price → Oil price	1.45	0.20
Oil price → Corn price	4.56	0.01
Corn price → Oil price	1.42	5.97 **
Oil price → Sorghum price	2.00	1.12
Sorghum price → Oil price	0.59	3.27 *
Corn demand → Oil price	3.22	11.8 **
Corn supply → Oil price	1.05	1.04
Oil price → Corn use in ethanol	1.23	11.29 **
Corn use in ethanol → Oil price	6.16	6.52

Notes: *, ** denote significance at the 10%, 5% level respectively.

Regarding the responses of crude oil price, Figure 4B shows that agricultural shocks did not have a significant impact on crude oil price during the first period. The situation changed during the second period, when corn use in ethanol shock could trigger a marginally significant response of oil price. The impacts of other corn demand shocks and corn supply shock were insignificant in the second quarter. In Table 3, corn use in ethanol, other corn demand, and corn supply do not Granger-cause crude oil price during the second period.

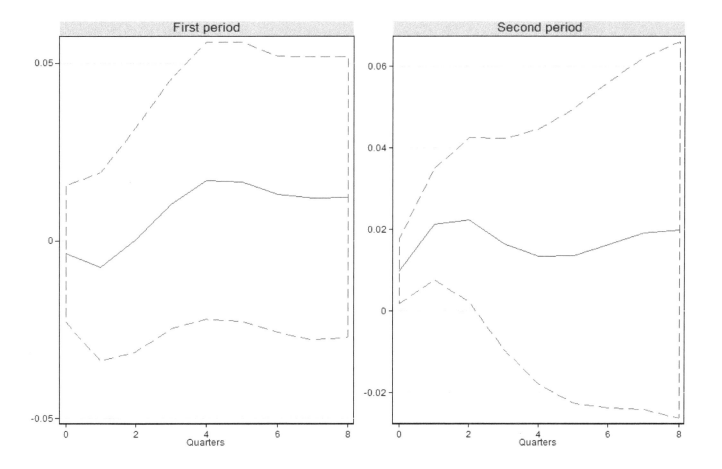

(A)

Figure 4. *Cont.*

First period

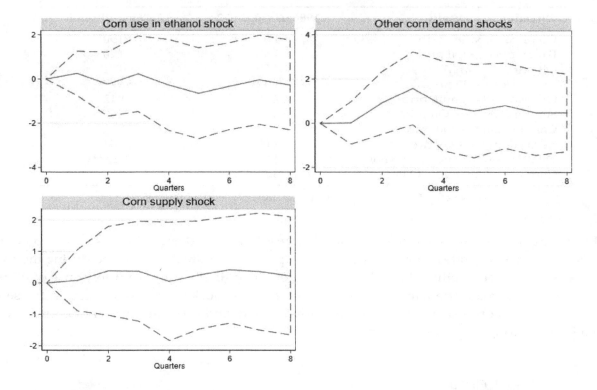

Second period

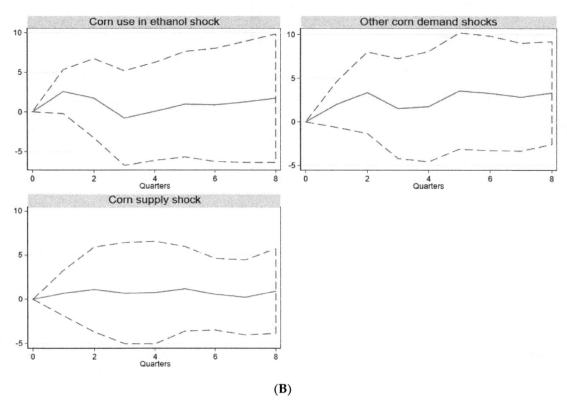

(B)

Figure 4. (**A**) Response of corn use in ethanol to oil price shocks. (**B**) Response of oil price to corn-related shocks. Notes: Red lines represent cumulative orthogonalized impulse–response functions while blue lines represent 95% confidence intervals.

5.4. The Contribution of Agricultural Shocks to Oil Price Changes

Table 4 quantifies the contribution of oil and corn-related shocks on crude oil price changes, using the method of forecasting error variance decomposition. We can see that other oil-specific demand shocks contributed the most, while the contribution of corn-related shocks was negligible during the first period. During the second period, even though other oil-specific demand shocks still contributed the most to oil price changes, its contribution reduced significantly. In contrast, the contribution of corn demand shocks increased almost fourfold, which contributed 18% to oil price variance and its contribution is comparable to the contribution of the aggregate demand during the second period. In general, the results suggest that corn demand shocks played a larger role in explaining oil price fluctuations, compared to the corn supply shock.

Table 5 shows the contribution of corn-related shocks after decomposing corn demand shocks into corn use in ethanol and other shocks. We can see that corn supply shock was the least important one among corn-related shocks during both periods. In the first period, we can see that other corn demand shocks contributed the most among corn-related shocks. However, during the second period, corn use in ethanol explained almost 10% of oil price changes and became the most important source of shocks among corn-related shocks. The results suggest that the transmission from the corn market to crude oil price is more likely to be explained by the direct biofuel channel than the indirect input cost channel during the second period.

5.5. The Impact of Corn Use in Ethanol on Corn Price and Corn Supply

Regarding the food versus fuel literature, various studies have found evidence that the expansion of biofuel may have a negative impact on food security and the welfare of the poor. In this study, Figure 5 shows the responses of corn price and corn supply to changes in corn use in ethanol.

During the first period, the response of corn supply to positive changes in corn use in ethanol was insignificant, while the response of corn price was significantly negative. The negative relationship between corn use in ethanol and corn price is more likely to reflect that corn use in ethanol might react to the future expectation of corn price fluctuation. In particular, the future expectation of a corn price increase may reduce the demand for corn use in ethanol.

During the second period, we can see that the response of corn price to positive shock on corn use in ethanol shock was insignificant. On the other hand, Figure 5 shows that increase in corn use in ethanol can trigger a positive response of corn supply. In general, the results show that corn use in ethanol had a limited impact on corn price during the second period. The reason for this might be that the increase in corn demand for ethanol triggered the expansion of corn production, which neutralized the pressure on corn price.

Table 4. Percentage contribution to oil price variation (before the decomposition of corn demand).

Quarters	First Period					Second Period				
	Oil Supply Shock	Aggregate Demand Shock	Other Oil-Demand Shocks	Corn Demand Shocks	Corn Supply Shock	Oil Supply Shock	Aggregate Demand Shock	Other Oil-Demand Shocks	Corn Demand Shocks	Corn Supply Shock
2	0.032	0.012	0.954	0.001	0.001	0.068	0.272	0.518	0.139	0.003
3	0.030	0.033	0.902	0.033	0.002	0.116	0.224	0.484	0.170	0.006
4	0.030	0.080	0.850	0.036	0.003	0.184	0.200	0.435	0.173	0.008
5	0.030	0.080	0.836	0.048	0.006	0.199	0.196	0.424	0.169	0.013
6	0.030	0.094	0.821	0.049	0.006	0.194	0.190	0.414	0.189	0.013
7	0.032	0.101	0.811	0.049	0.007	0.204	0.185	0.403	0.186	0.020
8	0.034	0.101	0.807	0.050	0.008	0.217	0.181	0.394	0.182	0.026

Table 5. Percentage contribution to oil price variation (after the decomposition of corn demand).

Quarters	First Period				Second Period			
	Oil-Related Shocks	Corn Use in Ethanol Shock	Other Corn Demand Shocks	Corn Supply Shock	Oil-Related Shocks	Corn Use in Ethanol Shock	Other Corn Demand Shocks	Corn Supply Shock
2	0.996	0.003	0.000	0.000	0.917	0.049	0.030	0.004
3	0.943	0.015	0.038	0.005	0.900	0.053	0.042	0.005
4	0.921	0.022	0.053	0.004	0.846	0.089	0.060	0.005
5	0.884	0.032	0.076	0.008	0.846	0.091	0.058	0.005
6	0.877	0.037	0.077	0.010	0.824	0.093	0.077	0.006
7	0.872	0.040	0.077	0.011	0.823	0.092	0.076	0.008
8	0.866	0.043	0.081	0.011	0.822	0.092	0.077	0.009

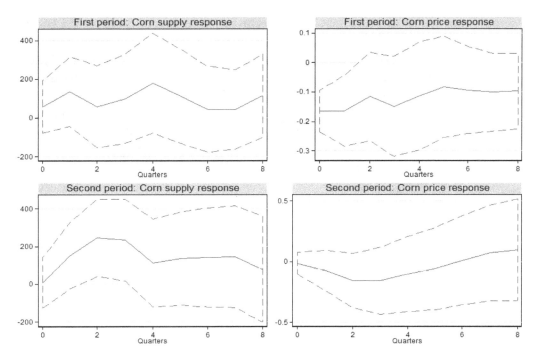

Figure 5. Response of corn supply and corn price to corn use in ethanol shocks. Notes: Red lines represent cumulative orthogonalized impulse–response functions while blue lines represent 95% confidence intervals.

5.6. Discussions

According to our results, there is a causality running from corn and sorghum prices to oil price and vice versa. The outcomes support the bidirectional relationship between agricultural commodities employed in biofuel production and crude oil price, as suggested by Su et al. (2019). On the other hand, our paper cannot find any correlation between barley and crude oil price, which supports the neutrality of agricultural commodity price to crude oil price changes (Nazlioglu and Soytas 2011, 2012; Ma et al. 2016; Fowowe 2016).

This study found evidence of causality running from the agricultural market to oil prices, which cannot be observed in some previous studies. A possible explanation is that the expansion of biofuel and the agricultural market has not been sufficiently significant to be observable during the sample periods in previous literature. As oil is a major market that is the fundamental driver of almost every sector in the economy, the biofuel and agricultural markets need to develop to a certain size to exert a significant impact on oil prices. On the other hand, the neutral relationship between barley price and oil price could be because barley is not directly related to biofuel production.

However, the story turns out a little different when the agricultural commodity price shocks are separated into supply and demand shocks. For the corn and sorghum case, we observed that agricultural demand shocks are mainly responsible for the impacts of the agricultural markets on the oil market. The outcomes suggest that the increases in agricultural demand have a positive impact on fuel demand. The reason for this might be the indirect input channel, as suggested by Ciaian and Kancs (2011). The input channel suggests that the agricultural markets have become more dependent on the fuel market, because crude oil price can have an impact on fertilizer and transportation costs. Another reason might be the direct biofuel channel, where the increase in biofuel production may add to the agricultural demand, which in return strengthens the increase in fuel demand and oil price (Ciaian 2011; Su et al. 2019).

For the barley case, even though the barley price was not a Granger cause for oil price, we observed that the response of oil price to barley supply shock was significant during the second period. The results support the hypothesis that when barley demand is inelastic, the productivity shock in the barley market may create an oversupply situation, which reduces the agricultural demand and therefore fuel demand (Ciaian 2011).

In general, our results confirm that both supply and demand shocks in the agricultural markets can lead to fluctuation in the crude oil market. We also confirmed that crude oil price can have a great impact on corn use in ethanol. The results support the hypothesis that the ethanol market is dependent on crude oil price (Chen and Saghaian 2015). On the other hand, corn use in ethanol can also cause crude oil prices in the second period. This outcome is in accordance with the direct biofuel channel that ethanol production expansion can increase fuel demand in the corn sector. Regarding the biofuel channel, Ciaian and Kancs (2011) argued that bio-ethanol production can impact crude oil price in two opposite directions. Firstly, an increase in corn demand due to biofuel production may increase the supply for corn. The increase in agricultural production due to an increase in corn demand may lead to the increase in oil demand. As result, an increase in corn demand due to bioethanol expansion will eventually lead to an increase in oil price, because of the rise in fuel demand. Secondly, biofuel production increases the total energy supply and, therefore, reduces oil price. Our empirical results show that an increase in corn use in ethanol can have a positive impact on both corn supply and oil price. Therefore, our study supports the hypothesis that bioethanol expansion may increase the dependency of the economy on fossil fuels.

Regarding the food versus fuel literature, our results show that an increase in corn use in ethanol cannot impact corn price, which contrasts with previous literature (Hao et al. 2017; Apergis et al. 2017; Chiu et al. 2016). On the other hand, we observed that an increase in corn use in ethanol can increase corn supply. This outcome partly explains why corn use in ethanol cannot impact corn price. Our results support the hypothesis that the expansion of biofuel production has greatly attracted farming resources to corn production (Büyüktahtakın and Cobuloglu 2015; De Martino Jannuzzi 1991; Fradj and Jayet 2016; Herrmann et al. 2017).

It was shown in the preliminary analysis that corn supply has increased significantly, while the other agricultural commodity supplies decreased dramatically during the second period. The expansion of corn and the shrinking of other agricultural commodity supplies happened during the same period as the expansion of biofuel production. These outcomes suggest that the expansion of biofuel production in recent years has caused the land use management to be shifted against the production of food crops. The increase in biofuel demand led to the expansion of certain agricultural commodities which are feedstocks of biofuel production. As agricultural resources are limited, the expansion of these crops may lead to the reduction of farming areas and other agricultural resources invested in other agricultural commodity productions, which creates supply disruptions and, finally, increases of several agricultural commodity prices. However, there should be more research in this direction before we can reach any conclusion. Future research should focus on the impact of corn production expansion on the supplies of non-biofuel agricultural commodities and their prices to validate the hypothesis.

In general, we observed that the effects of agricultural shocks only happened during the second period. However, the energy act is unlikely to be fully responsible for causing the agricultural shocks, as other major economic events happened in the same period, such as the global financial crisis, the food crisis, or even climate change. Therefore, a future study should investigate other sub-periods to identify the timeline of those shocks.

On the other hand, as biofuel enhancement continues in the future, it is likely to attract many real economic resources, which may have many drawbacks. Firstly, even though the initial objective of biofuel is to increase the energy supply and replace fossil fuel, the current farming machinery is still dependent on oil. Thus, to make biofuel more sustainable, future machinery needs to be more compatible with the use of biofuel. Secondly, growing more energy crops means that more non-arable land will be turn into arable land, which is costly to the environment. Lastly, as the profits of biofuel production increase, farmers will have more incentive to substitute food crops with energy crops, which will have negative effects on food security. These sources of drawbacks need to be dealt with to improve the long-term effectiveness of biofuel enhancement.

6. Concluding Remarks

This study investigated the impact of agricultural shocks in the period from 1986m1 to 2018m5 using the SVAR model. Our sample data was divided into two subsamples: 1986m1–2005m12 and 2006m1–2018m5. The paper found that agricultural shocks had an effect on oil price during the second period. The findings are consistent with the theoretical model that agricultural shocks can influence crude oil price through the indirect cost-push effect and direct biofuel channel. Furthermore, we decomposed the agricultural commodity price shocks into agricultural supply and demand shocks. The demand shocks were later separated into corn use in ethanol and other corn demand shocks. The outcomes from the impulse response function suggest that different agricultural shocks can have different effects on oil price. Firstly, positive agricultural supply shocks can have a negative impact on oil price due to the reduction in fuel demand. Secondly, agricultural demand shocks can have a positive effect on oil price, especially corn use in ethanol.

In particular, we could not find any significant response of the crude oil price to the agricultural shocks during the first period. However, the situation changed sharply during the second period, when agricultural shocks triggered a significant response in oil price. On the other hand, not every agricultural shock can have a significant impact on oil price. While oil price does not respond significantly to the shocks to the corn and sorghum supplies, the response of crude oil price to barley supply shock was significant during the second period. On the other hand, corn and sorghum demand shocks triggered a significant response in oil price in the second period.

We used the variance decomposition to quantify the contribution of agricultural demand shocks on oil price variations. The outcomes suggest that corn use in ethanol played an important role in the impact of corn demand shocks on oil price during the second period. The results support the direct biofuel channel, which suggests that the expansion of bio-energy production has made oil price vulnerable to corn demand shocks.

Overall, the paper's findings suggest that the links between agricultural market and oil prices have been strengthened since the issue of the Energy Policy Act of 2005. During this period, Table 6 shows that oil prices can influence agricultural prices, such as corn and sorghum prices, and increase the demand for corn use in ethanol. Oil prices also respond to shocks on agricultural supply, agricultural demand, and corn use in ethanol. In particular, the productivity shocks on barley supply can have a negative effect on oil prices. In corn and sorghum cases, agricultural demand shocks can have a positive impact on oil price. Moreover, corn use in ethanol plays an important role in the system, as the expansion of corn use in ethanol incentivizes growing more corn and increases the demand for oil in the agricultural sector. These findings are interesting because they show that biofuel expansion and an increase in size of the agricultural sector have become sufficiently significant to influence oil prices, which are the fundamental drivers for all sectors of the economy.

Table 6. Summary of findings.

Explanatory Variables	Dependent Variables				
	Oil Price	Agricultural Prices	Agricultural Supplies	Agricultural Demand	Corn Use in Ethanol
Oil price		+			+
Agricultural prices	+				
Agricultural supplies	−				
Agricultural demand	+				
Corn use in ethanol	+		+		

The policymakers in the agricultural and energy sectors can benefit from the findings of this paper. Firstly, the original purpose of the increase in bio-ethanol production is to reduce the dependency of the economy on fossil fuel. However, this strategy may have backfired because the increase in corn production due to the expansion of corn use in ethanol has led to a rise in fuel demand. Secondly, our results indicate that farmers have reacted to the rise in corn demand and increased the corn supply. Their decisions can affect the investment in growing other agricultural commodities, because agricultural resources such as land and water are limited. It will be interesting to study whether the increasing corn supply due to the expansion of corn use in ethanol can have an impact on the supplies and prices of other important agricultural commodities.

Author Contributions: Conceptualization, T.N.V.; methodology, D.H.V.; software, C.M.H.; formal analysis, T.N.V.; investigation, L.T.-H.V.; resources, C.M.H.; data curation, T.N.V., C.M.H. and L.T.-H.V.; writing—original draft preparation, T.N.V. and L.T.-H.V.; writing—review and editing, D.H.V.

Acknowledgments: We are grateful to the three anonymous referees for their constructive comments. We also thank the participants at the 3rd Vietnam's Business and Economics Research Conference VBER2019 (Ho Chi Minh City Open University, Vietnam, 18–20 July 2019) for their helpful suggestions. The authors wish to acknowledge financial supports from Ho Chi Minh City Open University. The authors are solely responsible for any remaining errors or shortcomings.

References

Adam, Pasrun, La Ode Saidi, La Tondi, La Ode, and Arsad Sani. 2018. The Causal Relationship between Crude Oil Price, Exchange Rate and Rice Price. *International Journal of Energy Economics and Policy* 8: 90–94.

Ahmadi, Maryam, Niaz Bashiri Behmiri, and Matteo Manera. 2016. How Is Volatility in Commodity Markets Linked to Oil Price Shocks? *Energy Economics* 59: 11–23. [CrossRef]

Allen, David E., Chialin Chang, Michael McAleer, and Abhay K Singh. 2018. A Cointegration Analysis of Agricultural, Energy and Bio-Fuel Spot, and Futures Prices. *Applied Economics* 50: 804–23. [CrossRef]

Apergis, Nicholas, Sofia Eleftheriou, and Dimitrios Voliotis. 2017. Asymmetric Spillover Effects between Agricultural Commodity Prices and Biofuel Energy Prices. *International Journal of Energy Economics and Policy* 7: 166–77.

Avalos, Fernando. 2014. Do Oil Prices Drive Food Prices? The Tale of a Structural Break. *Journal of International Money and Finance* 42: 253–71. [CrossRef]

Baumeister, Christiane, and Lutz Kilian. 2014. Do Oil Price Increases Cause Higher Food Prices? *Economic Policy* 29: 691–747. [CrossRef]

Baumeister, Christiane, and Lutz Kilian. 2016. Understanding the Decline in the Price of Oil since June 2014. *Journal of the Association of Environmental and Resource Economists* 3: 131–58. [CrossRef]

Bayramoğlu, Arzu Tay, Murat Çetin, and Gökhan Karabulut. 2016. The Impact of Biofuels Demand on Agricultural Commodity Prices: Evidence from US Corn Marketi&ii. *Journal of Economics* 4: 189–206.

Bentivoglio, Deborah, Adele Finco, and Mirian Bacchi. 2016. Interdependencies between Biofuel, Fuel and Food Prices: The Case of the Brazilian Ethanol Market. *Energies* 9: 464. [CrossRef]

Büyüktahtakın, Esra, and Halil I Cobuloglu. 2015. Food vs. Biofuel: An Optimization Approach to the Spatio-Temporal Analysis of Land-Use Competition and Environmental Impacts. *Applied Energy* 140: 418–34. [CrossRef]

Chang, Chia-lin, Michael Mcaleer, and Yu-ann Wang. 2018. Modelling Volatility Spillovers for Bio-Ethanol, Sugarcane and Corn Spot and Futures Prices. *Renewable and Sustainable Energy Reviews* 81: 1002–18. [CrossRef]

Chen, Bo, and Sayed Saghaian. 2015. The Relationship among Ethanol, Sugar and Oil Prices in Brazil: Cointegration Analysis with Structural Breaks. Paper presented at the 2015 Annual Meeting, Atlanta, GA, USA, January 31–February 3.

Chiu, Fan Ping, Chia Sheng Hsu, Alan Ho, and Chi Chung Chen. 2016. Modeling the Price Relationships between Crude Oil, Energy Crops and Biofuels. *Energy* 109: 845–57. [CrossRef]

Ciaian, Pavel. 2011. Food, Energy and Environment: Is Bioenergy the Missing Link? *Food Policy* 36: 571–80. [CrossRef]

Ciaian, Pavel, and d'Artis Kancs. 2011. Interdependencies in the Energy-Bioenergy-Food Price Systems: A Cointegration Analysis. *Resource and Energy Economics* 33: 326–48. [CrossRef]

Clemente, Jesus, Antonio Montañés, and Marcelo Reyes. 1998. Testing for a Unit Root in Variables with a Double Change in the Mean. *Economics Letters* 59: 175–82. [CrossRef]

Cooley, Thomas F., and Stephen F. LeRoy. 1985. Atheoretical Macroeconometrics: A Critique. *Journal of Monetary Economics* 16: 283–308. [CrossRef]

De Gorter, Harry, Dusan Drabik, and David R. Just. 2013. Biofuel Policies and Food Grain Commodity Prices 2006–2012: All Boom and No Bust? *AgBioForum* 16: 1–13.

De Martino Jannuzzi, Gilberto. 1991. Competition between Energy and Agricultural Production: A Discussion of a Country's Best Strategies. *Energy Economics* 13: 199–202. [CrossRef]

Dickey, David A., and Wayne A. Fuller. 1979. Distribution of the Estimators for Autoregressive Time Series with a Unit Root. *Journal of the American Statistical Association* 74: 427–31.

Dutta, Anupam. 2018. Cointegration and Nonlinear Causality among Ethanol-related Prices: Evidence from Brazil. *GCB Bioenergy* 10: 335–42. [CrossRef]

Dutta, Anupam, Juha Junttila, and Gazi Salah. 2018. Does Corn Market Uncertainty Impact the US Ethanol Prices? *GCB Bioenergy* 10: 683–93. [CrossRef]

Enciso, Sergio René Araujo, Thomas Fellmann, Ignacio Pérez Dominguez, and Fabien Santini. 2016. Abolishing Biofuel Policies: Possible Impacts on Agricultural Price Levels, Price Variability and Global Food Security. *Food Policy* 61: 9–26. [CrossRef]

Fowowe, Babajide. 2016. Do Oil Prices Drive Agricultural Commodity Prices? Evidence from South Africa. *Energy* 104: 149–57. [CrossRef]

Fradj, N. Ben, and P. A. Jayet. 2016. Land Use Policy Competition between Food, Feed, and (Bio) Fuel: A Supply-Side Model Based Assessment at the European Scale. *Land Use Policy* 52: 195–205. [CrossRef]

Han, Liyan, Yimin Zhou, and Libo Yin. 2015. Exogenous Impacts on the Links between Energy and Agricultural Commodity Markets. *Energy Economics* 49: 350–58. [CrossRef]

Hao, Na, Peter Pedroni, Gregory Colson, and Michael Wetzstein. 2017. The Linkage between the US Ethanol Market and Developing Countries' Maize Prices: A Panel SVAR Analysis. *Agricultural Economics* 48: 629–38. [CrossRef]

Herrmann, Raoul, Charles Jumbe, Michael Bruentrup, and Evans Osabuohien. 2017. Competition between Biofuel Feedstock and Food Production: Empirical Evidence from Sugarcane Outgrower Settings in Malawi. *Biomass and Bioenergy*. [CrossRef]

Jha, Shikha, and P. V. Srinivasan. 2001. Food Inventory Policies under Liberalized Trade. *International Journal of Production Economics* 71: 21–29. [CrossRef]

Kilian, Lutz. 2009. Not All Oil Price Shocks Are Alike: Disentangling Demand and Supply Shocks in the Crude Oil Market. *American Economic Review* 99: 1053–69. [CrossRef]

Kilian, Lutz. 2018. Measuring Global Economic Activity: Reply. pp. 1–5. Available online: https://sites.google.com/site/lkilian2019/research/data-sets (accessed on 15 March 2019).

Koirala, Krishna H., Ashok K. Mishra, Jeremy M. D. Antoni, and Joey E. Mehlhorn. 2015. Energy Prices and Agricultural Commodity Prices: Testing Correlation Using Copulas Method. *Energy* 81: 430–36. [CrossRef]

Kristoufek, Ladislav, Karel Janda, and David Zilberman. 2016. Comovements of Ethanol-related Prices: Evidence from Brazil and the USA. *Gcb Bioenergy* 8: 346–56. [CrossRef]

Kwiatkowski, Denis, Peter C. B. Phillips, Peter Schmidt, and Yongcheol Shin. 1992. Testing the Null Hypothesis of Stationarity against the Alternative of a Unit Root: How Sure Are We That Economic Time Series Have a Unit Root? *Journal of Econometrics* 54: 159–78. [CrossRef]

Lee, Junsoo, and Mark C. Strazicich. 2003. Minimum Lagrange Multiplier Unit Root Test with Two Structural Breaks. *Review of Economics and Statistics* 85: 1082–89. [CrossRef]

Lucotte, Yannick. 2016. Co-Movements between Crude Oil and Food Prices: A Post-Commodity Boom Perspective. *Economics Letters* 147: 142–47. [CrossRef]

Lumsdaine, Robin L., and David H. Papell. 1997. Multiple Trend Breaks and the Unit-Root Hypothesis. *Review of Economics and Statistics* 79: 212–18. [CrossRef]

Ma, Z., R. Xu, and X. Dong. 2016. World Oil Prices and Agricultural Commodity Prices: The Evidence from China. *Agricultural Economics (Zemědělská Ekonomika)* 61: 564–76. [CrossRef]

Mcphail, Lihong Lu. 2011. Assessing the Impact of US Ethanol on Fossil Fuel Markets: A Structural VAR Approach. *Energy Economics* 33: 1177–85. [CrossRef]

McPhail, Lihong Lu, Xiaodong Du, and Andrew Muhammad. 2012. Disentangling Corn Price Volatility: The Role of Global Demand, Speculation, and Energy. *Journal of Agricultural & Applied Economics* 44: 401–10. [CrossRef]

Natanelov, Valeri, Mohammad J. Alam, Andrew M. McKenzie, and Guido Van Huylenbroeck. 2011. Is There Co-Movement of Agricultural Commodities Futures Prices and Crude Oil? *Energy Policy* 39: 4971–84. [CrossRef]

Nazlioglu, Saban, and Ugur Soytas. 2011. World Oil Prices and Agricultural Commodity Prices: Evidence from an Emerging Market. *Energy Economics* 33: 488–96. [CrossRef]

Nazlioglu, Saban, and Ugur Soytas. 2012. Oil Price, Agricultural Commodity Prices, and the Dollar: A Panel Cointegration and Causality Analysis. *Energy Economics* 34: 1098–104. [CrossRef]

Nguyen, Van Phuc, and Duc Hong Vo. 2019. Macroeconomics Determinants of Exchange Rate Pass-Through: New Evidence from the Asia-Pacific Region. *Emerging Markets Finance and Trade*. [CrossRef]

Perron, Pierre. 1989. The Great Crash, the Oil Price Shock, and the Unit Root Hypothesis. *Econometrica: Journal of the Econometric Society* 57: 1361–401. [CrossRef]

Perron, Pierre, and Timothy J. Vogelsang. 1992. Nonstationarity and Level Shifts with an Application to Purchasing Power Parity. *Journal of Business & Economic Statistics* 10: 301–20.

Persson, U. Martin. 2015. The Impact of Biofuel Demand on Agricultural Commodity Prices: A Systematic Review. *Wiley Interdisciplinary Reviews: Energy and Environment* 4: 410–28. [CrossRef]

Phillips, Peter C. B., and Pierre Perron. 1988. Testing for a Unit Root in Time Series Regression. *Biometrika* 75: 335–46. [CrossRef]

Qiu, Cheng, Gregory Colson, Cesar Escalante, and Michael Wetzstein. 2012. Considering Macroeconomic Indicators in the Food before Fuel Nexus. *Energy Economics* 34: 2021–28. [CrossRef]

Saghaian, Sayed, Mehdi Nemati, Cory Walters, and Bo Chen. 2018. Asymmetric Price Volatility Transmission between US Biofuel, Corn, and Oil Markets. *Journal of Agricultural and Resource Economics* 43: 46.

Serra, Teresa, and David Zilberman. 2013. Biofuel-Related Price Transmission Literature: A Review. *Energy Economics* 37: 141–51. [CrossRef]

Su, Chi Wei, Xiao-Qing Wang, Ran Tao, and Oana-Ramona Lobonṭ. 2019. Do Oil Prices Drive Agricultural Commodity Prices? Further Evidence in a Global Bio-Energy Context. *Energy* 172: 691–701. [CrossRef]

To, Anh, Dao Ha, Ha Nguyen, and Duc Vo. 2019. The Impact of Foreign Direct Investment on Environment Degradation: Evidence from Emerging Markets in Asia. *International Journal of Environmental Research and Public Health* 16: 1636. [CrossRef] [PubMed]

To, Hang, and R. Quentin Grafton. 2015. Oil Prices, Biofuels Production and Food Security: Past Trends and Future Challenges. *Food Security* 7: 323–36. [CrossRef]

Vacha, Lukas, Karel Janda, Ladislav Kristoufek, and David Zilberman. 2013. Time–Frequency Dynamics of Biofuel–Fuel–Food System. *Energy Economics* 40: 233–41. [CrossRef]

Vo, Duc, Tan Vu, Anh Vo, and Michael McAleer. 2019. Modeling the Relationship between Crude Oil and Agricultural Commodity Prices. *Energies* 12: 1344. [CrossRef]

Vo, Anh, Quan Le, Phuc Nguyen, Chi Ho, and Duc Vo. 2018. Exchange Rate Pass-Through in ASEAN Countries: An Application of the SVAR Model. *Emerging Markets Finance and Trade*. [CrossRef]

Wang, Yudong, Chongfeng Wu, and Li Yang. 2014. Oil Price Shocks and Agricultural Commodity Prices. *Energy Economics* 44: 22–35. [CrossRef]

Zafeiriou, Eleni, Garyfallos Arabatzis, Paraskevi Karanikola, Stilianos Tampakis, and Stavros Tsiantikoudis. 2018. Agricultural Commodity and Crude Oil Prices: An Empirical Investigation of Their Relationship. *Sustainability* 10: 1199. [CrossRef]

Zhang, Zibin, Luanne Lohr, Cesar Escalante, and Michael Wetzstein. 2010. Food versus Fuel: What Do Prices Tell Us? *Energy Policy* 38: 445–51. [CrossRef]

Zhou, Wei, and Bruce A. Babcock. 2017. Using the Competitive Storage Model to Estimate the Impact of Ethanol and Fueling Investment on Corn Prices. *Energy Economics* 62: 195–203. [CrossRef]

Zivot, Eric, and Donald W. K. Andrews. 2002. Further Evidence on the Great Crash, the Oil-Price Shock, and the Unit-Root Hypothesis. *Journal of Business & Economic Statistics* 20: 25–44.

9

Enhancing Financial Inclusion in ASEAN: Identifying the Best Growth Markets for Fintech

Mark Kam Loon Loo⑩

Mihalcheon School of Management, Concordia University of Edmonton, Edmonton, AB T5B 4E4, Canada; mark.loo@concordia.ab.ca

Abstract: While most of the advanced economies are facing saturated markets, the Association of Southeast Asian Nations (ASEAN) has been touted a stable and attractive investment region averaging 5.4% growth since 1980. In 2013, ASEAN overtook China as the top foreign direct investment destination. Boasting the world's fifth largest economy with over 650 million people and 400 million reaching middle class, ASEAN has commendably transitioned from a subsistence economy to product and service industries. Despite the success, many live in marginalized areas without access to banking facilities. Advancing internet capability and availability present investors an opportunity to offer financial technology, or Fintech, to meet the need for financial services in this digital era. The aim of this research is to identify the countries with the highest need for financial inclusion and, hence, the best potential for Fintech growth. The results may help governments formulate policy that improves investment competitiveness. The methodology includes identifying relevant criteria and allocating weight to each criterion to evaluate the best international markets. The findings show Vietnam, Laos, and Cambodia as the countries with the highest potential. The associated risks and opportunities are discussed, followed by managerial implications, limitations, and recommendations for future research.

Keywords: ASEAN; financial inclusion; Fintech; risk; foreign direct investment; competitiveness

1. Introduction

ASEAN stands for the Association of Southeast Asian Nations comprising 10 members: Brunei, Cambodia, Indonesia, Laos, Malaysia, Myanmar, Philippines, Singapore, Thailand, and Vietnam. ASEAN has been outperforming the global growth rate averaging over 5.4% annual GDP since 1980, and in 2013, its foreign direct investment eclipsed China's. ASEAN has the world's fifth largest economy, third largest population with over 650 million, and a growing middle class reaching 400 million by 2020. The fast-emerging economies of Cambodia, Laos, Myanmar, and Vietnam average 7% growth. Business analysts agree that ASEAN is a high-growth region with strong intra-Asian trade, manufacturing supply chains with Northeast Asia, and massive infrastructure expansion over the next two decades. China's One Belt One Road, with three of five corridors across ASEAN connecting to some 60 countries, is expected to enhance ASEAN's competitiveness.

Christine Lagarde (Lagarde 2018), the International Monetary Fund (IMF) Managing Director, noted while ASEAN shows positive growth trends, ASEAN is subject to heightened competition, financial volatility, and technological advances such as digitalization, robotics, and artificial intelligence. ASEAN countries could navigate the difficult terrain by managing *uncertainty*, making economies more *inclusive*, and preparing for the *digital revolution*.

Although ASEAN countries have built stronger economic foundations that helped weather the global financial crisis, recent *volatility* in financial markets reminds policymakers to stay vigilant to manage uncertainties, and safeguard against volatile capital flows with bold reforms to make economies more resilient.

Many ASEAN countries have shifted from agriculture to advanced manufacturing and services but new growth models that are more *inclusive* are needed to sustain growth. ASEAN can work together to promote inclusive growth by increasing the quality of education and infrastructure, eliminating red tape and corruption, providing affordable childcare to encourage more women in workforce, and enhancing women's access to finance. However, all this will only go so far.

A McKinsey and Company (McKinsey and Company 2016) study found that 60% of current jobs comprise tasks will soon be automated. New growth models will rely on technological innovations from artificial intelligence to robotics, to biotechnology, to *fintech* or financial technology. Lee and Teoh (2015) argue that Fintech will bring about lower business costs and profit margins. An estimated 38% of the world population has no formal bank accounts and another 40% are underserved by banks, providing a huge potential market for Fintech firms.

With mobile payment systems, Fintech has become the new economy. Indonesia has a vibrant digital ecosystem with more than 1700 start-ups and *Go-Jek* is a transformation example from a ride-hailing app into a platform for mobile payments and other services. The Singapore Fintech Festival gathers some of the world's most dynamic entrepreneurs and innovators.

Fintech is the platform for the digital revolution that promotes financial inclusion. It is not just a boost to productivity, but also one that works for young and old, rich and poor, urban and remote communities to help create a smarter and fairer economy.

In ASEAN, only 50% of adults have an account at a financial institution and 264 million adults keep money at home and borrow from "loan sharks" at exorbitant interest rates. Rates of financial exclusion are higher among the poor, less-educated, and those living in rural areas. Recognizing the importance of financial inclusion for economic development, ASEAN leaders aim to achieve 70% account ownership by 2020 (Luna-Martinez 2016).

From the above discussion, there is a critical need to enhance Fintech to help ASEAN people access financial services to receive and save wages safely and build credit history. Which ASEAN countries would offer the greatest growth for financial inclusion to attract Fintech investors?

2. Objective

The objective of this research is to identify ASEAN markets that offer the best growth potential for financial inclusion to attract Fintech investors.

There are three associated research questions to guide the research project. What may be some factors that attract Fintech investors? How should markets be evaluated to determine the best potential for financial inclusion? What type of investors may value social returns over immediate profit in growing financial inclusion in ASEAN?

3. Literature Review

Financial inclusion is the process that ensures the ease of access, availability, and usage of formal financial system that offers equality of opportunities to access financial services to all members of a nation (Sarma 2008; Nanda and Kaur 2016) and access to a transaction account is a first step toward broader financial inclusion since a transaction account allows people to store money, and send and receive payments (World Bank 2019). This definition implies there is financial exclusion, and the (World Bank 2016) describes voluntary exclusion as a condition where the segment of the population or firms choose not to use financial services either because they have no need or due to cultural or religious reasons.

Involuntary exclusion may arise from an individual's insufficient income or high risk profile, discrimination by race, religion, or gender, market failures, and imperfections. The poor are excluded from wage-earning employment opportunities that traditional economic theory presupposes (Park and Mercado 2015). They live and work in the informal economy, not by choice but by necessity (Cull et al. 2014), managing a broad range of financial services by themselves to sustain livelihoods, build asset, and manage risks. They have limited financial access, which excludes them from the normal financial system.

3.1. Does Financial Inclusion Lower Income Inequality?

Many financial inclusion studies focused on the role of financial access in lowering poverty and income inequality.

A study in India provides empirical evidence that local differences in opening bank branches in rural unbanked population were associated with significant reduction in rural poverty (Burgess and Pande 2005). Cull, Ehrbeck, and Holle (Cull et al. 2014) suggest that financial access improves local economic activity.

Research in Mexico showed that rapid opening of Banco Azteca branches had a significant correlation with the region's economy leading to 7% increase in overall income levels compared to areas without Banco Azteca branches being opened (Bruhn and Love 2009). Ruiz (2013) explained that households were better able to smooth consumption and accumulate more durable goods in communities with Banco Azteca branches. At the same time, the proportion of households that saved money declined 6.6% in those communities, suggesting that households were able to rely on savings rather than available formal credit as a buffer against income fluctuation (Cull et al. 2014).

At the macroeconomic level, the literature suggests that the degree of financial intermediation is not only positively correlated with economic growth and employment under normal circumstances, but it is generally believed to casually impact economic growth (Levine 2000; Pasali 2013). The main mechanism for doing so is generally lower transaction costs and better distribution of capital and risk across the economy. Moreover, broader access to bank deposits can also have a positive effect on financial stability (Cull et al. 2014). However, Demetriades and Law (2006) indicated that the positive growth impact from financial intermediation does not hold in economies with weak institutional frameworks and nonexistent financial regulation.

3.2. Financial Inclusion in ASEAN

Financial inclusion could be measured in multiple dimensions, including account ownership, use of account, and financial account penetration. Table 1 shows the financial account penetration by percent of total adult population for ASEAN nations.

Table 1. Financial account penetration (% of total adult population).

Singapore	Malaysia	Thailand	Indonesia	Philippines	Vietnam	Lao PDR	Myanmar	Cambodia	Brunei
98%	85%	82%	49%	34%	31%	29%	26%	22%	NA

Source: The Global Findex Database (2017), World Bank. Data are not available for Brunei.

Lower levels of account ownership. While Singapore, Malaysia, Thailand, and Brunei have achieved almost universal financial inclusion, other countries in ASEAN face various challenges (Luna-Martinez 2016). From Table 1, Singapore, Malaysia, and Thailand have financial account penetration of over 75% while the rest of ASEAN range from 22% to 34%, which means at least two-thirds of their population do not have a bank account.

Wage payments mostly in cash. Only 29% of workers reported receiving monthly salaries through an account with a financial institution, and 71% are paid in cash, risky for employers and workers alike. Paying salary into employees' bank accounts is safer and builds credit histories to access new services, such as consumer credit, mortgages, education loans, and insurance products.

Figure 1 shows Singapore leads with less than 20% of adults receive wage in cash, followed by Malaysia at less than 50%, while the rest of ASEAN are over 70% (no data on Brunei). Singapore is on par with the Organization of Economic Cooperation and Development (OECD) comprising 35 countries. Overall, ASEAN has a higher percentage of adults who receive wage in cash at about 75% compared to East Asia Pacific at about 65%.

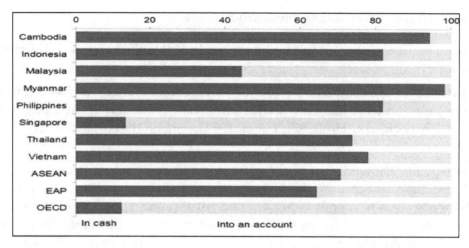

Figure 1. Adults receiving wage payments by method (%). Source: (Luna-Martinez 2016). "How to scale up financial inclusion in ASEAN countries".

Adoption of Electronic Payment. Only 30% of adults have a debit card and 9% have a credit card. Cash is used extensively including those with a bank account. Even among the banked population, penetration of non-cash payment tools is low. Table 2 shows the percent of adults with a debit card, credit card, and whether they are used.

Table 2. Adults with debit card and credit card (% of Total Adult Population 2014).

Card	Singapore		Malaysia		Thailand		Indonesia		Philippines		Vietnam		Lao PDR		Myanmar		Cambodia	
	Own	Used	Own	Used	Own	Used	Own	Used	Own	Used	Own	Used	Own	Used	Own	Used	Own	Used
Debit	89	78	41	19	58	7.9	26	8.5	21	12	27	3.1	6	2	1.7	0.4	5.4	0.7
Credit	35	31	20	17	5.7	3.7	1.6	1.1	3.2	2.2	1.9	1.2	3	2	NA	Na	2.9	2.3

Source: The Global Findex Database (2017), World Bank. Note: Lao PDR 2011 data. Data is not available for Brunei.

Singapore leads at 89% with a debit card and 78% used it, and 35% with a credit card and 31% used, followed by Malaysia and Thailand. The rest of ASEAN has below 30% debit card ownership and below 5% credit card ownership.

4. Methodology

From the above discussion, Singapore has the highest financial inclusion rate and while Fintech businesses continue to grow, it is a matured market with people owning and using multiple credit and debit cards. In contrast, there may be emerging ASEAN nations with a greater need for financial inclusion and offer a bigger opportunity. The objective is to identify the markets with the best potential to grow financial inclusion that attract Fintech investors.

The methodology is similar to evaluating international markets. However, the uniqueness of this methodology is that it does not seek to identify the most advanced Fintech markets but the markets that need financial inclusion most urgently. Hence, the methodology executes the societal marketing philosophy and fulfills the social responsibility mission.

The steps to determine the best growth market in ASEAN for Fintech to promote financial inclusion are described below.

1.   Identify the key factors that promote Fintech growth.
2.   Gather reliable data for key factors.
3.   Determine the scale to rate each factor.
4.   Allocate weight for the set of factors.
5.   Calculate and compare the scores for the ten ASEAN nations.
6.   Determine the best market(s) to grow financial inclusion and maximize equality.

4.1. Identify the Key Factors That Promote Fintech Growth

(Bart and Ayna 2014) proposed three key factors for Fintech success: Selection process and criteria, business support services, and network. Lee and Teoh (2015) identified LASIC for Fintech success: *Low margin, asset light, scalable, innovative,* and *compliance easy.* Chen, Chen, Yeh, and Tsaur (Chen et al. 2016) found that Taiwan finance customers had high expectations of information security and preferred high technology products with complex functions, demonstrating the customer's *use behavior* was influenced by *perceived usefulness,* not *perceived ease of use.*

The three studies adopted different approaches from evaluating external to internal factors, from support services and network to easy compliance to customer's perception of usefulness of Fintech facilities. While the discussions of these authors focused on building the success of the Fintech business, there is a need to determine the success factors that help identify the best growth nations in ASEAN that can help influence and accelerate financial inclusion in other ASEAN nations.

Table 3 shows the key factors that influence international market selection based on surveys by UNCTAD, Deloitte and Touche, International Finance Corporation, and FDI Markets (Elms 2017). The far left column categorizes the factors identified from the four surveys.

Table 3. Factors that influence international market selection.

Factor Category	Factors	UNCTAD	Deloitte & Touche	International Finance Corporation	FDI Markets
1. Market Size	Market size	Yes			
	Access to customers		Yes	Yes	Yes
	Market growth	Yes		Yes	Yes
	Regional market access	Yes			
2. Labor Market Efficiency	Skilled labor		Yes	Yes	Yes
	Management staff		Yes		
	Tech pros		Yes		
	Labor Cost	Yes			
3. Financial Market Development	Capital market access	Yes			
4. Institutions	Government support			Yes	Yes
	Government incentives	Yes		Yes	
	Regulations & business climate				Yes
5. Stability *(Fragile States Index)*	Stability	Yes	Yes		
	Crime and safety		Yes		
6. Ease of Doing Business	Ease of doing business		Yes		
7. Infrastructure	Infrastructure			Yes	Yes
	Utilities	Yes			
8. Technological Readiness	Technology				Yes
	Universities & Researchers				Yes

Source: Created by author, adapting from Elms (Elms 2017).

The ING Economics Department (ING Economics Department 2016) developed the fintech index methodology (FIM) comprising three *dimensions* and four *Sub-indices* with respective *indicators.* While the FIM used a set of data to determine the most advanced and commercial Fintech markets, this study seeks to identify the markets that need Fintech most to expand financial inclusion and, thus, needs a different approach in sourcing data to meet this objective.

This methodology undertakes a rigorous procedure to identify the markets with the highest potential to expand financial inclusion urgently to appeal to Fintech entrepreneurs. First, it determines the nations with low penetration and usage of credit and debit cards to facilitate cashless transactions. Second, it determines the most important factors for selecting markets with the best potential for growth such as ease of doing business and infrastructure, from the comparative surveys of four investment-related organizations as shown in Table 3. Third, it identifies sources of information that provide measurements for these factors as shown in the last column *data sources* in Table 4.

Table 4. Dimension, sub-index, indicators, and data sources for this study.

Dimension	Sub-Index	Indicators in ING FIM	Indicators for This Study	Data Sources
Demand	Urgency for Financial Inclusion	1. Unbanked 2. Credit gap 3. Poverty 4. Rural population	1. Financial Account Penetration	World Bank
Supply	Fintech Infrastructure	5. Mobile subscription density 6. Internet density 7. Electricity coverage 8. Grid reliability	2. Mobile telephone subscriptions 3. Internet users 4. Quality of Electricity 5. Technological Readiness	GCR 2017–2018
	Fintech Ecosystem	9. Start-up attractiveness	6. Ease of doing business 7. Starting a business 8. Market size 9. Labour market efficiency 10. Financial market development	World Bank (indicators 6 & 7) GCR 2017–2018 (indicators 8, 9 & 10)
Risk	Political & Regulatory Environment	10. Corruption index 11. Political stability, absence of violence & terrorism index 12. Strength of legal rights index	11. Institutions 12. Fragile States Index	GCR 2017–2018 (indicator 11) FSI (indicator 12)

Source: Adapting ING Fintech Index Methodology's indicators with Key Factors for Investment identified by investment surveys as per Table 3. GCR = Global Competitiveness Report by World Economic Forum. FSI = Fragile States Index by Fund for Peace.

4.2. Gather Reliable Data for Key Factors

Several global data sources were referenced. The World Competitiveness Yearbook (2017) by the International Institute of Management and Development covers 63 countries but excludes Brunei, Cambodia, Laos, Myanmar, and Vietnam. These countries were, however, included in the global competitiveness report (GCR) 2017–2018 by the World Economic Forum that ranked competitiveness of 137 economies and countries, the Global Findex Database 2017 by World Bank that ranked financial inclusion of 190 countries, and the Fragile States Index 2018 by Fund for Peace that measures the cohesion-economic-political-social stability of 178 countries. Table 4 shows the indicators drawn from these sources to form three *dimensions* and four *sub-indices*.

The specific indicators for this study that form the three *dimensions* and four *sub-indices* are discussed in the following.

4.2.1. Demand

The urgency for financial inclusion is measured by the *financial account penetration* (FAP) expressed in percentage of adults aged 15+ with a formal account at a bank, credit union, cooperative, post office, or microfinance institution (Kunt and Klapper 2013), available to all population segments irrespective of economic situation (Griffin 2017), especially marginalized rural markets (Lewis and Lindley 2015; Schlein 2017). The cumulative effect of digitally driven financial inclusion could boost GDP by 2% to 3% in markets like Indonesia and the Philippines, and 6% in Cambodia (Asian Development Bank 2014).

4.2.2. Supply: Fintech Infrastructure

The *internet* is dependent on *quality of electricity supply*, which powers connectivity. *Electricity* and *mobile subscription* indicators are provided by the second pillar, infrastructure, and *internet user % population* by the ninth pillar, technological readiness, in the global competitiveness report by the World Economic Forum. *Technological readiness* comprises all the important indicators that support financial inclusion such as *fixed broadband internet subscriptions, internet bandwidth*, and *mobile-broadband subscriptions*.

Quality of Electricity Supply (QES) refers to the availability and fitness to power devices important to the success of Fintech businesses. *Electricity* access refers to the percentage of people with stable access to electricity, and serves as a good proxy for other indicators of wealth and opportunity (Hanania et al. 2018). The 2017 World Bank Enterprise Survey identified electricity services as one of the biggest obstacles to business owners (Doing Business 2018: Reforming to Create Jobs 2018). *QES* data are provided by the second pillar, infrastructure, in GCR 2017–2018.

Mobile Cellular Telephone Subscriptions provides access to the public switched telephone network (PSTN) using cellular technology. It includes the number of postpaid and active prepaid accounts during the past three months and subscriptions that offer voice communications. It excludes subscriptions via data cards or USB modems, subscriptions to public mobile data services, and private trunked mobile radio, telepoint, radio paging, and telemetry services. (ITU World Telecommunication-ICT Indicators 2017). The second pillar, infrastructure, in the GCR 2017–2018 provides data for *mobile cellular telephone subscription per 100 population*.

Internet users % population refers to *percent of people* using internet from any location or purpose in the last three months via a desktop, laptop or tablet, mobile phone, games machine, and digital TV regardless of fixed or mobile network (GCR 2017–2018). Internet penetration increases trade and income growth (Chu 2013) and a 10% rise has been reported to increase GDP by 1.08% (The Economic Times 2015). With smartphones, the internet evolved the banking platform (Andrew 2015) into the internet of things (IoT) facilitating consumer banking, international trade financing, exchange of information, and customer authentication to increase legitimacy of transactions ("Fintech Trends: The Internet of Things," 12 January 2017 (Lazarova 2017)). The ninth pillar, **technological readiness**, provides data on *internet users by % population*, and six other important indicators of Fintech infrastructure.

For example, Singapore is ranked 25th in internet users due to its small population of 5 million but the other indicators put Singapore in the world's top five: Fifth for internet bandwidth, fourth for mobile broadband subscriptions, and second for FDI and technology transfer.

4.2.3. Supply: Fintech Ecosystem

While the ING FIM only provided *start-up attractiveness*, this study uses several measurements: Ease of doing business, starting a business, market size, labor market efficiency, and financial market development.

Ease of doing business **(EDB)** represents the reforms a country has undertaken such as infrastructure and legal systems over decades (Javadekar 2017) that influence international confidence (Wijaya 2017). A higher EDB index indicates higher investment friendliness in three ways: (1) Access to economic opportunities such as securing construction permits and electricity, registering property, getting credit, paying taxes, trading across borders, enforcing contracts, and resolving insolvency; (2) lower business set up costs with fewer steps to allow small and medium enterprises (SME) to use finances for post-setup operation; and (3) less corruption as bureaucracy can make official channels vulnerable to corruption, while simplifying the process accelerates economic growth (Naumann 2018). The World Bank's Global Findex Database 2017 provides data for ease of doing business.

Starting a business (SB) measures the paid-in minimum capital requirement, number of procedures, time, and cost for a SME limited liability firm to complete the procedures to start business and formally operate in the country's largest business city. A higher rank indicates more ease in starting a business. Table 5 shows starting a business is harder than doing business in ASEAN, for example, Malaysia' *EDB* is ranked 24 but *SB* is 111. (World Bank's Doing Business 2018: Reforming to Create Jobs 2018).

Market Size affects productivity since large markets allows economies of scale (GCR 2017–2018; Ozimek 2016; Aziz and Makkawi 2012). However, population cannot adequately explain market size efficiency; for example, Singapore has a population of 5 million but ranks 35th in market size in the world. The 10th pillar, market size, accounts for strength of domestic market, foreign markets, GDP, and exports as GDP%. Purchasing power is important to advance Fintech into more sophisticated transaction platforms.

Labor Market Efficiency refers to matching worker skills with suitable jobs and incentivizing human capital development with workers working efficiently and employers providing the right incentives (GCR 2017–2018). The seventh pillar, *labor market efficiency*, comprises 10 indicators including professional management, talent retention and attraction, effect of taxation, pay, and productivity to support Fintech growth.

Financial Market Development is defined as the depth of the intermediation system, including the availability and liquidity of credit, equity, debt, insurances, and other financial products (GCR 2017–2018). The eighth *pillar, financial market development*, measures eight factors that includes availability and affordability of financial services, ease of access to loans, venture capital availability, soundness of banks, securities of exchange regulations, and legal rights index.

Table 5. Factors, data source, and scaling method.

Dimension and Indicators	Data Source & Scaling Method

Demand
1. Financial Account Penetration

The Global Findex Database (2017), World Bank. 190 Ranks, Rank Range: 19
Reverse scale is applied: the lower the percent of account penetration, the higher the potential market for Fintech

% AP	Points	% AP	Points	% AP	Points
0–5	10	36–40	6.5	71–75	3
6–10	9.5	41–45	6	76–80	2.5
11–15	9	46–50	5.5	81–85	2
16–2	8.5	51–55	5	86–90	1.5
21–25	8	56–60	4.5	91–95	1
26–30	7.5	61–65	4	96–100	0.5
31–35	7	66–70	3.5		
		Note: AP = Account Penetration			

Supply: Fintech Infrastructure
2. Mobile Cellular Subscription/100 population *2nd Pillar Infrastructure*
3. Internet users *% population 9th Pillar Technological Readiness*
4. Quality of Electricity *2nd Pillar Infrastructure*
5. Technological Readiness *9th pillar*
Supply: Fintech Ecosystem
6. Market Size *10th Pillar*
7. Labor Market Efficiency *7th pillar-*
8. Financial Market Development *8th pillar*

Global Competitiveness Index 2017–2018
137 Ranks, Rank Range: 14

Rank	Points	Rank	Points	Rank	Points
1–7	10	50–56	6.5	99–105	3
8–14	9.5	57–63	6	106–112	2.5
15–21	9	64–70	5.5	113–119	2
22–28	8.5	71–77	5	120–126	1.5
29–35	8	78–84	4.5	127–133	1
36–42	7.5	85–91	4	134–137	0.5
43–49	7	92–98	3.5		

Supply: Fintech Ecosystem
9. Ease of Doing Business
10. Starting a Business

The Global Findex Database (2017), World Bank. 190 Ranks, Rank Range 19

Rank	Points	Rank	Points	Rank	Points
1–10	10	68–76	6.5	134–143	3
11–19	9.5	77–86	6	144–152	2.5
20–29	9	87–95	5.5	153–162	2
30–38	8.5	96–105	5	163–171	1.5
38–48	8	105–114	4.5	172–181	1
49–57	7.5	115–124	4	182–190	0.5
58–67	7	125–133	3.5		

Risk
11. Institutions *1st pillar* (scale same as Factors 1–7, (Global Competitiveness Report 2017–2018 2017))
12. Fragile States Index (*see right column*)

Fragile States Index (2018). 178 Ranks, Rank Range: 18
Reverse scale is applied as the higher the rank, the higher the risk

Rank	Points	Rank	Points	Rank	Points
1–9	0.5	64–72	4	127–135	7.5
10–18	1	73–81	4.5	136–144	8
19–27	1.5	82–90	5	145–153	8.5
28–36	2	91–99	5.5	154–162	9
37–45	2.5	100–108	6	163–171	9.5
46–54	3	109–117	6.5	172–178	10
55–63	3.5	118–126	7		

Note: Ranks = number of nations surveyed by the data source; Rank Range = number of Ranks divided by 10 nations, to nearest whole number.

4.2.4. Risk

FIM measures risk by the political and regulatory environment indexes such as *corruption, political stability, and strength of legal rights*. These indexes are covered by the first pillar, *institutions*, in the GCR. **Institutions** is the first pillar with 21 indicators including strength of investor protection, property rights, judicial independence, efficiency of legal framework in settling disputes and challenging regulations, ethical behavior, and protection of minority shareholders' interest (GCR 2017–2018).

The **Fragile States Index** (2018) assesses vulnerability comprehensively through four categories with 12 risk indicators: Cohesion (security apparatus, factionalized elites, group grievance), economic (economic decline, uneven economic development, human flight, and brain drain), political (state legitimacy, public services, human rights, and rule of law), and social (demographic pressures, refugees, external intervention).

4.3. Determine the Scale to Rate Each Factor

A scale of 1 as lowest to 10 as highest is awarded to the indicator rank for each nation. The scale developed is dependent on the number of countries in each survey, and *reverse scaling* may be applied, where the higher the rank, the lower the support for financial inclusion.

World Bank's ranking for 190 countries. For ease of doing business and starting a business, the 190 countries are divided by 10 (ASEAN members) and the resulting rank range is 19. As the rank does not have a decimal, Table 5 shows rank 1 to 10 gains 10 points and 11 to 19 gains 9.5 points, and so on.

The financial account penetration (FAP) shows percent of adult population with a bank account. 100% divided by 10 yields a range of 10. **Reverse scaling** will be applied. Countries with lower FAP have higher potential for financial inclusion. Table 4 shows countries with *up to 5%* FAP earns 10 points, 6% to 10% earns 9.5 points, and so on. There are no FAP data for Brunei but reporting for World Bank, Luna-Martinez (2016) advised *"Singapore, Malaysia, Thailand and Brunei have achieved almost universal financial inclusion ... "* Thus, an 82% penetration is accorded to Brunei, and 81% to 85% FAP earns 2 points for Malaysia, Thailand, and Brunei. Data for Myanmar are based on 2014/15 as no later data are available.

Global Competitiveness Report's ranking for 137 countries. With 137 divided by 10, the rank range is 13.7 rounded to 14. Table 4 shows rank 1 to 7 earns 10 points, rank 8 to 14 earns 9.5 points, and so on. This scale applies to the indicators in:

- Infrastructure: Mobile cellular subscriptions/*100 population* (*second pillar, infrastructure*), internet users *% population* (*ninth pillar, technological readiness*), quality of electricity (*second pillar, infrastructure*), and technological readiness (*ninth pillar*).
- Ecosystem: Market size (*10th pillar*), labor market efficiency (*seventh pillar*), and financial market development (*eighth pillar*).
- Risk: *Institutions* (*first pillar*).

The Fragile States Index's ranking of 178 countries. With 178 divided by 10, the range is 17.8 rounded to 18. **Reverse scaling** is applied as a higher rank means higher risk. Rank 1 to 9 earns 0.5 points, 10 to 18 earns 1 point, and finally, rank 172 to 178 earns 10 points.

Table 6 shows the FAP and ranks for each financial inclusion indicator, Table 7 shows the weight allocation, and Table 8 shows the respective points allocated for each indicator along with evaluative scores for the market with the best potential for financial inclusion.

Table 6. Financial account penetration and ranks for financial inclusion indicators.

Country	Financial Account Penetration %	Mobile Telephone Subscriptions	Internet Users	Quality of Electricity	Technological Readiness	Ease of Business	Starting a Business	Market Size	Labour Market Efficiency	Financial Market Development	Institution	Fragile State Index
Singapore	98	23	25	3	14	2	6	35	2	3	2	161
Malaysia	85	28	32	36	46	24	111	24	26	16	27	116
Thailand	82	5	86	57	61	26	36	18	65	40	78	77
Brunei	82	61	43	53	60	56	58	110	47	87	40	124
Indonesia	49	18	109	86	80	72	144	9	96	37	47	91
Vietnam	31	44	87	90	79	68	123	31	51	71	79	107
Philippines	34	88	74	92	83	113	173	27	84	52	94	47
Lao PDR	29	131	116	75	110	141	164	101	36	75	62	60
Cambodia	22	52	107	106	97	135	183	84	48	61	106	53
Myanmar*	26	135	137	118	138	171	155	60	73	138	133	22

Note: Myanmar* data for first eight factors from GCR 2014/15. Financial Account Penetration % Brunei estimated (Luna-Martinez 2016).

Table 7. Weight allocation for financial inclusion urgency, infrastructure, ecosystem, and risk.

Dimension	Sub-Index	Indicator for This Study	Weight 1	Weight 2
Demand	Urgency for Financial Inclusion	1. Financial Account Penetration	40%	50%
Supply	Fintech Infrastructure	2. Mobile telephone subscriptions 3. Internet users 4. Quality of Electricity 5. Technological Readiness	20%	20%
	Fintech Ecosystem	6. Ease of doing business 7. Starting a business 8. Market size 9. Labor market efficiency 10. Financial market development	20%	15%
Risk	Political & Regulatory Environment	11. Institutions 12. Fragile States Index	20%	15%

Sources: Created by author, adapting the ING FIM's three dimensions and four sub-indices.

Table 8. Countries with highest potential for financial inclusion (financial account penetration 50%).

Dimension	Demand		Supply: Fintech Infrastructure					Supply: Fintech Ecosystem						Risk			
Country	Financial Account Penetration %	50%	Mobile Telephone Subscriptions	Internet Users	Quality of Electricity	Technological Readiness	20%	Ease of Business	Starting a Business	Market Size	Labour Market Efficiency	Financial Market Development	15%	Institution	Fragile State Index	15%	Total 100%
Vietnam	7	35	7	4	4	5	9.8	7	4	8	7	5	9.4	5	6	7.9	62
Lao PDR	8	37.5	1	2	5	3	5.3	3	2	3	8	5	5.6	6	7	9.8	58
Cambodia	8	40	7	3	3	4	7.5	3	1	5	7	6	5.6	3	3	4.1	57
Philippines	7	35	4	5	4	5	8.5	5	1	9	5	7	6.9	4	3	4.9	55
Indonesia	6	27.5	9	3	4	5	10	7	3	10	4	8	8.3	7	6	9.4	55
Singapore	1	2.5	9	9	10	10	18.3	10	10	8	10	10	14.3	10	9	14.3	49
Malaysia	2	10	9	8	8	7	15.5	9	5	9	9	9	11.4	9	7	11.3	48
Myanmar	8	37.5	1	1	2	1	1.8	2	2	6	5	1	5.4	1	2	1.9	47
Brunei	2	10	6	7	7	6	12.8	8	7	3	7	4	9.0	8	7	10.9	43
Thailand	2	10	10	4	6	6	13	9	9	9	6	8	12.0	5	5	6.8	42

Source: Points allocated by ranks from Global Findex Database (2017), Global Competitiveness Report 2017–2018 2017 (2017); Fragile States Index (2018).

4.4. *Allocate Weight for the Set of Factors*

If the 12 factors have equal weight, Singapore would top the list. While sophisticated Fintech businesses can flourish, there is little room for financial inclusion as Singaporeans have a high FAP with high debit and credit cards ownership and usage.

As the goal is to achieve maximum financial inclusion to overcome inequality, demand is the most important factor to begin with: Financial account penetration (FAP). Table 7 below shows two weight approaches to identify the best growth potential markets for financial inclusion.

The first approach allocates 40% to FAP (demand) for financial inclusion urgency, and 20% each to infrastructure and ecosystem (supply) and political and regulatory nvironment (Risk). The second approach allocates 50% to FAP, 20% to infrastructure, and 15% each to ecosystem and political and regulatory environment.

4.5. *Calculate and Compare the Scores for the Ten ASEAN Nations*

When 40% weight was applied, the results from highest to lowest potential for financial inclusion: Vietnam, Singapore, Lao PDR, Indonesia, Malaysia, Cambodia, Philippines, Brunei, Thailand, and Myanmar. As discussed earlier, Singapore and Malaysia have achieved high financial inclusion, which does not achieve the objective of this study. Incremental weight at 45% was applied but yielded similar results.

In Table 7, the points are allocated according to the rank of each indicator and the corresponding weight for each dimension (Table 5). When 50% was applied to FAP, a significantly different result emerged as shown in Table 8.

4.6. *Determine the Best Market(s) to Grow Financial Inclusion and Maximize Equality*

Vietnam, Lao PDR (Laos), and Cambodia are the top three markets for financial inclusion. The Philippines and Indonesia are fourth and fifth.

4.6.1. Discussion

Vietnam, Laos, and Cambodia are the emerging markets in ASEAN that need help to reduce inequality through financial inclusion. Table 9 shows the sector share of GDP (% 2011) of the three countries, all with agriculture 35% or more, suggesting a high rural population that suffers financial exclusion. Cambodia is highest in services at 43%, followed by Laos at 37%, while Vietnam is highest in industry at 41%.

Table 9. Sector share of real gross domestic product (GDP) (%, 2011).

	Vietnam	Lao PDR	Cambodia
Agriculture	39%	43%	35%
Services	20%	37%	43%
Industry	41%	20%	21%

Source: Doubling Financial Inclusion in the ASEAN Region by 2020, UNCDF.

4.6.2. Opportunities

Ensuring adults have access to a bank account is a first step toward comprehensive financial inclusion, where people can make use of appropriate financial services, including savings, payments, credit, and insurance (Pazarbasiogl 2017). Table 10 shows the summary of supply and demand of financial services of the three countries based on the UNCDF's *Doubling Financial Inclusion in the ASEAN Region by 2020.* The data show great potential in all three countries to grow financial inclusion.

Table 10. Summary of supply and demand of financial services.

Country		Cambodia	Laos	Vietnam
	Population	16.3 Million	6.9 Million	96.5 Million
Method of savings (aged 15+, 2011)	Financial institution	0.8	19.4	7.7
	Savings club	4.3	8.1	5.1
Population having a bank account (%, 2011)	Urban	10.2	32	29.8
	Rural	2.4	20.2	16.5
	Aged 15–24	4.5	23	22.6
	Aged 25+	3.3	28.5	21.1
Mobile use (%, 2011)	Mobile penetration	96	87	99
	Mobile use to pay bills	0.1	0	3.6
	Mobile use to receive money	0.6	0	3.4
	Mobile use to send money	0.4	0	2.8
Banking sector statistics (2010)	Number of banks	36	26	101
	Market share of state-owned banks	0	67.4	47.7
	Number of branches	360	83	1988
	Number of ATMs	501	346	11700
	Number of branches (per 100,000 adults)	4	2.6	3.3
	Number of ATMs (per 100,000 adults)	5.1	4.3	17.6
	Assets/GDP ratio (%)	58	49.7	14

Source: *Doubling Financial Inclusion in the ASEAN Region by 2020*, UNCDF. Population data from (Worldometers 2018).

Table 10 shows the following financial inclusion opportunities:

- *Method of savings (% population aged 15+):* All three countries have less than 20% who saved with a financial institution. Laos has twice more savers in a financial institution at nearly 20% than Cambodia and Vietnam.

- *Population with a bank account*: Rural dwellers are twice lower than urban dwellers in a bank account ownership.

- *Banking sector statistics:* There are insufficient bank branches to meet needs. Cambodia leads by four branches *per 100,000 adults*. Laos has 67.4% *market share of state-owned banks* followed by Vietnam 47.7% but nil for Cambodia. Laos has the highest population of formally banked at nearly 20% but lowest in branches and ATMS per 100,000 adults.

- *Mobile use*: Despite mobile penetration from 87% upwards, *mobile use* to pay bills, receive, or send money is 0% in Laos, below 1% in Cambodia, and below 5% in Vietnam. There is great potential for mobile banking.

The data above provide a vast opportunity for growth in financial inclusion in the three countries. The following discusses the initiatives in each country to expand financial inclusion.

4.6.3. Vietnam

Vietnam has 96.5 million people and a density of 299 people per sq. km (compared to 8188 per sq. km in Singapore). Financial account penetration is 31% and 27% own a debit card and 1.9% a credit card (The Global Findex Database 2017, World Bank). Vietnam has the highest number of banks, bank branches, and ATMs compared to Laos and Cambodia.

Since 2016, the State Bank of Vietnam and World Bank have partnered to focus on shifting government payments to digital platforms, providing financial services to ethnic minorities and agricultural communities where poverty rates are above national average, and strengthening financial education to prepare the next generation for a modern financial marketplace.

Vietnam is among World Bank's 25 priority countries for financial inclusion efforts, where 39% of adults save outside the formal sector such as "under the mattress" or use informal savings clubs, and 65% send or receive remittances, and pay school fees or utility bills in cash. Some of the barriers to formal financial services include:

- Financial services are too far to access—6.2 million adults;
- Financial services are too expensive to use—2.2 million adults;
- Documentation requirements are prohibitive to open an account—2.3 million adults;
- Lack of trust in the financial sector—1.1 million adults.

Removing these barriers through appropriate legal and regulatory reforms can help move consumers from the informal to formal financial sector with great effect, as an improved policy environment could mean an estimated 48 million adults with transaction accounts. Furthermore, government-to-person (G2P) cash transfers can be digitized to reach an additional 3.7 million currently unbanked adults.

4.6.4. Lao PDR

Lao People Democratic Republic (Laos) has 6.9 million people with a density of 30 people per sq. km. An agricultural society with 80% of population in rural areas, the landlocked landscape of thick forests, rugged mountains, and fast flowing rivers makes physical and economic connectivity between communities difficult. Small-scale subsistence agriculture accounts for over 30% of GDP and employs 70% of population. In rural upland areas, the poverty rate is 43% compared with 28% in the lowlands. A mere 20% of the population in the lower 40% income segment have a formal bank account (Internationale Zusammenarbeit (GIZ)).

While Laos has experienced economic growth over the last decade, inequality has risen and financial inclusion remains low. Access to financial institutions is limited to 29% of population, 6% own a debit card, and 3% credit card (The Global Findex Database 2017). Laos has the third-lowest level of financial access in ASEAN (only Cambodia and Myanmar rank lower). Laos is working on increasing the supply of financial services such as access to ATMs and financial literacy programs.

To increase financial inclusion, the authorities introduced "Community Money Express" in 2015 to allow microfinance institutions to utilize commercial banks' branches to expand reach in the largely rural and agrarian country, a service launched by Banque pour le Commerce Exterieur Lao Public (BCEL), one of the country's leading banks. The UNCDF, in collaboration with the Bank of Lao PDR and Central Bank, have worked to design several initiatives:

- Making access to finance more inclusive for poor people to improve policy and regulatory environment, financial infrastructure, and capacity of financial service providers.
- Making access possible through evidence-based financial inclusion policy framework to diagnose financial inclusion disaggregated by gender, geographic location, and income level.
- Shaping inclusive finance transformations to accelerate financial inclusion and women's economic participation (UNCDF 2017).

4.6.5. Cambodia

Cambodia has 16.3 million people with a density of 92 people per sq. km. Financial account penetration is 22% and 5.4% with credit cards and 2.9% debit cards (The Global Findex Database 2017). In 2016, the United Nations Capital Development Fund (UNCDF) and partners conducted a survey on the accessibility and usage of Cambodian financial services among 3150 adults. The findings show:

- Financial exclusion: 29% use neither formal nor informal financial services.
- Informal services: Over one-third of the population use unregistered lenders or savings clubs.

- Formal inclusion: 59% with 24% of these using microfinance institutions (MFIs) and 17% banks; females 73% compared to males 69%; urban areas 74% and rural areas 69%.
- Access financial infrastructure: 75% in rural areas take over 30 min to access post offices, bank branches, and ATMs.
- Borrowings: 58% do not borrow to avoid debt; 54% turn to MFIs; 22% borrow from family and friends; 14% from a bank.
- Savings at time of survey: Over 50% no savings with 86% of these claiming no money left after basic living expenses.
- Those who save: Kept money at home or a secret hiding place, while 31% invested in livestock; 21% bought gold or jewelry for future re-sale profit. (MacGrath 2016).

Microfinance is used as a key driver of financial inclusion. The Cambodian Microfinancing program aims to increase financial literacy, improve governance and transparency, regulate the financial sector, and make financial services more affordable. Oxfam (2013), a global charitable organization, introduced savings-for-change (SfC) as a pro-poor savings-led microfinance product, and in 2017, over 140,000 people saved USD 5.7 million and 40 local organizations received training to provide the product. SfC is a community-organizing tool to support women transformative leadership to challenge social norms. Oxfam developed two approaches on financial inclusion and economic strengthening of poor women farmers and their families. The single approach provides financial services (loans and credits) for poor women and their families and financial education of households. The integrated approach provides skills-based education (financial literacy with social/life skills) and service on financial inclusion (SfC Group, MFIs, and banking).

Giving women access to affordable financial credit/savings, such as SfC groups, helps to boost self-esteem and leadership capacity, improve income and livelihoods through loans or share outs, invest in farms or businesses to increase household income and security, and create sustainable wellbeing for poor women and their families.

Like their work in Laos, UNCDF has designed similar programs to help increase financial inclusion in Cambodia:

- Shaping inclusive finance transformations to accelerate financial inclusion and women's economic participation, and advocate pro-poor policies, utilize big data analysis of Cambodia's top banks to understand customer service needs and gaps; invest in innovative business models to expand women's economic participation.
- Making access possible expands financial access for rural populations, and micro and small businesses.
- YouthStart Global convenes stakeholders to provide economic opportunities geared toward youth, including capacity-building in opportune sectors, increased access to financial and non-financial services, and access to information on integrated services available to youth.
- CleanStart supports clean energy policy development, and provides risk capital and technical assistance to competitively selected financial service providers and energy enterprises. This initiative supports low-income consumers to transition to cleaner and more efficient energy through access to financial services and payment mechanisms and will help contribute to achieving development goals on poverty and hunger, education, gender, health, and environmental sustainability.

4.6.6. Interventions with Most Impact

In a UNCDF consultation with CLMV market-leaders in financial inclusion, the participants were requested to rate the interventions with the greatest impact on improving the level of financial inclusion in each market. Points were allocated for each intervention out of a total of 100 for each country. Table 11 shows the interventions that participants rated as having the most impact and the explanations of these outcomes are presented below.

Table 11. The interventions that will double the level of financial inclusion by 2020.

Intervention	Cambodia	Laos	Vietnam
Improved function of state FI	4	**11**	**13**
Government payments	11	10	11
Regulatory	10	16	18
New distribution models	**21**	11	10
Mobile	**23**	**18**	14
Microfinance extension	16	19	19
Demand analysis	15	15	15
Total	100	100	100

Source: Doubling Financial Inclusion in the ASEAN Region by 2020, UNCDF.

- In Laos and especially Vietnam, state financial institutions play an important role in increasing financial inclusion. However, participants face challenges with securing appropriate engagement with state institutions to discuss financial inclusion.
- Leveraging the role of Government payments in promoting financial inclusion will be significant in all three markets but will generally account for less than 10% of progress towards the targets.
- Regulatory change is needed especially in Laos and Vietnam to progress in financial inclusion.
- New distribution models such as outsourced or non-branch based services were considered most important in Cambodia.
- For mobile-based service delivery, Cambodia and Laos offer the greatest potential for impact.
- Extending microfinance is highly significant for all three markets.
- Appropriate demand analysis needs to precede intervention efforts.

4.6.7. Risk and Investor Profiles

While the emerging nations of Vietnam, Laos, and Cambodia present exciting growth opportunities in financial inclusion, they also present risks associated with Fintech infrastructure, Fintech ecosystem, or stability. The ING Economics Department (2016) identifies three types of investors.

Commercial investors seek maximum return on investments. Risk-averse investors prefer a stable economy and the right ecosystem. Risk-loving investors are more willing to balance the risk with higher gains with markets that provide larger growth opportunities. These investors are generally investment funds and venture capitalists.

Social investors want to create both social impact and a financial return, seeking "double-bottom line" results. They are usually not-for-profit and for-profit funds, investment vehicles, government sponsored organizations, development banks, and social enterprises.

Donor organizations focus on maximizing social returns and are likely to invest in countries where financial exclusion is highest. They seek to identify the economies that have a better capacity to absorb their funds to create the most impact.

As a summary, the investors who may find Vietnam, Laos, and Cambodia as attractive markets for their funds will be donor organizations, followed by social investors, and risk-loving commercial investors.

5. Limitations

The main limitation is the availability of data of some nations. This may be due to political instability that prevent data gathering or a lack of research partners to collect the data in some nations. While care has been taken to ensure relevant data to help in evaluating markets with the best potential for financial inclusion, The Global Findex Database (2017) did not provide data on Brunei. Based on a World Bank online article that Brunei has achieved almost universal financial inclusion along with

Singapore, Malaysia, and Thailand, Brunei was allocated the same points as Malaysia and Thailand since Singapore is ahead in financial inclusion.

The findings support the UNCDF's efforts to expand financial inclusion in the CLMV. However, Myanmar did not surface in the results and instead the Philippines and Indonesia emerged as fourth and fifth most potential markets. This may be due to the fact that Myanmar's data were dated to 2014/2015 and may have changed since Myanmar won democracy in March 2016. Nevertheless, the Philippines and Indonesia are justified as two markets with high growth potential considering their huge populations of 103 million and 260 million, respectively, with many people facing financial exclusion living in the thousands of islands that make up each country,

Another limitation may be the conventional approach to maximize profit from investments. The findings present the conflict between maximizing social impact and financial returns. Singapore is the best market with state-of-the-art infrastructure and strong governance but offers little room to grow financial inclusion. The likely investors for Vietnam, Laos, and Cambodia would be donor organizations that seek to maximize social returns, followed by social investors who seek a mix of financial and social returns, and lastly, risk-loving commercial investors who prioritize higher gains in markets with larger growth opportunities.

6. Conclusions and Recommendations

The main contribution of this research lies in its originality of a research that seek not to maximize financial profit but financial inclusion for people in dire need for banking facilities to alleviate poverty and improve quality of life. This research fulfills the social responsibility mission while it offers high growth markets to Fintech entrepreneurs. While other research and their respective methodologies seek to determine the most advanced and commercial Fintech markets for gain, this research adopts rigorous filters that analyzes empirical data that identify (1) markets with lowest financial inclusion via data of ownership and usage of debit cards, (2) the most important investment attractiveness factors integrating findings from four reputable investment-related organizations, and (3) sources of information that provide measurements to the investment attractiveness factors. Fintech entrepreneurs who capitalize on this research's findings will reap returns from largely untapped markets while they help to achieve societal marketing goals.

The research also contributes to the economic growth of the nation. Governments with poor ratings such as in governance and risk indicators can take measures to improve the relevant factors, and devise investment incentives to draw foreign investment. Another contribution is the potential collaboration with economists and other specialists who analyze such data to propose policy to their governments which in turn need to operationalize the policy. This research operationalizes the constructs of risk, demand, and supply to draw investments to expand financial inclusion that will stimulate economic growth and stability. This research's methodology is a first to identify the best growth markets for financial inclusion that will appeal to Fintech entrepreneurs with profit or altruistic motivations, to help narrow the gap in income equality within a nation and between nations. The step-by-step market selection methodology based on empirical analysis makes it easier for investors to follow than econometric models that may limit the discussion to and among economists. Integrating the expertise of economists and marketing specialists may create research that build growth models for the nation.

There are two recommendations for future research. The first proposal is to investigate from the consumer perspective the reasons for low ownership and usage of debit cards. Except for Singapore with 89% of adult population owning a debit card followed by Thailand at 58% and Malaysia 41%, the rest are 25% or below. As for debit card usage, the statistics are even lower. For example, Thailand has 58% debit card ownership, higher than Malaysia at 41%. However, only 8% of Thais use a debit card compared to 19% of Malaysians. Except for Singapore, Malaysia and the Philippines were over 50% of debit card owners using the debit card, while the rest of ASEAN have less than 10% using the debit card although a larger percentage own a debit card.

Could one reason be the multitude of small businesses such as food vendors in Thailand who need cash to buy supplies to make food? If so, what conditions may allow the provision of handheld credit/debit card terminals to such vendors? What can governments do to promote a cashless society in a country where small businesses are the spine of the economy?

Singapore, Malaysia, and the Philippines use English as the official business language. Is there evidence that English helps accelerate the usage of debit cards, and financial inclusion in the ASEAN context? ASEAN people, like other Asian nations, have a Confucian philosophy of saving for the future. A perceptual and attitudinal study on cashless transactions may help uncover reasons for the low debit card usage.

The second recommendation is to investigate the challenges of financial inclusion from both industry and governance perspectives. Finance is an industry vulnerable to disruption by software because financial services are made of information rather than concrete goods. Data security remains a threat as regulators are concerned with hacking and the need to protect sensitive consumer and corporate financial data. Any data breach can ruin a Fintech firm's reputation. The Bank Secrecy Act and money transmission regulations represent an ongoing threat to Fintech companies.

Blockchains can help lower cost of transaction by sharing a digital ledger among competitors with the assurance that cryptocurrencies have a permanent record of transfers and ownership free from being tampered or hacked. Cryptocurrency, however, faces low consumer confidence as a practical and trusted currency for transaction. Moving data to the cloud may sound safe but seems risky as any online platform suffers the risk of hacking.

As the industry explores products and services based on innovations, diminishing margins is the most likely challenge in the face of increasing competition. There is greater operational risk in maintaining virtual operations, vulnerable to money-laundering and terrorism financing activities. The online financial sector is also an increasing target of distributed denial of service extortion attacks. Fintech companies often face doubts from financial regulators like issuing banks and the Federal Government. The research can identify the challenges and make recommendations how the industry and government could collaborate to balance the need for financial inclusion with the need for consumer and corporate data protection.

References

Andrew, Ryan. 2015. The Impact of Mobile on the Evolution of Fintech. Available online: https://www.gsma.com/digitalcommerce/the-impact-of-mobile-on-the-evolution-of-fintech (accessed on 13 December 2017).

Asian Development Bank. 2014. *Accelerating Financial Inclusion South-East Asia with Digital Finance*. Philippines: ADB.

Aziz, Abdul, and Bilal Makkawi. 2012. Relationship between Foreign Direct Investment and Country Population. *International Journal of Business and Management* 7. [CrossRef]

Bart, Clarysse, and Yusubova Ayna. 2014. Technology Business Incubation Mechanisms and Sustainable Regional Development, Proceedings. October 23. Available online: http://hdl.handle.net/1854/LU-6842877 (accessed on 30 November 2019).

Bruhn, Miriam, and Inessa Love. 2009. *The economic Impact of Expanding Access to Finance in Mexico (English)*. Finance & PSD Impact Evaluation Note; No. 9. Washington, DC: World Bank, Available online: http://documents.worldbank.org/curated/en/607591468280440182/The-economic-impact-of-expanding-access-to-finance-in-Mexico (accessed on 30 November 2019).

Burgess, Robin, and Rohini Pande. 2005. Do Rural Banks Matter? Evidence from the Indian Social Banking Experiment. *American Economic Review* 95: 780–95. [CrossRef]

Chen, Ming-Chih, Shih-Shiunn Chen, Hung-Ming Yeh, and Wei-Guang Tsaur. 2016. The Key Factors Influencing Internet Finances Services Satisfaction: An Empirical Study in Taiwan. *American Journal of Industrial and Business Management* 6: 748–62. [CrossRef]

Chu, Shan-Ying. 2013. Internet, Economic Growth and Recession. *Modern Economy* 4: 209–13. [CrossRef]

Cull, Robert, Tilman Ehrbeck, and Nina Holle. 2014. Financial inclusion and development: Recent impact evidence. In *Focus Note*. Washington, DC: CGAP, vol. 92.

Demetriades, Panicos, and Siong Hook Law. 2006. Finance, institutions and economic development. *International Journal of Finance and Economics* 11: 245–60. [CrossRef]

Doing Business 2018: Reforming to Create Jobs. 2018. A World Bank Group Flagship Report. The World Bank Group. Available online: http://documents.worldbank.org/curated/en/803361509607947633/Doing-Business-2018-Reforming-to-Create-Jobs (accessed on 29 November 2019).

Elms, Gregory. 2017. International Investments. Presentation by Gregory A. Elms, Field Director, Canada-Indonesia Trade and Private Sector Assistance Project (TPSA) at BINUS International Campus, Jakarta, Indonesia. December 4.

Fragile States Index. 2018. The Fund for Peace. Available online: https://fragilestatesindex.org/ (accessed on 29 November 2019).

Global Competitiveness Report 2017–2018. 2017. The World Economic Forum. Available online: http://www3.weforum.org/docs/GCR2017-2018/05FullReport/TheGlobalCompetitivenessReport2017%E2%80%932018.pdf (accessed on 29 November 2019).

Griffin, Oliver. 2017. How Fintech is Increasing Financial Inclusion. Raconteur. Available online: https://www.raconteur.net/finance/how-fintech-is-increasing-financial-inclusion (accessed on 29 November 2019).

Hanania, Jordan, Kailin Stenhouse, and Jason Donev. 2018. Energy Education: Access to Electricity. June 25. Available online: http://energyeducatfubion.ca/encyclopedia/Access_to_electricity (accessed on 29 November 2019).

ING Economics Department. 2016. The Fintech Index: Assessing Digital and Financial Inclusion in Developing and Emerging Countries. The ING Group. Available online: https://www.ing.nl/media/ING_EBZ_fintech-index-report_tcm162-116078.pdf (accessed on 29 November 2019).

Internationale Zusammenarbeit (GIZ) GmbH. 2012. Rural Finance in Laos: GIZ Experience in Remote Rural Access. Available online: https://www.microfinancegateway.org/sites/default/files/mfg-en-paper-rural-finance-in-laos-giz-experience-in-remote-rural-areas-dec-2012.pdf (accessed on 29 November 2019).

ITU World Telecommunication-ICT Indicators. 2017. World Telecommunication/ICT Indicator Database. Available online: https://www.itu.int/en/ITU-D/Statistics/Pages/publications/wtid.aspx (accessed on 29 November 2019).

Javadekar, Apoorva. 2017. Why the Ease of Doing Business Matters: Livemint. Available online: http://www.livemint.com/Opinion/ZFP18NIFAl8Up0s8FPQySL/Why-the-ease-of-doing-business-matters.html (accessed on 29 November 2019).

Kunt, Asli Demirgüç, and Leora Klapper. 2013. Measuring Financial Inclusion: Explaining Variation in Use of Financial Services across and within Countries. The World Bank. Available online: http://siteresources.worldbank.org/EXTDEC/Resources/469371-1367338460733/Brookings_Apr28.pdf (accessed on 29 November 2019).

Lagarde, Christine. 2018. ASEAN and the IMF: Working Together to Foster Inclusive Growth. Available online: https://www.imf.org/en/News/Articles/2018/02/25/sp022718-jakarta-MD-asean-and-the-imf-working-together-to-foster-inclusive-growth (accessed on 29 November 2019).

Lazarova, Dara. 2017. Fintech trends: The Internet of Things. January 12. Available online: https://www.finleap.com/insights/fintech-trends-the-internet-of-things/ (accessed on 30 November 2017).

Lee, David Kuo Chuen, and Gin Swee (Zhang Jinrui) Teoh. 2015. Emergence of FinTech and the LASIC principles. *Journal of Financial Perspectives* 3: 24–36. [CrossRef]

Levine, Ross. 2000. Finance and Growth: Theory and Evidence. In *Handbook of Economic Growth*, 1st ed. Edited by Philippe Aghion and Steven Durlauf. Amsterdam: Elsevier, vol. 1.

Lewis, Sue, and Dominic Lindley. 2015. *Financial Inclusion, Financial Education and Financial Regulation in the United Kingdom*. ADB Working Paper Series 544; Tokyo: Asian Development Bank Institute.

Luna-Martinez. 2016. How to Scale up Financial Inclusion in ASEAN Countries. The World Bank. Available online: https://blogs.worldbank.org/eastasiapacific/how-to-scale-up-financial-inclusion-in-asean-countries (accessed on 29 November 2019).

MacGrath. 2016. New Tool for Financial Inclusion. The Phnom Penh Post. Available online: https://www.phnompenhpost.com/business/new-tool-financial-inclusion (accessed on 13 July 2016).

McKinsey and Company. 2016. Challenges and Opportunities for Fintech in Germany. Available online: https://www.mckinsey.com/industries/financial-services/our-insights/fintech-challenges-and-opportunities (accessed on 29 November 2019).

Nanda, Kajole, and Mandeep Kaur. 2016. Financial Inclusion and Human Development: A Cross-Country Evidence. *Management and Labour Studies* 41: 127–53. [CrossRef]

Naumann, Friedrich. 2018. 3 Reasons Why Ease of Doing Business in a Country is Important. *The Friedrich Naumann Foundation for Freedom*. Available online: http://asia.fnst.org/content/3-reasons-why-ease-doing-business-country-important (accessed on 29 November 2019).

Oxfam. 2013. Saving for Change: Financial Inclusion and Resilience for the World's Poorest People. *Oxfam America*, May. Available online: https://www.oxfamamerica.org/static/oa4/oxfam-america-sfc-ipa-bara-toplines.pdf(accessed on 29 November 2019).

Ozimek, Adam. 2016. Why Is Population Growth Good for Businesses? Available online: https://www.forbes.com/sites/modeledbehavior/2016/10/23/why-is-population-growth-good-for-businesses/#4ff10a10297f (accessed on 23 October 2016).

Park, Cyn-Young, and Rogelio Mercado. 2015. Financial Inclusion, poverty and Income Inequality in Developing Asia. Available online: https://ssrn.com/abstract=2558936orhttp://dx.doi.org/10.2139/ssrn.2558936 (accessed on 29 November 2019).

Pasali, Selahattin Selşah. 2013. *Where Is the Cheese? Synthesizing a Giant Literature on Causes and Consequences of Financial Sector Development*. Washington, DC: The World Bank.

Pazarbasiogl, Ceyla. 2017. Vietnam's Financial Inclusion Priorities: Expanding Financial Services and Moving to a 'Non-Cash' Economy. The World Bank. Available online: https://blogs.worldbank.org/voices/vietnam-s-financial-inclusion-priorities-expanding-financial-services-and-moving-non-cash-economy (accessed on 29 November 2019).

Ruiz, Claudia. 2013. *From Pawnshops to Banks. The Impact of Formal Credit on Informal Households*. Washington, DC: The World Bank.

Sarma, Mandira. 2008. Index of Financial Inclusion. Indian Council for Research on International Economic Relations. Available online: http://www.icrier.org/pdf/Working_Paper_215.pdf (accessed on 29 November 2019).

Schlein, Michael. 2017. Fintech's Potential for Financial Inclusion: MoneyConf Panel. *Accion Ventures*. Available online: https://medium.com/accion/moneyconf-panel-fintechs-potential-for-financial-inclusion-87adaba1cd1d (accessed on 29 November 2019).

The Economic Times. 2015. How Internet Users Will Impact These Five Areas. February 26. Available online: https://economictimes.indiatimes.com/tech-life/how-internet-users-will-impact-these-five-areas/economy-financial-inclusion/slideshow/46376647.cms (accessed on 30 November 2019).

The Global Findex Database. 2017. Global Findex: The World Bank. Available online: https://globalfindex.worldbank.org/ (accessed on 29 November 2019).

UNCDF. 2017. Doubling Financial Inclusion in the ASEAN Region by 2020. Available online: http://www.finmark.org.za/wp-content/uploads/2016/01/ASEAN_doubling_financial_inclusion.pdf (accessed on 29 November 2019).

Wijaya, Ahmad. 2017. Investors Want Ease of Doing Business and Legal Certainty. *ANTARA News*. Available online: https://en.antaranews.com/news/113532/investors-want-ease-of-doing-business-and-legal-certainty (accessed on 29 November 2019).

World Bank. 2016. Financial Access. Available online: https://www.worldbank.org/en/publication/gfdr/gfdr-2016/background/financial-access (accessed on 30 November 2019).

World Bank. 2019. Financial Inclusion Is the Key to Enabler to Reducing Poverty and Boosting Prosperity. Available online: https://www.worldbank.org/en/topic/financialinclusion/overview/ (accessed on 28 November 2019).

World Competitiveness Yearbook. 2017. IMD Competitiveness Ranking 2017: IMD World Competitiveness Center. Available online: https://www.imd.org/wcc/world-competitiveness-center-rankings/competitiveness-2017-rankings-results/ (accessed on 29 November 2019).

Worldometers. 2018. Available online: http://www.worldometers.info/ (accessed on 15 June 2018).

10

Internationalization, Strategic Slack Resources and Firm Performance: The Case Study of Vietnamese Enterprises

Phuong V. Nguyen [1],*[iD], Hien Thi Ngoc Huynh [2], Hoa Doan Xuan Trieu [2][iD] and Khoa T. Tran [1]

[1] Center for Public Administration, International University-Vietnam National University, Ho Chi Minh City 700000, Vietnam

[2] The School of Business, International University-Vietnam National University, Ho Chi Minh City 700000, Vietnam

* Correspondence: nvphuong@hcmiu.edu.vn

Abstract: The study attempted to fill a gap in the research on international business by providing fresh evidence of the effect of the degree of internationalization on firm performance and the influence of organizational slack on this relationship. By applying a fixed-effects model to data from 569,767 Vietnamese enterprises from 2007 to 2015, a significant W-shaped linkage between internationalization and firm performance was revealed. Importantly, the results also emphasized the importance of three types of slack in the first stage of the internationalization process: absorbed slack human resources, other absorbed slack resources, and unabsorbed slack resources.

Keywords: performance; internationalization; organizational slack

JEL Classification: F12; F14; F21; F23

1. Introduction

As internationalization in recent decades has expanded the size of the market and enabled small firms to do business on a global scale, the expansion of the presence of enterprises in the international market is no longer a strange phenomenon (Ciravegna et al. 2014). Although larger firm size and reputation are often benchmarks and advantages for acceptance in the global market, smaller firms with excellent products and services have proved their dynamic strengths in assessing and meeting the demands of customers abroad, which include activeness, flexibility and network accumulation (Dasí et al. 2015; Ciravegna et al. 2014). As a result, there is great interest in whether foreign expansion is beneficial for enterprises, given their different sizes and capabilities, and numerous studies have sought to assess the relationship between foreign expansion and firm performance as well as its influencing factors in order to optimize this relationship (Cho and Lee 2018; Dasí et al. 2015; Glaum and Oesterle 2007; Pangarkar 2008; Zhang et al. 2018; Zhou 2018; Delios and Beamish 1999). However, despite recognizing the costs and benefits associated with the increasing degree of internationalization, these studies have raised more questions than answers due to the inconclusive findings and ongoing debates (Glaum and Oesterle 2007).

Once the cost of internationalization outweighs its benefits, the global expansion will negatively impact on performance, whereas positive effects occur when the benefits of internationalization dominate its cost (Denis et al. 2002; Kim and Mathur 2008). The dominance of costs or benefits depends strongly on a firm's capabilities, characteristics, strategies, and national context (Cho and Lee 2018; Lin et al. 2011; Zhou 2018). Prior studies have viewed internationalization favorably due to the fact of its positive linear effect on performance, which is attributed to greater market access, competitive advantage and financial success (Chen and Hsu 2010; Pangarkar 2008). However, others have found a negative linear relationship, suggesting threats of global expansion to firm performance due to the presence of foreignness liabilities such as fierce competition, high transaction costs, market volatility, and cultural diversity (Zhou 2017; Zhang et al. 2018).

New research on this issue acknowledging internationalization as a multi-stage process has also found a curvilinear relationship between internationalization and firm performance (Bobillo et al. 2010; Cho and Lee 2018; Contractor et al. 2003; Dutta et al. 2016; Lin et al. 2011; Pangarkar 2008; Zhou 2018). Empirical results have suggested that this curvilinear relationship is moderated by firm characteristics and behaviors, leading to an S-shaped relationship in the three-stage theory of Contractor et al. (2003) and the empirical results of others (Bobillo et al. 2010; Cho and Lee 2018; Lin et al. 2011; Riahi-Belkaoui 1998; Ruigrok et al. 2007), a U-shaped relationship (Assaf et al. 2012; Capar and Kotabe 2003; Chen and Tan 2012), an inverted U-shaped relationship (Chiao et al. 2006), or a W-shaped relationship for small firms (Zhou 2018). Further complicating the issue, some studies have attempted to distinguish different modes of internationalization according to product diversification strategy, including single-item export versus multi-item export. The results indicate that the single-item strategy generates more benefits for internationalizing firms in terms of performance enhancement and technology absorption (Agyei-Boapeah 2018; Sharma 2017).

Moreover, the relevant theoretical and empirical literature has recognized the importance of organizational slack as a strategic resource to relieve uncertainties and sustain firm performance in the global expansion process (Bourgeois 1981; Daniel et al. 2004; Lin et al. 2011; Tan and Peng 2003). Depending on the discretion and flexibility level, slack resources can be classified as high-discretion slack and low-discretion slack (Lin et al. 2011). Zhang et al. (2018) recently explored the moderating effects of three types of slack on the relationship between internationalization and performance: absorbed slack human resources (AHRs), other kinds of absorbed slack resources (OARs), and unabsorbed slack resources (USRs). While AHRs represent inimitable slack based on human capital accumulation, OARs reflect the surplus in business operations and are oriented toward extremely selective uses. By contrast, due to the fact of its high discretion, USRs are more likely to be used as buffers in implementing international ventures.

Compared to the rich literature on international economics focused on the internationalization performance of MNCs from advanced economies like Taiwan, Japan, and Europe, there is less evidence for the going-global performance of enterprises from emerging countries. The past three decades have witnessed rapid growth and remarkable transformation in emerging economies (EEs), and EE enterprises have benefited tremendously from global trade integration and economic convergence. One of these emerging markets is Vietnam, a developing country that has experienced recent success in trade and economic growth. The dynamic internationalization process of domestic enterprises has been a significant contributor to these successes. Due to the globalization efforts and incentive policies during the past two decades, the total export of manufactured goods has grown at an average of 10 percent per year, stimulating the development of internationalized firms and contributing to 80 percent of Vietnam's GDP in 2017 (Eckardt et al. 2018).

In contrast to the regression of globalization occurring in some countries in the Pacific and East Asia region, Vietnam has witnessed a renaissance in manufacturing and processing industries toward international expansion. A number of critical factors are responsible for this positive outcome. Among the most important of these factors is Vietnam's open trade policy, which has supported the process of internationalization of local enterprises. Vietnam, along with Singapore, holds the top position in East Asia for participating in bilateral and multilateral free trade agreements (FTAs) with the United States, Japan, Korea, and the European Union and is also a member of ASEAN and WTO. In early 2018, Vietnam and 11 other countries joined the Comprehensive and Progressive Agreement for Trans-Pacific Partnership (CPTPP). The above trade agreements are committed to drastically reducing tariffs, implementing domestic reforms, and opening up the economy to foreign investment (Eckardt et al. 2018).

In addition, Vietnam has taken advantage of its population structure through effective investments in human resources. Furthermore, to facilitate international integration, Vietnam has relentlessly invested in improving competitiveness and creating a favorable business environment for both domestic and foreign firms by lowering corporate income taxes, resulting in higher rankings in the World Economic Forum's Competitiveness Index and the World Bank's Favorable Business Environment. Vietnam has also invested in infrastructure, especially in transport, logistics, and electricity, to meet rising business demands. Last but not least, the emergence of the digital era has enabled smaller firms in Vietnam to go global by using digital networking channels and more innovative approaches (Coviello et al. 2017). However, Vietnam's commercial competitiveness, in terms of time-consuming costs, procedural fees and transaction costs for import-export activities, lags behind other countries in the region, particularly the major ASEAN countries (including Singapore, Malaysia, Thailand, and the Philippines). Despite the significant achievements of local internationalized enterprises nurtured in this emerging market, the manufacturing and processing industry in Vietnam is still relatively small and is mainly driven by foreign direct investment (FDI), which accounts for nearly 90 percent of exports. The higher level of internationalization and increasing foreign inflows in Vietnam have challenged the survival and affected the internationalization performance of local enterprises in different ways (Lin 2014).

While a rich body of previous empirical studies has focused on the internationalization performance of multinational enterprises (MNEs) from developed economies, there is a shortage of academic studies on mature and newly internationalized enterprises from EEs (Buckley et al. 2017). The rapid growth of MNEs and newly internationalized firms in EEs has challenged arguments that successful internationalization requires a well-established institutional framework, firm or country-specific resources and favorable market conditions (Buckley et al. 2017). It has been claimed that EE enterprises can overcome their deficiencies and perform more effectively in global expansion by exploiting their non-traditional capabilities, such as superior networking, resource recombination, linkages, and leverage (Contractor et al. 2007; Cuervo-Cazurra et al. 2018; Buckley et al. 2017). However, there is a lack of evidence on the role of firm behavior, specifically, how EE enterprises allocate and use their strategic organizational resources to pursue internationalization despite many uncertainties and deficiencies (Buckley et al. 2017). Furthermore, direct empirical evidence supporting the explanation of the relationship between organizational slack and firm performance is not available for EEs. To address these research gaps and contribute to the literature on international integration, this study aims to answer two research questions. First, we investigated whether there is a curvilinear (specifically a W-shaped) global expansion–performance relationship for Vietnamese enterprises. Second, we filled a gap in the literature on behavioral economics by exploring the impact of different types of organizational slack on internationalization performance. We found that the three types of slack recently delineated by Zhang et al. (2018), i.e., AHRs, OARs, and USRs, can capture human capital accumulation and the discretion level; in addition, we identified which type of slack was critical for international integration in Vietnam in each of the different stages of internationalization. The findings from this paper can be applied to Vietnam's neighboring EEs in East Asia and the Pacific region, including Thailand, Malaysia, Philippines, Myanmar, Cambodia, and Laos. The government and top management of MNEs and newly internationalized firms in these regions can use these findings to develop appropriate policies and implement effective strategies to sustain internationalization performance at the firm level.

2. Literature Review

2.1. Degree of Internationalization and Firm Performance

2.1.1. Degree of Internationalization

Although global expansion is recognized as a favorable means of overcoming imperfect home institutional factors, market, and firm or country deficiencies, it is a gradual, long-term process that accompanies a firm's accumulation of knowledge, experience, transformation of organizational structure, and networking over time (Hutzschenreuter and Matt 2017; Buckley et al. 2017; Cuervo-Cazurra et al. 2018). In the Uppsala model, these movements require a switch in a firm's commitment modes (Johanson and Vahlne 2009). However, success stories of born-global companies exhibiting a phase-skipping process abound. To further explain the situation, Håkanson and Kappen (2017) synthesized and compared the three main rooted theories of the process of internationalization based on behavioral economics, as summarized below: the main focus of the study, the Uppsala model described by (Johanson and Vahlne 1977) and revised in (Johanson and Vahlne 2009); the born-global model of (Madsen and Servais 1997); and a new formulation and introduction of the Casino model by (Håkanson and Kappen 2017).

In their formulation of the Uppsala model, Johanson and Vahlne (1977) focus on interpreting firms' increasing resource commitments as a result of higher experience and knowledge acquisition over incremental phases of internationalization expansion. In this model, international expansion is considered as an evolutionary process that is accumulative in nature; in this process, experiential learning and knowledge gain enable decision-makers to recognize opportunities, perceive potential risks, and calculate expansion costs to move forward (Vahlne and Johanson 2017; Santangelo and Meyer 2017). Interestingly, the wait-and-see strategy is a common practice of firms using the Uppsala model, as a commitment by these firms is strongly restrained by risks (Clarke and Liesch 2017). The framework of the Uppsala model includes change variables and state variables. With respect to change variables, commitment in term of resource allocation decisions always represents a tradeoff between the benefits and costs of internationalization under conditions of uncertainty and partial ignorance, and the commitment can be subsequently altered or adapted (Johanson and Vahlne 1977). Hence, this is considered an important source of another change variable—knowledge development in terms of learning, capacity, and trust-building.

State variables are classified into capability variables and commitment/performance variables, which have a cause–effect relationship with change variables. Operational capabilities are associated with privileged access to raw materials, capital, technology, governance systems, etc., to deal with the liability of foreignness. Dynamic capabilities, on the other hand, are inimitable, often accumulated through the learning process, and reveal the ability of the firm to combine its strengths and competencies to successfully respond to the rapidly changing environment. Finally, commitment variables comprise resource distribution decisions, and performance variables refer to the outcomes that are determined by knowledge development and internal/external capabilities (Santangelo and Meyer 2017; Vahlne and Johanson 2017).

The born-global model, by contrast, emphasizes the spirit of entrepreneurship in risk-taking ventures that seek to take advantage of international niche markets. In this case, pioneering companies aim to go global without a stable foundation based on domestic revenue. The born-global model is quite different from the Uppsala model, which is highly sensitive to uncertainties and pursues a gradually incremental process of internationalization (Håkanson and Kappen 2017). In the modern world, the born-global model appears to be supported by the wide range of internet-based innovative operational approaches and digital tools that can eliminate traditional weaknesses and internationalization costs and open new horizons for newly internationalized firms in global markets (Coviello et al. 2017). In this way, despite lacking a step-by-step approach and cautious practices, born-global companies can take advantage of their means-oriented flexibilities in implementing their internationalization strategy and capturing market opportunities (Chetty and Holm 2000).

The Casino model can be considered as a convergence of the Uppsala and born-global models, as it explains the internationalization process by synthesizing a special pattern based on certain characteristics of these two models (Håkanson and Kappen 2017). Although the Casino model is similar to the Uppsala model in terms of the initial development of a strong domestic base, this model's international expansion strategy is not restricted to market uncertainties and knowledge gaps. In this model, once the initial investments are made, the marginal cost of internationalization, for example, the marginal cost to establish a new subsidiary, diminishes over time. Similar to born-global enterprises, firms implementing the Casino model are very purposive and proactive in seeking existing opportunities. However, as in the Uppsala model, they prefer feasible market opportunities rather than uncertain ventures.

It is worth noting that a higher level of internationalization usually requires an incremental process from exports to the establishment of subsidiaries and coordination units abroad for production, marketing, and distribution and from neighboring markets to more distant markets (Johanson and Vahlne 1977, 2009; Vahlne and Johanson 2017). More importantly, improvements in resource commitment and knowledge development over time not only provide firms with a strong base for shifting to later phases of the internationalization process but also influence internationalization performance. Therefore, the Uppsala model seems to be a good fit for the main focus of the present study, which aims to explore firm-level internationalization performance across different incremental phases and investigate whether firms' behavior in terms of slack resource allocation impacts the global expansion process.

2.1.2. The Relationship between Internationalization Degree and Firm Performance

Beginning with McDougall (1989), the literature on international entrepreneurship initially focused on new ventures undertaken rapidly and proactively by multinational companies. Recent studies of international entrepreneurship have expanded to include firms' cross-border operations independent of their age and size (Zahra 2005; Jones et al. 2011; Schwens et al. 2018). In general, entrepreneurial internationalization is a business strategy by which companies seek an appropriate level of involvement in global integration to be successful (Lu and Beamish 2001; Schwens et al. 2018). Consistent with the trend in the field, this paper focuses on firms' degree of internationalization in terms of foreign sales.

Whereas early studies proposed a positive linkage between firms' internationalization and performance, later analyses have taken into account the benefits and costs of a globalization strategy (Autio et al. 2000; Marano et al. 2016). The latter view is particularly pertinent to international expansion due to the fact of its proactive, innovative, and risky nature (McDougall and Oviatt 2000). Thus, although international market entry enables firms to seek opportunities for growth and value creation, firms also face risk and failure in implementing such an entry, leading to both negative outcomes and a non-linear internationalization–performance relationship. In particular, the greater global expansion will generate additional negative impacts. High global integration may increase coordination and governance costs related to managing internationalization operations, enhance management's information processing needs, and challenge the allocation of management resources.

Two main theoretical streams have emerged to propose and describe the benefits of internationalization: theories of foreign direct investment (FDI) and theories of multinational firms. According to FDI theories, firms invest in foreign countries because of economic drivers such as low production costs, market expansion, financial markets, and incentive policies from host countries (Ruigrok and Wagner 2003). While researchers in industrial organization and international business usually concentrate on economies of scale and scope (Buckley and Casson 1976), scholars in financial economics emphasize portfolio diversification and its impact on firms' risk–return performance (Gaur and Delios 2015; Bausch and Pils 2009; Wiersema and Bowen 2008). In general, the international business field has yielded consensus in terms of the benefits of internationalization (Contractor et al. 2007). However, an essential question remains to be clearly answered: "What is the optimum degree of internationalization?"

In addition to its benefits, previous studies have stressed the costs of internationalization. Entry costs and risks in international business are mainly related to differences in language and cultural background among employees, implementing new marketing and promotion programs, seeking reliable foreign distributors or suppliers, and international compliance, among other concerns.

As doing international business generates benefits as well as costs, it is worth noting that the linkage between internationalization and performance relies on the distribution of benefits and costs in the internationalization process. As a result, a non-linear internationalization–performance relationship is likely to be the most reasonable. Previous studies have demonstrated a complex curvilinear relationship between the degree of internationalization (DOI) and performance. The DOI reflects a firm's exports to other countries (Hitt et al. 1997; Velez-Calle et al. 2018). Many previous studies have investigated the internationalization–performance relationship, with mixed empirical results: positive linear (Delios and Beamish 1999); negative linear (Denis et al. 2002; Kim and Mathur 2008); no significant linkage (Majocchi and Zucchella 2003); inverted U-shaped (Elango 2006); U-shaped (Chen and Tan 2012); inverted S-shaped (Cho and Lee 2018); S-shaped (Ruigrok et al. 2007); and U-shaped in large firms and W-shaped in small firms (Zhou 2018). Table 1 summarizes the commonly reported relationships.

Table 1. Empirical studies on the internationalization–performance link.

Author (Year)	Measurement of DOI	Empirical Results
Majocchi and Zucchella (2003)	Ratio of exports to total sales—Italian SMEs	No significant impact on ROA
Elango (2006)	Foreign sales to total sales—12 emerging markets	Inverted U-shaped relationship between DOI and performance
Ruigrok et al. (2007)	Foreign sales to total sales—Swiss multinational companies	S-shape was shifted to the right. The higher the DOI, the lower the performance
Chen and Tan (2012)	Percentage of total sales from foreign sales Percentage of total sales from within Asia excluding China Percentage of total sales from the Greater China region—Chinese firms	Weakly negative U-shaped link between Asian sales and firm performance Weak effect
Cho and Lee (2018)	Foreign sales to total sales—SMEs in Korea	Inverted S-shaped link between DOI and firm performance (supporting the three-stage international theory)
Velez-Calle et al. (2018)	Foreign sales to total sales (internationalization depth) Geographic zone index (international breadth)—firms in Latin America	U-shaped link Inverted U-shaped link
Zhou (2018)	The ratio of the number of overseas subsidiaries to the number of total subsidiaries—manufacturing firms in China	W-shaped in small firms and U-shaped in large firms
Cuervo-Cazurra et al. (2018)	Dummy variable that equals 1 if the firm has international operations—Argentina, Brazil, Chile, and Peru	The internationalization–performance linkage varied depending on the characteristics of the home and host countries

Notes: DOI: Degree of internationalization; ROA: Return on assets.

Given the number of empirical studies on the subject and the variety of outcomes, researchers have recently attempted to reconcile the theoretical arguments by suggesting that a U-shaped, inverted U-shaped, S-shaped or inverted S-shaped curve (a horizontal three-stage) may best represent the relationship between international expansion and corporate performance (see Table 1). However, researchers have not explained the reason that many enterprises, i.e., so-called "born-global" firms, devote all of their resources to achieving high global integration and why firms with greater global expansion have better performance. In particular, few studies in this field have explored emerging markets like Vietnam. Therefore, based on the evidence, we considered a fundamental W-shaped internationalization–performance link and investigated how enterprises' product diversification affects the global integration decision and the internationalization–performance link in the manufacturing industry of Vietnam. Moreover, this study attempted to determine the theoretical mechanism underlying the curvilinear relationship in Vietnam, which differs from those in other developed countries.

2.1.3. Four Stages of the Internationalization Process

From an evolutionary perspective, such as that adopted in the Uppsala model, early international developers often start with a low-commitment mode and are restrained to uncertainties and knowledge ignorance (Johanson and Vahlne 1977). In this adverse condition, they attempt to develop their knowledge and experiential learning to better perceive risks and recognize opportunities. This learning process incurs a cost burden, and an analysis of relevant studies illustrates that at the initial stage of foreign entry, firms seeking market expansion often experience upfront costs such as setting costs, administrative costs, and transaction costs (Hutzschenreuter and Matt 2017). The learning theory of Johanson and Vahlne (1977) considers internationalization an incremental process in which firms enhance organizational learning and improve knowledge as they enter foreign markets. Therefore, in the early stage of foreign market entry, firms are willing to pay high costs to obtain new market knowledge and adapt to foreign cultures, industry dynamics, and business environments (Johanson and Vahlne 2009; Zhou 2018). Although internationalization may generate a new income inflow, these benefits are not sufficient to offset the initial costs. In this early stage, firms do not yet benefit from economies of scale, as both the scope and scale of global operations are still small and inefficient (Santangelo and Meyer 2017). The first phase of the internationalization process is the most uncertain and challenging step and initially incurs a huge cost burden without any predictable outcome. However, this phase paves the way for later phases. Because internationalized firms are more exposed to risks and, thus, have a high probability of a loss or poor performance in the early period of foreign entry, we proposed that DOI was negatively associated with firm performance in the first stage of foreign entry.

In the second stage, firms allocating resources to increase DOI can gain economic benefits in diverse ways: accumulating and transforming innovative and useful knowledge, which can enable firms to improve capabilities and performance (Lu and Beamish 2001); obtaining competitive advantages throughout catch-up opportunities in global markets (McDougall and Oviatt 1996); and gaining benefits from economies of scale that are sufficient to compensate for the incremental costs of further foreign expansion. Upon further implementation of global expansion, firms increase market share throughout different foreign markets (Pangarkar 2008). In addition, with an increasing number of representatives in different countries, firms have the ability to reduce country risks derived from deviations in foreign, fiscal, and monetary policies. Moreover, in this second stage, going-global enterprises can exploit markets and seek resources in a more optimal way using a wide range of strategies and advantages, such as price discrimination, arbitrage, access to low-cost inputs or even exercising global market power (Rugman 2016; Contractor et al. 2007). Therefore, we expected that the relationship between DOI and firm performance was positive in the second stage.

In the third stage, as firms continue to implement global entry, DOI increases with the expanding number of overseas subsidiaries. Conflicts of interest among these subsidiaries may occur and lead to unattainable goals of the parent company. As a result, the subsidiaries could become competitors instead of collaborators (Porter 1976). Under this scenario, firms have to overcome considerable challenges in multinational organizational management. In addition, the diversity of culture among employees across countries may become an obstacle for cooperation and coordination toward common objectives (Contractor et al. 2003). When firms are in the third phase of the internationalization process, they face greater exposure to risks due to the large resource commitment and operations beyond an optimum number of nations with increasing governance costs (Vahlne and Johanson 2017). In this way, unexpected market variations or underperformance may accidentally defeat firms as they go beyond the optimal threshold. Therefore, firm performance may decrease in the third stage.

As an expansion of the three-stage theory outlined above, Zhou (2018) described the fourth stage. This fourth stage is consistent with findings by Contractor et al. (2003) that multinational firms will attempt to reform organizational operations to improve their performance. Previous studies have shown that if multinational firms successfully build up an international network, they can gain benefits from "arbitrage and leverage opportunities" in various markets via this network. Moreover, with investments in new technologies and innovative solutions, firms can enhance effective communication between employees of various cultural and knowledge backgrounds (Kogut 1989; Wernerfelt 1984; Hitt et al. 1997; Zhou 2018). Firms can organize short course training or seminars to promote their organizational culture and core values. The greater the internationalization, the more alternatives that are available to firms when responding to external environmental uncertainty (Trigeorgis and Reuer 2017). Moreover, at the fourth stage, highly internationalized firms have greater access to global resources, human competencies, and opportunities to practice various effective strategies using their global coverage and power (Trigeorgis and Reuer 2017). Hence, internationalization performance was expected to increase again in stage 4.

Thus, based on the above arguments, we propose that the link between DOI and performance is W-shaped:

Hypothesis 1. *The link between DOI and performance is non-linear (W-shaped): DOI is negatively associated with firm performance in the first stage; has a positive effect on performance in the second stage; is negatively associated with performance in the third stage; and positively impacts performance in the fourth stage.*

2.2. Organizational Slack and Internationalization Performance

Bourgeois and Singh (1983) propose that organizational slack is "composed of three interrelated but conceptually distinct dimensions: available, recoverable, and potential slack." The first includes resources that have not been incorporated into the technical design of the organization; the second comprises resources that "have already been absorbed into the system design as excess costs, but may be recovered during adverse time"; and the last involves "the capacity of the organization to generate extra resources from the environment, as by raising additional debt or equity capital." In particular, Nohria and Gulati (1997) define organizational slack as the "pool of resources in an organization that is in excess of the minimum necessary to produce a given level of organizational output." In addition, Singh (1986) separates slack into absorbed slack and unabsorbed slack. The first refers to excess costs in organizations, whereas the second encompasses excess, uncommitted liquid resources. Lee and Wu (2016) propose that absorbed slack "can be defined as slack committed to human resource, overhead expenses, the company's reputation, and other administrative costs. Unabsorbed slack can be defined as excess, uncommitted liquid assets, showing a firm's ability to meet current obligations with available resources." Therefore, recoverable slack was considered absorbed slack, and available slack was considered unabsorbed slack.

Previous studies have explored bundles of slack resources and illustrated their influence on firm outcomes. For instance, Mellahi and Wilkinson (2010) examined the effect of slack level on innovation output and found that downsizing of slack was temporally associated with innovation output. In an investigation of financial slack and research and development (R&D) investments, Kim et al. (2008) demonstrated that financial slack had an inverted U-shaped linkage with R&D investments. Other studies concentrated on examining the relationship between organizational slack and outcomes such as firm performance, R&D investments, innovation outcomes, firm growth, and corporate entrepreneurship (Bradley et al. 2011; George 2005; Tan and Peng 2003; Lee and Wu 2016).

Among recent empirical evidence on the extent to which bundles of financial and human resource slack contribute to firm performance and survival, Paeleman and Vanacker (2015) illustrated that neither parallel resource abundance (having slack in financial and human resources) nor parallel resource constraints (lacking slack in financial and human resources) are optimal for firm performance and survival. By contrast, Wiersma (2017) showed that slack leads to greater benefits, as the organization achieves many profitable investment opportunities. Their findings show that the total impact of available slack is positively associated with organizational performance, whereas the association of recoverable slack with performance is negative.

From the perspective of firm behavior, the allocation of slack resources is among the strategic decisions that can determine a firm's readiness to relieve internal and external challenges and provide possibilities for starting internationalization ventures (Lin and Liu 2012; Tan and Peng 2003; Bourgeois 1981). In this way, slack resources can be understood as a firm's tangible and intangible assets that are primarily used for contingency purposes (Bourgeois 1981). The availability of organizational slack also reflects firms' strategic decisions and resource commitment level for internationalization activities (Johanson and Vahlne 1977; Lin 2014). Understanding the moderating effect of organizational slack on the internationalization–firm performance relationship is very important because slack plays a key role in buffering internationalization ventures and promoting efficient strategies to deal with uncertainties and foreign liability (Zhang et al. 2018).

Depending on the specific characteristics and discretion level of the slack, Lin et al. (2011) divided organizational slack into two main types: high-discretion slack and low-discretion slack. By contrast, Zhang et al. (2018) estimated three important kinds of slack: AHR, OAR, and USR. While OAR and USR reflect financial slack in terms of flexibility and discretion level for use, AHR captures a firm's inimitable assets in terms of human capital accumulation and expertise. Therefore, this study takes into account the impact of these three types of slack on the internationalization–performance relationship for Vietnamese enterprises.

2.2.1. The Moderating Effect of Absorbed Slack Human Resources (AHRs)

As mentioned above, AHR (measured by the ratio of the number of employees to total sales) is considered a critical resource for implementing an internationalization plan. Absorbed slack human resources can be defined as a firm's long-term intangible assets established through accumulated human capital and expertise that are very difficult to imitate, such as sophisticated solutions, complete processes, experiences, disciplines, and professionals (Zhang et al. 2018; Dutta et al. 2016). For firms, learning, experience, and improvement require a long period. In addition, AHRs are extremely important for newly internationalized firms in the first stage of joining the global market, as this stage requires accumulated international experience and in-depth knowledge to overcome the challenges of foreign liability and cultural diversity (Lin and Liu 2012). Hence, AHRs are expected to enhance a firm's internationalization performance in the early stages.

However, the importance of AHRs may gradually fade away in later stages due to the increasing cost burden associated with the retention of highly qualified experts. The skills and knowledge of these experts are highly attached to specific tasks instead of multi-task diversification (Zhang et al. 2018). Therefore, as firms reach higher degrees of the internationalization process, AHRs may no longer be an advantage. However, the overall effect of AHRs on international performance at each stage is difficult to predict. From the theoretical aspects discussed above, we obtained the second hypothesis.

Hypothesis 2. *Absorbed slack human resources (AHRs) positively moderate the internationalization–performance relationship of Vietnamese enterprises.*

2.2.2. The Moderating Effect of Other Kinds of Absorbed Slack Resources (OARs)

The second type of slack, OARs, originate from the financial surplus from business operations (measured by the difference between working capital and the salary budget divided by total sales) and are allocated for very selective contingency use, particularly for relieving internal pressures (Daniel et al. 2004; Bourgeois 1981). This kind of slack is characterized by a low discretion level for use. Moreover, OARs in term of excess financial cashflow may be challenged by economic downturns, inefficient investments, or long payback periods during the firm's operation time. More importantly, internationalization requires firms to start new ventures under uncertain and unpredictable conditions, but OARs are oriented toward facilitating firm operations and absorbing shock (Zhang et al. 2018). Despite its disadvantages, OARs are a vital resource that enable firms to stabilize firm performance and eliminate shocks to sustain firm development. In this way, OARs are a key resource for opening new horizons for launching internationalization and maintaining firm performance when going global. Thus, we obtained the third hypothesis:

Hypothesis 3. *Other kinds of absorbed slack resources (OARs) positively moderate the internationalization– performance relationship of Vietnamese enterprises.*

2.2.3. The Moderating Effect of Unabsorbed Slack Resources (USRs)

Among the three types of slack, unabsorbed slack resources (USRs) appears to be the most uncommitted flexible type of additional resource in favor of implementing innovation and internationalization strategies (Nohria and Gulati 1996). The USRs are estimated by the ratio of current assets to current liabilities. While OARs are used to smooth daily operations by buffering internal pressures, USRs can enable firms to launch new ambitious goals, such as investing in new opportunities and diversifying products and markets (Lin 2014; Zhang et al. 2018). Because enterprises are often characterized by limited budgets and low access to abundant resources, the allocation of a firm's strategic organizational resources to USR has a very high opportunity cost and requires the right investment in truly feasible projects (Dutta et al. 2016). It is important to note that managers in enterprises are under extremely high pressure to ensure efficient portfolio and capital use, especially when implementing complex long-term strategies like international integration. Nevertheless, a higher level of USRs undeniably contribute to activating and facilitating the global expansion process. Thus, we obtained the fourth hypothesis:

Hypothesis 4. *Unabsorbed slack resources (USRs) positively moderate the internationalization–performance relationship of Vietnamese enterprises.*

3. Methodology

3.1. Data Sample

This study used data on all Vietnamese enterprises drawn from the General Statistics Office of Vietnam (GSO) database, which consists of annual reports of all enterprises operating in Vietnam, from 2007 to 2015. During the study period, GSO compiled 2,850,883 records belonging to approximately 900,000 operating firms listed by firm IDs. After filtering out samples not following basic Vietnamese standards, such as those with negative assets or a negative number of employees, we constrained for a suitable range according to the entire variable list to eliminate outliers. Finally, the data used for analysis contained a total of 1,732,265 samples of 569,767 Vietnamese firms, which accounted for 61% of the initial population. According to Vietnamese law, small enterprises have a total labor force under 100 and total assets under 20 billion VND (equivalent to 741 million EUR) or a total labor force under 50 and total assets under 50 billion VND (equivalent to 1852 million EUR). This kind of enterprise accounts for 91.51% of the sample. Similarly, medium enterprises have a total labor force under 200 and total assets under 100 billion VND (equivalent to 3704 million EUR) or a total labor force under 100 and total revenue under 300 billion for trading and service industries. Medium enterprises account for 8.49% of the sample.

3.2. Measurement

3.2.1. Firm Performance

Firm performance can be estimated based on accounting indexes or justification of managers. As a proxy for firm performance, this study used return on assets (ROA), which has been popularly used in many previous studies (Daniel et al. 2004; Zhang et al. 2018), in addition, to return on sales (ROS) or return on equity (ROE). Because of the characteristics of Vietnamese enterprises, which include limited financial management and a lack of financial capabilities, we strongly suggest using ROA to avoid the unobservable bias of ROE.

3.2.2. Internationalization

There are many ways to estimate firm DOI. The DOI can be calculated based on a firm's operations overseas, including its operation time in years, a number of overseas subsidiaries, or amount of outward FDI (Lu and Beamish 2004; Zhang et al. 2018). However, for Vietnamese enterprises, this measurement is not appropriate, as most Vietnamese enterprises do not operate abroad. Therefore, we estimated the DOI of enterprises by the ratio of total foreign sales to total revenue (Zhao and Ma 2016; Korsakienė and Tvaronavičienė 2012; Dutta et al. 2016).

3.2.3. Organizational Slack

Previous studies of the relationship between internationalization and firm performance have suggested an important role for organizational slack (Tan 2003; Lin and Liu 2012; Lin 2014; Zhang et al. 2018; Daniel et al. 2004; Bourgeois 1981; Dutta et al. 2016). Following Zhang et al. (2018), AHRs are measured as the ratio of the number of workers to total sales, USRs as the ratio of current assets to current liabilities, and OARs as the difference between working capital and total labor cost divided by total sales.

3.2.4. Control Variables

This study had four control variables: product diversification (PDIVER), experience in business (AGE), firm size (FIRM_SIZE), and technology gap (TECH_GAP). Bowen and Wiersema (2009); Chang and Wang (2007); Kumar et al. (2012), and Tallman and Li (1996) have described the impact of product diversification strategies on firm performance. Following Santarelli and Tran (2016), we estimate PDIVER by entropy. The AGE was represented by firm operating years, and FIRM_SIZE was measured by the natural logarithm of firm revenue. TECH_GAP was estimated by the gap between the firm average wage and the average wage of the industry. In addition, two dummy variables, YEAR and INDUSTRY, were introduced to prevent unobservable bias of the research model.

3.3. The Model

A research model was designed to investigate the relationship between internationalization and firm performance and the impact of the three types of organizational slack on this relationship. The main research model is as follows:

$$ROA_{it} = \beta_0 + \beta_1 DOI_{it} + \beta_2 DOI^2_{it} + \beta_3 DOI^3_{it} + \beta_4 DOI^4_{it} + \beta_5 AHR_{it} + \beta_6 OAR_{it} + \beta_7 USR_{it} + \beta_8 PDIVER_{it} + \beta_9 FIRM\text{-}SIZE_{it} + \beta_{10} AGE_{it} + \beta_{11} TECH\_GAP_{it} + \mu_i + \varepsilon_{it}$$

The model in this study was estimated by a fixed-effects-based regression following the results of a Hausman test (Hausman 1978) indicating that a fixed-effects regression was more appropriate than a random-effects regression for our dataset. The next step in the analysis procedure was to check for collinearity among the independent variables. As shown in Table 2, the correlations between independent variables were relatively low; all were less than 0.3 (Neter et al. 1990), indicating low bias and high reliability. The variance inflation factor (VIF) test was also used to test for collinearity in the research model. The mean VIF was 1.17, and the highest VIF was 1.67, which indicates that multicollinearity was not a problem in our model.

Table 2. Descriptive statistics and variable correlations.

	Mean	SD	ROA	DOI	AHR	OAR	USR	PDIVER	FIRM_SIZE	AGE	TECH_GAP
ROA	−0.003	0.178	1	-							
DOI	0.001	0.013	0	1	-						
AHRs	0.007	0.024	−0.0026 *	0.0008	1	-					
OARs	−0.762	0.717	0.0001	−0.0002	−0.0102 *	1	-				
USRs	0.023	0.910	−0.0001	0.0002	0.0193 *	0.0243 *	1	-			
PDIVER	0.031	0.154	0.0092 *	0.0107 *	−0.0071 *	0.0007	−0.0004	1	-		
FIRM_SIZE	8.305	1.822	0.0362 *	0.0368 *	−0.1290 *	0.0117 *	−0.0076 *	0.1452 *	1		
AGE	3.974	4.248	0.0402 *	0.0262 *	−0.0145 *	−0.0008	−0.001	0.1173 *	0.2387 *	1	-
TECH_GAP	−0.032	0.274	0.0118 *	0.0146 *	−0.0096 *	−0.0018 *	−0.0001	0.0150 *	0.1294 *	0.0153 *	1

Notes: ROA: Return on assets. DOI: Degree of internationalization. AHR: Absorbed slack human resources. OAR: Other kinds of absorbed slack resources. PDIVER: Product diversification. FIRM_SIZE: Firm size. AGE: Firm operating years. TECH_GAP: the gap between the firm average wage and the average wage of the industry. * p-value < 0.05.

4. Results and Discussion

To estimate the impact of DOI on firm performance, a fixed-effects-based regression model and random-effects model were first considered due to the fact of their popularity and appropriateness for panel data. The results of the Hausman test ($p = 0.000$) recommended the use of a fixed-effects model for our large unbalanced 2007–2015 panel data. However, according to two studies (Bell et al. 2018; Bell and Jones 2015), the Hausman test is not always optimal for determining the preferred model. An alternative approach to check the appropriateness of a fixed-effect versus random-effect model is provided by Mundlak (1978) work. The comparative advantage of the Mundlak approach to the Hausman test is that the former can be applied to scenarios with the heteroskedastic error or intragroup correlation. According to the Mundlak approach, a panel-level average of time-varying proxies is calculated and checked to determine whether the panel-level means are jointly equal to zero in the random-effects estimator with other covariates in the model. In the present study, the results of the Mundlak approach rejected the hypothesis that the coefficients of our model were jointly equal to 0, which implies that a correlation between the time-invariant unobservable bias and regressors exists and that the fixed-effect model would be more appropriate. The coefficients of Fixed Effect Model (FEM) and Random Effect Model (REM) that were used to conduct the Hausman test and Mundlak approach are illustrated in Appendix A. We also conducted firm clustering to reduce heteroskedasticity and autocorrection bias in the model. On the right-hand side of the equation, other important explanatory variables, such as organizational slack, product diversification, firm size, firm age, and technology gap, are comprehensively reviewed and added to avoid missing-variable status and enhance the possibility of explaining unobserved variants. Organizational slack is also used as a moderator to explore how this critical variable moderates the relationship between DOI and firm performance. The problems of heteroskedasticity and autocorrelation are eliminated by using industry/year clusters and dummies for ownership identities. Because the VIF was 1.17 (less than 10), there was no concern of multicollinearity in our estimation.

As the R^2 value of the quartic estimation was highest among the linear, quadratic, cubic, and quartic models, we report the quartic estimation of the DOI–performance relationship. First, as shown in Table 3, the coefficient of DOI was significantly negative ($\beta = -0.226$, $p < 0.01$). In other words, internationalization triggers a negative impact on firm performance in the first stage. On the contrary, the quadratic term of DOI shows the opposite trend in the second stage, with a significantly positive influence on firm performance ($\beta = 1.526$, $p < 0.01$). Interestingly, the magnitude of this upturn is quite strong and outweighs the initial loss. Next, the cubic coefficient of DOI indicated a significantly negative effect on firm performance in the third stage ($\beta = -2.836$, $p < 0.01$). The magnitude of the negative downturn in the third stage was quite large compared to the benefits in stage 2. Then, at the final stage, the quartic term of DOI indicated a significantly positive relationship between internationalization and performance ($\beta = 1.558$, $p < 0.01$), as the curve shifts up strongly again after the decline in the third stage. Therefore, the empirical evidence indicated a W-shaped curvilinear relationship between internationalization and firm performance across the four different stages, supporting the first hypothesis.

This result is consistent with that of Zhou (2018), who also found a W-shaped DOI–performance relationship for small Chinese firms from 2001 to 2014. Most studies measuring the curvilinear impact of DOI on performance have discovered an S-shaped relationship (Bobillo et al., 2010; Cho and Lee 2018; Lin et al. 2011) or U-shaped relationship (Assaf et al. 2012; Capar and Kotabe 2003; Chen and Tan 2012), and the present study is among the very few providing strong evidence that performance shifts toward a W-shaped trend under the presence of DOI. While the theory of Contractor et al. (2003) rejects the argument that "the more international integration, the more benefits", this study once again challenges the three-stage theory of Contractor et al. (2003) by supporting the fourth stage of internationalization. In this way, internationalization can start with an initial loss due to the presence of foreign liability before moving to the second prosperous stage with accumulated experiences and offset benefits. Moreover, internationalization does not end at the third stage, where performance continues to diminish with higher levels of internationalization, but recovers again and truly thrives in the fourth stage as a result of increasing maturity of international integration, which brings enormous improvements such as advanced technology upgrades, innovative solutions, effective networking, and within-organization communication (Hitt et al. 1997; Zhou 2018).

Table 3. The relationship between DOI and firm performance.

Fixed-Effects Model	
Dependent Variable	**ROA (Firm Performance)**
DOI (Degree of internationalization)	−0.226 *** (0.073)
DOI^2	1.526 *** (0.445)
DOI^3	−2.836 *** (0.828)
DOI^4	1.558 *** (0.466)
AHRs (absorbed slack human resources)	0.001 *** (0.000)
OARs (other kinds of absorbed slack resources)	−0.000 (0.000)
USRs (unabsorbed slack resources)	0.000 * (0.000)
PDIVER (product diversification)	−0.003 *** (0.001)
FIRM_SIZE (firm size)	0.004 *** (0.000)
AGE (firm age)	0.003 *** (0.000)
TECH_GAP (technology gap)	0.007 *** (0.001)
OWNERSHIP dummies	Yes
Industry dummies	Yes
Year dummies	Yes
_cons	−0.038 *** (0.004)
N	1,732,265
R-square	0.004

Standard errors in parentheses: * $p < 0.10$, *** $p < 0.01$.

Table 3 also shows that AHRs positively affect firm performance (β = 0.001, ρ < 0.01), while OARs had no influence on performance (β = −0.000, ρ > 0.1). The significantly positive relationship between USR and firm performance was quite weak, with a very small coefficient (β = 0.000, ρ < 0.1). From the perspective of firm behavior, on the one hand, high availability of slack resources may enable a firm to start its new ventures abroad and to tackle the uncertainties associated with a higher level of internationalization (Lin and Liu 2012; Lin et al. 2011). The AHRs are a critical determinant of the stimulation of firm performance and growth, as it reflects an inimitable resource via human capital accumulation (Tan and Peng 2003; Dutta et al. 2016). On the other hand, abundant slack may be a signal of inefficient capital use, which may trigger a negative impact on firm performance (Zhang et al. 2018). Because slack may originate from different strategic sources, the type of slack and its level of flexibility vary across industries.

In addition, product diversification had a significantly negative impact on firm performance ($\beta = -0.003$, $\rho < 0.01$). This finding indicates that the single-item strategy is a wiser choice for enterprises. By specializing in the best thing that it can produce, supply or serve, a firm can reach a higher position in its learning curve, generate more innovations, and achieve higher productivity and performance targets (Sharma 2017). In addition, scholars consider international diversification an essential strategic tool for firms entering global markets. Agyei-Bboapeah (2017) proposes that product-diversified firms may retain greater performance since they confront lower cash flow volatility. However, they can also experience poor performance if they have to deal with agency costs (Agyei-Boapeah 2018). Interestingly, the newly added variable of technology gap has a significantly positive coefficient, which may reflect the far lower technological level of Vietnamese enterprises compared with foreign firms in developed countries. Therefore, global integration may generate greater motivation and opportunities for Vietnamese enterprises to absorb knowledge spillovers and strengthen their production systems (Goh 2005).

The relationships between firm performance and other control variables representing firm characteristics, such as firm size ($\beta = 0.003$, $\rho < 0.01$) and firm age ($\beta = 0.007$, $\rho < 0.01$), are also significantly positive. Firm size was identified as a strong moderator of the DOI–performance relationship by Zhou (2018). Undoubtedly, firm size functions as a control variable in the present study, but it is closely linked to a firm's internal capabilities. Thus, the larger the firm, the greater its capabilities to deal with uncertainties and launch successful international campaigns. Firm age, on the other hand, can reflect the international experiences of the firm. Firms with rich international experiences are undeniably more likely to succeed in the global market (Hsu et al. 2013).

Figure 1 illustrates the W-shaped relationship between DOI and Vietnamese enterprises' performance from 2007 to 2015. Based on the figure and the estimation of extreme values, the first stage of the internationalization process is completed as the DOI of Vietnamese enterprises reaches approximately 9.9 percent. The second stage occurs between DOI of 9.9 percent and 44 percent. The third stage extends from DOI of 44 percent to 82.47 percent. The fourth stage occurs when DOI exceeds 82.47 percent. Firm performance is highest when the DOI of Vietnamese enterprises reaches approximately 44 percent. By contrast, firm performance is lowest when the DOI of Vietnamese enterprises reaches approximately 82.47 percent.

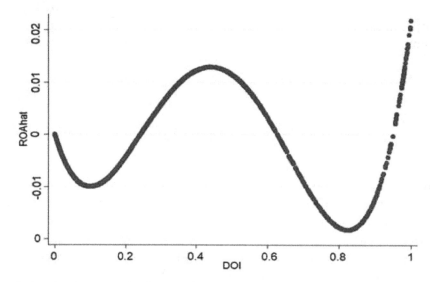

Figure 1. The relationship between the degree of internationalization and Vietnamese firms' performance from 2007 to 2015 (Notes: ROAhat is estimated according to the coefficients of regression results).

Table 4 presents the results for the potential moderating effects of the three types of organizational slack on the relationship between DOI and the performance of Vietnamese enterprises. Based on the observed W-shaped relationship between internationalization and firm performance, we estimated three thresholds of DOI in the population. We then separately analyzed the moderating effects of the organizational slack in each stage. First, the coefficients for the interaction term DOIxAHR are significantly positive for the first stage ($\beta = 46.057$, $\rho < 0.1$) and the second stage ($\beta = 173.585$, $\rho < 0.05$). Thus, a higher level of AHRs in the first two stages of the internationalization process will enhance the internationalization–performance relationship of Vietnamese enterprises. The large magnitudes of these terms imply a very strong moderating effect of AHRs. However, as the DOI reaches a higher percentage in the later stages, the results indicated that there was no influence of AHRs on the internationalization–performance relationship (stage 3: $\beta = -0.047$, $\rho > 0.1$; stage 4: $\beta = -0.043$, $\rho > 0.1$). This new empirical evidence is consistent with the results of Zhang et al. (2018), who found an inverted U-shaped moderating effect of AHRs. In summary, the second hypothesis is supported only in the first and second stages and not in the two later stages.

Table 4. The moderating effects of AHRs, OARs, and USRs across the four stages of internationalization.

	(Stage 1)	(Stage 2)	(Stage 3)	(Stage 4)
	ROA	ROA	ROA	ROA
DOI (degree of internationalization)	−0.227 ***	−0.174	−0.095 ***	−0.060 ***
	(0.072)	(0.136)	(0.023)	(0.021)
AHRs (absorbed slack human resources)	0.001 ***	−63.653 **	0.070	0.042
	(0.000)	(28.076)	(0.109)	(0.565)
OARs (other kinds of absorbed slack resources)	−0.000	−0.017	0.000	−0.000
	(0.000)	(0.016)	(0.000)	(0.000)
USRs (unabsorbed slack resources)	0.000 *	8.480 *	−0.807 **	0.029
	(0.000)	(4.678)	(0.344)	(0.088)
PDIVER (product diversification)	−0.003 ***	−0.027	−0.019	0.745
	(0.001)	(0.050)	(0.037)	(0.942)
DOIxAHR	46.057 *	173.585 **	−0.047	−0.043
	(26.030)	(75.865)	(0.176)	(0.575)
DOIxOAR	0.022 ***	0.063	−0.000	0.000
	(0.008)	(0.054)	(0.000)	(0.000)
DOIxUSR	13.621 ***	−23.096	1.443 ***	−0.029
	(3.885)	(18.781)	(0.555)	(0.089)
FIRM_SIZE	0.004 ***	−0.031	0.003	0.012 *
	(0.000)	(0.030)	(0.003)	(0.006)
AGE	0.003 ***	0.009	0.001 *	0.004 ***
	(0.000)	(0.008)	(0.001)	(0.001)
TECH_GAP	0.007 ***	0.112 **	0.006	−0.040
	(0.001)	(0.054)	(0.025)	(0.050)
_cons	−0.052 ***	0.209		
	(0.001)	(0.294)		
N	1,563,517	119,574	35,639	13,535
R^2	0.031	0.147	0.071	0.146

Standard errors in parentheses. * $p < 0.10$, ** $p < 0.05$, *** $p < 0.01$.

The early stages of the internationalization process are strongly supported by the presence of AHRs, which consists of accumulated human capital, expertise, international experiences, and innovative solutions (Dutta et al. 2016). In this way, the availability of AHRs represent an inimitable key for unlocking the door to global markets, which requires in-depth knowledge and experiences to deal with uncertainties and complexities (Zhang et al. 2018). However, in the later stages of internationalization, retaining highly qualified labor and experts represents an unexpected cost burden for enterprises, as these individuals tend to specialize in specific tasks and have difficulty in meeting new job requirements. This may partly explain why there is no influence of AHR on the internationalization–performance relationship.

Second, the interaction term DOIxOAR is only significantly positive in the first stage (β = 0.022, ρ < 0.01). This result indicated that there were no moderating effects of OARs on the internationalization–performance relationship beyond the first stage (stage 2: β = 0.063, ρ > 0.1; stage 3: β = −0.000, ρ > 0.1; stage 4: β = 0.000, ρ > 0.1). Because OARs are oriented for very selective use with a low discretion level, it is often used to relieve internal pressures and smooth firm operation rather than investing in new opportunities (Daniel et al. 2004; Bourgeois 1981). However, a firm should always have stable performance and a growth rate approaching sustainable development before pursuing an internationalization strategy. This makes OARs vital for going global, especially for the first stage of an internationalization launch. Thus, the third hypothesis is only supported in the first stage of the internationalization process.

Third, among the three types of slack, USRs are considered the key resource to help enterprises break limits and pursue ambitious targets, including an internationalization strategy. The results show that the coefficient of the interaction term DOIxUSR was significantly positive in the first (β = 13.621, ρ < 0.01) and third stages (β = 1.443, ρ < 0.01). In other words, USRs positively moderate the internationalization–performance relationship in the first and third stages of global expansion. By contrast, USRs did not affect the influence of internationalization on performance in the second (β = −23.096, ρ > 0.1) and fourth stages (β = −0.029, ρ > 0.1). Because USRs are characterized by their readiness and easy redistribution, it can facilitate the full exploitation of the expansion opportunities of internationalization regardless of geographical location and industry (Zhang et al. 2018; Nohria and Gulati 1996). Notably, firm performance decreases in stage 1 and stage 3 of the internationalization process due to the presence of foreign liability in stage 1 and under-controlled diversity in stage 3 (Contractor et al. 2003). As a result, USRs are more effective as a moderator in these stages to help the firm overcome international challenges.

4.1. Contributions

First, the findings contribute strong evidence for a W-shaped internationalization–performance linkage across the four different stages of internationalization. Specifically, Vietnamese enterprises' performance initially decreased in the first stage as a result of early barriers arising from foreign liability, followed by an increase in the second stage due to the higher market size and economies of scale. Next, firms again experienced a downward trend as DOI goes beyond the optimum threshold and triggers the negative impacts of loose governance control. However, instead of ending with this diminishing outcome at the third stage, the firm once again recovers and truly thrives in the fourth stage, when it successfully attains maturity in the learning curve. All three types of slack had positive influences on the relationship between internationalization and performance at the early stages of the internationalization process, especially at stage 1.

Interestingly, USRs, which are considered the most available slack in terms of discretion and readiness for implementing internationalization strategies, positively moderated the effect of internationalization on performance in stages 1 and 3. These stages appeared to be the most difficult stages faced by newly internationalizing firms. Moreover, the lower product diversification of Vietnamese enterprises was beneficial, as product diversification negatively affected firm performance. In addition, other explanatory variables related to firm characteristics, such as firm size, labor size, age, and technology gap, were significant determinants of enhanced firm performance.

The empirical results have practical contributions from a managerial perspective. First, a long-term action plan is very important in implementing internationalization strategies because firms face many uncertainties and complexities during this process. Reaching a higher level of internationalization forces firms to make strategic decisions on resource allocation that can determine their survival. Therefore, until their growth stabilizes, firms must be calm and avoid aggressive global expansion and

successfully nurture their internal capabilities. Second, as slack resources are extremely important in the initial stage of launching international integration, firms must allocate each type of slack efficiently and promptly to take advantage of internationalization without harming their daily business operations.

4.2. Limitations and Further Study

This paper has several limitations that may also provide scope for future studies. Because the enterprise dataset does include unlisted firms, the measurements of some interesting variables or multi-dimensional indicators of DOI may not fully capture the internationalization level of Vietnamese enterprises. Future studies employing smaller groups of listed enterprises with adequate data may provide new evidence. In addition, the measurement of AHRs of enterprises and their interaction term with DOI are presented in very small values. Consequently, the insignificant effects of these proxies are considerable limitations in this paper. Therefore, future studies should find appropriate measurements to overcome these limitations.

Moreover, intangible assets play a crucial role in many businesses, and the effect of human slack resources should be considered in this context. Thus, future research can investigate the interaction effect of human slack resources and R&D investment on firm performance.

5. Conclusions

This study attempted to fill a gap in the research on the international business of enterprises by investigating whether the relationship between internationalization and enterprise performance exhibits a W-shaped trend using unbalanced panel data of 569,767 Vietnamese enterprises from 2007 to 2015 (surveyed by GSO). While the implementation of international strategies requires a certain level of slack resources, enterprises are often characterized by limited resources. Thus, three types of organizational slack, i.e., AHRs, OARs, and USRs, and their interaction terms with DOI were added to an econometric model as moderators to examine whether each kind of slack and its inherent characteristics influence the internationalization–performance relationship. In addition, independent variables such as product diversification, firm size, firm age, product diversification, and technology gap were added to the right-hand side of the equation as important predictors of firm performance. If this paper could have one message, it would be to have entry strategies based on different types of local resources (Meyer et al. 2009). The higher the level of internationalization, the better the firms can make strategic decisions on resource allocation that can determine their survival. Since slack resources are so essential in the initial stage of global integration, the firms must allocate each type of slack efficiently and promptly to take internationalization business opportunities. This further illustrates that the importance of the global competitiveness has partly been established by internationalization strategies, which stimulates the economic growth and reduce poverty so important to nations (Tomizawa et al. 2019).

Author Contributions: P.V.N. developed the research topic and design, provided the literature review, and revised and corrected the final revision. H.T.N.H. wrote the methodology, conducted data analysis, and wrote discussions. H.D.X.T. was in charge of the programming code to filter the data, provided some explanations and wrote conclusions and limitations. K.T.T. wrote the introduction and provided some ideas to respond to the reviewers' comments.

Acknowledgments: We are grateful to the three anonymous referees for their constructive comments. We also thank the participants at the 3rd Vietnam's Business and Economics Research Conference VBER2019 (Ho Chi Minh City Open University, Vietnam, 18–20 July 2019) for their helpful suggestions. The authors wish to acknowledge financial supports from Ho Chi Minh City Open University. The authors are solely responsible for any remaining errors or shortcomings.

Appendix A

Table A1. The coefficients of Fixed Effect Model (FEM) and Random Effect Model (REM).

	Hausman		Mundlak
	FEM	**REM**	**REM vce (Robust)**
	ROA	**ROA**	**ROA**
DOI	−0.003	−0.002	−0.002
	(0.010)	(0.009)	(0.006)
AHRs	0.001 ***	0.001 ***	0.001 ***
	(0.000)	(0.000)	(0.000)
OARs	−0.000	−0.000	−0.000
	(0.000)	(0.000)	(0.000)
USRs	0.000	0.000	0.000 *
	(0.000)	(0.000)	(0.000)
PDIVER	−0.003 **	−0.002	−0.002 **
	(0.001)	(0.001)	(0.001)
FIRM_SIZE	0.004 ***	0.004 ***	0.004 ***
	(0.000)	(0.000)	(0.000)
LABOR_SIZE	0.003 ***	0.001 ***	0.001 ***
	(0.000)	(0.000)	(0.000)
AGE	0.003 ***	0.003 ***	0.003 ***
	(0.000)	(0.000)	(0.000)
TECH_GAP	0.007 ***	0.006 ***	0.006 ***
	(0.001)	(0.001)	(0.000)
mean_DOI	0.000	−0.075 ***	−0.075 ***
	(0.000	(0.021)	(0.015)
mean_AHR	0.000	−0.001 ***	−0.001 ***
	(0.000.)	(0.000)	(0.000)
mean_OAR	0.000	−0.000	−0.000
	(0.000)	(0.000)	(0.000)
mean_USR	0.000	−0.000	−0.000
	(0.000)	(0.000)	(0.000)
mean_PDIVER	0.000	0.007 ***	0.007 ***
	(0.000)	(0.002)	(0.002)
mean_FIRM_SIZE	0.000	−0.003 ***	−0.003 ***
	(0.000)	(0.000)	(0.000)
mean_AGE	0.000	−0.002 ***	−0.002 ***
	(0.000)	(0.000)	(0.000)
mean_TECH_GAP	0.000	−0.004 ***	−0.004 ***
	(0.000)	(0.001)	(0.001)
_cons	−0.051 ***	−0.017 ***	−0.017 ***
	(0.001)	(0.001)	(0.001)
N	1,732,265	1,732,265	1,732,265
R^2	0.004		

Notes: vce: variance-covariance matrix of the estimators. *** $p < 0.01$.

Table A2. Hausman test.

	(b)	(B)	(b-B)	sqrt(diag(V_b-V_B))
	est7	est6	Difference	SE
DOI	−0.0029642	−0.0020761	−0.0008881	0.0022336
AHR	0.0005098	0.0005713	−0.0000615	0.0000226
OAR	-1.50×10^{-9}	-2.15×10^{-9}	6.41×10^{-10}	2.78×10^{-9}
USR	1.01×10^{-6}	1.02×10^{-6}	-6.12×10^{-9}	6.96×10^{-7}
PDIVER	−0.0025694	−0.0018824	−0.000687	0.0002745
FIRM_SIZE	0.0037832	0.0040962	−0.000313	0.0000441
LABOR_SIZE	0.0031273	0.0006498	0.0024776	0.0002044
AGE	0.0030544	0.0030589	-4.53×10^{-6}	0.0000138
TECH_GAP	0.0070024	0.0062325	0.0007699	0.0001346

$\text{Chi}^2 = 180.36$. p-value = 0.000.

References

Agyei-Bboapeah, Henry. 2017. Easing Financing and M & A Investment Constraints: The Role of Corporate Industrial Diversification. *Annals of Economics & Finance* 18: 277–90.

Agyei-Boapeah, Henry. 2018. Foreign Acquisitions and Firm Performance: The Moderating Role of Prior Foreign Experience. *Global Finance Journal*. [CrossRef]

Assaf, A. George, Alexander Josiassen, Brian T. Ratchford, and Carlos Pestana Barros. 2012. Internationalization and Performance of Retail Firms: A Bayesian Dynamic Model. *Journal of Retailing* 88: 191–205. [CrossRef]

Autio, Erkko, Harry J. Sapienza, and James G. Almeida. 2000. Effects of Age at Entry, Knowledge Intensity, and Imitability on International Growth. *Academy of Management Journal* 43: 909–24. [CrossRef]

Bausch, Andreas, and Frithjof Pils. 2009. Product Diversification Strategy and Financial Performance: Meta-Analytic Evidence on Causality and Construct Multidimensionality. *Review of Managerial Science* 3: 157–90. [CrossRef]

Bell, Andrew, Malcolm Fairbrother, and Kelvyn Jones. 2018. Fixed and Random Effects Models: Making an Informed Choice. *Quality & Quantity* 53: 1051–74. [CrossRef]

Bell, Andrew, and Kelvyn Jones. 2015. Methods: Explaining Fixed Effects: Random Effects Modeling of Time-Series Cross-Sectional and Panel Data. *Political Science Research and Methods* 3: 133–53. [CrossRef]

Bobillo, Alfredo M., Felix López-Iturriaga, and Fernando Tejerina-Gaite. 2010. Firm Performance and International Diversification: The Internal and External Competitive Advantages. *International Business Review* 19: 607–18. [CrossRef]

Bourgeois, L. Jay, III. 1981. On the Measurement of Organizational Slack. *Academy of Management Review* 6: 29–39. [CrossRef]

Bourgeois, L. Jay, III, and Jitendra V. Singh. 1983. Organizational Slack and Political Behavior Among Top Management Teams. *Academy of Management Proceedings* 1: 43–47. [CrossRef]

Bowen, Harry P., and Margarethe F. Wiersema. 2009. *International and Product Diversification: Their Interrelationship and Impact on Firm Performance*. Discussion Paper Series; Charlotte: Vlerick Leuven Gent Management School.

Bradley, Steven W., Johan Wiklund, and Dean A. Shepherd. 2011. Swinging a Double-Edged Sword: The Effect of Slack on Entrepreneurial Management and Growth. *Journal of Business Venturing* 26: 537–54. [CrossRef]

Buckley, Peter J., and Mark Casson. 1976. A Long-Run Theory of the Multinational Enterprise. *The Future of the Multinational Enterprise*, 32–65. [CrossRef]

Buckley, Peter J., Jonathan P. Doh, and Mirko H. Benischke. 2017. Towards a Renaissance in International Business Research? Big Questions, Grand Challenges, and the Future of IB Scholarship. *Journal of International Business Studies* 48: 1045–64. [CrossRef]

Capar, Nejat, and Masaaki Kotabe. 2003. The Relationship between International Diversification and Performance in Service Firms. *Journal of International Business Studies* 34: 345–55. [CrossRef]

Chang, Shao-Chi, and Chi-Feng Wang. 2007. The Effect of Product Diversification Strategies on the Relationship between International Diversification and Firm Performance. *Journal of World Business* 42: 61–79. [CrossRef]

Chen, Homin, and Chia Wen Hsu. 2010. Internationalization, Resource Allocation and Firm Performance. *Industrial Marketing Management* 39: 1103–10. [CrossRef]

Chen, Stephen, and Hao Tan. 2012. Region Effects in the Internationalization–performance Relationship in Chinese Firms. *Journal of World Business* 47: 73–80. [CrossRef]

Chetty, Sylvie, and Desiree Blankenburg Holm. 2000. Internationalisation of Small to Medium-Sized Manufacturing Firms: A Network Approach. *International Business Review* 9: 77–93. [CrossRef]

Chiao, Yu Ching, Kuo Pin Yang, and Chwo Ming Joseph Yu. 2006. Performance, Internationalization, and Firm-Specific Advantages of SMES in a Newly-Industrialized Economy. *Small Business Economics* 26: 475–92. [CrossRef]

Cho, Jaeyoung, and Jangwoo Lee. 2018. Internationalization and Performance in Korean SMEs: The Moderating Role of Ownership Structure. *Asian Business & Management* 17: 140–66. [CrossRef]

Ciravegna, Luciano, Sara B. Majano, and Ge Zhan. 2014. The Inception of Internationalization of Small and Medium Enterprises: The Role of Activeness and Networks. *Journal of Business Research* 67: 1081–89. [CrossRef]

Clarke, James E., and Peter W. Liesch. 2017. Wait-and-See Strategy: Risk Management in the Internationalization Process Model. *Journal of International Business Studies* 48: 923–40. [CrossRef]

Contractor, Farok J., Vikas Kumar, and Sumit K. Kundu. 2007. Nature of the Relationship between International Expansion and Performance: The Case of Emerging Market Firms. *Journal of World Business* 42: 401–17. [CrossRef]

Contractor, Farok J., Sumit K. Kundu, and Chin Chun Hsu. 2003. A Three-Stage Theory of International Expansion: The Link between Multinationality and Performance in the Service Sector. *Journal of International Business Studies* 34: 5–18. [CrossRef]

Coviello, Nicole, Liena Kano, and Peter W. Liesch. 2017. Adapting the Uppsala Model to a Modern World: Macro-Context and Microfoundations. *Journal of International Business Studies* 48: 1151–64. [CrossRef]

Cuervo-Cazurra, Alvaro, Luciano Ciravegna, Mauricio Melgarejo, and Luis Lopez. 2018. Home Country Uncertainty and the Internationalization–performance Relationship: Building an Uncertainty Management Capability. *Journal of World Business* 53: 209–21. [CrossRef]

Daniel, Francis, Franz T. Lohrke, Charles J. Fornaciari, and R. Andrew Turner. 2004. Slack Resources and Firm Performance: A Meta-Analysis. *Journal of Business Research* 57: 565–74. [CrossRef]

Dasí, Angels, María Iborra, and Vicente Safón. 2015. Beyond Path Dependence: Explorative Orientation, Slack Resources, and Managerial Intentionality to Internationalize in SMEs. *International Business Review* 24: 77–88. [CrossRef]

Delios, Andrew, and Paul W. Beamish. 1999. Geographic Scope, Product Diversification, and the Corporate Performance of Japanese Firms. *Strategic Management Journal* 20: 711–27. [CrossRef]

Denis, David J., Diane K. Denis, and Keven Yost. 2002. Global Diversification, Industrial Diversification, and Firm Value. *Journal of Finance* 57: 1951–79. [CrossRef]

Dutta, Dev K., Shavin Malhotra, and Peng Cheng Zhu. 2016. Internationalization Process, Impact of Slack Resources, and Role of the CEO: The Duality of Structure and Agency in Evolution of Cross-Border Acquisition Decisions. *Journal of World Business* 51: 212–25. [CrossRef]

Eckardt, Sebastian, Viet Tuan Dinh, Annette I. De Kleine Feige, Duc Minh Pham, and Jung Eun Oh. 2018. *Taking Stock: An Update on Vietnam's Recent Economic Developments—Special Focus: Reform Priorities for Reducing Trade Costs and Enhancing Competitiveness in Vietnam*. Washington, DC: The World Bank.

Elango, Balasubramanian. 2006. An Empirical Analysis of the Internationalization–performance Relationship Across Emerging Market Firms. *Multinational Business Review* 14: 21–44. [CrossRef]

Gaur, Ajai, and Andrew Delios. 2015. International Diversification of Emerging Market Firms: The Role of Ownership Structure and Group Affiliation. *Management International Review* 55: 235–53. [CrossRef]

George, Gerard. 2005. Slack Resources and the Performance of Privately Held Firms. *Academy of Management Journal* 48: 661–676. [CrossRef]

Glaum, Martin, and Michael-Jörg Oesterle. 2007. Introduction: 40 Years of Research on Internationalization and Firm Performance: More Questions than Answers? *MIR: Management International Review* 47: 307–17. [CrossRef]

Goh, Ai Ting. 2005. Knowledge Diffusion, Input Supplier's Technological Effort and Technology Transfer via Vertical Relationships. *Journal of International Economics* 66: 527–40. [CrossRef]

Håkanson, Lars, and Philip Kappen. 2017. The 'Casino Model' of Internationalization: An Alternative Uppsala Paradigm. *Journal of International Business Studies* 48: 1103–13. [CrossRef]

Hausman, Jerry A. 1978. Specification Tests in Econometrics. *Econometrica: Journal of the Econometric Society* 46: 1251–71. [CrossRef]

Hitt, Michael A., Robert E. Hoskisson, and Hicheon Kim. 1997. International Diversification: Effects on Innovation and Firm Performance in Product-Diversified Firms. *Academy of Management Journal* 40: 767–98.

Hsu, Wen Tsung, Hsiang Lan Chen, and Chia Yi Cheng. 2013. Internationalization and Firm Performance of SMEs: The Moderating Effects of CEO Attributes. *Journal of World Business* 48: 1–12. [CrossRef]

Hutzschenreuter, Thomas, and Tanja Matt. 2017. MNE Internationalization Patterns, the Roles of Knowledge Stocks, and the Portfolio of MNE Subsidiaries. *Journal of International Business Studies* 48: 1131–50. [CrossRef]

Johanson, Jan, and Jan-Erik Vahlne. 1977. The Internationalization Process of the Firm—A Model of Knowledge Development and Increasing Foreign Market Commitments. *Journal of International Business Studies* 8: 23–32. [CrossRef]

Johanson, Jan, and Jan Erik Vahlne. 2009. The Uppsala Internationalization Process Model Revisited: From Liability of Foreignness to Liability of Outsidership. *Journal of International Business Studies* 40: 1411–31. [CrossRef]

Jones, Marian V., Nicole Coviello, and Yee Kwan Tang. 2011. International Entrepreneurship Research (1989–2009): A Domain Ontology and Thematic Analysis. *Journal of Business Venturing* 26: 632–59. [CrossRef]

Kim, Hicheon, Heechun Kim, and Peggy M. Lee. 2008. Ownership Structure and the Relationship Between Financial Slack and R&D Investments: Evidence from Korean Firms. *Organization Science* 19: 404–18. [CrossRef]

Kim, Young Sang, and Ike Mathur. 2008. The Impact of Geographic Diversification on Firm Performance. *International Review of Financial Analysis* 17: 747–66. [CrossRef]

Madsen, Tage Koed, and Per Servais. 1997. The Internationalization of Born Globals: An Evolutionary Process? *International Business Review* 6: 561–83. [CrossRef]

Kogut, Bruce. 1989. Research Notes and Communications a Note on Global Strategies. *Strategic Management Journal* 10: 383–89. [CrossRef]

Korsakienė, Renata, and Manuela Tvaronavičienė. 2012. The Internationalization of SMEs: An Integrative Approach. *Journal of Business Economics and Management* 13: 294–307. [CrossRef]

Kumar, Vikas, Ajai S Gaur, and Chinmay Pattnaik. 2012. Product Diversification and International Expansion of Business Groups: Evidence from India. *MIR: Management International Review* 52: 175–92. [CrossRef]

Lee, Chia Ling, and Hsu Che Wu. 2016. How Do Slack Resources Affect the Relationship between R&D Expenditures and Firm Performance? *R and D Management* 46: 958–78. [CrossRef]

Lin, Wen Ting. 2014. How Do Managers Decide on Internationalization Processes? The Role of Organizational Slack and Performance Feedback. *Journal of World Business* 49: 396–408. [CrossRef]

Lin, Wen Ting, and Yunshi Liu. 2012. Successor Characteristics, Organisational Slack, and Change in the Degree of Firm Internationalisation. *International Business Review* 21: 89–101. [CrossRef]

Lin, Wen Ting, Yunshi Liu, and Kuei Yang Cheng. 2011. The Internationalization and Performance of a Firm: Moderating Effect of a Firm's Behavior. *Journal of International Management* 17: 83–95. [CrossRef]

Lu, Jane W., and Paul W. Beamish. 2001. The Internationalization and Performance of SMEs. *Strategic Management Journal* 22: 565–86. [CrossRef]

Lu, Jane W., and Paul W. Beamish. 2004. International Diversification and Firm Performance: The S-Curve Hypothesis International Diversification and Firm Performance: The S-Curve Hypothesis. *Academy of Management Journal* 47: 598–609.

Majocchi, Antonio, and Antonella Zucchella. 2003. Internationalization and Performance: Findings from a Set of Italian SMEs. *International Small Business Journal* 21: 249–68. [CrossRef]

Marano, Valentina, Jean Luc Arregle, Michael A. Hitt, Ettore Spadafora, and Marc van Essen. 2016. Home Country Institutions and the Internationalization–performance Relationship: A Meta-Analytic Review. *Journal of Management* 42: 1075–1110. [CrossRef]

McDougall, Patricia Phillips. 1989. International versus domestic entrepreneurship: new venture strategic behavior and industry structure. *Journal of Business Venturing* 4: 387–400. [CrossRef]

McDougall, Patricia Phillips, and Benjamin M. Oviatt. 1996. New Venture Internationalization, Strategic Change, and Performance: A Follow-up Study. *Journal of Business Venturing* 11: 23–40. [CrossRef]

McDougall, Patricia Phillips, and Benjamin M. Oviatt. 2000. International Entrepreneurship: The Intersection of Two Research Paths. *Academy of Management Journal* 43: 902–6. [CrossRef]

Mellahi, Kamel, and Adrian Wilkinson. 2010. A Study of the Association between Level of Slack Reduction Following Downsizing and Innovation Output. *Journal of Management Studies* 47: 483–508. [CrossRef]

Meyer, Klaus E., Saul Estrin, Sumon Kumar Bhaumik, and Mike W. Peng. 2009. Institutions, Resources, and Entry Strategies in Emerging Economies. *Strategic Management Journal* 30: 61–80. [CrossRef]

Mundlak, Yair. 1978. On the Pooling of Time Series and Cross Section Data. *Econometrica: Journal of the Econometric Society* 46: 69–85. [CrossRef]

Neter, John, William Wasserman, and Michael H. Kutner. 1990. *Applied Statistical Models*. Burr Ridge: Richard D. Irwin, Inc.

Nohria, Nitin, and Ranjay Gulati. 1996. Is Slack Good or Bad for Innovation? *Academy of Management Journal* 39: 1245–64. [CrossRef]

Nohria, Nitin, and Ranjay Gulati. 1997. What Is the Optimum Amount of Organizational Slack? *European Management Journal* 15: 603–11. [CrossRef]

Paeleman, Ine, and Tom Vanacker. 2015. Less Is More, or Not? On the Interplay between Bundles of Slack Resources, Firm Performance and Firm Survival. *Journal of Management Studies* 52: 819–48. [CrossRef]

Pangarkar, Nitin. 2008. Internationalization and Performance of Small- and Medium-Sized Enterprises. *Journal of World Business* 43: 475–85. [CrossRef]

Porter, Michael E. 1976. Please Note Location of Nearest Exit: Exit Barriers and Planning. *California Management Review* 19: 21–33. [CrossRef]

Riahi-Belkaoui, Ahmed. 1998. The Effects of the Degree of Internationalization on Firm Performance. *International Business Review* 7: 315–21. [CrossRef]

Rugman, Alan M. 2016. Internalization as a General Theory of Foreign Direct Investment. *Inside the Multinationals 25th Anniversary Edition*, 18–33. [CrossRef]

Ruigrok, Winfried, Wolfgang Amann, and Hardy Wagner. 2007. The Internationalization–performance Relationship at Swiss Firms: A Test of the S-Shape and Extreme Degrees of Internationalization. *Management International Review* 47: 349–68. [CrossRef]

Ruigrok, Winfried, and Hardy Wagner. 2003. Internationalization and Performance: An Organizational Learning Perspective. *Management International Review* 43: 63–83. [CrossRef]

Santangelo, Grazia D., and Klaus E. Meyer. 2017. Internationalization as an Evolutionary Process. *Journal of International Business Studies* 48: 1114–30. [CrossRef]

Santarelli, Enrico, and Hien Thu Tran. 2016. Diversification Strategies and Firm Performance in Vietnam: Evidence from Parametric and Semi-Parametric Approaches. *Economics of Transition* 24: 31–68. [CrossRef]

Schwens, Christian, Florian B. Zapkau, Michael Bierwerth, Rodrigo Isidor, Gary Knight, and Rüdiger Kabst. 2018. International Entrepreneurship: A Meta-Analysis on the Internationalization and Performance Relationship. *Entrepreneurship Theory and Practice* 42: 734–68. [CrossRef]

Sharma, Chandan. 2017. Exporting, Access of Foreign Technology, and Firms' Performance: Searching the Link in Indian Manufacturing. *Quarterly Review of Economics and Finance* 68: 46–62. [CrossRef]

Singh, Jitendra V. 1986. Performance, Slack, and Risk Taking in Organizational Decision Making. *Academy of Management Journal* 29: 562–85. [CrossRef]

Tallman, Stephen, and Jiatao Li. 1996. Effects of International Diversity and Product Diversity on the Performance of Multinational Firms. *Academy of Management Journal* 39: 179–96. [CrossRef]

Tan, Justin. 2003. Curvilinear Relationship between Organizational Slack and Firm Performance:: Evidence from Chinese State Enterprises. *European Management Journal* 21: 740–49. [CrossRef]

Tan, Justin, and Mike W. Peng. 2003. Organizational Slack and Firm Performance during Economic Transitions: Two Studies from an Emerging Economy. *Strategic Management Journal* 24: 1249–63. [CrossRef]

Tomizawa, Aki, Li Zhao, Geneviève Bassellier, and David Ahlstrom. 2019. Economic Growth, Innovation, Institutions, and the Great Enrichment. *Asia Pacific Journal of Management*, 1–25. [CrossRef]

Trigeorgis, Lenos, and Jeffrey J. Reuer. 2017. Real Options Theory in Strategic Management. *Strategic Management Journal* 38: 42–63. [CrossRef]

Vahlne, Jan Erik, and Jan Johanson. 2017. From Internationalization to Evolution: The Uppsala Model at 40 Years. *Journal of International Business Studies* 48: 1087–102. [CrossRef]

Velez-Calle, Andres, Fernando Sanchez-Henriquez, and Farok Contractor. 2018. Internationalization and Performance: The Role of Depth and Breadth [Internacionalización y Desempeño de La Empresa: El Papel de La Profundidad y La Extensión]. *Academia Revista Latinoamericana de Administracion* 31: 91–104. [CrossRef]

Wernerfelt, Birger. 1984. A Resource-based View of the Firm. *Strategic Management Journal* 5: 171–80. [CrossRef]

Wiersema, Margarethe F., and Harry P. Bowen. 2008. Corporate Diversification: The Impact of Foreign Competition, Industry Globalization, and Product Diversification. *Strategic Management Journal* 29: 115–32. [CrossRef]

Wiersma, Eelke. 2017. How and When Do Firms Translate Slack into Better Performance? *British Accounting Review* 49: 445–59. [CrossRef]

Zahra, Shaker A. 2005. A Theory of International New Ventures: A Decade of Research. *Journal of International Business Studies* 36: 20–28. [CrossRef]

Zhang, Yufeng, Zhibo Yang, and Tao Zhang. 2018. Strategic Resource Decisions to Enhance the Performance of Global Engineering Services. *International Business Review* 27: 678–700. [CrossRef]

Zhao, Hongxin, and Jieqiong Ma. 2016. Founding Environment, Inward Internationalization, and Firm Performance: Evidence from Chinese Private Enterprises. *Journal of East-West Business* 22: 296–323. [CrossRef]

Zhou, Chao. 2017. Internationalization and Performance: The Role of State Ownership. *Applied Economics Letters* 25: 1130–34. [CrossRef]

Zhou, Chao. 2018. Internationalization and Performance: Evidence from Chinese Firms. *Chinese Management Studies* 12: 19–34. [CrossRef]

11

Corporate Social Responsibility and SMEs in Vietnam: A Study in the Textile and Garment Industry

Loan Thi-Hong Van [1,*] and Phuong Anh Nguyen [2]

[1] School of Advanced Study, Ho Chi Minh City Open University, Ho Chi Minh City 7000, Vietnam
[2] Graduate School, Ho Chi Minh City Open University, Ho Chi Minh City 7000, Vietnam; anhphuong262@gmail.com
*   Correspondence: loan.vth@ou.edu.vn

Abstract: This study explored the influence of factors on the implementation of corporate social responsibility (CSR) in companies. The study used a quantitative approach in which a survey was conducted. The final 250 among various respondents in the textile and garment industry were used. The final respondents were top-, middle-, and low-level managers in 250 small and medium enterprises (SMEs) in Vietnam. The results indicate that competitive context, social influences, the understanding of managers about CSR, and the internal environment of companies are the four drivers of CSR. In the four drivers, competitive context has the strongest impact on adopting CSR. The finding implies that stakeholders' pressure influences SMEs in this industry because of the high expectations from international stakeholders.

Keywords: corporate social responsibility; textile and garment industry; Vietnam

1. Introduction

Corporate social responsibility (CSR) has had a long history of development in the world (Carroll 2009). However, it is practiced differently in countries because of the different contexts (Nguyen et al. 2017; Omran and Ramdhony 2015; Gupta 2009). Most CSR studies take place in developed countries; thus, there is a need to examine CSR in developing countries (Eweje 2006). Research about CSR in Vietnam, a developing country, is sparse (Nguyen et al. 2017, Nguyen and Truong 2016). Current CSR research additionally focuses on large organizations rather than small and medium enterprises (SMEs) (Jenkins 2006; Morsing and Perrini 2009). It is hard to use the theories and practices of large enterprises on SMEs due to SMEs' characteristics (Davies and Crane 2010). Thus, there need to be more studies with findings which are useful and applicable to SMEs.

Research on CSR and SMEs has only recently emerged (Murrillo and Lozano 2006; Morsing and Perrini 2009; Vo 2012). Literature needs more studies on these topics. One of the research gaps is the engagement of CSR in SMEs (Murrillo and Lozano 2006; Vo 2012). Research is needed to explore why SMEs adopt CSR. Some researchers state that not many SMEs conduct CSR due to the lack of resources (see, e.g., Lepoutre and Heene 2006; Kusyk and Lozano 2007; Sweeney 2007; Nguyen and Pham 2016), or the lack of CSR understanding (Tran and Jeppesen 2016). Others say that SMEs implement CSR because of ethical reasons (Longo et al. 2005; Jenkins 2006), business performance and regulation (Williamson et al. 2006), relationship with the community and company image improvement (Longo et al. 2005), and capital and human resources (Nguyen and Pham 2016).

CSR was introduced in Vietnam in recent years (Hamm 2012; Tran and Jeppesen 2016), although its definition by Bowen was published in 1953 (Carroll 1979). Many Vietnamese companies have therefore had difficulties in adopting the concept due to their little CSR knowledge. For example, from January to May 2019, European countries refused 17 shipments of seafood from Vietnam because of the lack of knowledge relating to food safety and hygiene (Bach 2019). The wastewater emissions by the Formosa Plastics Corporation in the Ha Tinh province in 2016, and the food scandal by the Tan Hiep Phat Beverage Group in 2015, are other examples of the limitations of CSR knowledge. The disapprobation of stakeholders to these companies implies that stakeholders have taken notice of social responsibilities in spite of the fact that CSR is new to them (see Phương 2015; Quang et al. 2016; Nguyen and Truong 2016).

According to a survey by the General Statistics Office of General Statistics Office of Vietnam (2017), a large majority of companies in Vietnam are SMEs (98.1%). In Vietnam, SMEs are companies whose charter capital is below 10 billion Vietnam dong ($430,000) and whose number of employees is lower than 300 (Vietnamese Government 2001). Vietnam's textile and garment industry contributes to 10 percent of the national industrial values and creates 2.7 million jobs—this shows the importance of the industry in the Vietnamese economy. Additionally, a characteristic of the industry is that most companies have collaborated with international partners (Song 2018). These are our reasons for selecting the industry for our research. It may help to understand how to promote CSR in SMEs, which is little known (Murrillo and Lozano 2006). SMEs in other industries may not want to practice CSR, but SMEs in the textile and garment industry in Vietnam may do so due to the high expectations of their international stakeholders.

Although the industry exported products worth more than 36 billion US dollars in 2018—reaching the top three in the world, together with China and India (Song 2018)—problems still occurred relating to CSR. For example, in July 2019, the Big C supermarket, a foreign supermarket in Vietnam, announced that it was stopping its collaboration with 200 textile and garment SMEs because of product quality (Kieu 2019). These may show the lack of CSR in their business strategy. In SMEs, owners/managers have the power in their hands to make decisions in personal ways (Spence 1999). Therefore, this study explores the understanding of the CSR of Vietnamese managers in SMEs, in order to understand what CSR means in their companies, and which drivers force them to practice CSR. The purpose of this research was to study factors that affect the implementation of CSR in SMEs in the textile and garment industry in Vietnam. The study used a survey of 250 managers in 250 SMEs in Vietnam in the textile and garment industry. The results indicated that SMEs adopt CSR because of a competitive environment, social influences, the understanding of managers about CSR, and the internal environment of SMEs.

The next section of this article is a review of the existing literature on CSR and SMEs. Next, we elaborate on the collection of the data for the study. Then, we present our research findings and discuss them. The last part is a conclusion in which we show the limitations of the study and the implications for future research.

2. Theoretical Background and Hypotheses

CSR was defined as "the commitment of business to contribute to sustainable economic development, working with employees, their families, the local community, and society to improve their quality of life, in ways that are both good for business and good for development" (World Bank 2006). Campbell (2006) defined that "CSR sets a minimum behavioral standard that aims at doing no harm to stakeholders and if it has happened then rectifies it as soon as it is identified." Business companies have to have ethical behaviors, minimize negative influences, and maximize their benefits to society. They need to practice social responsibilities as per the requirements of stakeholders and society.

Garriga and Mele (2004) classified the theories used in CSR research into four groups: instrumental theories, integrative theories, political theories, and ethical theories. The first two groups focus on business management issues, whereas the last two concern society power and ethical codes. A large number of CSR studies use a management perspective, which concerns what motivates business organizations to become engaged in CSR (Basu and Palazzo 2008). One of the groups of integrative theories' stream is stakeholder management that focuses on stakeholder satisfaction. Research by Mitchell et al. (1997) showed that an organization's CSR activities affect its stakeholders' interest and behavior. This also means that the pressure of stakeholders (internal and external) can motivate organizations to conduct CSR activities. Internal stakeholders include staff, workers, and managers. Their opinions may influence the way to practice CSR in their companies. In other words, managers' ideas and their understanding of CSR can be a driver for CSR implementation in their organizations. External stakeholders can be associations, government agencies, the community, customers, partners, and suppliers (Akkucuk 2015). Most of Vietnam's textile and garment goods are exported, approximately 90 percent of the whole industry (Song 2018; Luu 2018), so international stakeholders may constitute a motive to put CSR into companies' business strategies due to competition—this is one of my research focuses.

Research about CSR was originally undertaken in developed countries (e.g., Carroll 1979, 1991; Carroll 2009); however, the CSR concept is now used in different parts of the world. Visser (2008) said that compared to developed countries, developing countries have different emphases of CSR domains because of "indigenous cultural traditions of philanthropy, business ethics ... " (p. 481). There is a call to study CSR in developing countries (such as Vietnam), in order to contribute knowledge to world literature (Eweje 2006; Carroll 2016). That is because CSR is influenced by the context where it is applied (Ortenblad 2016; Nguyen et al. 2017). In other words, social expectations about social responsibilities of business organizations in Vietnam may be different to those in developed countries. The way to practice CSR may differ from country to country due to the influence of social contexts. For example, Vietnamese organizations tend to donate to religious festivals and provide 13th month wages' rewards for employees around New Year because of social expectations (Tran and Jeppesen 2016). Social influences may be a motive affecting the implementation of CSR in developing countries such as Vietnam. Literature shows that little research on CSR in SMEs has been conducted (e.g., Tilley 2000; Jenkins 2006; Morsing and Perrini 2009). The reasons for this relate to the importance of large organizations in the economy (Tilley 2000). Researchers may think that SMEs can use the theories and practices of CSR that were drawn from the study findings of large enterprises. However, the characteristics of SMEs are different to those of large ones (Spence and Rutherford 2003). For example, in SMEs, in most cases, ownership and management are not separate, so owners have the power to decide all business activities based on their personal preferences (Spence 1999; Perez-Sanchez et al. 2003; Davies and Crane 2010). The acceptance of putting CSR in SMEs can depend on the opinions and understandings of owners/managers about CSR, and this issue needs more research. Another SME issue relates to the lack of financial resources (Kusyk and Lozano 2007; Sweeney 2007), which means that SMEs may not focus on investment into CSR immediately—this study examines this.

The concept of CSR has been present in Vietnam since 2002, when it was introduced by international organizations such as the World Bank (Tran and Jeppesen 2016). Research about CSR in Vietnam also began at the same time. My literature review shows that there is little research on it, particularly relating to SMEs. Most research focuses on customers' perception of CSR (see, e.g., Bui 2010; Thi and Van 2016; Tran et al. 2017; Van et al. 2019). In other words, it explored how Vietnamese customers understand CSR. Findings showed that the concept of CSR is still new to research participants. In addition, many studies in Vietnam used the CSR dimensions by Carroll (1991) such as economic, legal, ethical, and philanthropic responsibilities (see, e.g., Bui 2010; Thi and Van 2016). They have not pointed out drivers such as the internal environment of SMEs that impact the implementation of CSR in firms—this is explored in our research.

Our review on the available literature shows that research about CSR in Vietnam usually studies the views of consumers, rather than managers, especially relating to SMEs (see, e.g., Bui 2010; Thi and Van 2016; Tran et al. 2017; Van et al. 2019). Collecting CSR opinions by customers may be easier than that by managers—this implies that our research, which studies manager perspectives, may be invaluable for literature. The study by Tran and Jeppesen (2016) was one of the few exploring the voice of managers about CSR in SMEs in Vietnam. Tran and Jeppesen (2016) interviewed 20 managers and 125 workers in 20 Vietnamese textile, garment, and footwear firms. Their study explored the way to practice CSR in firms, such as physical environment, working conditions, wages, and benefits. Their research findings showed that CSR was not implemented in firms because financial resources were limited, and managers and workers did not understand the concept of CSR.

Nguyen and Pham (2016) are other researchers studying factors influencing the implementation of CSR in Vietnamese firms. Four factors, e.g., the regulatory system, knowledge of CSR, capital and human resources, were used for the test in their research. They sent a questionnaire to 207 firms in different business fields. Their research results showed that the only two factors affecting the way the firms practiced CSR are capital and human resources. As can be seen, SMEs in Vietnam may not be ready for the adoption of CSR due to cash limitations; however, in the industry of textiles and garments, they may be, due to the pressure of international partners or a competitive environment. Factors impacting the adoption of CSR in firms in Vietnam such as a competitive context, social influences, the understanding of managers about CSR and the internal environment of firms have not been the focus in these studies as of yet. Our research examines them from the view of managers who can play a decisive role in putting CSR in firms' developmental strategy.

As analyzed above, in order to study factors affecting the engagement of CSR in SMEs, the hypotheses were developed as follows:

H1. *An understanding of managers about CSR has a significant impact on the implementation of CSR in SMEs.*

H2. *The external and internal environment of SMEs positively affects their engagement in CSR. The environment consists of a competitive context, social influences, and the internal environment of companies.*

3. Method

Pilot tests and face-to-face interviews with four Vietnamese managers in the textile and garment industry were conducted to adjust, enhance, and validate the observed variables and the suggested measurement scales. Based on the feedback from the participants, all observed variables were corrected (see also Table 1).

Quantitative research was a survey on 330 top-, middle-, and low-level managers in different SMEs in Vietnam. We chose the firms based on the list of registered SMEs in the textile and garment industry provided by the Ho Chi Minh City Tax Department. The managers were not in the same companies. The surveys in Vietnamese, undertaken from March to October in 2017, were used for the study. After the returned questionnaires were reviewed and the invalid ones were eliminated, 250 valid answered questionnaires were coded to SPSS 23.0 for analysis purposes.

We measured CSR from the managers' perspectives using 5 factors with 25 observed items: the understanding of managers about CSR (4 variables: LĐ1, LĐ2, LĐ3, and LĐ4), the internal environment of companies (6 variables: MTNB1, MTNB2, MTNB3, MTNB4, MTNB5, and MTND6), competitive context (6 variables: MTCT1, MTCT2, MTCT3, MTCT4, MTCT5, and MTCT6), social influences (4 variables: MTVM1, MTVM2, MTVM3, and MTVM4), and the implementation of CSR in SMEs (5 variables: CSR1, CSR2, CSR3, CSR4, and CSR5). These variables were employed using research by Burke and Logsdon (1996), Spence et al. (2003), Murrillo and Lozano (2006), Porter and Kramer (2007), and Darnall et al. (2010). These were translated into Vietnamese. The scale was designed as a 5-point Likert scale, from 1—Totally disagree to 5—Totally agree (see Table 1). The study used Cronbach's alpha to test the reliability of the scale, exploratory factor analysis (EFA) to identify relationships between measured variables, and Pearson to study the correlation coefficient between dependent and independent variables (see also Section 4). The language used for the data collection and data analysis was Vietnamese. Thus, the codes for the items were named based on the Vietnamese language (Table 1). The findings of the research were translated into English for this paper.

Table 1. Descriptive statistics.

Code	Observed variable (*n* = 250)	N	Min	Max	Mean	Std. Deviation
	The implementation of CSR in SMEs					
CSR1	CSR is embedded in firms' business responsibilities.	250	2.0	5.0	3.35	0.691
CSR2	CSR has brought specific benefits for companies.	250	2.0	5.0	3.46	0.706
CSR3	Firms voluntarily practice CSR.	250	2.0	5.0	3.42	0.714
CSR4	Practicing CSR is a part of the strategy and business plan of companies.	250	2.0	5.0	3.48	0.695
CSR5	Firms have an annual report of CSR for stakeholders as required.	250	2.0	5.0	3.33	0.675
	The understanding of managers about CSR					
LĐ1	You understand and participate in CSR programs in your company.	250	2.0	5.0	3.54	0.910
LĐ2	You participate in evaluating the benefits of CSR in your company.	250	2.0	5.0	3.51	0.870
LĐ3	You understand that stakeholders (shareholders, employees, competitors, suppliers, customers) have an influence on the strategy and plans of your company.	250	2.0	5.0	3.46	0.957
LĐ4	You think that companies need to have responsibilities to their stakeholders.	250	2.0	5.0	3.48	0.875
	The internal environment of SMEs					
MTNB1	Employees put pressure on your companies in terms of implementing CSR in practice.	250	2.0	5.0	3.57	.839
MTNB2	Following labor laws and ensuring fair working conditions for employees have an influence on the practice of CSR in your company.	250	2.0	5.0	3.53	.870
MTNB3	Following health and safety policies and making a report about these have an influence on the practice of CSR in your company.	250	2.0	5.0	3.72	1.041
MTNB4	Policies to motivate employees to improve practical skills and competencies have an influence on the practice of CSR in your company.	250	2.0	5.0	3.61	.805
MTNB5	Listening to employees' opinions about important issues has an influence on the practice of CSR in your company.	250	2.0	5.0	3.58	0.857
MTNB6	CSR is a part of the marketing strategy of your company.	250	2.0	5.0	3.56	0.891
	Competitive context					
MTCT1	Customers have an influence on the strategy, plans and decisions of your company.	250	2.0	5.0	3.49	0.879
MTCT2	International partners have important requirements to the practice of CSR in your company.	250	2.0	5.0	3.50	0.970
MTCT3	Suppliers and business partners have an influence on the strategy, plans and decisions of your company.	250	2.0	5.0	3.52	0.906
MTCT4	Policies and standards of the industry and market about CSR have an influence on company.	250	2.0	5.0	3.52	0.915
MTCT5	Suppliers have an influence on the plans and decisions of CSR implementation in your company.	250	2.0	5.0	3.66	0.727
MTCT6	Formal and informal surveys of customer satisfaction have an influence on the practice of CSR in your company.	250	2.0	5.0	3.51	0.919
	Social influences					
MTVM1	Local communities have an influence on the strategy, plans and decisions of the CSR implementation in your company.	240	2.0	5.0	3.55	0.953
MTVM2	Governmental agencies have an influence on the strategy, plans and decisions of the CSR implementation in your company.	250	2.0	5.0	3.55	0.914
MTVM3	Associations and non-governmental organizations have an influence on the strategy, plans and decisions of the CSR implementation in your company.	250	2.0	5.0	3.59	0.906
MTVM4	Society has an influence on the strategy, plans and decisions of the CSR implementation in your company.	250	1.0	5.0	3.56	0.944

4. Research Findings

4.1. Descriptive Statistics

After we deleted items with missing data, our final sample of 250 respondents was used for analysis. Respondents were top managers (46.4%), middle managers (34.4%), and low-level managers (19.2%). They were from companies with fewer than 50 employees (4.8%), between 50 and 200 employees (45.6%), between 200 and 300 employees (42.8%), and over 300 employees (6.8%). In terms of charter capital, the majority of companies (65.6%) were below $430,000; the remaining ones (34.4%) were from $430,000 to $4,300,000. Almost all respondents were managers with more than three years' experience in the same position.

The statistical results described 25 observed items. The average value for the 25 observed items ranges from 3.33 to 3.72. Means are different between different components (see Table 1).

4.2. Cronbach's Alpha and EFA Analysis

The scale's reliability was tested via Cronbach's alpha. Cronbach's alphas of all variables were acceptable (>0.7). Item-total correlations were good (>0.3) (Table 2). Item reliability was also assessed by examining the factor loadings of each item with its respective latent variables. Kaiser–Meyer–Olkin (KMO) and Barlett's test was 0.852 for the all factors (sig. = 0.000 < 0.005). All observed items were eligible to be continued with EFA analysis.

Table 2. Cronbach's alpha of observed variables.

Observed Variable	Scale Mean if Item Deleted	Scale Variance if Item Deleted	Item-Total Correlations	Cronbach's Alpha if Item Deleted
Cronbach's Alpha The understanding of Managers about CSR (LĐ): 0.733				
LĐ 1	10.45	4.280	0.571	0.646
LĐ 2	10.48	4.684	0.482	0.697
LĐ 3	10.53	4.154	0.561	0.652
LĐ 4	10.50	4.661	0.485	0.695
Cronbach's Alpha The Internal Environment of companies (MTNB): 0.812				
MTNB1	18.01	10.659	0.591	0.779
MTNB2	18.05	10.335	0.627	0.771
MTNB3	17.85	9.532	0.619	0.773
MTNB4	17.96	11.368	0.417	0.802
MTNB5	18.00	10.622	0.580	0.781
MTNB6	18.01	10.598	0.553	0.787
Cronbach's Alpha Competitive Context (MTCT): 0.818				
MTCT 1	17.72	10.948	0.547	0.796
MTCT 2	17.71	10.134	0.619	0.781
MTCT 3	17.69	10.792	0.552	0.795
MTCT 4	17.69	10.527	0.592	0.786
MTCT 5	17.55	11.549	0.571	0.794
MTCT 6	17.71	10.400	0.616	0.781

Table 2. *Cont.*

Observed Variable	Scale Mean if Item Deleted	Scale Variance if Item Deleted	Item-Total Correlations	Cronbach's Alpha if Item Deleted
Cronbach's Alpha Social Influences (MTVM): 0.744				
MTVM 1	10.70	4.871	0.483	0.716
MTVM 2	10.69	4.680	0.580	0.660
MTVM 3	10.66	4.909	0.517	0.696
MTVM 4	10.69	4.609	0.570	0.666
Cronbach's Alpha The Implementation of CSR in SMEs (CSR): 0.850				
CSR 1	9.72	5.301	0.710	0.806
CSR 2	9.61	5.242	0.685	0.813
CSR 3	9.66	5.472	0.636	0.826
CSR 4	9.60	5.718	0.575	0.842
CSR 5	9.76	5.519	0.705	0.809

EFA analysis was conducted to examine whether the items produced proposed factors, and if the results support the proposed five-factor solution. According to statistics results, all variables were grouped into five components at eigenvalue >1 and a cumulative sum of squared loadings >50%. All factors loadings were higher than 0.5 except MTCT5, therefore, this observed variable was removed from the analysis. The five groups were named internal environment, competitive context, managers, social influences, and CSR. Hence, the measurement scale meets the satisfactory level of reliability and validity.

4.3. Correlation and Regression Analysis

The Pearson's analysis was used to analyze the linear correlation between the dependent variable and independent variables. The correlation number had to be between −1 and 1 (IBM 2016). Table 3 shows that the variables are linearly related. The lowest correlation with the dependent variable is MTNB (0.402), whereas the highest is MTCT (0.681) (see Table 3). In terms of the regression equation, the adjusted R square (0.652) in Table 4 explains that the independent variables actually affect the dependent variable. The ANOVA test (Table 5) shows that the survey results are significant.

Table 3. Correlations.

		CSR	LĐ	MTNB	MTCT	MTVM
CSR	Pearson Correlation Sig. (2-tailed)	1				
LĐ	Pearson Correlation	505 **	1			
	Sig. (2-tailed)	0.000				
MTNB	Pearson Correlation	0.402 **	0.329 **	1		
	Sig. (2-tailed)	0.000	0.000			
MTCT	Pearson Correlation	0.681 **	0.386 **	0.257 **	1	
	Sig. (2-tailed)	0.000	0.000	0.000		
MTVM	Pearson Correlation	0.611 **	0.404 **	0.383 **	0.343 **	1
	Sig. (2-tailed)	0.000	0.000	0.000	0.000	

** Correlation is significant at the 0.01 level (2-tailed).

Table 4. Model summary.

Model	R	R Square	Adjusted R Square	Std. Error of the Estimate
1	0.811 [a]	0.658	0.652	0.32987

[a] Dependent Variable: CSR.

Table 5. ANOVA.

	Model	Sum of Squares	df	Mean Square	F	Sig.
1	Regression	51.244	4	12.811	117.733	0.000 [b]
	Residual	26.660	245	0.109		
	Total	77.904	249			

[b] Predictors: (Constant), MTVM, MTCT, MTNB, LĐ.

4.4. Hypothesis Test

Linear regression was conducted to test research hypotheses and the results are presented in Tables 4–6. The results show that the model is consistent with the data set (Sig. = 0.000 < 0.05) and CSR factors explain 65.2 percent of the implementation of CSR in SMEs (see Table 4). The VIFs (variance inflation factors) <2 indicate that there is no multi-collinearity issue in the data set. Table 6 shows that the four independent variances (LĐ, MTNB, MTCT, and MTVM) with sig. <0.05 are linearly related with the dependent variance (CSR). Research hypotheses indicate that H1 and H2 are accepted at the significance level of 1 percent. This means that the understanding of managers about CSR, and the external and internal environment of SMEs positively affect their engagement in CSR.

Table 6. Coefficients.

Model	Unstandardized Coefficients		Standardized Coefficients	t	Sig.	Collinearity Statistics	
	B	Std Error	Beta			Tolerance	VIF
Constant	0.257	0.157		1.642	0.102		
LĐ	0.118	0.036	0.142	3.274	0.001	0.744	1.344
MTNB	0.105	0.036	0.119	2.871	0.004	0.810	1.234
MTCT	0.393	0.034	0.478	11.451	0.000	0.802	1.246
MTVM	0.276	0.035	0.344	7.923	0.000	0.739	1.353

5. Discussion

The research findings show that all proposed hypotheses were accepted. Impacts on the implementation of CSR in SMEs, are the understanding of managers about CSR, competitive context, social influences, and the internal environment of companies. Table 3 shows that MTCT and MTVM are the two strongest correlations with the dependent variance (CSR) compared to the others. Respondents highly value the relationships between SMEs' engagement in CSR, and competitive context and social influences (Table 6). The research hypothesis that the external environment (competitive context and social influences) positively affects SMEs' implementation of CSR was thus confirmed.

Table 3 also indicates that the correlations of LĐ and MTNT with the dependent variance were strong. The standardized coefficient of LĐ and MTNT (Table 6) showed significant relationships with the CSR variance. The proposed hypotheses about the influence of managers' CSR understanding and the internal environment of companies on the implementation of CSR in SMEs were confirmed.

The research findings showed that competitive context (observed variable MTCT) was the strongest driver to impact the strategy, plans, and decisions around CSR in SMEs (see Table 1, Table 3, and Table 6). This is a reason for SMEs to engage in CSR in order to reach their own business objectives.

The context here relates to customers, international partners, suppliers, business partners, policies and standards of the industry and market, and formal and informal surveys of customers. The large majority of goods (90%) in Vietnam's textile and garment industry are exported to other destinations such as the United States, Japan, and Europe (Song 2018; Duyen 2019). Thus, the expectations of external stakeholders, particularly international customers and business partners, may be important for companies in Vietnam in terms of the international standards of CSR and the industry. The pressure of shipment returns by European partners such as in 2018 (Bach 2019) can be an example to answer why competitive context is the most important impact on adopting CSR in companies. This finding is different to other research on CSR in SMEs (e.g., De Kok and Uhlaner 2001)—their research said that SMEs are often challenged from local rather than international markets and deal with less stakeholder stress. The difference can be due to the export market-specific characteristics of the industry in Vietnam. Another interesting point here is that SMEs have to put CSR in their business plans immediately because of stakeholder pressure and competitive context. Although SMEs have financial limitations compared to large enterprises (Kusyk and Lozano 2007; Sweeney 2007), they will adopt CSR soon owing to business requirements and stakeholders' satisfaction.

Social influences are ranked second among the four drivers (Table 1, Table 3, and Table 6). These are local communities, governmental agencies, associations, nongovernmental organizations, and society. This finding implies that there are requirements of society toward SMEs, meaning that companies are dependent on the society for their existence and developments. SMEs have to focus on social and political issues in their business activities. Vietnam is facing many pollution problems (World Health Organization 2018), so the society and local communities have put pressure on business companies due to fears around air and water pollution (see, e.g., Tan 2015; Le 2016; Ortmann 2017; Vinh 2019). Many environmental protest campaigns and movements have been organized by local people for many years. The campaigns led to the attention of governmental representatives in provinces and cities of Vietnam. Some provinces have thus established regulations on environmental issues. For example, Hue, a city in Central Vietnam, has a regulation on protecting the environment in the textile and garment industry (People's Committee of Hue 2018).

The understanding of managers about CSR is ranked third in the four factors (Table 6). Their understanding is about the influence of stakeholders on the strategy and plans of companies (Table 1). The respondents also agreed that participation in CSR programs and evaluating the benefits of CSR in companies is important for managers. The finding shows that there is a relationship between the implementation of CSR in companies and the understanding of managers about CSR (Table 6). This implies that the more managers understand CSR, the more they put CSR in their strategy and business plans (see also Table 1). In SMEs, decision-making tends to be based on the personal choices of managers (Spence 1999; Perez-Sanchez et al. 2003), so their understanding of CSR can support adopting CSR more directly and quickly than large companies do. This finding can help to consider that the CSR theories, which can successfully be applied to large enterprises, may need to be adjusted slightly for SMEs.

The last factor affecting the implementation of CSR in business is the internal environment of SMEs (Table 6). The managers in this study agreed that employees put pressure on their companies in terms of implementing CSR (Table 1). They also said that companies need to follow labor laws, health and safety policies, policies to motivate employees to improve practical skills and competencies, ensure fair working conditions for employees, and listen to employees' opinions. These issues have an influence on the strategy and plans of SMEs. As analyzed above, most companies in the textile and garment industry in Vietnam are exporters. Thus, they need to follow the standards of the CSR of countries where they supply goods. The majority of garment and textile goods are exported to other countries (Song 2018), therefore, international CSR standards (e.g., International Standards ISO 26000), which emphasize issues relating to employees, employment relationships, and labor practice, are all issues that the managers in this study were aware of. Moreover, Vietnam has recently had many protest campaigns relating to working conditions and employee wages (see, e.g., Dinh and Nguyen 2018).

For example, on 24 March 2018, thousands of workers in Pou Chen Corporation in the Dong Nai province, were on strike against the new salary policy that had been set by the company (Le 2018). Thus, internal environment is one of the drivers that force SMEs to engage in CSR.

Our research findings were different compared to those of other studies. For example, Tran and Jeppesen (2016) concluded that: "the CSR practices are not implemented because the business case for CSR in SMEs cannot be identified or because the western concept of CSR is not understood by managers and workers" (p. 605). However, our research found that SMEs adopt CSR due to the high expectations of stakeholders. The difference can be because of the research samples and time taken for data collection, even though the two studies explored CSR in the same field: the textile and garment industry. Tran and Jeppesen (2016) studied 20 managers in 20 firms, whereas our research surveyed 250 managers in 250 SMEs. Moreover, our research collected the data in 2017, while Tran and Jeppesen did theirs in 2011. This explains that the concept of CSR may now become popular in Vietnam and managers may recognize the importance of CSR for their business. In addition, our research found that competitive context, social influences, the understanding of managers about CSR, and the internal environment of SMEs are the four drivers influencing the implementation of CSR in SMEs. However, Nguyen and Pham (2016) said that SMEs only practice CSR if they have the cash and human resources. This implies that SMEs may not want to implement CSR due to the limitation of resources. Nevertheless, they can be ready to do it due to the pressure of international partners, competitive environment, local community, and society.

6. Conclusions

The relationship between the environment of SMEs and their engagement in CSR was tested in this research. The research also tested the link between the understanding of managers about CSR and the implementation of CSR in SMEs. The findings provide evidence of manager awareness about CSR practice in Vietnam. The research results indicated that competitive context, social influences, the internal environment of SMEs, and the understandings of managers about CSR are the four drivers of CSR. In the four drivers, competitive context has the strongest impact on adopting CSR in SMEs. This finding is different owing to the export market-specific characteristics of the textile and garment industry in Vietnam. The study results imply that stakeholder pressure influences companies due to the high expectations from international customers and partners, employees, local communities, and society. Another interesting finding relates to the characteristic of SMEs—personal decision making by managers/owners—in that the more managers/owners understand CSR and its benefits, the more CSR is incorporated in their business strategies. Although SMEs have financial limitations compared to large enterprises, SMEs can immediately add CSR to their business agenda because of stakeholder pressure and competitive context. This study provides evidence for the development of the theory of CSR that needs to consider more SMEs.

This study was conducted in Vietnam, where scholarship is emerging. This contributes to a broader understanding of CSR in SMEs, especially in the developing world. The research is also significant because it explores SMEs' engagement in CSR in a country where CSR is new to the public. Another contribution of this study relates to the research sample. The study collected data from the perspectives of SMEs, not those of large enterprises. In other words, our research findings reflect the view of SME managers who have an important role in making decisions about why firms need to add CSR to their business strategy. Finally, this research provides empirical evidence from the textile and garment industry. SMEs may have resource limitations, but they are ready to practice CSR due to the pressure of a competitive context and social influences.

There are limitations in this study that need to be considered in future research. Firstly, this study was conducted only in the textile and garment industry. Thus, generalizability of the research results is limited. Research in future should explore other industries so that it can discover similarities and differences among them. Secondly, our research surveyed SMEs only. Future studies need to examine large companies in order to compare the practice of CSR between SMEs and large enterprises in the developing world, such as in Vietnam. Finally, future studies should be cross-country to develop a better understanding of the use of CSR theories in different countries.

Author Contributions: Conceptualization, L.T.-H.V.; methodology, A.P.N.; software, A.P.N.; formal analysis, L.T.-H.V. and A.P.N.; investigation, A.P.N.; resources, L.T.-H.V.; data curation, A.P.N. and L.T.-H.V.; writing—original draft preparation, L.T.-H.V.; writing—review and editing, L.T.-H.V.

Acknowledgments: We are grateful to the three anonymous referees for their constructive comments. We also thank the participants at the 3rd Vietnam's Business and Economics Research Conference VBER2019 (Ho Chi Minh City Open University, Vietnam, 18-20 July 2019) for their helpful suggestions. The authors wish to acknowledge financial supports from Ho Chi Minh City Open University. The authors are solely responsible for any remaining errors or shortcomings.

References

Akkucuk, Ulas. 2015. *Handbook of Research on Developing Sustainable Value in Economics, Finance, and Marketing.* Hershey: IGI Global.

Bach, Hue. 2019. EU trả về 17 lô nông, thuỷ sản của Việt Nam (EU returned 17 agricultural products and seafood shipments of Vietnam). *VnEconomy*, May 6. Available online: http://vneconomy.vn/eu-tra-ve-17-lo-nong-thuy-san-cua-viet-nam-2019050612483513.htm (accessed on 1 August 2019).

Basu, Kunal, and Guido Palazzo. 2008. Corporate social responsibility: A process model of sense making. *Academy of Management Review* 33: 122–36. [CrossRef]

Bui, Thi Lan Huong. 2010. The Vietnamese consumer perception on corporate social responsibility. *Journal of International Business Research* 9: 75–87.

Burke, Lee, and Jeanne M. Logsdon. 1996. How corporate social responsibility pays off. *Long Range Planning* 29: 495–502. [CrossRef]

Campbell, John L. 2006. Institutional analysis and the paradox of corporate social responsibility. *American Behavioral Scientist* 49: 925–38. [CrossRef]

Carroll, Archie B. 1979. A three-dimensional conceptual model of corporate performance. *Academy of Management Review* 4: 497–505. [CrossRef]

Carroll, Archie B. 1991. The pyramid of corporate social responsibility: Toward the moral management of organizational stakeholders. *Business Horizons* 34: 39–48. [CrossRef]

Carroll, Archie B. 2009. A History of Corporate Social Responsibility Concepts and Practices. In *The Oxford Handbook of Corporate Social Responsibility*. Oxford: Oxford University Press, pp. 19–46.

Carroll, Archie B. 2016. *Carroll's Pyramid of CSR: Taking Another Look.* Springer Open. Available online: https://doi.org/10.1186/s40991-016-0004-6 (accessed on 15 March 2019).

Darnall, Nicole, Irene Henriques, and Perry Sadorsky. 2010. Adopting proactive environmental practices: The influence of stakeholders and firm size. *Journal of Management Studies* 47: 1072–93. [CrossRef]

Davies, Iain, and Andrew Crane. 2010. Corporate social responsibility in small-and media-size enterprises: Investigateing employee engagement in fair trade companies. *Business Ethics: A European Review* 19: 126–41. [CrossRef]

De Kok, Jan, and Lorraine M. Uhlaner. 2001. Organization context and human resource management in the small firm. *Small Business Economics* 17: 273–91. [CrossRef]

Dinh, Quan, and Lanh Nguyen. 2018. Hàng nghìn công nhân ngừng việc tập thể ở Đồng Nai (Thousands of workers stop working in Dong Nai Province). *Bao Moi*, August 25. Available online: https://baomoi.com/hang-nghin-cong-nhan-ngung-viec-tap-the-o-dong-nai/c/27446038.epi (accessed on 1 August 2019).

Duyen, Duyen. 2019. Vietnam đang xuất khẩu, nhập khẩu mặt hàng nào nhiều nhất với EU (Which are the largest items that Vietnam exports and imports from and to EU). *VnEconomy*, June 6. Available online: http://vneconomy.vn/viet-nam-dang-xuat-nhap-khau-mat-hang-nao-nhieu-nhat-voi-eu-2019062616412069.htm (accessed on 6 June 2019).

Eweje, Gabriel. 2006. The role of MNEs in community development initiatives in developing countries. *Business & Society* 45: 93–129.

Garriga, Elisabet, and Domenec Mele. 2004. Corporate social responsibility theories: Mapping the territory. *Journal of Business Ethics* 53: 51–71. [CrossRef]

General Statistics Office of Vietnam. 2017. Thông cáo báo chí kết quả chính thức Tổng điều tra kinh tế năm 2017 (News Release about the Official Result of the Economic Survey in Vietnam in 2017). Hanoi. Available online: https://www.gso.gov.vn/Default.aspx?tabid=382&idmid=&ItemID=18945 (accessed on 9 July 2019).

Gupta, Shruti. 2009. Perception of corporate social responsibilities: Perspectives from American and Indian consumers. In *Proceedings of the Third IIMA Conference on Marketing Paradigms for Emerging Economies, January 7–9*. Ahmedabad: Indian Institute of Management.

Hamm, Brigitte. 2012. Corporate social responsibility in Vietnam: Integration or mere adaptation? *Pacific News* 38: 4–8.

IBM. 2016. *SPSS @ Statistics 23.0*. Armonk: IBM Company.

Jenkins, Heledd. 2006. Small business champions for corporate social responsibility. *Journal of Business Ethics* 67: 241–56. [CrossRef]

Kieu, Linh. 2019. Big C Việt Nam nói gì việc tạm ngưng nhập hàng may mặc Việt? (What did Big C in Vietnam say about refusing the supply by the Vietnamese textiles and garment companies?). *VnEconomy*, July 3. Available online: http://vneconomy.vn/bigc-viet-nam-noi-gi-viec-tam-ngung-nhap-hang-may-mac-viet-20190703190543384.htm (accessed on 10 July 2019).

Kusyk, S. M., and J. M. Lozano. 2007. Corporate social responsibility and corporate performance: The case of Italian SMEs. *Corporate Governance* 5: 28–42.

Le, Hoang. 2016. Hàng trăm người đội mưa rét vây nhà máy phân bón ô nhiễm (Hundreds of people surrounded the polluted fertilizer factory in raining and freezing cold days). *Vnexpress*, March 11. Available online: https://vnexpress.net/thoi-su/hang-tram-nguoi-doi-mua-ret-vay-nha-may-phan-bon-o-nhiem-3368436.html (accessed on 11 July 2019).

Le, Lam. 2018. Công nhân Pouchen tràn ra QL1K phản đối chính sách tiền lương mới (Workers in Pouchen Corporation were in Highway 1K to protest against its new policy of salary). *Thanh Nien*, March 24. Available online: https://thanhnien.vn/thoi-su/cong-nhan-pouchen-tran-ra-ql1k-phan-doi-chinh-sach-tien-luong-moi-945191.html (accessed on 12 July 2019).

Lepoutre, Jan, and Aime Heene. 2006. Investigating the impact of firm size on small business social responsibility: A critical review. *Journal of Business Ethics* 67: 257–73. [CrossRef]

Longo, Mariolina, Matteo Mura, and Alessandra Bonoli. 2005. Corporate social responsibility and corporate performance: The case of Italian SMEs. *Corporate Governance* 5: 28–42. [CrossRef]

Luu, Quyen. 2018. Năm 'đột biến' của Ngành Dệt may Việt Nam (2018- a "sharp increased" year of the textiles and garment industry in Vietnam). In *Ministry of Industry and Trade of the Socialist Republic of Vietnam*; December 27. Available online: https://moit.gov.vn/tin-chi-tiet/-/chi-tiet/2018-nam-%C4%91ot-bien-cua-nganh-det-may-viet-nam-13523-16.html (accessed on 15 July 2019).

Mitchell, Ronald K., Bradley R. Agle, and Donna J. Wood. 1997. Toward a theory of stakeholder identification and salience: Defining the principle of who and what really counts. *Academy of Management Review* 22: 853–86. [CrossRef]

Morsing, Mette, and Francesco Perrini. 2009. CSR in SMEs: Do SMEs matter for the CSR agenda? *Business Ethics: A European Review* 18: 1–6. [CrossRef]

Murrillo, David, and Josep Lozano. 2006. SMEs and CSR: An approach to CSR in their own words. *Journal of Business Ethics* 67: 227–40. [CrossRef]

Nguyen, Minh, Stephen J. Kelly, and Jo Bensemann. 2017. Contextual factors affecting corporate social responsibility in an emerging country: A conceptual framework on the nature of the CSR concept in Vietnam. *ResearchGate*. Available online: http://www.researchgate.net/publication/317579309/ (accessed on 15 July 2019).

Nguyen, Thi Lanh, and Thi Ngoc Tram Pham. 2016. Các nhân tố tác động đến việc thực hiện trách nhiệm xã hội của các doanh nghiệp nhỏ và vừa Việt Nam (Factors influencing the implementation of CSR in Vietnamese SMEs). *Journal of Science* 6: 119–28.

Nguyen, My, and Minh Truong. 2016. The effect of culture on enterprise's perception of corporate social responsibility: The case of Vietnam. *Science Direct* 40: 681–87. [CrossRef]

Omran, Mohamed A., and Dineshwar Ramdhony. 2015. Theoretical perspectives on corporate social responsibility disclosure: A critical review. *International Journal of Accounting and Financial Reporting* 5: 38–55. [CrossRef]

Ortenblad, Anders. 2016. *Research Handbook on Corporate Social Responsibility in Context*. Northampton: Edward Elgar Publishing.

Ortmann, Stephan. 2017. *Environmental Governance in Vietnam: Institutional Reforms and Failures.* London, United Kingdom: Palgrave Macmillan.

Perez-Sanchez, D., J. R. Barton, and D. Bowder. 2003. Implementing environmental management in SMEs. *Corporate Social Responsibility and Environmental Management* 10: 67–77. [CrossRef]

Phương, Dung. 2015. Vụ Tân Hiệp Phát: "Con ruồi 500 triệu" và "bản án" 2.000 tỷ đồng (Tan Hiep Phat Corporation Case: "Butterfly in bottle" of 500 million VND and lost of 2000 billion VND). *Dan Tri*, December 19. Available online: http://dantri.com.vn/kinh-doanh/vu-tan-hiep-phat-con-ruoi-500-trieu-va-ban-an-2-000-ty-dong-20151218201416.htm (accessed on 15 July 2019).

People's Committee of Hue 2018. Quy định bảo vệ môi trường trong hoạt động dệt may công nghiệp trên địa bàn tỉnh Thừa Thiên Huế (Regulation for Protecting Environment in Textile and Garment Activities in Hue Province), Decision Number 30/2018/QĐ-UBND, 15/05/2018. Available online: https://huongvinh. thuathienhue.gov.vn/UploadFiles/TinTuc/2018/5/23/ubnd302018qdubnd2018pl1_signed.pdf (accessed on 16 July 2019).

Porter, Michael E., and Mark R. Kramer. 2007. Strategy and Society: The link between competitive advantage and corporate social responsibility. *Harvard Business Review* 84: 78–92.

Quang, Dai, Phi Long, and Hưng Tho. 2016. Hãy cứu du lịch biển miền trung (Please save sea tourism in Central Vietnam). *Lao Dong*. May 12. Available online: https://laodong.vn/thoi-su/hay-cuu-du-lich-bien-mien-trung-550511.bld (accessed on 15 July 2019).

Song, Ha. 2018. Xuất khẩu dệt may tăng đột biến, kim ngạch năm 2018 hơn 36 tỷ USD (Vietnamese Textile and garment exports have increased dramatically in 2018, reached more than 36 billion USD). *VnEconomy*. December 27. Available online: http://vneconomy.vn/xuat-khau-det-may-tang-dot-bien-kim-ngach-nam-2018-hon-36-ty-usd-2018122709311581.htm (accessed on 18 July 2019).

Spence, Laura J. 1999. Does size matter? The state of the art in small business ethics. *Business Ethics: A European Review* 8: 163–72. [CrossRef]

Spence, Laura J., René Schmidpeter, and André Habisch. 2003. Assessing social capital: Small and medium-sized enterprises in Germany and the UK. *Journal of Business Ethics* 47: 17–29. [CrossRef]

Spence, Laura J., and Robert Rutherford. 2003. Small business and empirical perspectives in business ethics: Editorial. *Journal of Business Ethics* 47: 1–5. [CrossRef]

Sweeney, Lorraine. 2007. Corporate social responsibility in Ireland: Barrier and opportunities experience by SMEs when undertaking CSR. *Corporate Governance* 7: 516–23. [CrossRef]

Tan, Luc. 2015. Dân phản đối nhà máy soda gây ô nhiễm (Local people protests factories that caused pollution). *Tuoi Tre Online*, August 1. Available online: https://tuoitre.vn/dan-phan-doi-nha-may-soda-gay-o-nhiem-786363.htm (accessed on 15 August 2019).

Tilley, Fiona. 2000. Small firm environmental ethics: How deep do they go? *Business Ethics: A European Review* 9: 31–40. [CrossRef]

Thi, QuyVo, and Phung Le Van. 2016. Consumers' perception towards corporate social responsibility and repurchase intention: A study of consumer industry in Vietnam. *Industrial Engineering & Management Systems* 15: 173–80.

Tran, Quan N., Thuy T. Le, and Ly Ngoc T. Huynh. 2017. Perception of Bank Customers towards Banking Corporate Social Responsibility in Vietnam. *International Research Journal of Finance and Economics* 161: 81–95.

Tran, Angie Ngoc, and Soren Jeppesen. 2016. SMEs in their own right: The views of managers and worker in Vietnamese textiles, garment and footwear companies. *Journal of Business Ethics* 137: 589–608. [CrossRef]

Vietnamese Government. 2001. Nghị định số 90/2001/NĐ-CP của Chính phủ: Nghị định về trợ giúp phát triển doanh nghiệp nhỏ và vừa (Decree number 90/2001/NĐ-CP by Vietnamese Government: Decree about helping SMEs). Available online: http://vanban.chinhphu.vn/portal/page/portal/chinhphu/hethongvanban? class_id=1&mode=detail&document_id=9917 (accessed on 5 March 2019).

Vinh, Quan. 2019. Người dân phản đối DN gây ô nhiễm môi trường nghiêm trọng (Local people protests against companies that caused serious pollution). *Kinh tế & Đô Thị*, August 4. Available online: http://kinhtedothi.vn/nguoi-dan-phan-doi-dn-gay-o-nhiem-moi-truong-nghiem-trong-346638.html (accessed on 5 August 2019).

Visser, Wayne. 2008. Corporate social responsibility in developing countries. In *The Oxford Handbook of Corporate Social Responsibility.* Edited by Andrew Crane, Abagail McWilliams, Dirk Matten, Jeremy Moon and Donald Siegel. New York: Oxford University Press, pp. 473–501.

Van, Thi-Hong Loan, Nguyen Huy Hoang, and Vo Hong Duc. 2019. Corporate Social Responsibility: A study on awareness of consumers in Vietnam. In *Review of Pacific Basin Financial Markets and Policies*. Singapore: World Scientific.

Vo, Linh Chi. 2012. Corporate social responsibility and SMEs: A literature review and agenda for future research. *Problems and Perspectives in Management* 9: 89–97.

Williamson, David, Gary Lynch-Wood, and John Ramsay. 2006. Drivers of Environmental Behaviour in Manufacturing SMEs and the Implications for CSR. *Journal of Business Ethics* 67: 317–30. [CrossRef]

World Bank. 2006. Our Commitment to Sustainable Development. Available online: http://siteresources.worldbank. org/ESSDNETWORK/Resources/481106-1129303936381/1777397-1129303967165/chapter4.html (accessed on 15 September 2019).

World Health Organization. 2018. More than 60000 Deaths in Viet Nam each Year Linked to Air Pollution. 02/05/2018. Available online: http://www.wpro.who.int/vietnam/mediacentre/releases/2018/air_pollution_ vietnam/en/ (accessed on 17 June 2019).

12

Exchange Rate Regime and Economic Growth in Asia: Convergence or Divergence

Dao Thi-Thieu Ha [1,*] and **Nga Thi Hoang** [2]

[1]   International Economics Faculty, Banking University Ho Chi Minh City, Ho Chi Minh City 70000, Vietnam
[2]   Office of Finance & Accounting, Ho Chi Minh City Open University, Ho Chi Minh City 70000, Vietnam; nga.ht@ou.edu.vn
*   Correspondence: daohtt@buh.edu.vn

Abstract: Exchange rates and exchange rate regimes in a constantly changing economy have always attracted much attention from scholars. However, there has not been a consensus on the effect of exchange rate on economic growth. To determine the direction and magnitude of the impact of an exchange rate regime on economic growth, this study uses the exchange rate database constructed by Reinhart and Rogoff. This study also employs the GMM (Generalized Method of Moments) technique on unbalanced panel data to analyze the effect of the exchange rate regime on economic growth in Asian countries from 1994 to 2016. Empirical results suggest that a fixed exchange rate regime (weak flexibility) will affect economic growth in the same direction. As such, results from the study will serve as quantitative evidence for countries in the Asian region to consider when selecting a suitable policy and an exchange rate regime to attain high economic growth.

Keywords: exchange rate regime; economic growth; Asia; Reinhart and Rogoff

1. Introduction

In a market economy with a flexible exchange rate, the exchange rate changes daily, or in fact, by the minute. The fluctuation in exchange rates has an impact on the economy (reflected by macroeconomic variables) and on society. As a result, in addition to policymakers and enterprises, the majority of the public pays attention to exchange rate changes. The selection of an appropriate exchange regime for a country is a very important issue, as it not only affects international finance but also a country's economic development.

In reality, different countries select different exchange rate regimes, and a country can have different exchange rate regimes at different points in time. There is not a universally suitable exchange rate regime for every country in the world. Some countries choose a floating exchange rate regime when the price of a country's currency relative to other currencies entirely depends on the supply and demand of related currencies. One of the representative countries with a floating exchange rate regime is Australia. In Australia, the Reserve Bank of Australia (RBA) does not intervene in the foreign exchange market except for in urgent situations, such as a speculative attack. Some countries may choose a fixed exchange rate (Hong Kong), while others, such as Vietnam, opt for a managed floating system.

From a theoretical angle, the theory of optimum currency areas by American economist Mundell (1961) states that a fixed exchange rate regime can enhance trade and output growth by devaluing the exchange rate and risk premium, while encouraging investment by lowering monetary value with interest rates. The criteria of the theory of optimum currency areas include trade interdependence, a converging trend of macro policies, flexibility of production factors, and uniform responses to shocks.

From an empirical angle, many scholars have examined how the exchange rate regime affects economic growth and have arrived at different conclusions. Empirical studies by Baxter and Stockman

(1989); Flood and Rose (1995); Ghosh et al. (2002); Mauro and Juhn (2002) argue that the choice of exchange rate regime has no effect on economic growth. However, the study by Husain et al. (2005) contends that a floating exchange rate regime is more stable and has a stronger relationship with growth, while a managed float in emerging economies is unstable and vulnerable to crises. On the other hand, studies by Mundell (1961); Dubas et al. (2005); and Bailliu et al. (2003) show contradictory results.

The current study is employed to supply additional empirical evidence on growth and exchange rate regimes for Asian countries. To the best of our knowledge, most of the studies used de jure data set on exchange rate regimes such as Husain et al. (2005); Domaç et al. (2004); and Eichengreen and Leblang (2003) but a limited number of studies conducted their research with de facto exchange rate regimes of Asian countries such as Coudert and Dubert (2005). To address this issue, in this paper, we contribute to the discussion by using the unique data set of the exchange rate regime classification by Reinhart and Rogoff (2004) with two types of measurement, by value and by group of dummy variables, to investigate the effect of exchange rate regime on economic growth. This study also covers all Asian countries with data availability.

Moreover, this paper pays much attention to Asian countries. Asia is one of the world's most dynamic economic regions and plays an essential role in the world's economy. Figure 1 shows that the growth rates of Asian countries are always much higher than the average growth of the world. Referring to papers on the exchange rate regime and economic growth, most studies focused either on all the world such as Ghosh et al. (1997); Moreno (2001); Levy-Yeyati and Sturzenegger (2003); Husain et al. (2005); and Dubas et al. (2005), or indispensable Asian countries which suffered from the financial crisis of 1997 such as Huang and Malhotra (2005); and Coudert and Dubert (2005). Moreover, the empirical evidence of Asian countries over the time period of the study confirms the theory of Mundell (1961) on optimum currency areas, which requires trade interdependence, convergence of macro policies, and flexibility in production factors. Asian countries are increasingly open to trade, and financial markets play an increasingly important part of the world economy. Asia also has a high number of emerging and developing countries. Therefore, the stability of currency values plays an important role in the balance of trade, thereby contributing positively to a country's economic growth. The choice of exchange rate regime ultimately aims to boost growth, improving the standard of living and executing international responsibilities. As a result, the study of these countries will provide many vital implications in the choice of exchange rate regime for Asian countries.

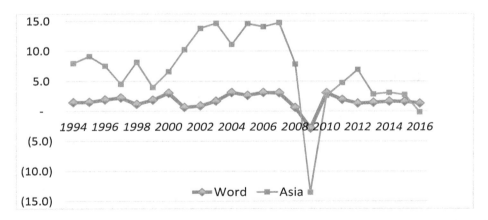

Figure 1. Average growth rate of GDP per capita of World and Asian countries in 1994–2016.

Despite these miraculous developments, Asian economies have fell into crisis in the 1990s. This currency crisis started Thailand in 1997 (Stiglitz 2000; Wang 1999; Wade 1998) then spread to the rest of southeast Asia, to the Taiwan, Hong Kong, Korea, Russia, and even countries such as Australia and New Zealand (Wade 1998; Jang and Sul 2002; Athukorala and Rajapatirana 2003). These countries were also affected by the 2008 economic crisis. The global economic crisis in 2008 saw the banks panic, with a sudden drop in lending in the US (Ivashina and Scharfstein 2010) cause recessions in many western countries (Burdekin et al. 2012; Barth et al. 2012), falling stock prices, and large-scale currency depreciation in the US and Europe, before spreading to other countries (Ivashina and Scharfstein 2010; Kotz 2009).

The contributions of this paper are as follows: (1) economic theory and empirical evidence provides conflicting predictions about the effects of exchange rate regimes on economic growth. This paper attempts to help close this gap by examining the effect of exchange rate regimes on economic growth using de facto exchange rate classification which is considered to be a better indicator for exchange rate policy; (2) This is a unique study using two datasets (the dataset of Reinhart and Rogoff, which reflects the foreign exchange market, and the dataset of Laeven and Valencia, which identifies the crisis year of each Asian country); (3) This research investigates the role of crisis (two measurement techniques of crisis) in the impact of exchange rate regimes on economic growth.

The rest of this paper is structured as follows: Section 2 presents a literature review. Section 3 presents the methods and data. Empirical results and a discussion are given in Section 4. Lastly, Section 5 includes some conclusions and policy recommendations.

2. Theoretical Reviews on the Effect of Exchange Rate on Economic Growth

2.1. Exchange Rate Regime

According to Ilzetzki et al. (2017) and International Monetary Fund (IMF), types of exchange rate regime classification based upon official statements of the jure policy include (1) exchange arrangement with no separate legal tender; (2) currency board arrangement; (3) conventional peg arrangement; (4) stabilized arrangement; (5) crawling peg; (6) crawling-like arrangement; (7) pegged exchange rate within horizontal bands; (8) floating; (9) free floating; and (10) other managed arrangements.

Since the IMF classification of exchange rate regimes is based on information provided by member countries, it does not reflect the differences between the actual implementation versus the official statements. According to Rose (2011), there are some other de facto exchange rate regime classifications such as Levy-Yeyati and Sturzenegger (2003); Reinhart and Rogoff (2004) (RR); and Shambaugh (2004). The ratio of observations is similar between these methodologies of classifications and IMF one is 59%, 59%, and 68% respectively. RR classification is based on market-determined exchange rates, dividing regimes into 5 groups: (1) the fixed exchange rate regime: a fixed regime that is announced and maintained, with monetary policy pegged to foreign policy; (2) the peg regime: the central exchange rate is pegged to another currency on a fixed rate with a small margin of fluctuation, the central bank is ready to intervene to maintain the rate, central bank may intervene but not frequently; (3) the managed float regime: the exchange rate is determined by the market, which means there is no officially announced exchange rate though the government has an underlying target exchange rate; the central bank proactively intervenes to soften the fluctuations; (4) the free float regime: the exchange rate is entirely determined by the market as the central bank has no underlying target rate and does little intervention; and (5) the "free-falling" regime: a regime that can be any type legally but the country is in fact suffering from a crisis.

International Monetary Fund (IMF) presents a set of common principles regarding the size of the economy, openness, diversification of production/export, diversification of export market, difference between domestic and external inflation, extent of economic development, finance, extent of freedom in capital movement, exchange rate fluctuation, and trustworthiness of policies to control inflation. The choice of an appropriate exchange rate regime depends on the characteristics of each country and may vary with time.

2.2. Theoretical Background and Previous Studies on Exchange Rate Regime and Economic Growth

Ghosh et al. (1997); Bailliu et al. (2003); and Jakob (2016) point out that economic theory which explains how the exchange rate regime affects economic growth is relatively modest. Theories mainly refer to the exchange rate regimes that can affect trade, investment, and productivity, and thereby affect growth. Furthermore, the magnitude of these effects is upon the development level of each country. Two notable theories concerning this relationship are the theory of optimum currency areas (OCA) of Mundell (1961) and Penne hypothesis of Balassa (1964); Samuelson (1964). The leading theoretical basis for exchange rate regime selection is the theory of OCA, first proposed by Mundell (1961) and McKinnon (1963). According to his theory, a fixed exchange rate regime can promote trade and output growth by devaluing the exchange rate and risk insurance premium, while encouraging investment by lowering the monetary value with interest rate. However, on the other hand, it reduces trade growth potential and output growth by suspending, delaying, or slowing the necessary relative price adjustment process. The Balassa–Samuelson hypothesis is also considered to be a well-known theory indirectly explaining exchange rate regime, trade, and growth. The Penne effect is explained by productivity increases in the tradable sector tending to be higher than that of non-tradable ones. In turn, the productivity increases are expected to contribute to higher growth rates of prices in the tradable sector. Moreover, exchange rates tend to appreciate in countries with high growth rate and be underestimated in countries with low growth rate (Balassa 1964; Samuelson 1964).

Because theories do not present the foundations of the relationship between exchange rate regimes and economic growth, the research framework is built on neoclassical economic growth theory, endogenous growth theory, and empirical evidence.

For economic theory, the neoclassical theory by Solow (1956) introduces labor and technology into the growth equation with decreasing marginal returns to production factors. The production function is $Y = f(K, L, R, T)$ in which Y = output (GDP), K = capital, L = labor force, R = natural resources and T = technology. According to Mankiw et al. (1995), capital does not flow to developing countries to make use of the high rates of return, as Solow and subsequently Lucas (1988) have predicted. Countries that invest more in physical and human capital will not only achieve an income in the steady state that is higher than in Solow's model, but also continue to grow at a faster rate. This means that the growth rate is not simply a reflection of external factors such as labor force growth rate or rate of global technological change, but also an endogenous variable in the model. Since then, economists have developed more sophisticated models and brought many endogenous variables into the model. This contribution has formed the research of Lucas (1988); Romer (1986); Romer (1990).

For empirical evidence, there are various studies on the impact of exchange rate regime on economic growth. The studies using descriptive statistics on panel data have provided very different results. Baxter and Stockman (1989) examined 49 countries in the 1946–1984 period, concluding that the impact does not exist. Meanwhile, a study by Mundell (2002), which looked into the 1947–1993 period in the US, Japan, Canada, and European countries, and a study by Moreno (2001), which investigated 98 developing countries in East Asia in 1974–1999, show a same-direction impact. Ghosh et al. (1997) conducted a study on 145 countries in the 1960–1990 period, which found no clear impact.

Following the studies using descriptive statistics, many post-2002 studies opt to use econometric models, most commonly pooled ordinary least squares. Similar to those using descriptive statistics, the econometric studies yield inconsistent results on the impact of exchange rate regime on economic growth.

A lot of the studies, with different data types, different time periods, and different estimation techniques, find no conclusive evidence on whether exchange rate regime makes a difference to economic growth. Huang and Malhotra (2005) used regression on panel data of 18 developed countries in 1976–2001. Domaç et al. (2004) employed the switching estimation technique for 22 different countries in different time periods in 10 years in the 1990s. Garofalo (2005) used OLS and 2SLS for Italy in the 1861–1998 period.

Besides the studies that give inconclusive results, there are studies that prove the inverse relationship between the fixed extent of the exchange rate and economic growth, such as Husain et al. (2005), Levy-Yeyati and Sturzenegger (2003) (183 countries in 1974–2000), and Eichengreen and Leblang (2003) (21 countries in 1880–1997). Most notably, Husain et al. (2005) argues that a floating exchange rate regime is more stable and has a strong relationship with economic growth. This is because richer and more financially developed countries benefit more from the flexibility of the exchange rate system. On the other hand, as developing countries are less sensitive to the capital markets, a pegged exchange rate regime brings lower inflation and more stability for the economy, even though this regime is least stable and more susceptible to risks when crises occur.

In particular, Levy-Yeyati and Sturzenegger (2003) examined the relationship between growth and exchange rate regime of 183 countries in the post-Bretton–Woods era between 1974 and 2000. Developing countries that have a less flexible exchange rate regime have a slower growth rate and more volatile output fluctuation. Meanwhile, in industrial countries, exchange rate regime does not have any impact on growth. Even though this result is later rebutted by Bleaney and Francisco (2007) as having a weak basis, it prompts much thinking on the diverging or converging nature of the effect of exchange rate regime on economic growth.

Contrary to this viewpoint, according to the theoretical analysis by Mundell (1961), who establishes the foundation of the theory of exchange rate regime selection, a fixed exchange rate regime can enhance trade and output growth rate by devaluing the exchange rate and risk premium, while encouraging investment by lowering the monetary value with interest rate. Criteria to achieve this include trade interdependence among countries in the area, a converging trend in macro policies, flexibility of production factors, and uniform responses to shocks. This result is supported by empirical studies conducted by Dubas et al. (2005); De Grauwe and Schnabl (2005); Bailliu et al. (2003); and Baldwin (1989). In their study, Ghosh et al. (2002) state that "one of the most surprising discoveries is that the growth results of a fixed exchange rate regime are not worse than the floating regimes". Dubas et al. (2005) prove that there is a meaningful symmetrical effect between fixing the exchange rate and economic growth.

Notably, countries with exchange rate regimes that show "fear of floating" (in which the exchange rate regime is announced to be floating but exposes characteristics of a fixed regime) have a significantly higher growth rate than other countries. Other than in developing countries, De Grauwe and Schnabl (2005) point out that a fixed exchange rate does not reduce economic growth in Central and East European countries, and that it is unconvincing to think that joining the European common currency area will dampen economic growth. In support of this argument, Baldwin (1989) i n his analysis of the European monetary union asserts that a common currency such as the euro can stimulate economic growth in Europe by reducing the exchange rate premium on capital within the continent. In addition to the effect of exchange rate regime, economic growth is affected by other factors, which are compiled in Table 1.

Table 1. List of explanatory variables used in previous studies.

Author	Time and Region Regime	Independent Variables	Methods	Results
Baxter and Stockman (1989)	1946–1984; 49 countries; pegged and floating		Comparative	No effect
Mundell (2002)	1947–1993; US, Japan, Canada, EC, other Europe; De jure		Descriptive statistics	Positive
Moreno (2001)	1974–1999; 98 East Asian developing countries; De facto		Descriptive statistics	Positive
Ghosh et al. (2002)	1960–1990; 145 countries; De jure		Descriptive statistics	Unclear relationship

Table 1. *Cont.*

Author	Time and Region Regime	Independent Variables	Methods	Results
Levy-Yeyati and Sturzenegger (2003)	1974–2000; 183 countries; De facto	investment/GDP; terms of trade; Government spending; political instability; average initial GDP; population; trade openness; enrollment rate of secondary school; dummy variable for the region and exchange rate regime	OLS; 2SLS	Negative
Eichengreen and Leblang (2003)	1880–1997; 21 countries; de jure	income per capita/total income, enrollment rate of primary, and secondary students, capital control, dummy exchange rate regime	GMM	Negative
Bailliu et al. (2003)	1973–1998; 60 countries; de facto and de jure	initial GDP, investment rate/GDP, number of secondary students, real government spending/GDP, trade openness, M2/GDP, private sector credit/GDP, domestic credit/GDP, net private capital/GDP, exchange rate dummy variable	GMM	Positive
Domaç et al. (2004)	10 years (1990s, different period for each country); 22 transition countries; de jure	net government spending, lagged financial openness, inflation, number of years in socialism, urbanization degree, the proportion of trade in CMEA	Switching estimation technique	Depend on development level
Husain et al. (2005)	1970–1999; 158 countries; De jure	Investment/GDP; Trade openness; term of trade growth, average years of schooling, tax rates, net government spending; initial average annual income/gross income; population growth; population; exchange rate dummy variable	OLS	Developing countries: positive Developed countries: Negative, emerging: insignificant
Garofalo (2005)	1861–1998; Italy; De facto	investment/GDP; Government spending; political instability; initial GDP; population; trade openness; enrollment rate of secondary school students; dummy variable for the region and exchange rate regime	OLS; 2SLS	Depend on development level
Dubas et al. (2005)	1960–2002; 180 countries; De facto	initial GDP, initial population, population growth, investment /GDP; civil responsibility, trade openness; terms of trade, dummy variables for transition countries, Latin America and Africa, time dummy variables, exchange rate dummy variables	REM	Positive
Huang and Malhotra (2005)	1976–2001; 12 developing Asian countries and 18 developed European countries; De facto	financial crisis, trade openness; initial GDP, fertility rate, enrollment rate of secondary school students, dummy exchange rate regime	Pooled OLS	Depend on development level
Coudert and Dubert (2005)	1990–2011; 10 Asian countries	initial GDP, investment/GDP, population, trade openness, education spending	2SLS	Positive
De Grauwe and Schnabl (2005)	1994–2002; 10 Eastern Europe countries; de facto	investment rate/GDP; export, net government spending/GDP; Short-term capital/GDP ratio, EU-15 real growth rate, exchange rate dummy variable	GMM	Positive
Bleaney and Francisco (2007)	1984–2001; 91 developing countries; de facto	growth rate, time, exchange rate regime (all are dummy)	Pooled OLS	Negative

Source: Authors' synthesis.

3. Data and Model

3.1. Data

The study spans the 1994–2016 period and covers 46 countries according to geographical classification of the World Bank (Appendix A, column 1). Among them, 34 countries have sufficient data on the exchange rate regimes following RR classifications (Column 2), and 23 countries were present in systemic banking crisis data of Laeven and Valencia (2018). Therefore, all available data studies the impact of exchange rate regimes on economic growth. Moreover, Georgia and Russia were considered to be "dual market in which parallel market data is missing" in 1997, 1998 and 1997, 1998, 2011–2016, respectively. Data comprises an unbalanced panel with 525 observations.

Most variables, such as economic growth, trade openness, government expenditure, and education, are extracted from the World Development Indicator database (WDI) of World Bank.

Exchange rate regime (ER), the independent variable in the model, is the measurement of the exchange rate policies of various countries, and taken from the publications of Reinhart and Rogoff at http://www.carmenreinhart.com, a website updated by the two professors. They re-classify actual exchange rate regimes based on reports of member countries to IMF. According to Reinhart and Rogoff (2004), exchange rate regimes are sorted from the most rigid to the most flexible {1; 2; 3; 4; 5} = {fixed; pegged; managed float; free float; "free-fall"}.

Crisis data is updated in the database on systemic banking crises presented in Laeven and Valencia (2018) and can be downloaded at https://sites.google.com/site/laevenl/des. This data set provides more comprehensive information of the crisis over time. In contrast to other research, this dataset points out the crisis year of each country. The descriptive variables are presented in Table 2.

Table 2. A summary of variables.

Variables	Definition	Calculation
	Dependent variable	
$Y_{i,t}(g)$	Economic growth	Growth rate of GDP per capita (measured in USD with 2010 as the base year)
	Independent variable	
$Y_{i,t-1}$		GDP per capita of the year preceding year t
ER	Exchange rate regime	taking on the values 1, 2, 3, 4, 5
CRISIS	Crisis	dummy variables: 1 in crisis year (model 1)
		dummy variables: 1 in 1997 and 2008 (model 2)
OPEN	Trade openness	(Export + Import)/GDP
GOV	Government spending	General government final consumption expenditure (% of GDP)
EDU	A measurement of human capital	Total secondary school enrollment/Total population
GDP initial	A measurement of catching-up process	Ln (Real GDP per capita of 1993)

3.2. Research Model

Drawing from the theoretical basis and empirical studies, and from the process of trial and error, the research model is constructed with the following factors: (1) GDP per capital growth; (2) exchange rate regime; (3) frequency of monetary crisis, magnitude of crisis; (4) openness of the economy; (5) government spending; and (6) human capital. To examine the impact between exchange rate regime and economic growth, the study is based on theoretical and empirical studies (Table 1), and makes use of the two approaches, in which Model 1 uses a proportionate variable for exchange rate regime while Model 2 uses dummy variables for types of exchange rate regime as follows:

Model 1:

$$Y_{i,t(g)} = a + Y_{i,t-1} + \mu_1 ER + \mu_2 CRISIS + \mu_3 OPEN + \mu_4 GOV + \mu_5 EDU + GDPinitial + \varepsilon \qquad (1)$$

Model 2:

$$Y_{i,t(g)} = a + Y_{i,t-1} + \mu_{11}dregime_1 + \mu_{12}dregime_2 + \mu_{13}dregime_3 + \mu_{14D}dregime_4 + \mu_2 CRISIS + \\ \mu_3 OPEN + \mu_4 GOV + \mu_5 EDU + GDPinitial + \varepsilon \qquad (2)$$

In which:

- Crisis is a dummy variable reflecting the effect of the global financial crisis of 2008 and Asian financial crisis of 1997 on output (Ma and Lin 2016). In addition to Ma and Lin (2016), the currency crisis of 1997 was recognized in the studies of Stiglitz (2000); Wang (1999); Wade (1998); Jang and Sul (2002); and Athukorala and Rajapatirana (2003) while the financial crisis of 2008 was emphasized in the studies of Ivashina and Scharfstein (2010); Munir (2011); Kotz (2009). To cross check and increase the reliability of empirical evidence, this study uses another database of crisis, which is introduced and updated by Laeven and Valencia (2018).
- Openness reveals trade openness level. The effect of trade openness is not clear cut. Studies supporting fixed exchange rates suggest that the fixed exchange rate will reduce exchange rate risk, thus stimulating trade, investment, and especially technology transfer, increasing the openness of the economy and in turn promoting economic growth (Moreno 2001; De Grauwe and Schnabl 2005; Sachs et al. 1995). Unsupported studies such as Bailliu et al. (2003); Domaç et al. (2004) suggest that the flexible exchange rate will smooth the adjustment to shocks, thereby quickly and easily and absorbing economic shocks, enhancing the expected growth. They also pointed out that when uncertainty exists, trade and investment activities will become hesitant and many countries are claimed as mentioned in McKinnon (1963); Calvo and Reinhart (2002). In particular, Rodriguez and Rodrik (2000) could not find any linkage. However, given that most countries in our sample have based their development strategy on exports, a positive impact can be expected.
- Government spending and education enrollment should have a positive impact on growth, since such expenditure is generally viewed as an improvement in investment and human capital and helps to increase the factors of production. Both variables are represented by the resources in standard economic growth model.
- GDP initial is designed to stand for the catching-up process. According to neoclassical theory, initial per-capita income has a negative relationship with economic growth (Bailliu et al. 2003; Huang and Malhotra 2005; Coudert and Dubert 2005). Countries with a lower level of initial per-capita growth will grow faster than higher ones because they must go out of their steady state and must catch up.

For estimation technique, initially, the study uses pooled OLS estimation. However, a heteroskedasticity test using the Greene test (Greene 2000), and autocorrelation test using Wooldridge (2010) and Drukker (2003) show the presence of heteroskedasticity and autocorrelation. Moreover, the relationship between government spending and economic growth is theoretically endogenous, as confirmed by Lee and Gordon (2005) and Halko et al. (2012). Moreover, the existence of endogeneity in the model has been demonstrated in background theory. Endogenous problems in the model are mentioned by Garofalo (2005). In addition, the simultaneous relationship between economic growth and the exchange rate regime is also mentioned in the study of Levy-Yeyati and Sturzenegger (2003), and potential two-way causality between economic performance and the exchange rate regime also are pointed out by Bailliu et al. (2003).

As a result, this study will conduct the regression using the GMM (Generalized Method of Moments) on unbalanced panel data. According to results from Arellano and Bond (1991) and

Arellano and Bover (1995), GMM is an effective solution to control for autocorrelation of residuals, heteroskedasticity and endogeneity, ensuring that the estimation is strong and robust.

4. Analysis and Discussion of Results

4.1. Descriptive Statistics of Data

From Table 3, it can be seen that the standard variations are not too high compared to the mean values. The data are relatively uniform, with no presence of anomaly. A sample size of 525 observations is a large size in statistics according to Green (1991).

Table 3. Descriptive statistics of variables.

Variable	Sample Size	Mean	Standard Variation	Min	Max
Y	525	3.56	4.99	−20.78	32.99
GDP initial	525	4212.14	7890.64	180.19	35,451.30
ER	525	2.34	1.06	1.00	5.00
OPEN	525	81.52	37.92	16.10	220.41
GOV	525	14.02	4.87	5.46	33.92
EDU	525	8.54	2.33	3.98	14.14

The average economic growth of the countries being studied is 3.56 in the 1994–2016 period. Since a standard variation of 4.99 is not too high compared to the mean, the growth in this period is relatively stable. Tajikistan has the lowest growth rate of (−22.48%) in 1994. Azerbaijan has the highest growth rate of 33.03% in 2006.

Figure 1 shows that the trend in the growth rate of countries and territories in Asia is similar to that of the world economy, with two slowdowns in 1997–1998 and 2008–2009.

In the Asian region, the exchange rate regime is very diverse. During the period of research, most countries are under pegged or managed to float regimes: Kazakhstan, Kyrgyz, Sri Lanka, and Vietnam follow pegged exchange rates (except for crisis time); Brunei, Israel, and Turkey adopted managed flow; the others apply both. Small countries or demand economy countries adopt fixed regimes such as Lebanon (23 years), Jordan (21 years), Azerbaijan (19 years), Kuwait (14 years), and China (12 years). The "free-fall" exchange rate regimes most frequently occurred in 1994, 1995 (8 countries), 1996 (5 countries), 1997, 1998 (3); in other years, only 1999 (2), 2001, 2002, 2015 (1 countries) occurred, and no countries face free-fall in the remaining years. The application of free-fall exchange rate mechanisms in Asian countries is probably considered to be an indicator for the fluctuations in their financial markets. The most common regime is pegged and managed float. This data also shows that before the 1997 crisis countries often chose either fixed or floating exchange rates, also called "hollow middle" according to Hernández and Montiel (2001) or bipolar (Fischer 2001) or corner solutions (Calvo and Reinhart 2002). All five worst-hit Asian economies, except for Japan (Hernández and Montiel 2001), pegged their currencies to USD (McKinnon and Schnabl 2003).

After the crisis, the countries involved are more floating than before: after falling into free-fall in 1998, Korea moved to managed float so far, Indonesia moved from free-fall to managed float (1998) and pegged (2006), Thailand from fixed to managed float (1998), and the Philippines shift to both managed and pegged. As can be seen, with the strong impact of the crisis on economic growth, many countries have changed their exchange rate regime selection. Not only the five most affected countries (Korea, Malaysia, Indonesia, Thailand, and the Philippines) but also the remaining others must be changed. This movement is also consistent with Ilzetzki et al. (2017); Hernández and Montiel (2001); Coudert and Dubert (2005); Grewal and Tansuhaj (2001); Rajan (2012); Hernández and Montiel (2001); and Ellis and Gyoerk (2019).

Although shifting to the more floating mechanism, the movement of the exchange rate regimes of Asian countries shows the "fear of floating" tendency, which announces floating in theory but still keeps fixed in practice. Currently, in 2016, the dominant exchange rate regime remains pegged and managed (9 countries) followed by fixed and "free-fall" and pegged (with 3 countries of each). Only Japan maintained an exchange rate of "free float" during the period 2004–2016 and Malaysia adopted this regime only in 2008.

4.2. Analysis of Results

Results of the GMM model following the Arellano Bond test on AR(1) and AR(2) correlation of the first different order satisfy the conditions as p-value AR(1) < 0.05 and p-value AR(2) > 0.05 (see Table 4). At the same time, the Hansen test for the validity of the GMM model based on instrumental variables is sufficient and valid at 5% significant level. Hence, the GMM model is highly reliable for the analysis.

Table 4. Regression results of panel data.

	GMM (Model 1)	GMM (Model 2)
y	0.357 ***	0.368 ***
	(5.36)	(0.069)
er_regime	−0.938 ***	−1.044 ***
	(−2.64)	(0.298)
lnigdppc	−0.0002	−0.000
	(−0.86)	(0.000)
Open	0.020	0.021
	(1.21)	(0.018)
Gov	−0.039	−0.037
	(−0.29)	(0.130)
EDU	0.863 ***	0.862 ***
	(5.13)	(0.160)
Crisis	−4.868 ***	−0.919
	(−2.78)	(0.605)
cons	−3.116	−3.085
	(−1.20)	(2.618)
AR(1)	0.000	0.000
AR(2)	0.133	0.214
Hansen	1.000	1.000

Notes: ***, **, and * denote significance at the level of 1%, 5%, 10% respectively. Figures in parenthesis denote *t* statistics.

In the first model (financial crisis measured by dummy variables for the crisis year) and the second model (using dummy variables for 1997 and 2008), it can be seen from the results that the higher the ER value, the lower the growth rate at 5% significant level. Specifically, when the exchange rate regime as classified by Reinhart and Rogoff (2004) increases by 1, the average growth rate decreases by 0.938% and 1.044% respectively (Table 4). Therefore, the more flexible the regime, the lower the growth rate. Moreover, the inconsistent results of the two models (using dummy variables in 1997 and 2008 and using the above dataset) show that Asian countries are quite different, so the simultaneous selection of two years of 1997 and 2008 as the crisis year is not reasonable.

Regarding control variables, they are significant, and expected. The study finds same-direction impacts exerted by the openness of the economy (OPEN) and human capital (EDU) on economic growth. On the other hand, government spending (GOV), economic crises (CRISIS), and GDP per capita of previous year have a negative relationship with growth.

While controlling the likely impact of human capital, government spending, crisis, economic openness, the econometric results reveal that the empirical evidence supports the hypothesis that the more flexible the exchange rate regime, the lower the growth rate. This result persists after changing methods of measurement exchange rate regimes (Model 1 and 2) and correcting for endogeneity by using GMM.

The empirical evidence of Asian countries in 1994–2016, which shows that countries with less flexible exchange rate regimes have a higher growth rate, concurs with an empirical study by Dubas et al. (2005), which states that economic growth will be high under a fixed exchange rate regime.

The more fix, the more growth is quite strange in the context of the increase in capital flows and the increase in trade openness. This may be because small countries, which have high trade and financial openness, are easily affected by world economy fluctuations, and choose more fixed exchange regimes to ensure stability. In addition, many countries in the study experienced two shocks in 1997 and 2008, thus having more experience in adjusting the exchange rate (not anchoring with a currency, using foreign exchange reserves to avoid currency speculation). Moreover, most countries in the sample are leading exporting countries; nevertheless, they keep the exchange rate stable to gain from trade and then higher growth.

These findings are consistent with the results of Levy-Yeyati and Sturzenegger (2003), and Huang and Malhotra (2005) that countries with lower levels of development will have higher growth when applying a more fixed exchange rate regime. This conclusion is also in line with the judgment of Rose (2011); Calvo and Reinhart (2002) that small economies often pursue fixed exchange rate regimes.

Results of the study are also consistent with the fundamental values of the theory of OCA by Green (1991), as well as with other studies undertaken in the past on various regions in different time periods. Therefore, the results of this study can serve as quantitative evidence for Asian countries that are deliberating on the choice of appropriate exchange rate policies and regime to achieve high economic growth.

5. Conclusions and Policy Recommendations

The question of whether exchange rate regimes influence the performance of Asian countries has attracted attention among researchers. However, the number of these studies in Asia is relatively limited and the answer is controversial. Thus, this paper adds to the literature by supplying new evidence on the impact of exchange rate regimes on economic growth. Using unbalanced panel data of 23 economies over 23 years, we find that a country with a less flexible exchange rate regime will have a higher growth rate.

With this result, the study suggests that the approach in government's choice of policy is to intervene in the exchange rate to lower the flexibility, depending on the ability of each government. To do this, policymakers should prepare the tools of exchange rate intervention, such as foreign exchange reserve or the power and effectiveness of the central bank. Moreover, depending on the context, when formulating exchange rate policies, governments should look at trade interdependence, convergence of macro policies, flexibility of production factors, and uniformity of responses to economic shocks in comparison to other countries.

In addition, passively adopting a fixed exchange rate mechanism is a failure of this mechanism. Therefore, it is necessary to have flexible policies, and a good strategy for this adjustment. The experience of countries that have experienced crisis shows that developing countries should stay away from corner solutions, i.e., solutions that are at the poles, either too floating or fixed to sole currency.

It is worth noting that although our empirical results prove the abovementioned hypothesis, the theoretical foundations underlying this impact largely remain absent due to the lack of robustness check to extended period of time as well as sub-samples. Therefore, pointing out detailed information on financial crises and expanding the sample size by increasing the number of countries being observed, thus increasing the years under observation, should be undertaken in future research.

Author Contributions: Conceptualization, D.T.-T.H.; Methodology, N.T.H. and D.T.-T.H.; Software, N.T.H.; Validation, N.T.H. and D.T.-T.H..; Formal Analysis, N.T.H.; Investigation, N.T.H. and. D.T.-T.H.; Resources, N.T.H.; Data Curation, N.T.H. and D.T.-T.H.; Writing—Original Draft Preparation, N.T.H. and D.T.-T.H.; Writing—Review & Editing, D.T.-T.H.; Visualization, N.T.H. and D.T.-T.H.; Supervision, D.T.-T.H. All authors have read and agreed to the published version of the manuscript.

Acknowledgments: We are grateful to the anonymous referees for their constructive comments. We also thank the participants at the 3rd Vietnam's Business and Economics Research Conference VBER2019 (Ho Chi Minh City Open University, Vietnam, 18–20 July 2019) for their helpful suggestions. The authors are solely responsible for any remaining errors or shortcomings.

Appendix A

Table A1. List of Countries under Observation in the Study.

NO.	Country	RR	LV	NO.	Country	RR	Crisis
1	Afghanistan			24	Lebanon	x	x
2	Armenia	x	x	25	China, Macao	x	
3	Azerbaijan	x	x	26	Malaysia	x	x
4	Bahrain	x		27	Maldives		
5	Bangladesh			28	Mongolia	x	x
6	Bhutan	x		29	Myanmar		
7	Brunei Darussalam	x		30	Nepal	x	x
8	Cambodia	x		31	Oman	x	
9	China	x	x	32	Pakistan		
10	Georgia	x	x	33	Philippines	x	x
11	China, Hong Kong	x		34	Qatar		
12	India	x	x	35	Russia	x	x
13	Indonesia	x	x	36	Singapore		
14	Iran	x		37	Sri Lanka	x	x
15	Iraq			38	Syrian Arab Republic		
16	Israel	x	x	39	Tajikistan	x	
17	Japan	x	x	40	Thailand	x	x
18	Jordan	x	x	41	Timor-Leste		
19	Kazakhstan	x	x	42	Turkey	x	x
20	Korea	x	x	43	United Arab Emirates		
21	Kuwait	x	x	44	Vietnam	x	x
22	Kyrgyz	x	x	45	West Bank and Gaza	x	
23	Laos	x		46	Yemen		

References

Arellano, Manuel, and Stephen Bond. 1991. Some tests of specification for panel data: Monte Carlo evidence and an application to employment equations. *The Review of Economic Studies* 58: 277–97. [CrossRef]

Arellano, Manuel, and Olympia Bover. 1995. Another look at the instrumental variable estimation of error-components models. *Journal of Econometrics* 68: 29–51. [CrossRef]

Athukorala, Prema-Chandra, and Sarath Rajapatirana. 2003. Capital inflows and the real exchange rate: A comparative study of Asia and Latin America. *World Economy* 26: 613–37. [CrossRef]

Bailliu, Jeannine, Robert Lafrance, and Jean-François Perrault. 2003. Does exchange rate policy matter for growth? *International Finance* 6: 381–414. [CrossRef]

Balassa, Bela. 1964. The purchasing-power parity doctrine: A reappraisal. *Journal of Political Economy* 72: 584–96. [CrossRef]

Baldwin, Robert E. 1989. The political economy of trade policy. *Journal of Economic Perspectives* 3: 119–35. [CrossRef]

Barth, James R., Apanard Prabha, and Greg Yun. 2012. The Eurozone financial crisis: Role of interdependencies between bank and sovereign risk. *Journal of Financial Economic Policy* 4: 76–97. [CrossRef]

Baxter, Marianne, and Alan C. Stockman. 1989. Business cycles and the exchange-rate regime: Some international evidence. *Journal of Monetary Economics* 23: 377–400. [CrossRef]

Bleaney, Michael, and Manuela Francisco. 2007. Exchange rate regimes, inflation and growth in developing countries—An assessment. *The BE Journal of Macroeconomics* 7. [CrossRef]

Burdekin, Richard C. K., James R. Barth, Frank M. Song, and Zhongfei Zhou. 2012. China after the Global Financial Crisis. *Economics Research International* 2012. [CrossRef]

Calvo, Guillermo A., and Carmen M. Reinhart. 2002. Fear of floating. *The Quarterly Journal of Economics* 117: 379–408. [CrossRef]

Coudert, Virginie, and Marc Dubert. 2005. Does exchange rate regime explain differences in economic results for Asian countries? *Journal of Asian Economics* 16: 874–95. [CrossRef]

De Grauwe, Paul, and Gunther Schnabl. 2005. Exchange rate regimes and macroeconomic stability in Central and Eastern Europe. In *Euro Adoption in Central and Eastern Europe: Opportunities and Challenges*. Washington, DC: International Monetary Fund, pp. 41–60.

Domaç, Ilker, Kyle Peters, and Yevgeny Yuzefovich. 2004. *Does the Exchange Rate Regime Matter for Inflation? Evidence from Transition Economies*. Policy Research Working Paper. Ankara: Research and Monetary Policy Department, Central Bank of the Republic of Turkey, p. 2641.

Drukker, David M. 2003. Testing for serial correlation in linear panel-data models. *The Stata Journal* 3: 168–77. [CrossRef]

Dubas, Justin M., Byung-Joo Lee, and Nelson C. Mark. 2005. *Effective Exchange Rate Classifications and Growth (No. w11272)*. Cambridge: National Bureau of Economic Research.

Eichengreen, Barry, and David Leblang. 2003. Exchange rates and cohesion: Historical perspectives and political-economy considerations. *JCMS: Journal of Common Market Studies* 41: 797–822. [CrossRef]

Ellis, Colin, and Emilia Gyoerk. 2019. Investigating the Economic and Financial Damage around Currency Peg Failures. *Journal of Risk and Financial Management* 12: 92. [CrossRef]

Fischer, Stanley. 2001. Exchange rate regimes: Is the bipolar view correct? *Journal of Economic Perspectives* 15: 3–24. [CrossRef]

Flood, Robert P., and Andrew K. Rose. 1995. Fixing exchange rates a virtual quest for fundamentals. *Journal of Monetary Economics* 36: 3–37. [CrossRef]

Garofalo, Paolo. 2005. *Exchange Rate Regimes and Economic Performance: The Italian Experience (No. 10)*. Rome: Banca d'Italia.

Ghosh, Atish R., Anne-Marie Gulde, Jonathan D. Ostry, and Holger C. Wolf. 1997. *Does the Nominal Exchange Rate Regime Matter? (No. w5874)*. Cambridge: National Bureau of Economic Research.

Ghosh, Atish R., Anne-Marie Gulde-Wolf, and Holger C. Wolf. 2002. *Exchange Rate Regime: Choices and Consequences*. Cambridge: MIT Press.

Green, Samuel B. 1991. How many subjects does it take to do a regression analysis. *Multivariate Behavioral Research* 26: 499–510. [CrossRef]

Greene, William H. 2000. *Econometric Analysis*, 4th ed. International Edition. Upper Saddle River: Prentice Hall, pp. 201–15.

Grewal, Rajdeep, and Patriya Tansuhaj. 2001. Building organizational capabilities for managing economic crisis: The role of market orientation and strategic flexibility. *Journal of Marketing* 65: 67–80. [CrossRef]

Halko, Marja-Liisa, Markku Kaustia, and Elias Alanko. 2012. The gender effect in risky asset holdings. *Journal of Economic Behavior & Organization* 83: 66–81.

Hernández, Leonardo, and Peter Montiel. 2001. *Post-Crisis Exchange Rate Policy in Five Asian Countries: Filling in the" Hollow Middle"? (No. 1–170)*. Washington, DC: International Monetary Fund.

Huang, Haizhou, and Priyanka Malhotra. 2005. Exchange rate regimes and economic growth: Evidence from developing Asian and Advanced European Economies. *China Economic Quarterly-Beijing* 4: 971.

Husain, Aasim M., Ashoka Mody, and Kenneth S. Rogoff. 2005. Exchange rate regime durability and performance in developing versus advanced economies. *Journal of Monetary Economics* 52: 35–64. [CrossRef]

Ilzetzki, Ethan, Carmen M. Reinhart, and Kenneth S. Rogoff. 2017. *Exchange Arrangements Entering the 21st Century: Which Anchor Will Hold? (No. w23134)*. Cambridge: National Bureau of Economic Research.

International Monetary Fund (IMF), ed. 2006. *Annual Report on Exchange Arrangements and Exchange Restrictions*. Washington, DC: International Monetary Fund, vol. 2006.

Ivashina, Victoria, and David Scharfstein. 2010. Bank lending during the financial crisis of 2008. *Journal of Financial Economics* 97: 319–38. [CrossRef]

Jakob, Brigitta. 2016. Impact of exchange rate regimes on economic growth. *Undergraduate Economic Review* 12: 11.

Jang, Hoyoon, and Wonsik Sul. 2002. The Asian financial crisis and the co-movement of Asian stock markets. *Journal of Asian Economics* 13: 94–104. [CrossRef]

Kotz, David M. 2009. The financial and economic crisis of 2008: A systemic crisis of neoliberal capitalism. *Review of Radical Political Economics* 41: 305–17. [CrossRef]

Laeven, Luc, and Fabian Valencia. 2018. *Systemic Banking Crises Revisited*. Washington, DC: International Monetary Fund.

Lee, Young, and Roger H. Gordon. 2005. Tax structure and economic growth. *Journal of Public Economics* 89: 1027–43. [CrossRef]

Levy-Yeyati, Eduardo, and Federico Sturzenegger. 2003. To float or to fix: Evidence on the impact of exchange rate regimes on growth. *American Economic Review* 93: 1173–93. [CrossRef]

Lucas, Robert E., Jr. 1988. On the mechanics of economic development. *Journal of Monetary Economics* 22: 3–42. [CrossRef]

Ma, Yong, and Xingkai Lin. 2016. Financial development and the effectiveness of monetary policy. *Journal of Banking & Finance* 68: 1–11.

Mankiw, N. Gregory, Edmund S. Phelps, and Paul M. Romer. 1995. The growth of nations. *Brookings Papers on Economic Activity* 1: 275–326. [CrossRef]

Mauro, Paolo, and Grace Juhn. 2002. *Long-Run Determinants of Exchange Rate Regimes: A Simple Sensitivity Analysis (No. 2–104)*. Washington, DC: International Monetary Fund.

McKinnon, Ronald I. 1963. Optimum currency areas. *The American Economic Review* 53: 717–25.

McKinnon, Ronald, and Gunther Schnabl. 2003. Synchronised business cycles in East Asia and fluctuations in the yen/dollar exchange rate. *World Economy* 26: 1067–88. [CrossRef]

Moreno, Ramon. 2001. Pegging and Macroeconomic Performance in East Asia. *ASEAN Economic Bulletin* 18: 48–63.

Mundell, Robert A. 1961. A theory of optimum currency areas. *The American Economic Review* 51: 657–65.

Mundell, Robert A. 2002. Exchange-rate systems and economic growth. In *Monetary Standards and Exchange Rates*. London: Routledge, pp. 27–52.

Munir, Kamal A. 2011. Financial crisis 2008–2009: What does the silence of institutional theorists tell us? *Journal of Management Inquiry* 20: 114–17. [CrossRef]

Rajan, Ramkishen S. 2012. Management of exchange rate regimes in emerging Asia. *Review of Development Finance* 2: 53–68. [CrossRef]

Reinhart, Carmen M., and Kenneth S. Rogoff. 2004. The modern history of exchange rate arrangements: A reinterpretation. *The Quarterly Journal of Economics* 119: 1–48. [CrossRef]

Rodriguez, Francisco, and Dani Rodrik. 2000. Trade policy and economic growth: A skeptic's guide to the cross-national evidence. *NBER Macroeconomics Annual* 15: 261–325. [CrossRef]

Romer, Paul M. 1986. Increasing returns and long-run growth. *Journal of Political Economy* 94: 1002–37. [CrossRef]

Romer, Paul M. 1990. Endogenous technological change. *Journal of Political Economy* 98: S71–S102. [CrossRef]

Rose, Andrew K. 2011. Exchange rate regimes in the modern era: Fixed, floating, and flaky. *Journal of Economic Literature* 49: 652–72. [CrossRef]

Sachs, Jeffrey D., Andrew Warner, Anders Åslund, and Stanley Fischer. 1995. Economic reform and the process of global integration. *Brookings Papers on Economic Activity* 1995: 1–118. [CrossRef]

Samuelson, Paul A. 1964. Theoretical notes on trade problems. In *The Review of Economics and Statistics*. Cambridge: MIT Press, pp. 145–54.

Shambaugh, Jay C. 2004. The effect of fixed exchange rates on monetary policy. *The Quarterly Journal of Economics* 119: 301–52. [CrossRef]

Solow, Robert M. 1956. A contribution to the theory of economic growth. *The Quarterly Journal of Economics* 70: 65–94. [CrossRef]

Stiglitz, Joseph. 2000. What I learned at the world economic crisis. The Insider. *The New Republic* 17: 2000.

Wade, Robert. 1998. The Asian debt-and-development crisis of 1997–?: Causes and consequences. *World Development* 26: 1535–53. [CrossRef]

Wang, Hongying. 1999. The Asian financial crisis and financial reforms in China. *The Pacific Review* 12: 537–56. [CrossRef]

Wooldridge, Jeffrey M. 2010. *Econometric Analysis of Cross Section and Panel Data*. Cambridge: The MIT Press.

13

CO$_2$ Emissions, Energy Consumption and Economic Growth: New Evidence in the ASEAN Countries

Anh The Vo [1,*] , **Duc Hong Vo** [1] **and Quan Thai-Thuong Le** [2]

[1] Business and Economics Research Group, Ho Chi Minh City Open University,
Ho Chi Minh City 70000, Vietnam; duc.vhong@ou.edu.vn

[2] Office of Cooperation and Research Management, Ho Chi Minh City Open University,
Ho Chi Minh City 70000, Vietnam; quan.ltt@ou.edu.vn

* Correspondence: anh.vt@ou.edu.vn

Abstract: The members of the Association of Southeast Asian Nations (ASEAN) have made several attempts to adopt renewable energy targets given the economic, energy-related, environmental challenges faced by the governments, policy makers, and stakeholders. However, previous studies have focused limited attention on the role of renewable energy when testing the dynamic link between CO$_2$ emissions, energy consumption and renewable energy consumption. As such, this study is conducted to test a common hypothesis regarding a long-run environmental Kuznets curve (EKC). The paper also investigates the causal link between carbon dioxide (CO$_2$) emissions, energy consumption, renewable energy, population growth, and economic growth for countries in the region. Using various time-series econometrics approaches, our analysis covers five ASEAN members (including Indonesia, Myanmar, Malaysia, the Philippines, and Thailand) for the 1971–2014 period where required data are available. Our results reveal no long-run relationship among the variables of interest in the Philippines and Thailand, but a relationship does exist in Indonesia, Myanmar, and Malaysia. The EKC hypothesis is observed in Myanmar but not in Indonesia and Malaysia. Also, Granger causality among these important variables varies considerably across the selected countries. No Granger causality among carbon emissions, energy consumption, and renewable energy consumption is reported in Malaysia, the Philippines, and Thailand. Indonesia experiences a unidirectional causal effect from economic growth to renewable energy consumption in both short and long run and from economic growth to CO$_2$ emissions and energy consumption. Interestingly, only Myanmar has a unidirectional effect from GDP growth, energy consumption, and population to the adoption of renewable energy. Policy implications have emerged based on the findings achieved from this study for each country in the ASEAN region.

Keywords: ASEAN; CO$_2$ emissions; economic growth; EKC; energy consumption; Granger causality; VECM

JEL Classification: C22; C32; Q43; Q56

1. Introduction

The Association of Southeast Asian Nations (ASEAN) has experienced a profound economic transformation, attained high economic growth, and become the most dynamic economic area in the world in recent years (De Grauwe and Zhang 2016). The region, which is home to around 630 million people and has gross domestic production (GDP) of approximately US$2.4 trillion, plays a large role in boosting regional integration and cooperation in East Asia and is becoming a driving force behind global growth, according to the fifth ASEAN energy outlook, in 2017. This economic development requires an enormous supply of energy, which heavily depends on fossil fuel with the consequence of environmental degradation.

In its 2017 report on the Southeast Asia energy outlook, the International Energy Agency (IEA) highlighted that achieving stable economic growth, meeting energy demand in a secure, affordable, and sustainable manner, as well as maintaining an acceptably low level of environment degradation, are multiple challenges that the governments in the Southeast Asia nations encounter. Many ASEAN countries have made tremendous efforts to tackle those challenges. A wide range of policies aimed at the adoption and use of renewable energy have been implemented as a result of not only the influence of the Paris Agreement but also the national plans for energy consumption. The fifth ASEAN energy outlook indicated that the members of the ASEAN countries have made several attempts to adopt targets for renewable energy. For example, Indonesia has developed and implemented a plan to increase new and renewable energy as a share of total primary energy supply (TPES) to 23 percent in 2025 and approximately 30 percent in 2050, and the country expects to reduce greenhouse gas (GHG) emissions to under 30 percent by 2020 below the business-as-usual level. Malaysia has set a target for increasing the capacity of renewable electricity supply to around 8 percent of total installed capacity by 2020 and decreased the ratio of GHG emissions to GDP by 35 percent by 2030, compared to the level in 2005. In its national renewable energy program roadmap to 2030, the Philippine government set a goal for every source of renewable energy that will triple the installed capacity of renewables-based supply by 2030 compared to its 2010 level, together with controlling GHG and stabilizing it at less than 16 percent of the business-as-usual level. Thailand has the more profound objective of increasing renewable energy to 30 percent of total energy usage by 2036 in power generation, heating, and transport fuel consumption. These efforts in the expansion of renewable energy use to rebalance the energy mix could depend significantly on a country's resource availability, energy security, and environmental targets. On these grounds of these strong, committed and ambitious policies formulated and implemented by various ASEAN nations, it is the claim of this paper that it is vitally important to understand the relationship among economic growth, energy demand, renewable energy use, and environmental degradation in the context of gradual population growth. Findings from this paper will enhance greatly understanding and rationales for policies from these ASEAN nations and other emerging markets.

The context of economic growth in the region raises the question of the environment in the EKC hypothesis. This hypothesis stipulates that an increase in a country's income leads to a corresponding increase in the level of CO_2 emissions at the early stage of economic development, but in the later stage, the impact is reversed at a certain income threshold. The adoption of environmentally harmful technology in economic activities, lack of awareness of environmental problems, and the goal of higher profit in premature economic development can explain the parallel pattern in the level of per capita income and environmental degradation at this stage. However, higher per capita income, improved social indicators, and safer technology in the mature stage create a turning point in the growth-environment nexus (Zoundi 2017).

Many scholars have tested the EKC in the context of the ASEAN region focused only on economic growth, energy consumption, and CO_2 emissions. For instance, Tang and Tan (2015) confirmed the validity of the EKC hypothesis in Vietnam over the 1976–2009 period. Yet Al-Mulali et al. (2015) found no evidence to support the existence of the EKC over the 1981–2011 period, and Shahbaz et al. (2019) arrived at the same conclusion for the period 1976 to 2016. Ozturk and Al-Mulali (2015) failed to confirm the validity of the EKC but found a U-shaped relationship between economic growth and CO_2 emissions in Cambodia in 1996–2012 period. Begum et al. (2015) reached the same conclusions as those from Ozturk and Al-Mulali (2015) in a study for Malaysia over the 1980–2009 period. In contrast, Saboori et al. (2016) found the opposite result, supporting the existence of the EKC in Malaysia. Saboori and Sulaiman (2013) used a recently developed cointegration approach based on the autoregressive distributed lag (ARDL) model to examine the cointegration among economic growth, CO_2 emissions, and energy consumption in five ASEAN countries over the 1971–2008 period. They supported the EKC hypothesis in Singapore and Thailand, found a U-shaped relationship (the inverted EKC hypothesis) in Indonesia and the Philippines. The different levels of economic development may reflect their mixed results although these countries are housed in the same region.

The paper makes significant contributions to the contemporary literature on this important issue. Our attempt is to supplement empirical evidence in relation to an EKC hypothesis in the ASEAN region. Although numerous scholars have investigated the link between economic growth, energy consumption, and environmental degradation, little attention has been paid to renewable energy, which has emerged as an alternative source of fossil fuel energy. The only exception is a study from Liu et al. (2017), who analyzed Granger causality among per capita CO_2, economic growth, renewable and nonrenewable energy consumption, and agricultural value added in four ASEAN members—Indonesia, Malaysia, the Philippines, and Thailand—over the 1970–2013 period. Their findings show a long-run relationship among those variables but a turning point in the EKC hypothesis is not observed. As such, our empirical study will bridge the gap on this important link. We critically examine the relationship among economic development, energy consumption, environmental degradation, and population growth in the ASEAN region. A special focus on renewable energy usage is the most significant contribution of the paper.

Useful insights on renewable energy also benefit the governments, policy makers, and stakeholders in the ASEAN region in dealing with economic, energy-related and environmental challenges. The EKC hypothesis and the causality between economic growth, energy consumption and CO_2 emissions were tested using a panel of ASEAN countries in previous studies (e.g., Heidari et al. 2015; Le and Quah 2018; Lean and Smyth 2010; Nasreen and Anwar 2014). These studies ignored the usage of renewable energy in the context that ASEAN countries have a strong desire for such kind of energy in coming years. Also, pooling a panel of countries in a whole sample can potentially suffer a difficulty in relation to policy implementations on this important link. The ASEAN countries vary considerably in terms of economic development and size as well as their targets for renewable energy. Thus, it is essential to analyze the interrelationship among economics, energy consumption, environmental degradation, the use of renewable energy for a case-by-case country. A thorough understanding of this interrelationship at a country level enables the governments not only to design proper strategies for sustainable economic development, energy security, and environmental protection but also to achieve an optimal, effective, and efficient level of consumption and supply of renewable energy.

To achieve our objectives, a common validity of the EKC hypothesis is tested in the long run and investigate the causal link between CO_2 emissions, energy consumption, renewable energy, population growth, and economic growth for five ASEAN members, including Indonesia, Myanmar, Malaysia, the Philippines, and Thailand over the 1971–2014 period. The selection of countries is based on data availability. We use several econometrics techniques on time series, including advanced cointegration tests, two long-run estimators—the fully modified ordinary least squares (FMOLS) and the dynamic ordinary least squares (DOLS)—and a causality test based on the vector error correction model (VECM) framework. Using these techniques will strengthen the validity of our conclusions.

The paper is organized as follows. Following this Introduction, Section 2 discusses relevant theories and empirical studies related to the EKC hypothesis as well as the causal relationship among the variables of interests. The methodology is presented in Section 3, while Section 4 describes the data and empirical results. Our conclusions are discussed in Section 5.

2. Literature Review

2.1. The Environmental Kuznets Curve (EKC) Hypothesis

To date, many studies on the EKC hypothesis have failed to reach a consensus; some failed to reject the null hypothesis of the validity of the EKC while others found supporting evidence. One major factor causing such an unclear conclusion is the econometrics testing method, the countries in the sample, and the period studied in the analysis.

Several studies have reported mixed evidence on the EKC hypothesis using a country panel over a particular time period with the use of CO_2 emissions as pollutants. The EKC appears to be present in the member countries of the Organization for Economic Cooperation and Development (OECD) (Bilgili et al. 2016; Jebli et al. 2016), in G-7 countries (Raza and Shah 2018), in the European Union region (Dogan and Seker 2016), in Central America (Apergis and Payne 2014), among a wide group of developed and developing countries globally (Ibrahim and Law 2014), as well as in Asia (Heidari et al. 2015). Other scholars failed to confirm the validity of the EKC hypothesis based on empirical evidence in both developed and developing countries (Apergis et al. 2010).

The same pattern of inconclusive findings in relation to the EKC hypothesis with the use of CO_2 emissions is observed in various studies on a particular country using time-series data. Supporting evidence is observed in France (Iwata et al. 2010), Indonesia (Sugiawan and Managi 2016), China (Jalil and Mahmud 2009; Jayanthakumaran and Liu 2012), and Pakistan (Shahbaz et al. 2015; Shahzad et al. 2017). Other papers failed to confirm the validity of EKC—for instance, Soytas et al. (2007) found no presence of the EKC in the US, which is further supported by Dogan and Ozturk (2017), even when taking a structural break into consideration.

The most striking characteristic in earlier empirical studies is that they used the same sample of a country with different timespans and econometrics techniques but come to a completely different conclusion regarding the EKC hypothesis. One example is a study for Malaysia, where Saboori et al. (2016) confirmed the presence of the EKC over the 1980–2008 period, while Ali et al. (2017), Begum et al. (2015), and Gill et al. (2018) presented the opposite outcome. A contradictory finding is observed in Vietnam (Tang and Tan 2015; Al-Mulali et al. 2015) and in Turkey (Pata 2018; Soytas et al. 2007).

Another potential factor contributing to the mixed findings arising from previous empirical studies on the validity of the EKC hypothesis is the proposed model tested with diverse additionally controlled variables. Various factors have been added to a traditional EKC model. These variables include energy consumption (Le and Quah 2018; To et al. 2019), trade openness (Halicioglu 2009; Halicioglu and Ketenci 2018; Jayanthakumaran and Liu 2012; Ozturk and Acaravci 2013), financial development (Dogan and Seker 2016; Dogan and Turkekul 2016; Shahbaz et al. 2013), population (Dong et al. 2018; Zoundi 2017), and urbanization (Ozturk and Al-Mulali 2015; Dogan and Turkekul 2016; Saidi and Mbarek 2016). Other studies integrated all sorts of variables and used them to test the EKC hypothesis (Ozatac et al. 2017; Pata 2018). For example, Ozatac et al. (2017) confirmed the EKC hypothesis in Turkey over the 1971–2013 period, integrating energy consumption, trade openness, financial development, and urbanization into the proposed model. So, the role of these variables should not be ignored in testing the EKC hypothesis.

Many studies investigated the relationship between energy use and the amount of CO_2 emissions produced by economic development. Some scholars have tested the link between economic growth and carbon emissions (Nguyen and Kakinaka 2019). The role of renewable energy in the EKC hypothesis has gained attention among scholars as part of efforts to reverse the effects of environment degradation. It is well recognized renewable energy sources have many benefits in terms of increased energy security, sustainable economic growth, and pollution reduction (Şener et al. 2018).

Contemporary studies have also employed the variable of renewable energy in models testing the EKC hypothesis. Raza and Shah (2018) confirmed the EKC hypothesis in the G7 countries due to the trade openness and renewable energy consumption based on panel data over the 1991–2016 period. Pata (2018) confirmed the EKC hypothesis using a model including renewable energy, urbanization, and financial development in Turkey over the 1974–2014 period after controlling for structural breaks over the selected period.

The adoption of parametric approach in testing the EKC hypothesis may face the problem of misspecification. As such, the nonparametric strand of the EKC literature has emerged to further explain the mixed results as it does not require the specification of a functional form (Shahbaz et al. 2017). Using a novel nonparametric econometrics approach is expected to yield a more insightful understanding of the EKC literature. For example, Azomahou et al. (2006) revealed a contradict result in relation to the EKC hypothesis using both parametric and non-parametric method. While the estimation of a parametric specification supported the EKC, the non-parametric approach opposed to the parametric finding. Similarly, when employing a non-parametric approach in the MENA region, Fakih and Marrouch (2019) found the none-existence of an EKC in contrast to the findings from Arouri et al. (2012), who presented evidence of EKC relationship between CO_2 emissions and GDP. Recently, based on a nonparametric approach with the data over nearly two centuries, Shahbaz et al. (2017) argued for an existence of the EKC in six out of the G-7 countries—Canada, France, Germany, Italy, UK and the US with an exception for the case of Japan. Recently, Kalaitzidakis et al. (2018) used a semiparametric smooth coefficient model to investigate the impact of CO_2 emissions on economic growth, as measured by total factor productivity, among a set of the Organization for Economic Co-operation and Development (OECD) countries during the 1981–1998 period. Their results reported a robust non-linear relationship between these variables and showed that CO_2 emissions contributes marginally to productivity growth, approximately 0.07 percent on average. These findings highlighted the nature of nonlinearity in the relationship between income and environment degradation.

2.2. *The Causal Link between Renewable Energy Use, Economic Growth, and Environmental Degradation*

From a theoretical perspective, a causal link is observed between the use of renewable energy, economic growth, and environmental degradation. Higher income raises demand for energy consumption and consequently exacerbates degradation of the environment. Increasing concerns about energy security and global warming, in turn, create greater pressure for the use of renewable energy. Renewable energy is an ideal substitute for fossil fuels and results in fewer CO_2 emissions (Bilgili et al. 2016). As such, sustainable economic growth is compatible with the use of renewable energy.

On the empirical aspect, the directional effect among renewable energy consumption, economic growth, and environmental degradation varies considerably across studies. Some scholars recognized a unidirectional causal effect. The short-run unidirectional casual effect from renewable energy consumption to CO_2 emissions was found in 25 African countries by Zoundi (2017), in BRICS (Brazil, Russia, India, China, and South Africa) countries by Sebri and Ben-Salha (2014). Shafiei and Salim (2014) showed unidirectional causality from renewable energy consumption to CO_2 emissions in the long run in 29 OECD member countries between 1980 and 2011.

The same pattern was observed in Bilgili et al. (2016) in a smaller sample of 17 OECD countries in the 1977–2010 period. Additionally, Sadorsky (2009) demonstrated that increases in real per capita income and per capita CO_2 emissions led to an increase in the use of renewable energy in the long run in the G7 countries. Based on a sample of nine developed countries, Saidi and Mbarek (2016) revealed a unidirectional effect from renewable energy consumption to economic growth, but in the long run, they Granger-cause each other. In contrast, Jebli et al. (2016) observed short-run Granger causality from economic growth to renewable energy.

Several studies revealed reverse causality among economic growth, renewable energy, and CO_2 emissions. Apergis et al. (2010) reported a bidirectional causal relationship between each pair of three variables of interest in seven Central American countries both in the short and long run. Raza and Shah (2018) found that economic growth is positively associated with CO_2 emissions in the long run, as well as the reverse causality from CO_2 emissions to renewable energy consumption in G7 countries. The bidirectional Granger causality between renewable energy and CO_2 emissions is observed by Dogan and Seker (2016) in 15 EU member countries in the short run and by Dong et al. (2017) in BRICS countries in the long run.

In consistency with studies that use panel data on several countries over a long period, an investigation on Granger causality in particular countries presents mixed directions, either unidirectional or bidirectional. A unidirectional effect from renewable energy to CO_2 emissions is observed in the US (Jaforullah and King 2015), Denmark and Finland (Irandoust 2016), Indonesia (Sugiawan and Managi 2016), and Algeria (Belaid and Youssef 2017). Recently, using a VECM-based Granger-causality test, Bekhet and Othman (2018) found unidirectional causality from CO_2 emissions to renewable energy in Malaysia. Reverse causality is observed in Sweden and Norway by Irandoust (2016). The varying patterns in the directional effect among economic growth, renewable energy, and CO_2 emissions demonstrate the need for more investigation on the complicated relationship among those variables.

3. Methodology

3.1. Model Specification and Data Source

Stern (2004) proposed three causes of the EKC relationship via the scale, technique, and composition effects. The scales effect implies the expansion of production which will lead to a corresponding increase in the amount of polluted emissions. The component effect postulates the heterogeneity of pollution intensities across industries. The technique effect indicates the improvement of the state of technology which will lead to a lower pollutant generated. This can be achieved through either a higher productivity, meaning a reduction of inputs for a given output, or lowering emissions per unit of input with innovations. On the ground of those effects, in this paper, we shed a light on the importance of using renewable energy for the growth-environment nexus using the following model specification.

$$LnCO_{2t} = \alpha_0 + \alpha_1 LnY_t + \alpha_2 LnY_t^2 + \alpha_3 LnEC_t + \alpha_4 LnRE_t + \alpha_5 LnPOP_t + \varepsilon_t \qquad (1)$$

in which CO_2 represents per capita CO_2 emissions at year t. EC_t is per capita energy consumption; RE_t is per capita consumption of renewable energy; Y_t and Y_t^2 denote real per capita GDP and the square of real per capita GDP at year t, respectively; and POP_t is the population of the country at year t. The residuals ε_t are assumed to be normally distributed and white noise.

We focus on long-run coefficients ($\alpha_i, i = 1, \ldots, 4$), which indicate the effect of the independent variables—economic growth, use of renewable energy, and population size—on the dependent variable, CO_2 emissions. α_1 and α_2 are expected to be positive and negative, respectively, so that the EKC hypothesis holds. An increase in the consumption of renewable energy is expected to mitigate CO_2 emissions, thus α_3 is expected to be negative while the impact of population growth on CO_2 emissions is expected to be positive, as higher population growth is more likely to raise CO_2 emissions.

All the data on the five ASEAN countries including Indonesia, Myanmar, Malaysia, the Philippines, and Thailand are collected from the World Bank's World Development Indicators, over the 1971–2014 period. Renewable energy is proxied by combustible renewables and waste. Income is measured by real per capita GDP in constant 2010 US dollars. Population is total population, and CO_2 emissions is total CO_2 emissions from energy consumption in millions of metric tons, which is converted into kilograms per capita. Table 1 describes the data, with all variables transformed into their natural logarithmic form.[1]

---

[1] We have rescaled all the variables so that a number of values falls between zero and one. As such, these values are negative when taking the logarithm.

Table 1. Data description.

Variable	Observations	Mean	Std. Dev.	Minimum	Maximum
Indonesia					
$LnCO_2$	44	−0.04	0.53	−1.11	0.94
LnY	44	0.58	0.43	−0.22	1.31
LnY^2	44	0.51	0.50	0.00	1.71
$LnEC$	44	−0.61	0.37	−1.21	−0.12
$LnREC$	44	−0.02	1.78	−3.06	1.98
$LnPOP$	44	5.21	0.23	4.77	5.54
Myanmar					
$LnCO_2$	44	−1.73	0.29	−2.29	−0.88
LnY	44	−1.14	0.64	−1.79	0.24
LnY^2	44	1.70	1.11	0.00	3.21
$LnEC$	44	−1.26	0.07	−1.37	−0.99
$LnREC$	44	−1.11	0.64	−1.89	0.39
$LnPOP$	44	3.69	0.20	3.30	3.95
Malaysia					
$LnCO_2$	44	1.31	0.58	0.41	2.08
LnY	44	1.62	0.47	0.72	2.34
LnY^2	44	2.85	1.51	0.52	5.48
$LnEC$	44	0.34	0.56	−0.65	1.09
$LnREC$	44	0.49	0.54	−0.66	1.35
$LnPOP$	44	2.94	0.31	2.40	3.41
Philippines					
$LnCO_2$	44	−0.24	0.16	−0.66	0.05
LnY	44	0.50	0.16	0.25	0.92
LnY^2	44	0.27	0.19	0.06	0.84
$LnEC$	44	−0.79	0.06	−0.90	−0.67
$LnREC$	42	1.75	1.08	−0.88	2.62
$LnPOP$	44	4.16	0.30	3.61	4.61
Thailand					
$LnCO_2$	44	0.54	0.75	−0.68	1.53
LnY	44	0.92	0.57	−0.05	1.72
LnY^2	44	1.16	1.00	0.00	2.96
$LnEC$	44	−0.20	0.57	−1.02	0.69
$LnREC$	44	−0.35	0.33	−1.47	0.18
$LnPOP$	44	4.02	0.17	3.64	4.23

Notes: Std. Dev. is standard deviation. All variables are in logarithm.

3.2. Cointegration Tests

We examine the long-run relationship among the variables of interest employing the traditional Johansen cointegration approach and the bounds-testing approach to cointegration. The first test is proposed by Johansen (1988) and further developed by Johansen and Juselius (1990) while the second approach, a relatively new technique based on the ARDL model, is constructed by Pesaran et al. (2001). Using two well-known cointegration tests yields a more robust conclusion, and between the two, the ARDL bounds-testing approach has greater advantages (Sebri and Ben-Salha 2014). First, the ARDL technique works well with a small sample such as ours, and it can test a cointegrating relationship among underlying regressors and a regressand with uncertainty as to whether they are I(0) or I(1) (Narayan 2005; Pesaran et al. 2001). Second, the ARDL bounds-testing approach can address potential endogeneity problems, thus yielding an unbiased long-run estimation and interpreting the short-

and long-run effects with a single regression (Sebri and Ben-Salha 2014). Based on Equation (1), the ARDL-based approach to cointegration can be represented as follows:

$$
\begin{aligned}
\Delta LnCO_{2t} = \gamma_0 \ &+ \sum_{i=1}^{k1} \gamma_{1i}\Delta LnCO_{2t-i} + \sum_{i=0}^{k2} \gamma_{2i}\Delta LnY_{t-i} + \sum_{i=0}^{k3} \gamma_{3i}LnY_{t-i}^2 \\
&+ \sum_{i=0}^{k4} \gamma_{4j}\Delta LnRE_{t-i} + \sum_{i=0}^{k5} \gamma_{5i}\Delta LnPOP_{t-i} + \varnothing_{11}LnCO_{2t-1} \\
&+ \varnothing_{12}LnY_{t-1} + \varnothing_{13}LnY_{t-1}^2 + \varnothing_{14}LnRE_{t-1} + \varnothing_{15}LnPOP_{t-1} + \epsilon_t
\end{aligned}
\tag{2}
$$

where Δ denotes the first difference of the selected variables while γ_{1i} and $\varnothing_{1i}$ $(i = 1, \ldots, 4)$ are the estimated parameters. ki $(i = 1, \ldots, 4)$ are the optimal lag length determined by Akaike's information criterion (AIC), and ϵ_t is an error term of white noise.

Under the ARDL model as expressed in Equation (2), Pesaran et al. (2001) proposed two standard cointegrating tests, namely, the F- and t-statistics, for the purpose of testing a null hypothesis of no cointegration. These tests examine the significance of the lagged level of the regressors on the regressand using a univariate equilibrium correction mechanism. The confirmation of conintegration checks whether all the estimated coefficients of the lag level equal zero. That is, the t-statistics test the null hypothesis $\varnothing_1 = 0$ against the alternative $\varnothing_1 \neq 0$, whereas the F-statistics test the null hypothesis $\varnothing_i = 0$ $\left(i = \overline{1,4}\right)$ against the alternative of at least $\varnothing_i \neq 0$ $(i = 1, \ldots, 4)$. If the estimated F-statistic is smaller than the lower-bound critical value (larger than an upper one), then the null hypothesis is rejected (accepted); otherwise, there knows no conclusion.

Pesaran et al. (2001) supplemented the critical value bounds for the F- and t-test in their analysis, but Narayan (2005) used a simulation method to reproduce critical values for the ARDL bounds test with a small sample size (between 30 and 80 observations). As the time span of our study is quite short, we refer to Narayan (2005)'s critical values for confirmation of a cointegrating relationship among the variables in the proposed model. Before calculating these two statistics, we ensure that the error terms are serially uncorrelated and homoskedastic and select optimal lags using AIC.[2]

3.3. Granger-Causality Test

To test whether a cointegrating relationship exists among CO_2 emissions, energy consumption, the use of renewable energy, income, and the square of income, and population size, we perform a long-run Granger-causality test in the framework of the VECM. The VECM specification provides both short- and long-run Granger-caused relationships among all the variables. Equation (1) is revised with a VECM framework as follows:

$$
\begin{aligned}
\Delta LnCO_{2t} = \pi_0 \ &+ \sum_{j=1}^{n} \pi_{1j}\Delta LnCO_{2t-j} + \sum_{j=0}^{n} \pi_{2j}\Delta LnY_{t-j} + \sum_{j=0}^{n} \pi_{3j}LnY_{t-j}^2 \\
&+ \sum_{j=0}^{n} \pi_{4j}\Delta LnRE_{t-j} + \sum_{j=0}^{n} \pi_{5j}\Delta LnPOP_{t-j} + \varphi_1 ECT_{t-1} + \epsilon_{1t}
\end{aligned}
\tag{3}
$$

$$
\begin{aligned}
\Delta LnY_t = \delta_0 + \ &\sum_{j=0}^{n} \delta_{1j}\Delta LnCO_{2t-j} + \sum_{j=1}^{n} \delta_{2j}\Delta LnY_{t-j} + \sum_{j=0}^{n} \delta_{3j}\Delta LnY_{t-j}^2 \\
&+ \sum_{j=0}^{n} \delta_{4j}\Delta LnRE_{t-j} + \sum_{j=0}^{n} \delta_{5j}\Delta LnPOP_{t-j} + \varphi_2 ECT_{t-1} + \epsilon_{2t}
\end{aligned}
\tag{4}
$$

$$
\begin{aligned}
\Delta LnY_t^2 = \theta_0 + \ &\sum_{j=0}^{n} \theta_{1j}\Delta LnCO_{2t-j} + \sum_{j=0}^{n} \theta_{2j}\Delta LnY_{t-j} + \sum_{j=1}^{n} \theta_{3j}\Delta LnY_{t-j}^2 \\
&+ \sum_{j=0}^{n} \theta_{4j}\Delta LnRE_{t-j} + \sum_{j=0}^{n} \theta_{5j}\Delta LnPOP_{t-j} + \varphi_3 ECT_{t-1} + \epsilon_{3t}
\end{aligned}
\tag{5}
$$

---

[2] For details of the procedures in the bounds test, see earlier studies, such as Pesaran et al. (2001) and Vo et al. (2019).

$$\Delta LnRE_t = \beta_0 + \sum_{j=0}^{n} \beta_{1j}\Delta LnCO_{2t-j} + \sum_{j=0}^{n} \beta_{2j}\Delta LnY_{t-j} + \sum_{j=0}^{n} \beta_{3j}\Delta LnY_{t-j}^2$$
$$+ \sum_{j=1}^{n} \beta_{4j}\Delta LnRE_{t-j} + \sum_{j=0}^{n} \beta_{5j}\Delta LnPOP_{t-j} + \varphi_4 ECT_{t-1} + \epsilon_{4t} \tag{6}$$

$$\Delta LnPOP_t = \rho_0 + \sum_{j=0}^{n} \rho_{1j}\Delta LnCO_{2t-j} + \sum_{j=0}^{n} \rho_{2j}\Delta LnY_{t-j} + \sum_{j=0}^{n} \rho_{3j}\Delta LnY_{t-j}^2$$
$$+ \sum_{j=0}^{n} \rho_{4j}\Delta LnRE_{t-j} + \sum_{j=1}^{n} \rho_{5j}\Delta LnPOP_{t-j} + \varphi_5 ECT_{t-1} + \epsilon_{5t} \tag{7}$$

where Δ denotes the first difference of the selected variables, and n is the number of optimal lags. The residuals ($\epsilon_{it}, i = 1, \ldots, 5$) are assumed to be serially independent with a zero mean and a finite covariance matrix. ECT_{t-1}, the error correction term (ECT), is its one-period lagged estimation derived from the long-run regression in Equation (1).

Within the VECM framework, short-run Granger causality from income to CO_2 emissions is tested via the null hypothesis that all the coefficients of income and the square of income in Equation (3) are zero, simultaneously. So, we test $\pi_{2j} = \pi_{3j} = 0$ $\forall n$, using the Wald test. Rejection of the null hypothesis means that a unidirectional causal effect exists from income to CO_2 emissions. To confirm whether CO_2 emissions Granger-cause income, after estimating Equations (3) and (4), we test the significance of $\delta_{1j} = \theta_{1j} = 0$ $\forall n$ using the Wald test. If we find at least $\delta_{1j} \neq \theta_{1j} \neq 0$, we can conclude that a unidirectional causal effect exists from CO_2 emissions to income. Furthermore, a rejection of both $\pi_{2j} = \pi_{3j} = 0$ $\forall n$ and $\delta_{1j} = \theta_{1j} = 0$ $\forall n$ implies a bidirectional Granger-causal relationship between income and CO_2 emissions. Meanwhile, acceptance of these conditions illustrates that the two variables of interest have no causal relationship. A similar procedure can be performed for each pair of variables in Equations (3)–(7) to examine the Granger causality.

The long-run Granger-causality test is based not only on the conditions in short-run Granger causality but also a coefficient of the ECT. Specifically, we test the significance of $\varphi_1 = \pi_{2j} = \pi_{3j} = 0$, and rejecting this test indicates that income Granger-causes CO_2 emissions in the long run. Similarly, a rejection of the test $\varphi_2 = \varphi_2 = \delta_{2j} = \theta_{3j} = 0$ means a reverse Granger-caused relationship from CO_2 emissions to income in the long run. Using the same procedure, we examine the long-run Granger-caused relationship between other pairs of variables in the equations.

If Equation (1) shows no cointegration, we do not examine long-run causality. Instead, we conduct a short-run Granger-causality test using the vector autoregression (VAR) framework, in which we take the first difference of the variables to ensure that the data are stationary for our analysis.

4. Empirical Results and Discussions

4.1. Results of Unit-Root and Cointegration Tests

We begin our analysis by checking whether the time series of the given variables is stationary because regressing non-stationary variables leads to spurious estimation. We employ the Dickey–Fuller generalized least squares (DF-GLS) unit-root test by Elliott et al. (1996). The DF-GLS test is a modified version of traditional augmented Dickey–Fuller (ADF) test (Dickey and Fuller 1979), in which the time series is transformed via a GLS regression before the test is performed. Thus, it is perceived to be more robust and significantly powerful than the ADF test.

Table 2 illustrates the DF-GLS tests for all the variables of interest, namely CO_2 emissions, energy consumption, the use of renewable energy, income and the square of income, and population size. We find that the five ASEAN countries including Indonesia, Myanmar, Malaysia, the Philippines, and Thailand reject the null hypothesis of containing a unit root in population size at level. In other words, this variable is stationary or integrated I(0) although relatively week evidence is observed in Thailand at a level of 10 percent significance. Meanwhile, the test for the remaining variables—CO_2 emissions, energy consumption, renewable energy consumption, real income, and the square of real income—rejects the null hypothesis at the first difference, meaning they are integrated at I(1).

Table 2. The results of unit-root tests.

Country	Variable	Level			1st Difference			Order of Integration
		DF-GLS	DF	PP	DF-GLS	DF	PP	
Indonesia	$LnCO_2$	−2.13	−3.08	−2.96	−3.97 ***	−6.00 ***	−6.02 ***	I(1)
	lnY	−2.03	−1.98	−2.24	−3.26 **	−4.80 ***	−4.74 ***	I(1)
	LnY^2	−0.78	−0.33	−0.60	−3.38 **	−4.83 ***	−4.77 ***	I(1)
	$LnEC$	−1.29	−1.24	−1.22	−3.81 ***	−3.63 **	−6.68 ***	I(1)
	$LnREC$	−1.18	−0.65	−0.86	−3.09 *	−5.30 ***	−5.26 ***	I(1)
	$LnPOP$	−5.81 ***	−7.57 ***	−4.16 **	−3.86 ***	0.55	−0.35	I(0)
Myanmar	$LnCO_2$	−1.01	−1.57	−1.50	−2.99 *	−5.01 ***	−4.71 ***	I(1)
	lnY	−1.50	−0.15	−0.59	−1.86	−3.06	−3.12	I(2)
	LnY^2	−2.33	−1.22	−1.71	−1.84	−3.32 *	−3.78 **	I(1)
	$LnEC$	−1.50	−0.21	−0.95	−2.36	−3.51 *	−3.53 *	I(1)
	$LnREC$	−0.93	−1.32	−1.11	−3.86 ***	−7.13 ***	−7.37 ***	I(1)
	$LnPOP$	−6.07 ***	−2.38	−1.52	−5.54 ***	0.24	−1.28	I(1)
Malaysia	$LnCO_2$	−1.91	−2.02	−2.11	−3.31 **	−7.86 ***	−7.79 ***	I(1)
	lnY	−1.68	−2.20	−2.35	−3.01 *	−5.75 ***	−5.72 ***	I(1)
	LnY^2	−2.01	2.24	−2.38	−3.22 **	−5.98 ***	−5.96 ***	I(1)
	$LnEC$	−1.69	−1.84	−1.72	−3.89 ***	−7.03 ***	−7.39 ***	I(1)
	$LnREC$	−1.92	−1.81	−1.97	−3.96 ***	−5.17 ***	−5.08 ***	I(1)
	$LnPOP$	−3.59 **	−3.71 **	1.53	−2.96 *	−1.49	−1.78	I(0)
Philippines	$LnCO_2$	−1.89	−1.44	−1.74	−2.81	−5.70 ***	−5.79 ***	I(1)
	lnY	−1.22	0.04	−0.69	−3.07 *	−3.56 **	−3.52 *	I(1)
	LnY^2	−0.81	1.78	0.84	−2.63	−3.53 *	−3.52 *	I(1)
	$LnEC$	−2.04	−2.49	−2.53	−2.51	−8.62 ***	−8.33 ***	I(1)
	$LnREC$	−1.93	−1.57	−1.69	−2.60	−3.67 **	−3.58 **	I(1)
	$LnPOP$	−6.67 ***	6.10 ***	3.42 ***	−3.99 ***	−1.67	−1.92	I(1)
Thailand	$LnCO_2$	−1.54	−0.74	−1.17	−3.14 *	−4.48 ***	−4.44 ***	I(1)
	lnY	−1.81	−0.71	−1.29	−2.85	−4.04 **	−4.04 **	I(1)
	LnY^2	−1.81	−2.35	−2.41	−3.02 *	−4.33 ***	−4.34 ***	I(1)
	$LnEC$	−2.01	−1.60	−1.97	−2.39	−4.8 ***	−4.91 ***	I(1)
	$LnREC$	−4.79 ***	−5.36 ***	−5.27 ***	−5.17 ***	−8.97 ***	−10.1 ***	I(1)
	$LnPOP$	−2.94 *	−6.60 ***	4.04 ***	−5.05 ***	−1.36	−2.02	I(0)

Notes: For comparison purposes, we use the Dickey–Fuller Generalized Least Square (DF-GLS), augmented Dickey–Fuller (ADF) and Phillips Pearson (PP) tests with a constant and trend. The DF-GLS test is based on two lags and the remaining tests have three lags. ***, **, and * denote significance level of 1%, 5%, and 10%, respectively. In corresponding to these significant levels, the DFGLS test critical values are −3.77, −3.19, and −2.89 while the ADF and PP tests have interpolated critical values of −4.24, −3.52, and −3.20.

Our study uses two advanced cointegration tests, namely, the Johansen cointegration test developed by Johansen and Juselius (1990) and the bounded approach to cointegration by Pesaran et al. (2001). We then conduct a Granger-causality test with a multi-equation framework to examine whether a causal relationship exists among the variables of interest. In other words, when a long-run relationship exists among the selected variables, we use a VECM; otherwise, we use a vector autoregressive model (VAR).

Table 3 presents the results of the two cointegration tests, in which Panel A presents the Johansen method and Panel B depicts the bounds-testing approach. First, the Johansen test results show that both the maximum lambda and trace statistics are statistically significant at least at the 5 percent level of significance, indicating that the null hypothesis of no cointegration is rejected and that a long-run relationship among the variables exists in all of the selected countries. Interestingly, Indonesia, Myanmar, and Malaysia have as many as three conintegrating vectors in the test. Second, both the F- and t-statistics fail to confirm a cointegrating relationship among CO_2 emissions, energy consumption, renewable energy consumption, income and the square of income, and population size in the Philippines and Thailand, but not in Indonesia, Myanmar, and Malaysia. Because all the variables in the model are integrated at different levels, the bounds cointegration approach appears to be more appropriate for testing a long-run relationship and yields more consistent results. As such, we rely on the bounds approach rather than the Johansen cointegration test to reach our final conclusions about the long-run relationship.

Table 3. Results of the cointegration tests.

ASEAN Countries		Indonesia		Myanmar		Malaysia		Philippines		Thailand	
Ho	H1	λ	trace	λ	trace	λ	trace	λ	trace	λ	trace
				Panel A: Johansen cointegration test							
r = 0	r ≥ 1	84.42 **	186.27 **	91.29 **	201.37 **	54.22 **	152.94 **	67.90 **	167.58 **	49.73 **	117.12 **
r ≤ 1	r ≥ 2	46.51 **	101.85 **	54.58 **	110.08 **	43.64 **	98.72 **	41.53 **	99.68 **	34.12 **	67.40
r ≤ 2	r ≥ 3	31.71 **	55.33 **	24.37	55.50 **	25.19	55.08 **	33.00 **	58.15 **	15.06	33.27
r ≤ 3	r ≥ 4	14.59	23.62	22.23 **	31.14 **	17.3	29.89 **	15.61	25.14	9.43	18.21
r ≤ 4	r ≥ 5	8.22	9.03	8.36	8.90	11.76	12.59	9.38	9.53	6.05	8.77
r ≤ 5	r ≥ 6	0.81	0.81	0.54	0.54	0.83	0.83	0.16	0.16	2.72	2.72
				Panel B: Bound cointegration test							
		F-stat	t-stat	F-stat	t-stat	F-stat	t-stat	F-stat	t-stat	F-stat	t-stat
Ho: No cointegration		8.24 ***	−6.37 ***	8.09 ***	−3.81 *	5.04 **	−3.98 *	3.25	−3.07	3.03	−1.14
Model		ARDL (1, 1, 2, 1, 1, 1)		ARDL (1, 2, 2, 1, 1, 2)		ARDL (1, 1, 1, 1, 1, 2, 1)		ARDL (1, 1, 2, 1, 1, 2)		ARDL (1, 1, 1, 1, 1, 1)	

Notes: λ is max lambda value. Panel A shows the Johansen cointegration test by Johansen and Juselius (1990) and Panel B indicates the Bound cointegration test by Pesaran et al. (2001). Due to the small sample size, the critical values for the bounds test in Panel B refer to Narayan (2005), rather than Pesaran et al. (2001). The values are in the third case of the bounds test, which includes unrestricted intercept and no trend. ***, **, and * denote a significance level of 1%, 5%, and 10%, respectively. ASEAN: Association of Southeast Asian Nations.

4.2. Results of Long-Run Relationship

Because of the confirmation of the cointegration test in Indonesia, Myanmar, and Malaysia, we use the FMOLS and DOLS to estimate the long-run relationship with a particular stress on testing the EKC hypothesis as well as on investigating the impact of energy consumption, renewable energy consumption, and population growth on CO_2 emissions. Table 4 shows the estimation results for the long run relationship. Our findings support the presence of an EKC only in Myanmar, as both the FMOLS and DOLS have provided consistent results in which estimated coefficients are statistically positive for income per capita and negative for its square transformation. Because of conflicting results between the FMOLS and DOLS estimators, we did not come to a conclusive result about the EKC hypothesis in Indonesia and Malaysia.[3]

Table 4. The results from long-run estimations.

Variable	Indonesia	Myanmar	Malaysia
FMOLS			
LnY	0.66 ***	−0.12	0.87 ***
LnY^2	−0.09 **	−0.35 ***	0.08
$LnEC$	0.47 ***	1.72 ***	0.43 **
$LnREC$	−0.15 ***	−0.0003	−0.0004
$LnPOP$	1.58 ***	−0.89 ***	−0.62 *
Const	−8.32 ***	4.15 ***	1.35
DOLS			
LnY	−0.68 ***	0.43 ***	−0.78
LnY^2	0.15 ***	−0.41 ***	0.64 ***
$LnEC$	1.76 ***	2.8 ***	0.8 ***
$LnREC$	−0.27 ***	−0.49 ***	−0.14 **
$LnPOP$	3.6 ***	−1.84 ***	−0.86 **
Const	−18.19 ***	10.33 ***	1.87 *

Notes: ***, **, and * indicate significance levels of 1%, 5% and 10%, respectively.

Our mixed results on the EKC hypothesis in the selected ASEAN countries are in line with previous studies on the region. Some scholars are in favor of the EKC hypothesis. For example, Saboori and Sulaiman (2013) did confirm it in Singapore and Thailand and Saboori et al. (2016) revealed the same conclusion for the case of Malaysia. Our findings in Myanmar support this strand of an EKC literature. In contrast, Saboori and Sulaiman (2013) failed to confirm the EKC hypothesis in Indonesia, Malaysia, and the Philippines while Al-Mulali et al. (2015) reached the same outcome using the Vietnamese data over the 1981–2011 period. Our results are in line with this trend of empirical evidence as we found no conclusion of the EKC hypothesis in the long run in Indonesia, Malaysia, Thailand and the Philippines.

In the long run, the driving forces behind carbon emissions vary considerably from one surveyed country to another. In Indonesia, energy consumption is a contributing factor to CO_2 emissions, and the use of renewable energy mitigates their impact. The population growth also leads to higher carbon emissions. Similar patterns are observed in the driving determinants of CO_2 emissions in Myanmar and Malaysia, whose level of CO_2 emissions is positively associated with energy consumption and negatively related to population growth. The adoption of renewable energy in these two countries would help

---

[3] It should be noted that although the coefficients of the income per capita and its square form are appropriate in terms of signs and significance levels, the estimation results could be spurious if there is a failure of cointegration of the conventional EKC estimation. The spurious regression is caused not by the quadratic function form, but by the fundamental trend relationship between income per capita and pollutants (Wang 2013). Thanks to the confirmation of the two advanced cointegration tests, our regressions do not suffer spurious estimations.

mitigate the negative environmental impact by reducing the quantity of CO_2 emissions, though the findings are less supported by the FMOLS estimator because of the statistically insignificant coefficients.

4.3. Results of Granger-Causality Tests

Table 5 reveals the causality effect of the variables of interests adopted in this paper. In Indonesia, Myanmar, and Malaysia, we see both long- and short-run causality but only a short-run causal relationship in the Philippines and Thailand. In general, the five countries included in our sample have considerable differences in the causality effect, as shown in Figure 1. In Malaysia, the neutrality effect on one another is observed among energy consumption, renewable energy, and CO_2 emissions in the short and long run, and a causal effect is reported from economic growth to CO_2 emissions and energy consumption. GDP growth unidirectionally Granger causes not only energy consumption but also carbon emissions, and a feedback effect is found between GDP growth and population growth. These findings imply that GDP growth is a key determinant of the amount of energy consumption and environmental degradation. Consistent with our results, Ang (2008) posited that there was an impact of economic growth on energy consumption for Malaysia over the 1971–1999 period.

In Indonesia, GDP growth also plays a key role in causing energy consumption, carbon emissions, and renewable energy use. Economic growth and population growth cause each other. Unidirectional causality is found from energy consumption to population growth and from carbon emissions to energy consumption in both the short and long run. Our results are consistent with those of Sugiawan and Managi (2016) in supporting a unidirectional effect from GDP growth to carbon emissions in the long run in Indonesia. However, unlike Sugiawan and Managi (2016), we detect unidirectional causality from GDP growth to the use of renewable energy, which further supports the EKC hypothesis, as found in earlier studies (Bento and Moutinho 2016).

Several interesting findings are found for Myanmar. It has a complicated causality relationship among five selected variables, and renewable energy usage seems to be an issue of concern as it is significantly affected by different determinants. Specifically, a statistically strong inter-relationship is seen among carbon emissions, GDP growth, population growth, and energy consumption as a bidirectional causal relationship exists between each pair of those variables, except for unidirectional causality from energy consumption to carbon emissions. Additionally, the country has a unidirectional causal relationship from energy consumption, GDP growth, and population growth to renewable energy consumption in both the short and long run.

With respect to the short-run causal relationship among the selected variables in the Philippines and Thailand, the feedback hypothesis is confirmed between economic growth and population growth. Carbon emissions, energy consumption, and renewable energy use do not cause one another. The Philippines has a unidirectional effect from economic growth to energy consumption as well as to carbon emissions, and Thailand does not show any causal effect among these three variables. Population growth is observed to cause both energy consumption and renewable energy use in the Philippines, whereas population growth and energy consumption cause each other in Thailand.

In summary, we found a unidirectional causality running from economic growth to CO_2 emissions in Indonesia, Malaysia, and the Philippines, a bidirectional causality in Myanmar, and no causal relationship between these two variables in Thailand. Our findings are different from those from Azam et al. (2015) as they reported no causal relationship between these two variables in Indonesia, Thailand, Singapore, and the Philippines with an exception being a unidirectional causality from economic growth to CO_2 emissions in Malaysia.

Table 5. Results of Granger-causality test.

Null Hypothesis	Short-Run Granger-Causality Test					Long-Run Granger-Causality Test		
	Indonesia	Myanmar	Malaysia	Philippines	Thailand	Indonesia	Myanmar	Malaysia
$\Delta LnCO_2 \neq \Delta LnEC$	6.20 *	1.52	0.52	0.13	4.22	6.62 *	2.80	0.52
$\Delta LnCO_2 \neq \Delta LnREC$	0.35	3.67	1.97	1.44	4.85 *	0.42	4.48	2.02
$\Delta LnCO_2 \neq \Delta LnY, \Delta LnY^2$	1.77	12.88 **	4.26	6.23	6.95	1.78	14.08 **	4.40
$\Delta LnCO_2 \neq \Delta LnPOP$	2.1	7.39 **	5.91 *	0.17	4.44	2.1	9.15 **	6.95 *
$\Delta LnEC \neq \Delta LnCO_2$	0.34	12.24 ***	3.50	0.54	5.62 *	3.45	24.60 ***	3.91
$\Delta LnEC \neq \Delta LnREC$	2.34	5.60 *	0.35	1.00	2.86	3.86	20.99 ***	1.22
$\Delta LnEC \neq \Delta LnY, \Delta LnY^2$	1.54	25.8 ***	5.17	1.71	1.44	6.52	27.57 ***	5.27
$\Delta LnEC \neq \Delta LnPOP$	8.06 **	22.74 ***	1.91	3.87	1.29	9.00 **	25.66 ***	3.10
$\Delta LnREC \neq \Delta LnCO_2$	0.96	3.56	3.83	0.02	0.46	2.85	4.05	4.06
$\Delta LnREC \neq \Delta LnEC$	0.44	0.23	2.41	1.04	3.50	2.29	3.56	3.02
$\Delta LnREC \neq \Delta LnY, \Delta LnY^2$	4.09	3.87	0.79	5.87	18.48 ***	4.36	9.47 *	0.98
$\Delta LnREC \neq \Delta LnPOP$	2.93	2.73	1.19	1.21	9.17 **	3.84	3.38	1.33
$\Delta LnY, \Delta LnY^2 \neq \Delta LnCO_2$	4.93	14.08 ***	9.58 **	17.7 ***	6.22	37.3 ***	28.67 ***	12.00 *
$\Delta LnY, \Delta LnY^2 \neq \Delta LnEC$	6.69	13.52 ***	6.46	15.77 ***	5.01	36.65 ***	24.56 ***	12.55 *
$\Delta LnY, \Delta LnY^2 \neq \Delta LnREC$	10.77 ***	11.08 **	3.10	2.34	4.28	34.82 ***	11.61 *	9.43
$\Delta LnY, \Delta LnY^2 \neq \Delta LnPOP$	22.41 ***	3.96	11.72 **	17.35 ***	19.68 ***	52.13 ***	12.17 *	12.57 *
$\Delta LnPOP \neq \Delta LnCO_2$	0.12	13.03 ***	0.98	19.29 ***	2.70	0.93	18.93 ***	94.44 ***
$\Delta LnPOP \neq \Delta LnEC$	0.13	15.17 ***	18.04 ***	15.07 ***	9.7 ***	0.59	19.63 ***	63.13 ***
$\Delta LnPOP \neq \Delta LnREC$	2.09	19.48 ***	6.38 **	2.88	0.19	2.09	22.61 ***	69.21 ***
$\Delta LnPOP \neq \Delta LnY, \Delta LnY^2$	6.71	21.26 ***	18.13 ***	31.45 ***	9.47 **	32.22 ***	21.41 ***	87.40 ***

Notes: ***, **, and * indicate significance levels of 1%, 5% and 10%, respectively.

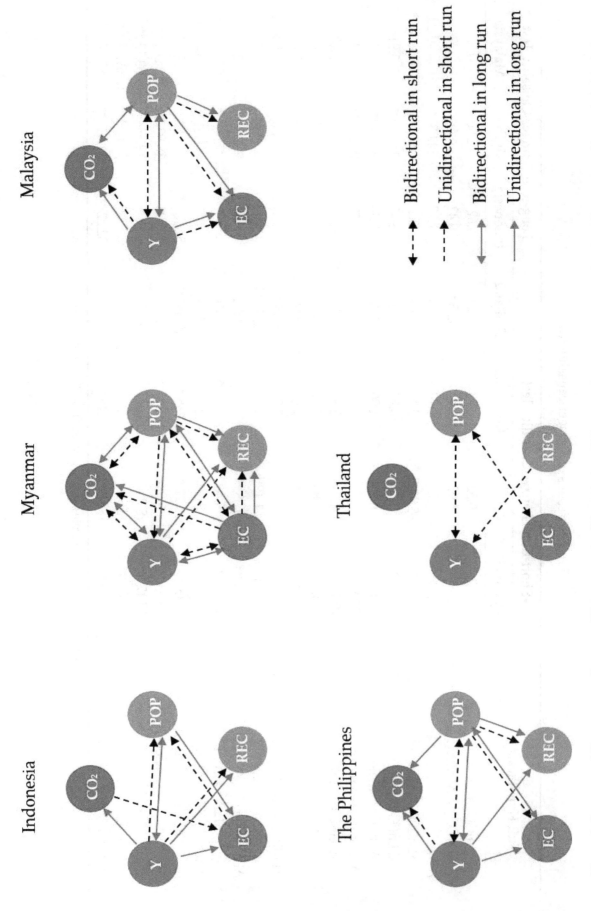

Figure 1. Summary of Granger causality tests. CO_2—per capita CO_2 emissions; EC—per capita energy consumption; Y: real per capita GDP and its square form; POP—population growth rate; REC—per capita consumption of renewable energy.

5. Concluding Remarks and Policy Implications

By using the ARDL bounds test of cointegration, the Johansen cointegration test, and the Granger-causality test based on both VECM and VAR framework, this paper examines a long-run relationship and direction of Granger causality between economic growth, energy consumption, renewable energy usage, environment degradation (i.e., carbon dioxide emissions), in a multivariate model including population growth as an additional variable. Also, we test the validity of a well-known EKC hypothesis using two long-run estimators, FMOLS and DOLS. Our sample consists of five ASEAN members: Indonesia, Myanmar, Malaysia, the Philippines, and Thailand. The primary reasons we conduct the study are the lack of empirical studies that examines the remedial role of renewable energy to address the increasing CO_2 emissions in the region. In addition, we observe and respond to the desire and efforts made by the governments in these countries to achieve their energy mix targets, with a major focus on renewable energy in recent years.

The main findings of this paper can be summarized as follows. First, a cointegrating relationship exists among economic growth, energy consumption, renewable energy usage, environment degradation in Indonesia, Myanmar, and Malaysia but not in the Philippines and Thailand. The validity of the EKC hypothesis is confirmed in Myanmar, but not in Indonesia and Malaysia because of the inconsistent results from the FMOLS and DOLS. Second, the outcomes from the Granger-causality test vary considerably across the selected countries, among variables such as economic growth, energy consumption, renewable energy use, CO_2 emissions, and population growth. The Granger-causality test was performed with the VECM framework with variables that have a long-run relationship; otherwise the VAR framework was adopted. Our findings serve as a critically empirical source of inputs for policy suggestions and implementation to balance sustainable economic growth, conserve energy, and preserve the environment.

The findings from this paper can be used in future research and for public policy purposes. The varying characteristics of different countries cause them to develop and implement different paths to achieving the proposed renewable energy targets in the short run and long run. Our findings appear to imply that academic studies in the future should examine the relationship among GDP growth, energy use, carbon emissions, renewable energy consumption, and other macroeconomics factors, including population growth for each country separately.

The varying findings across ASEAN countries can be a useful source of policy implications. No Granger causality is found among carbon emissions, energy consumption, and renewable energy consumption in Malaysia, Thailand, and the Philippines. This implies that the current level of renewable usage is not sufficient enough to mitigate the level of CO_2 emissions and to support the total of energy usage in these two countries. Malaysia experiences a unidirectional Granger caused from economic growth to energy consumption and to CO_2 emissions which indicates energy still plays a vitally important part in the country's economic development while pollution degradation creates a concern. This policy implication could be applied for the case of Indonesia in which economic growth is observed to have a unidirectional impact not only on CO_2 emissions and energy consumption but also on renewable energy in the long run. Furthermore, for the case of Thailand, no links among economic growth, CO_2 emissions, energy consumption and renewable energy usage were found in the short run. Not only does Myanmar have a unidirectional effect from GDP growth, energy consumption, and population growth to the adoption of renewable energy, but the country also has the particular causal effect among the variables, most of which bidirectionally cause one another. Our results show that there is a trade-off between higher level of economic growth and higher levels of CO_2 emissions as well as energy consumption. More importantly, the usage of renewable energy in curbing environment degradation gains little assistance. Our study reinforces a view that while the current level of renewable energy usage is an ineffective measure for environment protection, a transformation toward less polluted renewable energy would be crucial to achieve goals of sustainable development in Malaysia as mentioned by Gill et al. (2018).

The paper has a limitation that a number of observations are relatively small, making a traditional causality test less powerful. Like previous studies, the data for analyzing the relationship among energy consumption, economic growth and environment degradation rely on the World Bank indicators, starting in 1970. Using the so-called bootstrap causality test to deal with small sample size can be a proper robustness check. This opens a potential for future studies on a single country.

Author Contributions: Conceptualization, D.H.V.; Methodology, D.H.V.; A.T.V.; Software, A.T.V.; L.Q.T.T.; Validation, D.H.V.; Formal Analysis, A.T.V.; L.Q.T.T.; Investigation, A.T.V.; Resources, D.H.V.; Data Curation, L.Q.T.T.; Writing—Original Draft Preparation, A.T.V.; L.Q.T.T.; Writing—Review and Editing, D.H.V.; Visualization, A.T.V.; Supervision, D.H.V.; L.Q.T.T.; Project Administration, A.T.V.; Funding Acquisition, A.T.V.

Acknowledgments: We are grateful to the three anonymous referees for their constructive comments. We also thank the participants at the 3rd Vietnam's Business and Economics Research Conference (Ho Chi Minh City Open University, Ho Chi Minh City, Vietnam, 18–20 July 2019) for their helpful suggestions. The authors wish to acknowledge financial supports from Ho Chi Minh City Open University. The authors are solely responsible for any remaining errors or shortcomings.

References

Ali, Wajahat, Azrai Abdullah, and Muhammad Azam. 2017. Re-visiting the environmental Kuznets curve hypothesis for Malaysia: Fresh evidence from ARDL bounds testing approach. *Renewable and Sustainable Energy Reviews* 77: 990–1000. [CrossRef]

Al-Mulali, Usama, Behnaz Saboori, and Ilhan Ozturk. 2015. Investigating the environmental Kuznets curve hypothesis in Vietnam. *Energy Policy* 76: 123–31. [CrossRef]

Ang, James B. 2008. Economic development, pollutant emissions and energy consumption in Malaysia. *Journal of Policy Modeling* 30: 271–78. [CrossRef]

Apergis, Nicholas, and James E. Payne. 2014. Renewable energy, output, CO_2 emissions, and fossil fuel prices in Central America: Evidence from a nonlinear panel smooth transition vector error correction model. *Energy Economics* 42: 226–32. [CrossRef]

Apergis, Nicholas, James E. Payne, Kojo Menyah, and Yemane Wolde-Rufael. 2010. On the causal dynamics between emissions, nuclear energy, renewable energy, and economic growth. *Ecological Economics* 69: 2255–60. [CrossRef]

Arouri, Mohamed El Hedi, Adel Ben Youssef, Hatem M'henni, and Christophe Rault. 2012. Energy consumption, economic growth and CO_2 emissions in Middle East and North African countries. *Energy Policy* 45: 342–49. [CrossRef]

Azam, Muhammad, Abdul Qayyum Khan, B. Bakhtyar, and Chandra Emirullah. 2015. The causal relationship between energy consumption and economic growth in the ASEAN-5 countries. *Renewable and Sustainable Energy Reviews* 47: 732–45. [CrossRef]

Azomahou, Theophile, François Laisney, and Phu Nguyen Van. 2006. Economic development and CO_2 emissions: A nonparametric panel approach. *Journal of Public Economics* 90: 1347–63. [CrossRef]

Begum, Rawshan Ara, Kazi Sohag, Sharifah Mastura Syed Abdullah, and Mokhtar Jaafar. 2015. CO_2 emissions, energy consumption, economic and population growth in Malaysia. *Renewable and Sustainable Energy Reviews* 41: 594–601. [CrossRef]

Bekhet, Hussain Ali, and Nor Salwati Othman. 2018. The role of renewable energy to validate dynamic interaction between CO_2 emissions and GDP toward sustainable development in Malaysia. *Energy Economics* 72: 47–61. [CrossRef]

Belaid, Fateh, and Meriem Youssef. 2017. Environmental degradation, renewable and non-renewable electricity consumption, and economic growth: Assessing the evidence from Algeria. *Energy Policy* 102: 277–87. [CrossRef]

Bento, João Paulo Cerdeira, and Victor Moutinho. 2016. CO_2 emissions, non-renewable and renewable electricity production, economic growth, and international trade in Italy. *Renewable and Sustainable Energy Reviews* 55: 142–55. [CrossRef]

Bilgili, Faik, Emrah Koçak, and Umit Bulut. 2016. The dynamic impact of renewable energy consumption on CO_2 emissions: A revisited Environmental Kuznets Curve approach. *Renewable and Sustainable Energy Reviews* 54: 838–45. [CrossRef]

De Grauwe, Paul, and Zhaoyong Zhang. 2016. The rise of China and regional integration in East Asia. *Scottish Journal of Political Economy* 63: 1–6. [CrossRef]

Dickey, David A., and Wayne A. Fuller. 1979. Distribution of the estimators for autoregressive time series with a unit root. *Journal of the American Statistical Association* 74: 427–31.

Dogan, Eyup, and Ilhan Ozturk. 2017. The influence of renewable and non-renewable energy consumption and real income on CO_2 emissions in the USA: Evidence from structural break tests. *Environmental Science and Pollution Research* 24: 10846–54. [CrossRef] [PubMed]

Dogan, Eyup, and Fahri Seker. 2016. Determinants of CO_2 emissions in the European Union: The role of renewable and non-renewable energy. *Renewable Energy* 94: 429–39. [CrossRef]

Dogan, Eyup, and Berna Turkekul. 2016. CO_2 emissions, real output, energy consumption, trade, urbanization and financial development: Testing the EKC hypothesis for the USA. *Environmental Science and Pollution Research* 23: 1203–13. [CrossRef]

Dong, Kangyin, Renjin Sun, and Gal Hochman. 2017. Do natural gas and renewable energy consumption lead to less CO_2 emission? Empirical evidence from a panel of BRICS countries. *Energy* 141: 1466–78. [CrossRef]

Dong, Kangyin, Gal Hochman, Yaqing Zhang, Renjin Sun, Hui Li, and Hua Liao. 2018. CO_2 emissions, economic and population growth, and renewable energy: Empirical evidence across regions. *Energy Economics* 75: 180–92. [CrossRef]

Elliott, Graham, Thomas J. Rothenberg, and James H. Stock. 1996. Efficient tests for an autoregressive unit root. *Econometrica* 64: 813–36. [CrossRef]

Fakih, Ali, and Walid Marrouch. 2019. Environmental Kuznets Curve, a Mirage? A Non-parametric Analysis for MENA Countries. *International Advances in Economic Research* 25: 113–19. [CrossRef]

Gill, Abid Rashid, Kuperan K. Viswanathan, and Sallahuddin Hassan. 2018. A test of environmental Kuznets curve (EKC) for carbon emission and potential of renewable energy to reduce green house gases (GHG) in Malaysia. *Environment, Development and Sustainability* 20: 1103–14. [CrossRef]

Halicioglu, Ferda, and Natalya Ketenci. 2018. Output, renewable and non-renewable energy production, and international trade: Evidence from EU-15 countries. *Energy* 159: 995–1002. [CrossRef]

Halicioglu, Ferda. 2009. An econometric study of CO_2 emissions, energy consumption, income and foreign trade in Turkey. *Energy Policy* 37: 1156–64. [CrossRef]

Heidari, Hassan, Salih Turan Katircioğlu, and Lesyan Saeidpour. 2015. Economic growth, CO_2 emissions, and energy consumption in the five ASEAN countries. *International Journal of Electrical Power and Energy Systems* 64: 785–91. [CrossRef]

Ibrahim, Mansor H., and Siong Hook Law. 2014. Social capital and CO_2 emission–output relations: A panel analysis. *Renewable and Sustainable Energy Reviews* 29: 528–34. [CrossRef]

Irandoust, Manuchehr. 2016. The renewable energy-growth nexus with carbon emissions and technological innovation: Evidence from the Nordic countries. *Ecological Indicators* 69: 118–25. [CrossRef]

Iwata, Hiroki, Keisuke Okada, and Sovannroeun Samreth. 2010. Empirical study on the environmental Kuznets curve for CO_2 in France: The role of nuclear energy. *Energy Policy* 38: 4057–63. [CrossRef]

Jaforullah, Mohammad, and Alan King. 2015. Does the use of renewable energy sources mitigate CO_2 emissions? A reassessment of the US evidence. *Energy Economics* 49: 711–17. [CrossRef]

Jalil, Abdul, and Syed F. Mahmud. 2009. Environment Kuznets curve for CO_2 emissions: A cointegration analysis for China. *Energy Policy* 37: 5167–72. [CrossRef]

Jayanthakumaran, Kankesu, and Ying Liu. 2012. Openness and the Environmental Kuznets Curve: Evidence from China. *Economic Modelling* 29: 566–76. [CrossRef]

Jebli, Mehdi Ben, Slim Ben Youssef, and Ilhan Ozturk. 2016. Testing environmental Kuznets curve hypothesis: The role of renewable and non-renewable energy consumption and trade in OECD countries. *Ecological Indicators* 60: 824–31. [CrossRef]

Johansen, Søren. 1988. Statistical analysis of cointegration vectors. *Journal of Economic Dynamics and Control* 12: 231–54. [CrossRef]

Johansen, Søren, and Katarina Juselius. 1990. Maximum likelihood estimation and inference on cointegration—With applications to the demand for money. *Oxford Bulletin of Economics and Statistics* 2: 170–209. [CrossRef]

Kalaitzidakis, Pantelis, Theofanis Mamuneas, and Thanasis Stengos. 2018. Greenhouse emissions and productivity growth. *Journal of Risk and Financial Management* 11: 38. [CrossRef]

Le, Thai-Ha, and Euston Quah. 2018. Income level and the emissions, energy, and growth nexus: Evidence from Asia and the Pacific. *International Economics* 156: 193–205. [CrossRef]

Lean, Hooi Hooi, and Russell Smyth. 2010. CO_2 emissions, electricity consumption and output in ASEAN. *Applied Energy* 87: 1858–64. [CrossRef]

Liu, Xuyi, Shun Zhang, and Junghan Bae. 2017. The impact of renewable energy and agriculture on carbon dioxide emissions: Investigating the environmental Kuznets curve in four selected ASEAN countries. *Journal of Cleaner Production* 164: 1239–47. [CrossRef]

Narayan, Paresh Kumar. 2005. The saving and investment nexus for China: Evidence from cointegration tests. *Applied Economics* 37: 1979–90. [CrossRef]

Nasreen, Samia, and Sofia Anwar. 2014. Causal relationship between trade openness, economic growth and energy consumption: A panel data analysis of Asian countries. *Energy Policy* 69: 82–91. [CrossRef]

Nguyen, Kim Hanh, and Makoto Kakinaka. 2019. Renewable energy consumption, carbon emissions, and development stages: Some evidence from panel cointegration analysis. *Renewable Energy.* 132: 1049–57. [CrossRef]

Ozatac, Nesrin, Korhan K. Gokmenoglu, and Nigar Taspinar. 2017. Testing the EKC hypothesis by considering trade openness, urbanization, and financial development: The case of Turkey. *Environmental Science and Pollution Research* 24: 16690–701. [CrossRef] [PubMed]

Ozturk, Ilhan, and Ali Acaravci. 2013. The long-run and causal analysis of energy, growth, openness and financial development on carbon emissions in Turkey. *Energy Economics* 36: 262–67. [CrossRef]

Ozturk, Ilhan, and Usama Al-Mulali. 2015. Investigating the validity of the environmental Kuznets curve hypothesis in Cambodia. *Ecological Indicators* 57: 324–30. [CrossRef]

Pata, Ugur Korkut. 2018. Renewable energy consumption, urbanization, financial development, income and CO_2 emissions in Turkey: Testing EKC hypothesis with structural breaks. *Journal of Cleaner Production* 187: 770–79. [CrossRef]

Pesaran, M. Hashem, Yongcheol Shin, and Richard J. Smith. 2001. Bounds testing approaches to the analysis of level relationships. *Journal of Applied Econometrics* 16: 289–326. [CrossRef]

Raza, Syed Ali, and Nida Shah. 2018. Testing environmental Kuznets curve hypothesis in G7 countries: The role of renewable energy consumption and trade. *Environmental Science and Pollution Research* 25: 26965–77. [CrossRef]

Saboori, Behnaz, and Jamalludin Sulaiman. 2013. CO_2 emissions, energy consumption and economic growth in association of Southeast Asian Nations (ASEAN) countries: A cointegration approach. *Energy* 55: 813–22. [CrossRef]

Saboori, Behnaz, Jamalludin Sulaiman, and Saidatulakmal Mohd. 2016. Environmental Kuznets curve and energy consumption in Malaysia: A cointegration approach. *Energy Sources, Part B: Economics, Planning, and Policy* 11: 861–67. [CrossRef]

Sadorsky, Perry. 2009. Renewable energy consumption, CO_2 emissions and oil prices in the G7 countries. *Energy Economics* 31: 456–62. [CrossRef]

Saidi, Kais, and Mounir Ben Mbarek. 2016. Nuclear energy, renewable energy, CO_2 emissions, and economic growth for nine developed countries: Evidence from panel Granger causality tests. *Progress in Nuclear Energy* 88: 364–74. [CrossRef]

Sebri, Maamar, and Ousama Ben-Salha. 2014. On the causal dynamics between economic growth, renewable energy consumption, CO_2 emissions and trade openness: Fresh evidence from BRICS countries. *Renewable and Sustainable Energy Reviews* 39: 14–23. [CrossRef]

Şener, Şerife Elif Can, Julia L. Sharp, and Annick Anctil. 2018. Factors impacting diverging paths of renewable energy: A review. *Renewable and Sustainable Energy Reviews* 81: 2335–42. [CrossRef]

Shafiei, Sahar, and Ruhul A. Salim. 2014. Non-renewable and renewable energy consumption and CO_2 emissions in OECD countries: A comparative analysis. *Energy Policy* 66: 547–56. [CrossRef]

Shahbaz, Muhammad, Qazi Muhammad Adnan Hye, Aviral Kumar Tiwari, and Nuno Carlos Leitao. 2013. Economic growth, energy consumption, financial development, international trade and CO_2 emissions in Indonesia. *Renewable and Sustainable Energy Reviews* 25: 109–21. [CrossRef]

Shahbaz, Muhammad, Nanthakumar Loganathan, Mohammad Zeshan, and Khalid Zaman. 2015. Does renewable energy consumption add in economic growth? An application of autoregressive distributed lag model in Pakistan. *Renewable and Sustainable Energy Reviews* 44: 576–85. [CrossRef]

Shahbaz, Muhammad, Muhammad Shafiullah, Vassilios G. Papavassiliou, and Shawkat Hammoudeh. 2017. The CO_2–growth nexus revisited: A nonparametric analysis for the G7 economies over nearly two centuries. *Energy Economics* 65: 183–93. [CrossRef]

Shahbaz, Muhammad, Ilham Haouas, and Thi Hong Van Hoang. 2019. Economic growth and environmental degradation in Vietnam: Is the environmental Kuznets curve a complete picture? *Emerging Markets Review* 38: 197–218. [CrossRef]

Shahzad, Syed Jawad Hussain, Ronald Ravinesh Kumar, Muhammad Zakaria, and Maryam Hurr. 2017. Carbon emission, energy consumption, trade openness and financial development in Pakistan: A revisit. *Renewable and Sustainable Energy Reviews* 70: 185–92. [CrossRef]

Soytas, Ugur, Ramazan Sari, and Bradley T. Ewing. 2007. Energy consumption, income, and carbon emissions in the United States. *Ecological Economics* 62: 482–89. [CrossRef]

Stern, David I. 2004. The rise and fall of the environmental Kuznets curve. *World Development* 32: 1419–39. [CrossRef]

Sugiawan, Yogi, and Shunsuke Managi. 2016. The environmental Kuznets curve in Indonesia: Exploring the potential of renewable energy. *Energy Policy* 98: 187–98. [CrossRef]

Tang, Chor Foon, and Bee Wah Tan. 2015. The impact of energy consumption, income and foreign direct investment on carbon dioxide emissions in Vietnam. *Energy* 79: 447–54. [CrossRef]

To, Anh Hoang, Dao Thi-Thieu Ha, Ha Minh Nguyen, and Duc Hong Vo. 2019. The impact of foreign direct investment on environment degradation: Evidence from emerging markets in Asia. *International Journal of Environmental Research and Public Health* 16: 1636. [CrossRef] [PubMed]

Vo, Duc Hong, Son Van Huynh, and Dao Thi-Thieu Ha. 2019. The importance of the financial derivatives markets to economic development in the world's four major economies. *Journal of Risk and Financial Management* 12: 35. [CrossRef]

Wang, Yi-Chia. 2013. Functional sensitivity of testing the environmental Kuznets curve hypothesis. *Resource and Energy Economics* 35: 451–66. [CrossRef]

Zoundi, Zakaria. 2017. CO_2 emissions, renewable energy and the Environmental Kuznets Curve, a panel cointegration approach. *Renewable and Sustainable Energy Reviews* 72: 1067–75. [CrossRef]

Permissions

All chapters in this book were first published in MDPI; hereby published with permission under the Creative Commons Attribution License or equivalent. Every chapter published in this book has been scrutinized by our experts. Their significance has been extensively debated. The topics covered herein carry significant findings which will fuel the growth of the discipline. They may even be implemented as practical applications or may be referred to as a beginning point for another development.

The contributors of this book come from diverse backgrounds, making this book a truly international effort. This book will bring forth new frontiers with its revolutionizing research information and detailed analysis of the nascent developments around the world.

We would like to thank all the contributing authors for lending their expertise to make the book truly unique. They have played a crucial role in the development of this book. Without their invaluable contributions this book wouldn't have been possible. They have made vital efforts to compile up to date information on the varied aspects of this subject to make this book a valuable addition to the collection of many professionals and students.

This book was conceptualized with the vision of imparting up-to-date information and advanced data in this field. To ensure the same, a matchless editorial board was set up. Every individual on the board went through rigorous rounds of assessment to prove their worth. After which they invested a large part of their time researching and compiling the most relevant data for our readers.

The editorial board has been involved in producing this book since its inception. They have spent rigorous hours researching and exploring the diverse topics which have resulted in the successful publishing of this book. They have passed on their knowledge of decades through this book. To expedite this challenging task, the publisher supported the team at every step. A small team of assistant editors was also appointed to further simplify the editing procedure and attain best results for the readers.

Apart from the editorial board, the designing team has also invested a significant amount of their time in understanding the subject and creating the most relevant covers. They scrutinized every image to scout for the most suitable representation of the subject and create an appropriate cover for the book.

The publishing team has been an ardent support to the editorial, designing and production team. Their endless efforts to recruit the best for this project, has resulted in the accomplishment of this book. They are a veteran in the field of academics and their pool of knowledge is as vast as their experience in printing. Their expertise and guidance has proved useful at every step. Their uncompromising quality standards have made this book an exceptional effort. Their encouragement from time to time has been an inspiration for everyone.

The publisher and the editorial board hope that this book will prove to be a valuable piece of knowledge for researchers, students, practitioners and scholars across the globe.

List of Contributors

Laura Calvet
IN3—Computer Science Department, Universitat Oberta de Catalunya, 08018 Barcelona, Spain
Business Department, International University of Valencia, 46002 Valencia, Spain

Rocio de la Torre
INARBE Institute, Public University of Navarre, Campus de Arrosadia, 31006 Pamplona, Spain

Anita Goyal
Indian Institute of Management, Lucknow 226013, India

Mage Marmol
Euncet Business School, 08225 Terrassa, Spain

Angel A. Juan
IN3—Computer Science Department, Universitat Oberta de Catalunya, 08018 Barcelona, Spain
Euncet Business School, 08225 Terrassa, Spain

Luce Brotcorne
INRIA Lille—Nord Europe, Parc scientifique de la Haute Borne 40, av. Halley-Bât A, 59650 Villeneuve d'Ascq, France

Qu Wei
ICT for City Logistics and Enterprises Center, Politecnico di Torino, 10129 Turin, Italy

Mariangela Rosano
ICT for City Logistics and Enterprises Center, Politecnico di Torino, 10129 Turin, Italy
CARS@Polito, Politecnico di Torino, 10129 Turin, Italy

Guido Perboli
ICT for City Logistics and Enterprises Center, Politecnico di Torino, 10129 Turin, Italy
CARS@Polito, Politecnico di Torino, 10129 Turin, Italy
CIRRELT, Pavillon André-Aisenstadt, Montreal, QC H3T 1J4, Canada

Thang Cong Nguyen and Tan Ngoc Vu
Business and Economics Research Group, Ho Chi Minh City Open University, Ho Chi Minh City 70000, Vietnam

Nguyen Dang Le
Department of Financial Informatics and Statistics, Ministry of Finance, Ho Chi Minh City 700000, Vietnam

Pham Trung-Kien
Faculty of Economics, Binh Duong University, 504 Binh Duong Avenue, Binh Duong Province 590000, Vietnam

Nguyen Minh Ha
The Business and Economics Research Group, Ho Chi Minh City Open University, 97 Vo Van Tan Street, District 3, Ho Chi Minh City 700000, Vietnam

Quan Minh Quoc Binh
Faculty of Economics and Public Management, Ho Chi Minh City Open University, 97 Vo Van Tan Street, District 3, Ho Chi Minh City 700000, Vietnam

Pham Phi Dang
Department of Planning and Investment Binh Thuan Province, 290 Tran Hung Dao Street, Phan Thiet City 800000, Vietnam

Phuong Duy Nguyen
Ho Chi Minh City Market Surveillance Department, Vietnam Directorate of Market Surveillance, Ho Chi Minh City 72400, Vietnam

Hoang Huy Nguyen
Vietnam—The Netherlands Economics Program, Ho Chi Minh City 7000, Vietnam

Chi Minh Ho
Business and Economics Research Group, Ho Chi Minh City Open University, Ho Chi Minh City 7000, Vietnam

Mark Kam Loon Loo
Mihalcheon School of Management, Concordia University of Edmonton, Edmonton, AB T5B 4E4, Canada

Phuong V. Nguyen and Khoa T. Tran
Center for Public Administration, International University-Vietnam National University, Ho Chi Minh City 700000, Vietnam

Hien Thi Ngoc Huynh and Hoa Doan Xuan Trieu
The School of Business, International University-Vietnam National University, Ho Chi Minh City 700000, Vietnam

Loan Thi-Hong Van
School of Advanced Study, Ho Chi Minh City Open University, Ho Chi Minh City 7000, Vietnam

Phuong Anh Nguyen
Graduate School, Ho Chi Minh City Open University, Ho Chi Minh City 7000, Vietnam

Dao Thi-Thieu Ha
International Economics Faculty, Banking University
Ho Chi Minh City, Ho Chi Minh City 70000, Vietnam

Nga Thi Hoang
Office of Finance & Accounting, Ho Chi Minh City
Open University, Ho Chi Minh City 70000, Vietnam

Anh The Vo and Duc Hong Vo
Business and Economics Research Group, Ho Chi
Minh City Open University, Ho Chi Minh City 70000,
Vietnam

Quan Thai-Thuong Le
Office of Cooperation and Research Management, Ho
Chi Minh City Open University, Ho Chi Minh City
70000, Vietnam

Index

Leverage Model, 100, 102-103, 105-107

M
Microfinance, 143, 151-153
Multicollinearity, 65-66, 81, 168, 170

O
Organizational Slack, 158-160, 165-166, 168, 170, 172-173, 175, 177, 179-180

P
Pecking Order Theory, 99-102, 104, 107-109
Price Shocks, 119, 124, 128, 131, 133-136
Production Expansion, 112-113, 116, 132
Profits, 3, 7, 10, 19, 63, 79, 82, 132

R
Renewable Energy, 21, 110-111, 113, 115, 210-215, 218-219, 221-222, 224-229

S
Social Investors, 153-154
Stock Market, 51, 102, 108
Supply Shocks, 115, 124, 133, 135

T
Trade Openness, 48, 51, 59, 92-93, 95, 97, 115, 202-203, 206, 213, 228-229
Trade-off Theory, 99-103, 107-109
Transaction Cost, 7, 75-77, 79, 81-84

U
Urbanization, 61-66, 68-70, 73-74, 213, 227-228

V
Variance Inflation Factor, 81, 168
Volatility, 110, 112-113, 116, 134-137, 159, 172